FOUNDATIONS OF
COUNSELING PEOPLE

FOUNDATIONS OF COUNSELING PEOPLE

A Guide for the Counseling, Psychological, and Helping Professions

By

MICHAEL E. ILLOVSKY, PH.D.

Western Illinois University
Macomb, Illinois

CHARLES C THOMAS · PUBLISHER, LTD.
Springfield · Illinois · U.S.A.

Published and Distributed Throughout the World by

CHARLES C THOMAS • PUBLISHER, LTD.
2600 South First Street
Springfield, Illinois 62704

© 2013 by CHARLES C THOMAS • PUBLISHER, LTD.

ISBN 978-0-398-08863-7 (hard)
ISBN 978-0-398-08864-4 (paper)
ISBN 978-0-398-08865-1 (ebook)

Library of Congress Catalog Card Number: 2012037178

With THOMAS BOOKS *careful attention is given to all details of manufacturing
and design. It is the Publisher's desire to present books that are satisfactory as to their
physical qualities and artistic possibilities and appropriate for their particular use.*
THOMAS BOOKS *will be true to those laws of quality that assure a good name
and good will.*

Printed in the United States of America
SM-R-3

Library of Congress Cataloging-in-Publication Data

Illovsky, Michael E.
 Foundations of counseling people : a guide for the counseling, psychologi-
cal, and helping professions / by Michael E. Illovsky.
   p. cm.
 Includes bibliographical references and index.
 ISBN 978-0-398-08863-7 (hard) -- ISBN 978-0-398-08864-4 (pbk.) --
ISBN 978-0-398-08865-1 (ebook)
 1. Counseling--Vocational guidance. I. Title.

BF636.64.I55 2013
158.3--dc23

                                                                    2012037178

PREFACE

The United States, like the rest of the world, is interacting more with people from other cultures. U.S. influence is spreading globally. We are increasingly providing services to clients who are not Caucasian or of European heritage. Our educational programs have been active in training both domestic students of diverse ethnic backgrounds as well as foreign students. These factors contribute to the need for those who provide counseling to understand the elements involved in interacting with a wide spectrum of people.

This book provides a brief synopsis on such topics as common factors, values, universals, cross-cultural competence, and models, approaches, and psychological perspectives of human behavior (theories of personality). The emphasis is on material that relies more on the use of the scientific method and data instead of anecdotal and experiential literature. Material is provided in the form of results and conclusions, and not – usually – in the form of describing the research itself. For the reader who is interested in obtaining information from which statements are derived, there are references to investigate the material further. Information is garnered from such fields as animal studies, counseling, cross-cultural ethnology, education, evolutionary psychology, linguistics, medicine, medical anthropology, physics, psychology, psychological anthropology, and religion.

There are frequent cross-cultural examples in this book. This does not mean that the material is relevant only for those from other cultures. We are all members of cultural groups. What is appropriate for other cultures is usually appropriate for domestic service providers and their clients. Such a perspective enables those who do counseling to consider the cultural aspects of their clients when they provide services to Euro-Americans and to non-Euro-Americans.

The psychological, counseling, and cross-cultural literature often warn the reader of the problems involved in counseling people of different ethnic groups. There are caveats concerning racism, ignorance, ethnocentricity, bias, and so forth; these statements are often directed at Caucasian and middle-class counselors. This is one perspective. Another perspective can also be considered. That is, many counselors have personal and professional characteristics that are helpful in their interactions with those who are apparently dissimilar from them. In many other fields of study (e.g., linguistic, anthropology, and education), there are those who advocate the relativistic view and those who advocate the universal view. The relativist view is that each culture is unique and general approaches are viewed as inappropriate and inaccurate. The universal view is that there are commonalities (universals) among peoples and these commonalities can serve as a basis for interacting with a wide range of people. The psychological and counseling literature has focused on the relativistic view and neglected the universal view. This book presents the view that many counselors have some of the skills, life experiences, and knowledge to provide services to diverse groups of people. However, this does not mean that everyone should be providing counseling – certainly not: providing counseling entails doing so in an ethical and competent manner. When they counsel others, professional counselors have to abide by the ethical and professional standards of the American Counseling Association (2005), and psychologists have to abide by those of the American Psychological Association (2002a). That is, they have to provide services within the boundaries of their training, experience, competence, skills, and credentials. These are important standards that need to be adhered to. When interacting with any client, those who provide counseling have to examine their knowledge and skills and determine if they are the appropriate providers of care.

Various terms are used frequently in this book. The term "counselor" is used in two ways: it is used to refer to professionals whose role and function is to specifically provide counseling services, and it is also used in a more generic sense to refer to a person who gives advice especially professionally (Counselor, 2011). Similarly, the term "counseling" can refer to professional counselors' interactions with clients (American Counseling Association, 2010; Counseling, 2011), or it can refer to more generic interactions: "advice given especially as a result of consultation" (Counsel, 2011). People in many fields engage in counseling in the generic sense – especially those in the helping professions, e.g., medicine, education, social work, and the ministry. The term "U.S. Americans" is used to refer to people living in the United States. These people are predominantly influenced by European ways of thinking and perceiving. The term "Euro-American" is used in reference to U.S. Americans of European ancestry. The term "cross-culture" (and cross-cultural) is used to describe interactions with those of other cultures – this is just one of many terms used by different authors (Gerstein, Heppner, Ægisdóttir, Seung-Ming, Norsworthy, 2009a). Another term that is used in this book is "therapy." This refers to treatment especially of bodily, mental, or behavioral disorders (Therapy, 2011). This work is often done by psychologists. Counselors and counseling usually do not entail working with clinical pathologies; whereas, psychologists and therapy do. However, many psychologists do counseling, and many counselors do therapy. In this book, the terms "counselor" and "psychologist" are used interchangeably, just as the terms "therapy" and "counseling" are used similarly. The term "client" shall be used to refer to the person receiving counseling services. Occasionally there will be changes in the terms used to describe similar groups (e.g., referring to a group as Caucasians or Whites, or to African-Americans as Blacks); this is usually done in order to keep the same terms as the authors of the studies used. In regard to the use of the word "culture," there are many definitions (Kroeber & Kluckhohn, 1952), and there are many forms and dimensions of it (Cohen, 2009). In the professional psychological and counseling literature in the U.S., the term culture is often used in reference to ethnic groups (for example, when used in the context of cross-cultural studies, it most often refers to studies of different ethnic groups). However, culture has a more general meaning, and the term is used in this book both in reference to ethnic groups as well as in reference to factors in the person's environment. One set of definitions of culture refers to the values, conventions, or social practices associated with a particular field, activity, or societal characteristic (Culture, 2012a). It can consist of language, ideas, beliefs, customs, taboos, codes, institutions, tools, techniques, works of art, rituals, ceremonies, and symbols (Culture, 2012b). This term overlaps with other terms that can be used similarly, such as ecological counseling (Conyne & Cook, 2004), ecological psychology (Gibson & Pick, 2003; Heft, 2010), ecological psychotherapy (Fuchs, 2007; Willi, 1999), ecological systems theory, and bioecology (Bronfenbrenner, 1979, 2005), environmental psychology (Barker & Gump, 1964), and naturalistic psychology − of William James and John Dewey (Chemero, 2009). These terms are used by different people at different times but usually refer to environmental influences on the person. One aspect of culture is clear: it is not a static phenomena, it is constantly changing (Nanda & Warms, 2009).

The focus of the material in this book is on the aspects of humans that are conducive to interactions. For the most part, it ignores those aspects we often do not view favorably − e.g., the "killer ape" parts of us that are aggressive and destructive (Ardrey, 1961; Dart, 1953; Vendramini, 2009). This is not to say that these elements are not within humankind. In fact, humans have these propensities. We frequently experience these feelings and behaviors, and we often treat clients with problems in these areas. However, if the propensity to kill and destroy were the dominant features of humans, then they would not exist today. The fact that humans have not perished and have multiplied exponentially, suggests there are other factors (such as cooperation and caring − along with availability of resources) that allowed them to survive through the millenniums. It is understandable why the aggressive aspect of humans has received so much attention in history and in our everyday lives: it is strident, and the consequences can be horrendous. However, in recent years, there has been greater awareness and research on the cooperative and prosocial aspects of humans (Axelrod & Hamilton, 1981; Burtsev & Turchin, 2006; Frank, 1998; Hamilton, 1964; Lumsden & Wilson, 1981; Sachs, 2004; Skyrms, 1996; Wilson, 1975, 1979).

The reader is reminded that the focus of this book is on the concepts. The concepts are of long-term relevance – concepts such as: helping behaviors are ingrained in humans and in many other animals; humans have a long history in learning about others; in learning about others, we are learning about ourselves; in counseling, in addition to the therapeutic interaction, there are a myriad of other factors occurring; mental health professionals have a responsibility to examine what they are doing and to be aware of the influences on them; and mental health professionals have an obligation to seek ways to improve their services.

M.E.I.

CONTENTS

FOUNDATIONS OF
COUNSELING PEOPLE

Chapter 1

FOUNDATIONS OF HELPING BEHAVIORS

Helping others is the basis of counseling. Helping behaviors have their basis in genes and early behavioral patterns. Animals exhibit these behaviors, including those most similar to us: monkeys and apes. In addition, our early ancestors, the Cro-Magnons, and those related to us, such as the Neanderthals, also exhibited helping behaviors. These helping behaviors provide a basis for one person helping another. These helping behaviors are exhibited in all cultures. In terms of cross-cultural counseling, this means people have the capacity to understand why someone (e.g., the counselor) may want to help.

There are many terms used to describe helping behaviors. And there are many forms of helping behaviors. For example, altruism has been defined as a helping behavior. Among the definitions of "altruism" (2010) is that it is behavior that is not beneficial to or may be harmful to itself but that benefits others. This differs from other helping behaviors – which may or may not entail sacrifice. Other terms used to describe helping behaviors include: prosocial, benevolent, caring, compassionate, and humanitarian. There are differentiations among these terms but for the sake of parsimony, I will not go into the details. For the most part, these terms, along with the terms "helping behaviors," will be used similar to the various definitions of "help" (2011) from *Merriam-Webster's dictionary*: 1: to give assistance or support; 2a: to make more pleasant or bearable: improve, relieve; 3a: to be of use to: benefit; b: to further the advancement of: promote; 4a: to change for the better.

ANIMAL STUDIES (ALTRUISTIC BEHAVIORS)

Among the many forms of helping are altruistic behaviors. Arguably, most therapists do not usually engage in altruistic behaviors; that is, they get gains from helping others – such as getting money and appreciation. However, studies on altruism provide insight into some of the foundations of helping behaviors. In the studies that follow, researchers sometimes use the term altruism to describe altruistic behaviors and at other times the term is used to describe helping behaviors. Origins of what has been defined as altruistic behaviors have been traced to the cellular level. For example, Nedelcu and Michod (2006) found the *Volvox carterii*, a primitive multi-cellular creature that has the capacity to reproduce, gives up this function to take on other functions (such as swimming) to help the larger organism survive. The RegA gene causes this to happen. They found genes similar to RegA in a one-celled creature, *Chlamydomonas reinhardtii*. This organism is believed to be closely related to Volvox's single-celled ancestor. The most similar DNA sequence they identified was Crsc13. Of course, one distinction between the behaviors of these organisms and humans is the matter of volition: the behaviors of these organisms do not entail thinking, will power, and decision-making, whereas, these features are present in humans.

Dawkins (1976) used the term "selfish gene" to describe why an organism might sacrifice itself to perpetuate its genes. According to this theory, the gene uses the organism to perpetuate itself, rather than the gene serving as a vehicle to perpetuate the organism. Thus, organisms might cooperate and help others because the other organisms have genes that perpetuate the altruistic organism.

Studies have found helping and altruistic behaviors in many species. For example, these behaviors are exhibited in insects (Hamilton, 1975) and birds (Gould & Vrba, 1982; Jamieson, 1989; Sherman, 1988; Sober, 1984; White, Lambert, Miller, & Stevens, 1991; Williams, 1966). Okasha's (2008) statement of altruistic behaviors is informative and provides perspective: "Altruistic behavior is common throughout the animal kingdom, particularly in species with complex social structures" (para. 2), e.g., ants, wasps, bees, termites, vampire bats, and numerous bird species. An example of animal studies indicating altruistic behaviors is that of Burkart, Fehr, Efferson, and van Schaik (2007). They studied altruistic behaviors among marmoset monkeys. The monkeys were in two separate cages, with one monkey able to provide food (crickets) to a nonfood monkey. The monkey with the food would provide food to the nonfood monkey even though the food-distributing monkey received no gain from doing this. These monkeys spontaneously provided food to nonreciprocating, nongenetically related marmoset monkeys.

Thus, there is evident that helping behaviors, in this case altruistic behavior, exist on cellular to more complicated levels. It is evident through naturalistic observation as well as through experimental conditions in laboratories.

EARLY ANCESTORS

There is evidence that early hominids took care of their injured and sick. Their remains indicate they survived medical conditions and injuries because they were helped and sustained by others. The evidence is based on such studies those of Gracia ct al. (2009). They studied the remains of Homo heidelbergenis living about 530,000 years ago. Lebel et al. (2001) investigated Neanderthals living 175,000 years ago. Solecki (1972) reported on the remains of a Homo erectus who lived 1.7 million years ago. And Zollikofer, Ponce de León, Vandermeersch, and Lévêque (2002) investigated the remains of Neanderthals living 36,000 years ago. These are among the many studies (Alper, 2003; Bailey, 1987; Constable, 1973; Schwartz, 1993; Smithsonian Institution National Museum of Natural History, 2009; Tattersall, 2007; Winkelman, 2000) indicating evidence of early prosocial behaviors.

Spikins, Rutherford, and Needham (2010) wrote that their research and their review of the archaeological evidence indicate a four stage model for the development of human compassion. The first stage began six million years ago, it was at this time that the common ancestor of humans and chimpanzees first experienced empathy for others and motivation to help them. In the second stage, from about 1.8 million years ago, Homo erectus' emotions became integrated with rational thought – compassion and grieving behaviors were exhibited. The third stage, occurring 500,000 and 40,000 years ago, showed evidence that humans such as Homo Heidelbergensis and Neanderthals committed to the welfare of others. There was long-term investment in adolescence; hunting behaviors indicated cooperation and dependence on each other, and there was evidence of the caring of others over long periods of time. In the fourth stage, starting 120,000 years ago, modern humans extended compassion to strangers, animals, objects, and abstract concepts.

GENETIC AND NEUTROLOGICAL BASIS
OF HELPING BEHAVIORS

The ubiquitousness and importance of prosocial behaviors suggest that these behaviors are ingrained in humans. There are indications that altruistic behaviors are part of human genetic DNA as well as that of other species (Batson & Shaw, 1991; De Waal, 2009; Gardner, West, & Barton, 2007; Hamilton, 1972, 1975; Kerr, Feldman, & Godfrey-Smith, 2004; Lehmann & Keller, 2006; Maynard Smith, 1998; Nedelcu & Michod, 2006; Pizzari & Foster, 2008; Rosenberg, 1992; Rushton, 1991; Sober & Wilson, 1998; Toth et al., 2007; Trivers, 1971, 1985). Considerable research has been conducted on the neurological aspects of prosocial and empathetic behaviors (Decety & Jackson, 2006; Hoffman, 1981; Jackson, Brunet, Meltzoff, & Decety, 2006; Kalisch et al., 2005; Levenson & Ruef, 1992). Studies indicate many areas of the brain are involved in these behaviors, e.g., functional magnetic resonance imaging (fMRI) brain scans indicate the posterior superior temporal cortex (pSTC) is involved in altruistic behaviors (Tankersley, Stowe, & Huettel, 2007). Members of the Pongid line (the great apes – which include the chimpanzee, gorilla, and orangutan) show evidence of engaging in comforting and helping behaviors toward other primates that are suffering (Boesch, 1992; Goodall, 1986; DeWaal, 1996). In primates, the call for help is mediated through neurological and chemical processes – limbic and prefrontal regions: increased [18F]-fluoro-2-deoxy-d-glucose uptake in the right dorsolateral prefrontal cortex and decreased uptake in the amygdala (Fox, Oakes, Shelton, Converse, Davidson, & Kalin, 2005). Such mechanisms would not exist unless it serves a function to elicit another basic response – in this case, a helping response from another primate. Keltner (2009) stated that our mammalian and hominid evolution consist of tendencies toward kindness, generosity, compassion, gratitude, and self-sacrifice. These are part of our neurological and genetic composition, as well as part of our social practices. Keltner wrote that the vagus nerve seems to be adapted for altruistic behavior. It activates such parts of the body as the heart, lungs, liver, and digestive organs. Activating the vagus nerve can produce a feeling of expansive warmth in the chest. Some refer to the vagus nerve as "the nerve of compassion" (Porges, 2003, 2005). It may connect to the release of oxytocin, a neurotransmitter involved in bonding. Children with high vagus nerve activity are more cooperative and likely to give to others (Eisenberg, Fabes, & Spinrad, 2006). Keltner (2009) wrote that our capacities for virtue, cooperation, and our moral sense are old in evolutionary terms. Carter, Ahnert, Grossmann, Hrdy, Lamb, Porges, and Sachser (2006) state that it is deep in the neural circuitry of our mammalian roots.

The propensity to share the same feelings that others are experiencing (i.e., the feeling of empathy) is an aspect of emotions that can facilitate helping behaviors. Empathic responses have been found in mammals. For example, mice that see other mice in pain become more sensitive to pain when it is inflicted on them (Jordan & Mogil, 2006). Humans react similarly when they see pain inflicted on others (Danziger, Faillenot, & Peyron, 2009). Researchers have found that when monkeys observe other monkeys performing a task, the same neurons ("mirror neurons") activate in the observing monkey as in the monkey performing the task (Rizzolatti & Craighero, 2004). The same effect has been found with humans, not only with behaviors but also with emotions and sensations (Gallese, 2003; Goldman, 2006; Iacoboni, Molnar-Szakacs, Gallese, Buccino, Mazziotta, & Rizzolatti, 2005; Iacoboni, Woods, Brass,

Bekkering, Mazziotta, & Rizzolatti, 1999; Kappeler & van Schaik, 2006; Keysers, Wicker, Gazzola, Anton, Fogassi, & Gallese, 2004; Meltzoff & Prinz, 2002; Rizzolatti, 1995; Rizzolatti, Craighero, & Fadiga, 2002; Stueber, 2006; Wicker, Keysers, Plailly, Royet, Gallese, & Rizzolatti, 2003). In a book on empathy, De Waal (2009) wrote that one of the characteristics of primates (and that includes humans) is to engage in synchrony and mimicry. That is, humans have the tendency to synchronize and mimic others in behaviors and sensations – such as laughter and yawning. Smith's (Smith & Smith, 1966; Waldemar, 2006) research in the area of behavioral cybernetics demonstrated that our behavioral and physiological responses often coincide with those who interact with us. Counselors have long known of this effect – e.g., when dealing with an angry client, if the counselor maintains composure and responds in a calm manner, the angry client might also calm down. These are among the myriad of data demonstrating that people respond to the feelings around them. One of these feelings that is common to humans is empathy. This feeling can be both innate and learned. Clients can experience these feelings in response to the plight of others. Therefore, if a counselor plays an empathic and helping role, it is within the framework of humans in other cultures to understand this behavior.

CHILDREN

Research indicates that children exhibit prosocial behaviors early in their development (Jaeggi, Burkart, & Van Schaik, 2010; Kappeler & Van Schaik, 2006; Warneken & Tomasello, 2006). Warneken, Hare, Melis, Hanus, and Tomasello's (2007) studies indicated that there may be innate factors involved in helping behaviors. In their studies, they found that if experimenters dropped objects, 18-month-old infants (and chimpanzees) were able to interpret that help was needed and would retrieve the object and return it to the experimenter. Because this behavior was found in both human infants and chimpanzees, there are expectations that it was also present in their common ancestor – existing more than six million years ago. In another study, Benenson, Pascoe, and Radmore (2007) investigated four-, six-, and nine-year-old children and found altruistic behaviors among them. In their studies, they gave children stickers. Pre-trials indicated that the children liked these stickers. Each child said that the stickers were valued. The children were told they could give the stickers to another child they did not know, or they could keep the stickers for themselves. The researchers made sure that the children knew that nobody – including the researchers, parents, teachers, and others – was aware whether the child kept the stickers or gave them away. Under these anonymous conditions, with no gain for themselves, the children nevertheless gave away some of their prized stickers. The researchers wrote that their results were similar to studies done in diverse cultures, and with nonhumans. Eisenberg, Fabes, and Spinrad (2006) wrote that prosocial behaviors go through stages and depend on circumstances. For example, in their studies of children, they found sharing increased with age – but not with helping or providing emotional support. Altruistic and helping behaviors might be exhibited for different reasons as the person develops. Kohlberg (Duska & Whelen, 1975; McDevitt & Ormrod, 2007) wrote that moral development also goes through stages: obedience and punishment orientation; self-interest orientation, interpersonal accord and conformity, authority and social-order maintaining orientation, social contract orientation, and universal ethical principles.

SOCIAL ORIGINS OF HELPING BEHAVIORS

There are many possible origins and reasons for the existence and perpetuation of helping behaviors. For example, they could originate from the desire to propagate one's gene pool. William D. Hamilton (1996) has written of the "inclusive fitness theory," which explains altruistic behavior in terms of people's (and animals') tendency to want to sacrifice and help those with genes most similar to their own. It is interesting to note whether the "inclusive fitness theory" can be expanded to constructs and concepts; that is, are people more likely to help and sacrifice for those with similar values, religion, and so on, as themselves? This is a feasible application because those who are more similar to us on factors such as these are more likely to share similar gene pools.

Another explanation for helping is that it is a function of reciprocity (Bowles & Gintis, 2004; Charness & Rabin, 2002; Hoffman, McCabe, & Smith, 1998; Rabin, 1993). All people are vulnerable to getting hurt and sick. If they look after others who need help, they may be able to receive help when they need it themselves.

Helping behaviors might be facilitated by the grooming that is seen among many animals (Löttker, Huck, Zinner, & Heymann, 2007; Roger, Powell, & Fried, 1992; Russell & Lummaa, 2009; Silk, 2007). Grooming can serve many functions. It helps bond a group. It helps get rid of insects and other material that might jeopardize the well-being of the animal. Groups that do not have grooming behaviors might be more susceptible to dissention and disease.

The most prevalent explanation for helping behaviors is that it originates from the parent-child bond (Broad, Curley, & Keverne, 2006). Those who nurture, sacrifice, and protect their offspring increase the likelihood that their genes will survival. These behaviors are learned by their offspring and can serve as a template, or model, that extends to helping others.

MODERN PEOPLE/HOMO SAPIENS

As with the findings of Homo erectus and Neanderthals, researchers found remains of Cro-Magnons (e.g., Smithsonian National Museum of Natural History, 2007) indicating survival of medical conditions that needed community support to allow the individual to convalesce, heal, and live. It should be noted that "Cro-Magnon" is an older term. There are attempts to abandon the term because it inaccurately implies that Cro-Magnons are different from present-day humans – they are not. All indications are that they are the same as us. Nowadays the term 'Anatomically Modern Human' (AMH) or 'Early Modern Human' (EMH) is a more accurate designation of these Upper Paleolithic human beings living circa 35,000 to 10,000 years ago.

All cultures provide recourse to relieve suffering (Fabrega, 2004; Gielen, Fish, & Draguns, 2004). In these cultures, there were individuals who serve the functions and roles of counseling others (Bolles, 1993; Campbell, 1959; Canadian Mental Health Association, 2010; Frank, 1998; Frazer, 1922; Hearnshaw, 1989; Krippner, 2002; Wachtel & Messer, 1998). Rudnick (2002) wrote that "There is little doubt that various forms of mental healing or shamanism would have began in pre-historic times" (p. 8). He stated that the work of psychotherapists existed in various forms approximately one hundred thousand years ago, and that each culture in recorded history had its own way of treating mental illness/mental disorder through its own belief system. There were individuals who provided counseling, advice, guidance, mediation, healing, and divinations. They had such names as: kadji (Australian aborigine); Machi (Mapuche – South America); yaskomo (Waiwai – Amazonia); curanderos (Peru); Hatałii (Navajo – Native American); sangoma (Zulu); shamans (Evenki, Manchu-Tungus); Nuru and Yuta (Ryukyu Islands – Okinawa); Ngakpas or Ngakmas/mos (Tibet); mudangs and baksoo mudangs (Korean); Druids (Britain); jardalanin (Oroqen shaman assistant); Heyoka (Lakota); Ayahuasqueros (Peru); and "witch" doctors, medicine people, elders, priests, augurs, and astrologers (Moodley & West, 2005).

Specialized Roles and Functions

In the past and the present, most counseling occurs outside the realm of professional services. Family, relatives, friends, and community members often provided guidance and advice. With the advent of communal living and surplus, there was greater specialization. As people increasingly lived above subsistence levels, the surplus provided greater support for specialization. Individuals could perform such specialized functions as healing others, interpreting phenomena (e.g., interpreting bones, chicken entails, and stars), and acting as intermediaries or gateways to spirits and the divine. They arrived at these positions through various means. In some cultures, they attained their position because they had an interest in the specialty and developed the appropriate skills. In other cultures, they attained their positions because people perceive them as having these skills. Some attained their positions through hereditary. Others obtained their positions because they had access to the necessary resources (e.g., a college education). Usually, before individuals could exercise their skills, most cultures required the initiate to undergo some form of apprenticeship.

The roles and functions of "counselors" vary among cultures. In the preface of their book, Gielen, Fish, and Draguns (2004) wrote that the world's first healers had combined religious, healing, divination, and psychotherapeutic functions. However, in more modern times, different specialists take care of the body, mind, and soul (e.g., as physicians, psychologists, and priests). Fish (2004) stated that societies had various methods of dealing with people with physical, biological, and psychological differences. They were punished, injured, killed, imprisoned, burnt, isolated, quarantined, exiled, or ignored. There was also the view that the problem could be helped, improved, or cured – e.g., through psychotherapy. Many cultures attribute special qualities to those who help others, e.g., people believe the shaman, or counselor, knows the right rituals, or has the knowledge or interpretive skills, to perform their functions. In the developed countries, these special qualities are associated with having the imprimatur of an academic diploma.

Differences in the Manifestation of Prosocial Behaviors

The degree to which prosocial behaviors are manifested differ among individuals and cultures. Among individuals it might differ because of innate biological propensities, internalized norms, learned behaviors, modeling, or social expectations. Some of these same factors are also at work with the variation of prosocial behaviors among cultures. Cultures differ in the way prosocial behaviors are expressed, defined, and exhibited. They differ in the degree to which they help others (Dovidio, Schroeder, Penner, & Piliavin, 2006). Levine, Norenzayan, and Philbrick (2001) found such factors as the country's economic conditions influenced helping behaviors, e.g., citizens in countries with higher rates of productivity were less likely to help (though the study on which this statement is based did not find statistical significance). Countries that have cultural values to help strangers were more likely to help. For example, unlike all other European countries occupied by the Germans in World War II, Albania was the only country where every Jew who lived there, or who sought asylum there, survived. It was the only German occupied European country where the Jewish population increased at the end of the war. The behavior of the Albanians is attributed to the cultural value of "besa" (Gershman, 2008; Sarner, 1972). Besa is commonly referred to as word of honor (in this context, to take care of those in need and to be hospitable). Because of this value, many Albanians were willing to risk their lives to protect those who came to them for help.

Not only do cultures differ in prosocial behaviors, there are also intra-cultural variations – and different reasons for the behaviors to be exhibited. Gurven, Zanolini, and Schniter (2008) studied pro-social behaviors using the Dictator Game. In the Dictator Game, one person (the dictator) had a resource and had the option of sharing it with another person (Buss, 2005). The dictator could keep all the money or share; results indicated some dictators shared and others do not. The researchers studied the Tsimane Amerindians living in the lowlands of the Amazonian region of Bolivia. They found differences among villages in how much the dictator shared. They attributed differences to be a function of variations in social expectations and norms of fairness.

Human Ethos

The value and importance of prosocial behaviors is evident in their prevalence in human ideals. The ideal of caring for one's fellow being has a significant presence in many religions. For example, love for others is one of the main pillars of Christianity. Christianity derived this and other ideals and concepts from Judaism. Compassion for one's fellow human being and for the suffering of others is one of the main tenets of Buddhism. Buddhism derived these and other values from Hinduism. Those of the Islamic faith are extolled to love Allah, the prophet Muhammad, the Koran (*also spelled Qur'an*), the faithful, and the family (interpreted either as love for Muhammad's family, or love of one's own family and community). The ancient Greeks used the terms agape, philia, and eros to describe various types of love (Helm, 2009; Moseley, 2010). These terms have been used differently by people at different times – usually to connate love, or affection, ranging from sensual to transcendental (e.g., of the physical).

It should be noted that even though love, affection, and compassion are concepts and behaviors that are familiar to people in many cultures, the counselor's good intentions may not be perceived as such. There are many possible reasons for this. For example, people might not notice the counselor's good intentions, or people might misinterpret or have a deleterious interpretation of the behavior. Therefore, the client might not respond in a positive manner just because the counselor has intentions to help and to be beneficial.

Chapter 2

COMMON ASPECTS OF COUNSELING

During the incipient modern psychotherapy movement, many scholars of human behavior were interested in other cultures (Kaplan & Sadock, 2003). For example, Freud's (2000) book, *Totem and Taboo: Resemblances Between the Mental Lives of Savages and Neurotics,* was an examination of the psychological aspects of such societies as those of the Australian aborigines. Published in German in 1913, he applied psychoanalysis to the fields of archaeology, anthropology, and religion. He wrote four essays dealing with other cultures: *The Horror of Incest*; *Taboo and Emotional Ambivalence*; *Animism, Magic and the Omnipotence of Thoughts*; and *The Return of Totemism in Childhood.* Jung was another example of a person at the beginning of the modern psychological movement who was interested in other cultures. He traveled throughout the world and studied Chinese philosophy. He investigated common elements in the unconscious, and universals (1968, 1990; Jacobi, 1973; Kast, 1992; Segal, 1998; van Eenwyk, 1997). He found universal expressions of archetypes (symbols) expressed in dreams, art, and literature. Frazer's (1922) multivolume *Golden Bough* aroused interest and controversy. The anthropologist made comparative studies of mythology, religion, folklore, and magic. He wrote about rites, beliefs, superstitions, and taboos of early cultures and Christianity. He had a substantial impact on many fields, including literature, religion, and psychology – e.g., Carl Jung's collective unconscious was preceded by Fraser's identification of story motifs common to many cultures.

In the past 75 years or so, there was more of an interest in delineating the common and effective ingredients of psychotherapy. These were investigated in common factors, universals, and cross-cultural studies. The common factors literature often dealt with the common elements among the various therapeutics approaches and techniques. The literature on universals often dealt with applications across cultures. The more recent cross-culture literature focused more on recommended or suggested guidelines for dealing with people of other cultures. However, there is no agreement or rule as to the use of these terms, and they are often used without apparent consideration for their distinction.

COMMON FACTORS

Sprenkle and Blow (2004) wrote that most authors attribute Rosenzweig (1936) as the person who first addressed the issue of common factors in therapy. Rosenzweig (1936) found no particular therapeutic approach superior to others. He found the common factor among successful therapists was a warm, respectful, and friendly relationship with the client. In recent years, there has been an upsurge in the exploration and proposals of common factors in psychological treatment (Asay & Lambert, 2004; Bachelor & Horvath, 2004; Bordin, 1979; Frank & Frank, 1991; Hubble, Duncan, & Miller, 1999; Lambert, 1992; Luborsky, Singer, & Luborsky, 1975; Schofield, 1988; Snyder, Scott, & Cheavens, 1999; Tallman & Bohart, 2004; Tolle, 2004; Wampold, Mondin, Moody, Stich, Benson, & Ahn, 1997). The following are some of those who have written on common factors in effective therapy.

Fischer, Jome, and Atkinson (1998) wrote that common factors in psychotherapy and healing are as follows: (a) the therapeutic relationship – personal qualities of the healer that induce trust and expectation to be healed; (b) shared worldview – the more the counselor and client understand each other's values, perceptions, ways of categorizing, and explanations, the more likely positive change will occur; (c) client expectations – the more the client expects that the counselor can help the client, and the greater the credibility that the counselor has the ability to change, the more likely change will occur; and (d) ritual or intervention – the more the client and counselor believe that a certain ritual, intervention, or technique is relevant and effective, the more likely it will work.

Frank's seminal *Persuasion and Healing* (1961; Frank & Frank, 1991) presented the case that all psychotherapies consist of the following: an emotional and confiding relationship, the perception that the setting is therapeutic, the client's belief that the counselor can be trusted to provide help, the counselor's explanation of the problem, and the counselor providing a method for cure. Frank (1974) also presented the view that the essence of effective treatment is to deal with clients' feeling and perception of demoralization, e.g., deal with clients' feeling that they lack the ability to deal with the problem and that there is no hope or meaning. Similarly, Klein (1996) attributed the efficacy of therapies to the latter factors.

Garfield (1973) studied the basic ingredients or common factors in psychotherapy. He wrote that "such common factors as hope, expectation of change, trust, an emotional relationship, the facilitation of emotional arousal, catharsis, receiving information, the social impact of the healer, etc. might be variables cutting across all schools of psychotherapy, and they might be potent variables making for change" (p. 10).

Grencavage and Norcross (1990) classified common factors into (a) client characteristics – these are factors that the client brings into therapy that can have an impact, e.g., socioeconomic background, religion, gender, motivation, and expectations; (b) counselor qualities – these are counselor characteristics that can influence therapy – e.g., the degree to which client and counselor share the same demographics, theoretical orientation, experience, and education; (c) change processes – such as the acquisition of new insight or behaviors; (d) treatment structure – the use of particular theory, approach, or technique to deal with the problem; and (e) therapeutic relationship – the degree to which the counselor and client can work together to solve the client's problem.

Lambert (1992a) proposed four factors to account for therapeutic change: extra-therapeutic, common factors, expectancy or placebo, and techniques. Hubble, Duncan, and Miller (1999) expanded on Lambert's (1992a) four factors. Their four factors are client/extra-therapeutic factors, relationship factors, placebo hope/expectancy factors, and model/techniques factors. Client factors are endogenous to the client, such as motivation, and strengths. Extra-therapeutic factors are those that are outside the client, such as family support and a good job. Lambert reports that 40 percent of outcome variance is attributed to client/ extra-therapeutic factors. Relationship factors are those involved in the therapeutic alliance between the counselor and the client. Lambert (1992a) reports that 30 percent of outcome variance is attributed to counselor-client interaction factors. Placebo hope/expectancy factors are the influences of expectations of participants in therapy, e.g., expectations that therapy will help and belief in the counselor's skills and explanations. Lambert attributes 15 percent of outcome to these factors. Finally, the fourth factor are the models and techniques used by the counselor. These are the specific factors used by the counselor to help the client. Lambert (1992a) suggested that 15 percent of therapeutic effects are due to these factors. Luborsky et al. (2002) examined 17 meta-analyses of comparisons of treatments. They found an effect size of 0.2 was due to specific therapy techniques. According to Wampold (2001), at least 70 percent of therapeutic effects that contribute to client outcome are due to common factors – or are general effects.

Lambert and Bergin (1994) concluded that the common factors accounting for effective treatment across approaches are (a) support factors – the counselor provides support, reassurance with the present situation and with attempts at changing behaviors; (b) learning factors – the counselor helps the client learn ways to view the problem as well as solutions to them, and the counselor also provides skills information, advice, and possibly better ways of problem solving; and (c) action or behavioral factors – the counselor helps the client implement new and different ways of dealing with the problem.

Lin (1994) reviewed the research on common factors in counseling. Four constructs comprising common factors were found:

1. Client's characteristics. According to outcome research results, 40 percent of improvement in clients is because of this factor (Asay & Lambert, 1999; Lambert, 1992a, 1992b; Sexton, Whiston, Bleuer, & Walz, 1997). Client characteristics include inner resources, religious influence, motivation, goals, determination, openness to change and ideas, having skills to change, expectations, and desire to change.

2. Counselor's characteristics. These include such factors as counselor's warmth, empathy, unconditional positivity, traits of support, caring, acceptance, respect, expectations for improvement, persuasive abilities, attention, understanding and encouragement, use of psychological interventions in both theory and practice, and playing an active role in client improvement. Also included in counselor's characteristics are the counselor's status or reputation; competence; ability to be integrated, mature, genuine, and congruent; ability to provide a nonthreatening, trusting, and safe or secure atmosphere; and acceptance of the client.

3. Process of change. This consists of the counseling relationship, counseling techniques, placebo, hope, expectancy, and rituals. The therapeutic relationship is essential to therapeutic change. Important aspects of this are an emotionally charged confiding relationship with a helping person, including a good relationship with elements of accurate empathy, positive regard, nonpossessive warmth, and congruence or genuineness. Counseling techniques consist of combinations of affective, experiential, cognitive and behavioral elements. The techniques provide support for changes, as well as facilitate learning new or different ways to approach or resolve the problem, and help with the implementation of skills learned in therapy. The enhancement of the placebo effects, hope, and expectations are also important parts of the process of change – this is reported to contribute about 15 percent to therapy outcome (Asay & Lambert, 1999; Lambert, 1992a, 1992b). These can be enhanced by such factors as the degree to which the client and counselor believe in and are committed to the therapeutic approach and techniques, and the stimulation of the clients' self-healing processes by such influences as hope, and expectations. Rituals can play an important role in bringing about therapeutic changes. Rituals can enhance credence in the counselor's ability, buttress reasons for what is being done, and facilitate the therapeutic effects of the placebo, hope, and expectations.

4. Counseling context. The setting in which therapy occurs can enhance or detract from therapeutic changes. The setting can facilitate new learning, feelings of safety, and heighten the client's expectation for change.

Luborsky, Singer, and Luborsky (1975) compared the effectiveness of various psychotherapeutic approaches. They found no clear indication that there was a more effective approach among the various therapies. They wrote that the common factors in effective therapies consisted of a plausible explanation for the problem, which also provides a guide for future behavior, a helping relationship, "nonspecifics" such as suggestions (e.g., as to what to do for the problem), and abreaction (the ability of the client to express the problem – e.g., in words, and behavior).

Rogers (1957; Wyatt, 2001) believed that the counselor's attitude, not skills and knowledge, is the therapeutic agent in bringing about change. If the counselor exhibits empathy, warmth, and genuineness, these are essential and sufficient conditions for therapeutic change. Truax and Carkhuff (1967) followed suit with Rogers' ideas. Their approach, known as a client-centered, person-centered, nondirective, or Rogerian approach, presents Roger's core conditions differently, e.g., depicting them as congruence, empathy, and unconditional positive regard (Encyclopedia of Mental Disorders, 2009). Brown, Cameron, and Brown (2008) also wrote that the relationship with the counselor accounts for most of the outcome in treatment variance.

Stricker (2012) lists the common factors in psychotherapy as: (a) there is a therapeutic alliance; (b) the client has prior exposure to difficulties; (c) there is corrective emotional experience which enables the client to deal with the problem in a new or better manner; (d) the counselor and client have expectations of therapeutic change; (e) the counselor has such qualities as attention, empathy, and positive regard; and (f) the counselor provides an explanation of the problem to the client.

Jackson (1999) studied Western psychological healing from antiquity to the present. The writer found the common and essential ingredients consisted of a relationship between the healer and the sufferer; the healer was authoritative and listened to the sufferer, the healer directly or indirectly steered the sufferer (e.g., through approval or disapproval, suggestions, and interpretations), the healer consoled and comforted, the healer provided support for the expression of the sufferers' thoughts and feelings, and the sufferer shared thoughts and feelings as well as developed self-understanding.

One of the themes mentioned in the common factors literature is the importance of the relationship. There are sections of this book that deal with factors that facilitate and inhibit this process. These include: placebo effects, values, communication and cognitive processes, approaches and techniques, and client characteristics.

UNIVERSALS

Uncovering universal truths, guidelines, values, certainties, etc., has been an endeavor in numerous fields, e.g., many involved in philosophy, religion, linguistics, education, mathematics, evolution, game theory, and personality theory have tried to delineate universals (Armstrong, 1989; Klima, 2008; Loux, 2001; MacLeod & Rubenstein, 2006; Moreland, 2001; Russell, 1997). It has been a long source of debate and analysis for such influential people as Abelard (Marenbon, 1997), Aristotle (Perin, 2007), Averroes (also known as Ibn Rushd; Leaman, 1998), Berkeley (Margolis, 1982), Boethius (Klima, 2008), James (1918), Maimonides (1904), Moore (O'Connor, 1982), Ockham (Burns, 1913), Peirce (Perez-Teran Mayorga, 2007), Plato (Nehamas, 1975), Roscellinus (also known as Roscelin; Marias, 1967), Spinoza (Haserot, 1950), and Wittgenstein (1994). Those who support the idea that there are universals are contrasted with those who think there are no universals. For instance, universalists have been contrasted with relativists, realists with nominalists (terms used in philosophy), objects with primary quality with those of secondary quality (terms used in physics), evolutionists with proponents of the Standard Social Science Model (SSSM), culture-general with culture-specific, etic with emic, syntonic with dystonic, and so on. There are variations within and between the proponents of these views. Those who subscribe to the idea that there are similarities among people and cultures believe there are universals that transcend cultures. Those who have the view that each environment is unique and shapes the individual, e.g., the Standard Social Science Model, often view the mind as a "blank slate" (Barkow, Cosmides, & Tooby, 1992). They attribute less valence to biological and evolutionary factors. An example of a universal view are those who subscribe to biogenetic structuralism (Laughlin & d'Aquili, 1974). They view the evolution of the nervous system and brain structures (which are universal structures) as the basis of what goes on inside and outside the human body, like language, culture, thoughts, images, feelings, and pathologies. Pinker (2002) had a universal view and reacting against the tabula rasa perspective of the brain, wrote that evolution shapes behavior (based on brain process) rather than culture inscribing on the blank slate of the brain. For the most part, this book will use the terms and their cognates of "universal" in contrast to "relative." In a review of the literature, one point is obvious: if a universal is proposed, there will be challenges to it, there will be exceptions, and there will be disagreement.

The literature on universals covers many different approaches. Some investigate specific behaviors and factors, while others offer broad, general models and approaches. There are proposals for many types of universals. For example, there have been proposals of the universal innateness of language (Pinker, 1994), color vision (Zeki, 1993), ability to detect cheaters (Cosmides,

1989), and ability to monitor being gazed at (Scaife & Bruner, 1975). Brown (1991) lists hundreds of universals – these frequently have updates, additions, and modifications. Brown's universals range from abstraction in speech and thought, to vowel contrasts, and world view. He puts his universals into the categories of language and cognition, society, myth, ritual and aesthetics, and technology. There are other ways to categorize these universals. Of course, religions have presented their universals as well. The advent of the Abrahamic belief systems (Judaism, Christianity, and Islam), espoused monotheistic, universal, and singular truths. Whereas, Eastern belief systems (such as Hinduism, Buddhism) espoused multiple avenues to the Truth/Godhead (Smith, 1958). Those who adhere to the various psychological schools of thought often proclaim or assume their approaches are universally applicable. For example, Freud considered people's psychosexual development, the id, ego, superego, and the unconscious as applicable to everyone. Jung, considered the collective unconscious and archetypes as universals. Adler proposed the striving for superiority. McClelland, Murray, and Wiggins offered intimacy and status. James wrote about the multitudes of instincts. Skinner presented basic learning mechanisms. And so on.

Among those who use a psychological perspective to study people in other cultures are the cross-cultural psychologists and the cultural psychologists. Lonner (1980, 2000) wrote of the differences between the two. He wrote that the cross-cultural psychologists are inherently universal in their thinking, and cultural psychologists consider thoughts and behaviors to be the result of unique interactions with specific environments. Cross-cultural psychologists generally examine culture and try to determine the universality of what they observe (Berry, Poortinga, Segall, & Dasen, 1992; Cole, 1996; Hofstede, 2001; Laungani, 2007; Jahoda, 1993; Smith, Bond, & Kağitçibaşi, 2006; Williams & Best (1990). Whereas, cultural psychologists consider culture and mind to be inseparable. Culture influences the mind, and the mind influences culture; there are no universal laws (Bruner, 1990; Fiske, Kitayama, Markus, & Nisbett, 1998; Markus & Kitayama, 1991; Nesbitt, 2003; Nisbett & Cohen, 1996; Shore, 1996, Shweder, 1991; Shweder & Levine, 1984; Triandis, 1989). Helfrich (1999) presented a model that attempts to resolve the dissonance between the etic (can be applied to other cultures) and emic (within the culture) approaches. The model, using the triarchic resonance principle, considered the interactions of culture, the individual, and ecological task. "According to this framework, every observable behavior takes the specific form of interaction between the three components individual, task and culture. Culture exists independently of the individual and the task and remains relatively stable" (Spering, 2001, p. 10).

There are various classification schemes for universals. Norenzayan and Heine (2005) wrote that there are four universals. They are in a hierarchy of claims to universality, ranging strongest to weakest: (a) accessibility universals, (b) functional universals, (c) existential universals, and (d) nonuniversals. Accessibility universals are cognitively available to most people in most cultures, e.g., dealing with numbers. Functional universals are cognitively available to people in all cultures; they have the same use in all cultures, and vary in the extent of their use across cultures, e.g., dealing with social hierarchies, and trade. Existential universals are cognitively available to all "normal" adults in all cultures, and can vary in the ways and frequency of its use, e.g., the way people classify flowers might be based on different rules and criteria. And nonuniversals are psychological processes that do not meet the standards of existential processes, e.g., arithmetic reasoning is different between abacus and nonabacus users.

Prince (1980) explored the universal components of psychotherapy. They are listed as the following: there is a worldview shared by the healer and person being healed, the healer provides a culturally meaningful explanation of the problem, there is social influence through such avenues as suggestion, and there are self-healing and self-correcting elements in the sufferer.

The manner in which the Human Relations Area Files (HRAF) organized its information can provide insight into universals. The Human Relations Area Files (HRAF) serves as a repository of cultural anthropology data for an international consortium of universities, colleges, and research institutions. It provides information for the cross-cultural study of human behavior, society, and culture. Their material is organized into: (a) basic information; (b) history, prehistory, and culture change, (c) language and communication; (d) economy, food, and resource exploitation; (e) technology and material culture; (f) marriage, family, kinship, and social organization; (g) social relationships; (h) life cycle; (i) sexuality and reproduction; (j) political organization and behavior; (k) justice, law, and social problems; (l) international and interethnic relations; (m) religion; (n) health, illness, medicine, and death; (o) education and knowledge; (p) arts; and (q) recreation. The categories they developed to organize the data might reflect universals that can be applied to all cultures.

In terms of universal statements, common factors, and cross-cultural guidelines, these should be accepted with caution. International studies of values (e.g., Union of International Associations, 2009a; World Values Survey, 2009a) indicate that what is evident to people in one culture, is not necessarily agreed upon when submitted to the scrutiny of other cultures. For the most part, universal statements, common factors, and cross-cultural guidelines are made within the confines of certain journals, books, presentations, and professional circles. They have not been submitted to world opinion to the same degree as some of the studies of values. If they were submitted, it is possible that the guidelines are not as readily apparent and agreed upon.

This lack of clarity can be considered a weakness by those who like guidelines, and it does not inspire confidence in the ability of scholars and science to be definitive. However, it might also provide a more valid perception of humans; that is, the cultures they live in, and the individuals in them, are multidimensional and have different aspects to them. Among the problems in trying to develop definitive statements, general narratives, algorithms, scripts, schemas, and templates about people and cultures is that both the behavior (e.g., by the client) and the person doing the observing (e.g., the counselor) can change with time, place, and situation; also, making general statements can leave out relevant characteristics and information. Our quest for universals and for guidelines reflects our desire to have more certainty in what we do, and it appeases our insecurities. However, even if there were universals, it would be inadvisable to assume they are always applicable – for example, it would seem that every parent would want medical interventions to save their child's life; however, there are some people whose beliefs do not allow this (Migden & Braen, 1998; Sloan & Ballen, 2008). Our theories and models may provide us with direction and with the perception that we understand phenomena; however, we should also consider that just because we think we know what is going on does not necessarily mean that this is indeed the case.

It is little wonder that the social sciences have problems determining whether or not there are universals and getting agreement. The physical sciences offer some illustration of the problems in viewing, measuring, and categorizing phenomena. Freedman (2010) wrote of scientific theories: "Expert pronouncements so often turn out to be exaggerated, misleading, or flat-out wrong" (p. 56). In quantum mechanics, Heisenberg's (Hilgevoord, 2006) uncertainty principle states that with certain pairs of physical properties, the more precisely one property (such as position) is known, the less precisely the other property (such as velocity) is known – one cannot measure both simultaneously with accuracy or certainty. With humans, we are trying to measure, interpret, and understand multiple factors. Erwin Schrödinger's (Scott, 1967) theory of superposition (from quantum process and wave function) lets us know that whether something exists or not depends on the observer – the observation or measurement itself affects an outcome, so that the outcome as such does not exist unless the measurement is made – this phenomenon is sometimes called quantum indeterminacy or the observer's paradox. With humans, we have to consider that what we observe is through the eyes of the observer, and it does not necessarily reflect the viewed object as it is – this means what the object is depends on who is doing the observing. Even though it is questionable to apply physics and quantum mechanics to human behavior, these examples provide insight into the problems we face in the mental health field where the observer and the observed are so mutable. The delineations of universals are also constrained by the Zeitgeist and parameters of our times (Freedman, 2010; Kuhn, 1962); that is, the perspectives, values, and paradigms of our times limit us. In addition, our exposure to previous literature influences us: we act and react to the ideas presented in the literature – making it difficult to see phenomena in a very different light, e.g., Mischel (1973) reported numerous studies indicating how professional education can hinder the accurate diagnosing of mental disorders. One of Wittgenstein's (1967, 1994) views is that concepts interfere with our perceptions of a more accurate picture of phenomena. There is also the perspective that there are constraints to the way we think about universals because we engage in thinking which places information into our limited categories (Adams, Ambady, Nakayama, & Shimojo, 2011; Cangelosi & Harnad, 2001; Damper & Harnad, 2000, Goldstone, 1994; Harnad, 2005; Macrae & Bodenhausen, 2000).

One aspect of therapy is more apparent these days: therapy can modify universals. We have many examples from the area of biology of how environment affects basic, common, biological universals. For example, universally, we all need to eat. However, environmental factors such as diet can change our development and chemistry, e.g., if children are deprived of certain nutrients they may become anemic or have problems with their bones; another example is that human bodies share in common the capacity to make cells, but smoking cigarettes can exacerbate this capacity and induce cancer. Because of the plasticity of the brain and because humans are capable of adapting, psychotherapeutic intervention can induce fundamental changes.

There are a number of possible ways to view human, universal, and relativistic behaviors. One perspective is that humans are capable of learning and exhibiting a wide range of thoughts, feelings, and behaviors. This would include the ability to exhibit universal and relativistic behaviors, based on the circumstances. The expression of these behaviors can be facilitated or hindered by endogenous and exogenous factors. For instance, the tendency to feel anxious (a universal phenomena) may be influenced by low levels of gamma-aminobutyric acid (an endogenous factor), and whether one is in a hostile environment (an exogenous factor). Another perspective is that humans are engaged in a dialectic process; that is, there is a continuous action and reaction process among points of view (e.g., universal and relativistic). If one view prevails, this will give rise to the other view, and if there is a synthesis of these views, there will be a counterpoint to the synthesis, which will result in another perspective, and so on.

It is obvious that human behavior and the perception of universals are dependent on the viewer's reference point. Those who view people from a universal perspective will see universals, and those who have a relativistic perspective will see phenomena from that point of view – just as Rogerians look at therapy from the perspective of relationships, behaviorists look at behaviors, and psychoanalysts look at past experiences. Perhaps an approach to take is that provided by Jainism. This Indian philosophy uses the term "anekantavada" to describe the perspective that any assertions should be conditional, e.g., accompanied by the terms "maybe," "perhaps," and "from one point of view" (Dundas, 2002; Koller, 2000). This is similar to the perspective of such Western schools of thought as skepticism, agnosticism, and relativism – in general, it is more of a scientific approach.

Various authors have written about how to deal with contrasting views. Bezanson and James (2007) wrote that culture-general and culture-specific approaches to counseling are false dichotomies. They wrote about building on the commonalities of the culture-general approach, and having an understanding of the differences provided by a culture specific approach. They propose taking a hermeneutics approach that integrates the two approaches. Draguns (1995) rejected the universalist and relativist dichotomy in analyzing abnormal behavior. The author wrote that psychological manifestations are a combination of both common and culture-specific factors. Winkelman (2009) writes in a similar vein. In his chapter on "Transcultural Psychiatry and Indigenous Psychology" (Chapter 6), he states that culture and biology produce universal and cultural specific psychological characteristics and mental illness/disorder. Levy (2004) wrote that the evolutionary psychologists have presented the Standard Social Science Model as a "straw man" to contrast their theory with. He wrote that both sides of the nature-nurture debate are interactionists, and that everyone agrees that genomes and other developmental resources are involved in human behavior and that the environment plays a role, e.g., it influences how the genome is expressed. The difference between the two views is not one of either the evolutionist (universal) or the Standard Social Science Model (relativist) position; rather, it is a matter of the degree of influence the factors in each view plays.

There are other factors that are not mentioned in the literature that can facilitate and inhibit both universal and relativist perspectives. The advent of nationalism and ethnic identification can induce a relativistic perspective. From this perspective, each group might foster the perception that they are different from others, with unique identities, values, customs, traditions, and histories. Such identification can facilitate a sense of belonging and indigenous pride. Also, a relativistic view can help those with more resources justify and distinguish themselves from others, e.g., they have more because they work harder or are more deserving. A universal approach would facilitate the feeling that people belong to a world community and decrease the "them" versus "us" distinction. It could promote a greater sense of sharing and empathy. Thus, the universal and relativist views can have economic, social, and political aspects to them.

CROSS-CULTURAL LITERATURE

The diasporas of the original inhabitants of Africa into all parts of the world suggests that even in their early inception, humans were moving, exploring, learning, and experiencing new and different encounters (Tishkoff et al., 2009). There have been military, nomadic, trade, religious, exploratory, exploitive, and other interactions, among regions of the world for millenniums. Early in oral and written history, there were accounts of people going beyond their borders. For example, Herodotus (1998) of Halicarnassus around 430 B.C.E. wrote *The Histories* in which he describes the Greeks, Persians, Babylon, Upper Egypt, Thrace, Scythia (southern Russia), Crimea, Cyrene, Asia minor, southern Italy, and Aegean islands. Alexander III of Macedon (356 B.C.–323 B.C.) invaded Asia Minor, Syria, Egypt, Assyria and Babylonia, Persia, and India (Wilcken & Borza, 1967). His incursions influenced the countries he invaded, as well as the surrounding countries. He had scholars with him; they learned about other cultures, and they helped spread Hellenism. Marco Polo, a merchant in the 1200s, went to central Asia and China (Yule & Cordier, 1923). Friar Julian, in 1235 traveled to the lands of the Magyars and Volga Bulgaria (Guzman, 1996). Giovanni da Pian del Carpine in 1245, Ascelin of Lombardia also in 1245, André de Longjumeau in 1249, and William of Rubruck in 1253 (Hakluyt Society, 1990) visited the Mongols – going through such areas as central Europe, the Middle East, and northern and central Asia (including China). Between 1095 and 1291, the Europeans conducted the crusades – with campaigns continuing into the fifteenth century in Spain and eastern Europe. Their activities opened European culture and trade to the Middle East, North Africa, and various parts of Asia (Gabrieli & Costello, 1984; Hallam, 1989; Macron, 1979; Riley-Smith, 1999; Tyerman, 2006). Europe obtained information from their contacts with the Arab countries in such subjects as art, architecture, medicine, agriculture, music, language, education, law, technology, classic texts (such as the reintroduction of the works of Aristotle), science, philosophy, theology, literature, aesthetics, algebra, and chemistry. Around 1440, the advent of Gutenberg's printing press enabled the spreading of information to increased numbers of people. From the Renaissance (14th to 17th century), to the Industrial Age (18th to 19th century), a host of travelers and explorers expanded our horizons. Cabeza de Vaca (1993), 1490–1560; Christopher Columbus (Crosby, 1987), 1451–1506; John Cabot (also known as Giovanni Caboto; Pope, 1997), 1450?–1499; David Livingstone (Ross, 2002), 1813–1873; Ferdinand Magellan (Baker; 1993), 1480–1521; James Cook (Beaglehole, 1974; Rienits & Rienits, 1968), 1728–1779; and Richard Burton (Farwell, 1988; Rice, 1990), 1821– 1890, explored various parts of the world.

Europeans were not the only ones crossing boundaries and studying other cultures. There were many people in other cultures traveling, exploring, trading, learning, and conquering. For example, around 4300 B.C.E.–3200 B.C.E., there are indications that the Harappa culture, part of the Indus Valley Civilization, interacted with southern Turkmenistan and northern Iran. The influence of the Early Harappan period (about 3200 B.C.E.–2600 B.C.E.) was found in central Asia and the Iranian plateau (Neyland, 1992; Parpola, 2005; Possehl, 1982; Ratnagar, 2006). There were pre-Columbian transoceanic contacts between the Americas, Europe, Africa, Asia, and Oceania – approximately 9,000 to 12,000 years ago (Fagan, 1987; Fell, 1984; Hey, 2005; Huffman, n.d.; Ingstad, 1969; Jairazbhoy, 1974; Sorenson & Raish, 1996; Riley, Kelly, Pennington, Rands, 1971). The moral messages of the Indian ruler, Ashoka (304 B.C.–232 B.C.), of the Maurya Dynasty, was spread to many cultures and reached as far as ancient Rome and Egypt (Avari, 2007; Dhammika, 1993). There are various accounts of Jews traveling and settling in China during the Han dynasty in 206 B.C. to 220 A.D., the Zhou dynasty in the sixth century B.C., and the Tang dynasty in seventh to eighth century (Bareket, 2002; Gil, 1976; Guang, n.d.; Shapiro, 2007; Xu, 2003). There were maritime and overland routes interconnecting the east, south, and western Asia, the Mediterranean, North and Northeast Africa, and Europe though such routes as the Silk Road (Curtin, 1998; Elisseeff, 2000; Foltz, 2010; "Silk Road," 2009; Whitfield, 1999; Wood, 2004; Wriggins, 2004) which extended from China to the Mediterranean Sea. Chinese and Indians crossed their mutual borders for a variety of reasons, e.g., Faxian in 399, Xuanzang in 627, and Yijing in 671 (Sen, 2006) were among the hundreds of Chinese monks visiting India. Moslem conquests (632–732) and trade opened up interactions with Arabia, Asia, Africa, and Europe. They were in such areas as greater Syria, Palestine, Iraq, Persia, central Asia, Turkey, the Indian subcontinent, southeast Asia, inner Asia and eastern Europe; North Africa, Horn of Africa, East Africa, western Africa; the Iberian Peninsula, and the Balkans (Donner, 1981; Eaton, 1990; Esposito, 2010; Karsh, 2006; Krämer, Matringe, Nawas, & Rowson, 2007; Madelung & Daftary 2008-2010; Nicolle, 2009; Zaimeche, 2004). In the ninth century, the Persian geographer ibn Khordadbeh (Israeli, 2000; Meri & Bacharach 2005) wrote *Kitāb al Masālik w'al Mamālik* (*The Book of Roads and Kingdoms*). He describes peoples and cultures in various parts of the world. He wrote about the Abbasid Caliphate, the southern Asian coast, the Andaman Islands, Malaysia, Java, Tang China, Unified Silla (Korea), and Japan. Abu Rayhan al-Biruni (Ahmed, 1984; Scheppler, 2006), living around 973 to 1050, wrote detailed comparative studies on the anthropology of religions, peoples and cultures in the Middle East, Mediterranean, and especially the Indian subcontinent. The conquests of Genghis Khan (1162–1227) and his successors resulted in the largest contiguous empire in the history of the world. It spanned Asia, Africa, and Europe. At its greatest extent it stretched from the Danube to the Sea of Japan (or East Sea) and from the Arctic to Southeast Asia, covering 12,741,000 square miles. Commerce, technology, and ideas flowed back and forth (Brent, 1976; Kahn & Cleaves, 1998; Ratchnevsky, 1991; Turnbull, 2003). Ibn Battuta (Dunn, 2005) who was a Moroccan, Berber, and Muslim scholar (1304–1368?) traveled to North Africa, West Africa, eastern and southern Europe, the Middle East, India, central and Southeast Asia, and China. The Chinese navigator Zheng He (Dreyer, 2006; Filesi, 1972; Hays, 2008; Levathes, 1997; Zheng He, 2010) made seven voyages (1405–1433) exploring India, Indonesia, Southeast Asia, and Africa – e.g., Vietnam, Sumatra, Malacca, Sri Lanka, Malabar Coast, Thailand, Bangladesh, Malaysia, and the Maldives. These are examples of the myriads of minglings occurring throughout human history.

In nineteenth century Europe, there was a surge in cross-cultural studies (Levinson & Ember, 2009). Anthropologists such as Tylor (Bohannan, 1969; Lowrie, 1917) contributed to cultural evolutionism and social anthropology. Morgan (Moses, 2009) wrote about kinship, social structure, social evolution, and the ethnography of the Iroquois. Murdock (1949) ushered in modern cross-cultural studies. He established such data gathering systems as the Human Relations Area Files (Ember, 1997), the Ethnographic Atlas (Murdock, 1967) and, along with D. R. White, developed the Standard Cross-Cultural Sample (Murdock & White, 1969) to improve statistical analysis in the sampling of cultures.

In the contemporary literature (e.g., Cehner, 2008; Fries, 2002; Gerstein, Heppner, Ægisdóttir, Seung-Ming, & Norsworthy, 2009a; Van Maanen, 1996; World Health Organization, 1997), there are many terms, prefixes, and suffixes used to indicate the study of other cultures, including: ethno, cultural, multicultural, cross-cultural, intercultural, diversity, multiethnic, pluralistic, transcultural, holocultural, hybridity, and cultural heterogeneity. There are differences among these terms and various countries and writers use different terms or use them differently. Even within a particular country, the same term can be used differently. For example, in the United States, multicultural refers to groups within a nation or group, whereas cross-cultural refers to interactions beyond the country or social group, yet the term cross-cultural is often used in reference to domestic groups. Cross-cultural research can take the form of comparisons of case studies, controlled comparisons (e.g., with a variable to be investigated), and comparisons of samples (Ember & Ember, 1998, 2001; MacFarlane, 2004) – the latter often used in anthropology, sociology, psychology, economics, and political science.

The psychological and counseling literature does not exist in isolation and are influenced by other areas of study – such as anthropology, biology, and medicine. In the fields of mental health and therapy there have been numerous models, approaches, techniques, and guidelines for the provision of services to people of different cultures. Guidelines have been provided by such groups as the American Psychological Association (2002b), the Association of Multicultural Counseling and Development (Arredondo, Toporek, Brown, Jones, Locke, Sanchez, & Stadler, 1996), and others (Constantine & Sue, 2005). Some of the principle guidelines include the following: the counselor should have self-knowledge, the counselor should be knowledgeable about the client's culture, and the counselor should obtain the skills and knowledge to provide therapy and counseling to the client.

Vontress (1988) wrote that there are five cultures that influence people: (a) the universal culture that is based on biological functions – sex/reproduction, eating, sleeping, work, and death, (b) the ecological culture based on climatic factors – food, clothing, (c) the national culture – language, values, education, governance, (d) the regional culture – ways of existence associated with a geographic region or culture which influence how people relate to environment, fellows, and themselves, and (e) the racioethnic community culture – the demands, expectations, values, and mode of existence of one's community. He states that counseling is a human to human interaction. It is not the mechanics of the relationship, approaches, and techniques. The human to human interaction is based on shared concerns; with the same physical and psychological needs; with love, appreciation, sympathy, and respect. He states the most productive approach is the Socratic Method, in which the counselor probes the client to help discover ways to live effectively.

A number of books and articles have been written on cultural competence and working with ethnic, and other groups (Clauss-Ehlers, 2009; Pope-Davis, Coleman, Liu, & Toporek, 2003). Balcazar, Suarez-Balcazar, and Taylor-Ritzler (2009) reviewed the literature for cultural competence in order to provide guidelines and recommendations for the training of rehabilitation practitioners. They examined 259 peer-reviewed articles and book chapters. Forty-two publications were identified that referred to cultural competence models, of these 18 were unique in their models. Their synthesis of the literature resulted in the depiction of cultural competence skills as the ability to communicate effectively; the ability to recognize the verbal and nonverbal cues of the other culture; the ability to negotiate the other person's beliefs, practices, and culture with the counselor's profession; have flexibility; utilize active listening skills; utilize interpersonal warmth; have sensitivity; present reflection skills; and utilize nonverbal communications.

Sue (2001) offered a multidimensional model of cultural competence (MDCC). The model takes into consideration individual and group awareness of the counselor's own personality and group influences as well as that of the client's – including such factors as universal commonalities, group similarities and differences, individual uniqueness, genetic endowment, non-shared experiences, culture, disability, ethnicity, geographic location, age, socioeconomic status, gender, sexual orientation, marital status, religious preference, common life experiences, ability to use symbols, biological and physical similarities, and self-awareness. Sue wrote:

> A proposed multidimensional model of cultural competence (MDCC) incorporates three primary dimensions: (a) racial and culture-specific attributes of competence, (b) components of cultural competence, and (c) foci of cultural competence. Based on a 3 (Awareness, Knowledge, and Skills) × 4 (Individual, Professional, Organizational, and Societal) × 5 (African American, Asian American, Latino/Hispanic American, Native American, and European American) factorial combination. (p. 790)

Fish (2004) saw six themes in examining cross-cultural commonalities in therapy and healing: (a) industrialization and globalization – these are the changes in a group or client's culture because of outside influences, e.g., the impact of industrialization, globalization, and Westernization; (b) social structure, economics, and power – these are the social, economic, political, and power structures that impact on the client's group; (c) cultural factors – consists of the definitions of cultural norms and deviance in which the client exists; (d) the interactional perspective – consists of the influences of the social matrix, e.g., the family and other groups; (e) expectancy and placebo – refers to the influence of what the client expects of self, treatment, and the counselor; and (f) learning and cognition – consists of the use of the general psychological principles of behavior change, e.g., the use of the principles of shaping, extinction, modeling, and reinforcement in changing cognition and behavior.

Fukuyama (1990) reported the common themes of "special populations." She defined people in the special population as those who are not white, male, middle-class, heterosexual, able-bodied, and young. These included visible ethnic minority groups, gay men and lesbians, disabled or "differently abled" persons, women, elderly persons, and poor persons. Those in the special populations share in common discrimination and oppression, problems with identity development and self-esteem, and need for validation of personal experience and empowerment. She directs her article to counselor educators. She recommended teaching students about all forms of oppression (e.g., sexism, and homophobia), integrating these teachings into the core curriculum, and working them into other disciplines. She encouraged counselors to break out of their cultural cocoons by daily unlearning some things and by taking risks.

Tseng (2003) wrote about the characteristics of a cultural competent counselor. He stated that in addition to standard clinical competence, the cultural competent counselor has qualities that include cultural sensitivity, cultural knowledge, cultural empathy, culture-relevant relations and interaction, and ability for cultural guidance (p. 3). Tseng (1999) wrote that to provide culture-relevant psychotherapy, therapists should be willing to change in their approaches and techniques, and reconsider their theoretical and philosophical orientation.

Lin (2010) wrote of the cultural and ethnic issues in psychopharmacology; both the instrumental and symbolic effects of treatment are addressed. The statements made about psychopharmacology are applicable to psychotherapy as well:

> Remarkable interindividual and intracultural variations coexist with ethnic/cultural differences. That is, while the majority of members of a population group fall on one side of the distribution, and those of another group on the other side, there are always exceptions. Neglect of such overlaps may lead to overgeneralization of research findings, which, in turn, could contribute to cultural stereotyping and consequent stigmatization. (p. 2)

Each population has groups and individuals who do not subscribe to the larger group's values and perceptions. Groups such as women, those who are considered to have a disability, lesbians, gays, transsexuals, men, those of mixed heritage, veterans, the poor, the rich, the educated, the domestic and foreign born, and a host of other people might differentiate themselves from the general population by particular characteristics. Within the United States, there are those who state that they do not share much in common with their fellow U.S. Americans. They say they reject U.S. American values and culture, e.g., fundamentalists, the Amish, and the radical left and right. Similarly, there are those outside the United States who believe they do not share much in common with their larger cultural cohorts. This does not mean to imply that subgroups are necessarily entirely different from the main culture. Most often, they share the same values as the larger group – except in those areas that pertain to the differences that set them apart. In addition, a person does not have to be in a subgroup to have differences with the larger group. There are many individuals who differ from the main cultural group but they are not identified as belonging to a subgroup – they might be referred to by such names as independent, rebels, quirky, eccentric, odd, peculiar, strange, unconventional, unorthodox, or unusual.

In general, the cross-cultural literature provide guidelines and characteristics that can help in interactions with diverse individuals and groups. However, the counselor should be sensitive to the unique difference of individuals in all groups.

EXTRA-THERAPEUTIC EFFECTS

The literature on common factors often mentions extra-therapeutic effects. That is, in addition to the prescribed therapeutic agent (e.g., the herb, incantation, music, medicine, or psychological technique), other therapeutic effects may occur. There are no definitive definitions of the terms used to describe these effects. The delineation between therapeutic and "extra-therapeutic" is in many ways an arbitrary one. The "extra-therapeutic" effects may occur unintentionally or they may be used intentionally, e.g., the diploma on the therapist's wall may be intentional placed there to enhance the credibility of the counselor – and thus increase the probability of a placebo effect. Many of these extra-therapeutic effects are the result of the client and therapist's expectations. Sometimes the terms used to describe the various extra-therapeutic effects seem to describe similar phenomena (the effects of expectations). At other times, there are nuances that separate the terms, or they may depict different phenomena. Part of the reason for these ambiguities is because authors and areas of study use the terms differently and there is no definitive arbitrator to delineate the terms.

Placebo/Expectancy Effects

Of all the extra-therapeutic effects, the most well known and the one with a large amount research, is the placebo effect. The medical literature, especially drug literature, has paid considerable attention to the effects, ethics, and neurological mechanisms involved. Lin (2010) attributes most of the effectiveness of indigenous and alternatives medical treatments to placebo effects. However, there are relatively few studies of its effects across cultures. It is likely that many of the findings of the placebo effects in the medical and drug fields can be generalized to psychotherapy. For example, the medical and drug literature has found that some people respond to the placebo effect, and others do not; and the degree to which it works depends on the person's expectations (influenced by such factors as learning and memory) and genetic dispositions. The type of placebo used and its purpose (e.g., for pain relief or for ulcer treatment) can also contribute to its effects. It is not clear if there is any type of personality that is more or less susceptible to the effects of the placebo (Doongaji, Vahia, & Bharucha, 1978; Hoffman, Harrington, & Fields, 2005). From an evolutionary perspective, placebos may be one of the mechanisms to facilitate self-healing.

The term "placebo" is Latin for "I shall please." One definition of a placebo is "a substance or procedure that has no inherent power to bring about a particular effect" (Stewart-Williams & Podd, 2004). Another is another definition presented: any situation in which a person's belief in a treatment affects the outcome (Breedlove, Rosenzweig, & Watson, 2007; Critelli & Neumann, 1984). An example of the placebo effect is a client taking an inert pill. If the client believes the pill will reduce pain, it might have that effect (Wall, 1999). The belief might cause opioids to release in the brain, having the same effect as being administered the painkiller (e.g., morphine). However, the mind does not necessarily interpret and have expectations that are conducive to treatment. It can also react in a manner that is detrimental (O'Connell, 1983). The term "nocebo ("I will harm") effects" refer to adverse reactions to the placebo (Kennedy, 1961; Stewart-Williams & Podd, (2004). Whereas, the placebo may have neutral or positive effects (e.g., the person feels no pain after taking an inert pill), the nocebo effect could facilitate an undesirable, unpleasant reaction (e.g., the person feels more pain after taking an inert pill).

Placebos occur because the client's values, perceptions, and other internal and external factors contribute to the acquisition of expectations. There are two components usually associated with the placebo: (a) there is an expectancy aspect to it, and (b) its effects are mediated through a psychological mechanism. That is, the way the mind processes the information accounts for its effects. It is evident that the placebo effects are not just "psychological" and in the "mind." There are neurological, physiological, chemical, and other overt and measurable processes involved. In any given circumstance, there is no certainty as to whether there will be a placebo effect, and one cannot predict how much of an effect it will have. Not everyone concurs that there is a placebo effect – or if there is, they question if it is of any clinical significance. For example, Hróbjartsson and Gøtzsche's (2001) investigated 130 clinical trials in the medical and psychological literature and found little or no placebo effect. Wampold and Imel (2007) refuted Hróbjartsson and Gøtzsche's interpretation of the data. In terms of empirical evidence, data, and effect size of placebos, they are open to different interpretations – the title of Hunsley and Westmacott's (2007) article illustrates this: "Interpreting the Magnitude of the Placebo Effect: Mountain or Molehill?" How does the placebo effect work? Benedetti, Mayberg, Wager, Stohler, and Zubieta (2005) wrote: "The placebo effect is a psychobiological phenomenon that can be attributable to different mechanisms, including expectation of clinical improvement and Pavlovian conditioning. Thus, we have to look for different mechanisms in different conditions, because there is not a single placebo effect but many" (p. 10390).

Medical Effects

The delineation of placebo effects into medical and psychological is somewhat arbitrary because the two are closely connected. For example, the physician's behavior in administering a drug might have a psychological effect on the client – that is, have a placebo effect. Also, physicians and psychologists often treat the same conditions – such as depression, stress, anxiety, and pain; therefore, the psychologist's intervention could have a "medical" effect. One can make a case that most medical conditions have a psychological component and thus can come under the influence of the placebo effect.

The magnitude of the placebo effects depends on the problem, treatment conditions, characteristics of the person who is treating, who is being treated, and a host of other variables. Measures consist of subjective perceptions (e.g., asking people what they feel) as well as objective indices (e.g., measuring neurological and chemical responses). Studies indicate placebo effects provide relief in depression, ulcers, headaches, hypertension, the common cold, anxiety, angina pectoris, and many other conditions. Beecher's (1955) review of medical conditions found the placebo effects have an average effectiveness of 35.2, plus or minus 2 percent. Connelly's (1987) study of biomedical research indicates placebo effects vary from 0–100 percent. Lin (2010) reported 30 percent to 50 percent of participants in psychopharmacological studies show the effects of placebo. He reported that new drugs usually need to show an additional 10 percent to 20 percent efficacy over placebo effects for approval for marketing and clinical use. Moerman's (2000) study of the placebo effect on ulcers, anxiety, and blood pressure found high variability among cultures (e.g., Brazil and Germany). The magnitude of the effect with one group did not necessarily predict the same size effect on another group. Kirsch et al. (2008) meta-analyses of antidepressant found the medications had only modest effect over placebo treatment. Jopling (2008) came to the same conclusion.

Psychological Effects

There are various views of the placebo effect in psychological treatment. There are those who support the view that the effects of psychotherapy are basically because of the placebo effect (Shapiro, 1971; Shapiro & Morris, 1978; Rosenthal & Frank, 1956; Pentony, 1981; Luborsky, Singer, & Luborsky, 1975). O'Connell (1983) viewed psychotherapy as a form of placebo effect that facilitates the client's own capacity for self-maintenance and change. Lambert and Barley's (2001) summary of therapeutic outcome found that 40 percent of the variance was due to outside factors, 15 percent to expectancy effects, 15 percent to specific therapy techniques, and 30 percent of variance was predicted by the therapeutic relationship/common factors. Hubble, Duncan, and Miller (1999) separated psychotherapy factors that contribute to therapeutic change and outcomes into four categories: client intrapsychic factors and factors within the client's life (said to account for 40% of change), therapeutic relationship factors (30%), the model/technique used by the counselor

(15%), and expectancy or placebo effects of likeability (15%). Miller, Duncan, and Hubble (1997) determined that extra-therapeutic factors account for 40 percent of the variance of therapeutic outcome.

Neurological Aspects

There are many studies of the neural structures, systems, and biochemicals involving the way the brain processes the placebo effect (e.g., Benedetti, Mayberg, Wager, Stohler, & Zubieta, 2005; Doongaji, Vahia, & Bharucha, 1978; Lucki, 1998; Oken, 2008; Schultz, 2006). There is consensus that each type and variant of a placebo engenders concomitant unique neurological actions. For example, Oken's (2008) investigation of placebo analgesia indicated that opiate and dopamine neurotransmitters were involved. There was activation of such areas of the brain as the anterior cingulate cortex, dorsolateral prefrontal cortex, and basal ganglia. If the patient is motivated and the intervention is novel, there may be an increase in the placebo effect. The author wrote that learning and memory parts of the brain may also play a role. Placebos for depression affect many of the same areas of the brain as antidepressants – with the addition of the prefrontal cortex (Mayberg et al., 2002; Leuchter, Cook, Witte, Morgan, Abrams, 2002). Caffeinated coffee placebos increased bilateral dopamine in the thalamus (Kaasinen, Aalto, Någren, & Rinne, 2004). Inexperienced drug users who expected an intravenous injection of methylphenidate have increased release of dopamine in the ventral cingulate gyrus and nucleus accumbens in the brain (Volkow, 2006). It is likely that the dopamine system plays a role in the placebo effect because of its association with rewards (Schultz, 2006), and the serotonin system may also be involved because of its relationship with mood and stress (Lucki, 1998).

Operationalizing Placebo Effects

O'Connell (1983) wrote about the conditions under which the placebo effects may occur. He divides the conditions into the necessary and sufficient conditions:

Necessary Conditions:

1. There is an unequal relationship between the administrator of the placebo and the recipient.
2. The recipient acquiesces in the relationship.
3. The recipient consciously or unconsciously processes the information that the administrator provides.
4. There is some shared commonality between the administrator and the

recipient, e.g., beliefs, and assumptions.
5. The administrator evokes in the recipient enthusiasm for the healing ritual, confidence in the healer, trust in the placebo agent, and expectancy of success.

Sufficient Conditions:

1. The previous necessary conditions.
2. The administrator's information is processed into the recipient's own way of thinking.
3. The administrator engages in some activity that culminates in
4. The prescriptive agent or activity.

Patterson (1985) took a social psychology perspective, contending that the placebo effects occur because of the client's perception of the counselor's expertness, attractiveness, and trustworthiness. The first factor, expertness, consists of those elements that induce the client's perception of the counselor's competence, knowledge, and skills. The second factor, attractiveness, consist of the elements that attract the client and counselor to each other, such as similarities in values, opinions, and background. The third factor, trustworthiness, consists of methods and techniques that facilitate the client's expectations that therapeutic change will occur because of the counselor's influence. In addition, there are core conditions the counselor provides that facilitate certain therapeutic changes: empathic understanding, respect or warmth, and therapeutic genuineness. These conditions facilitate self-disclosure and self exploration. They enable the client to solve problems and make changes. They enable the client to engage in productive psychological development.

Many authors have written of the need to establish a therapeutic alliance with the client and for the counselor to change and adapt to the client's attitudes, values, and culture (Carter, 2006; Frank & Frank, 1991; Hill, 2004; Stark, 1999; Wampold, 2000). In terms of the therapeutic relationship, Ackerman and Hilsenroth (2003) identified counselor characteristics that contributed positively as flexibility, honesty, respectfulness, trustworthiness, confidence, warmth, interest, and openness. The techniques that contribute positively to the relationship include exploration, reflection, accurate interpretation, noting of past successes, and attending to the client's experiences.

Other Examples of Expectancy Effects

Vroom (1964) defines expectancy as "a momentary belief concerning the likelihood that a particular act will be followed by a particular outcome" (p. 17). The placebo effects are part of a spectrum of effects based on client expectations. The placebo and similar effects share the common feature in that "performance or other significant objective effects come from (nonobjective) causes of humans simply expecting something" (Draper, 2008, para. 1). These are effects in which what one expects to happen increases the probability that it will happen (Jastrow, 1900; Peters, 1987; Rosenthal & Jacobson, 1968, 1992; Stewart, LaDuke, Bracht, Sweet, & Gamarel, 2003). Some examples of other expectancy effects include the following:

The Hawthorne effect, also known as observer effect, experimenter effect, and reflectivity, refers to the phenomena where people change their behavior because they are aware that they are participating in a study. The term "Hawthorne" derives from studies at the Hawthorne Works (Mayo, 1949), where researchers found that when they manipulated variables (any kind) in workers' environment, productivity increased. For example, researchers varied lighting, they allowed workers to chose with whom they worked, they varied break time intervals, they provided food, they shortened the workday, and they changed supervisory practices. All these changes increased productivity. One interpretation of these phenomena is that the workers improved because they were aware that they were being studied – and not because of the changes introduced by the researchers. Another interpretation is that the workers changed their behaviors because the experiment elicits certain behaviors.

The John Henry effect is part of the Hawthorne effect (James, 1994; Mertens, 2005; Oyserman, Uskula, Yodera, Nesse, & Williams, 2007; Saretsky, 1975; Straub, 2006). This effect occurs when one group (e.g., the control group) puts in more effort (e.g., does better) to demonstrate they are as good as or better than the group with whom they are comparing themselves (e.g., the experimental group). Whereas the Hawthorne effect increases productivity in the target group (the group that received the treatment intervention), the John Henry effect (Zdep & Irvine, 1970) has the opposite of the Hawthorne effect: the control group compares itself to the experimental group and puts in extra effort to get the same or better results as the experimental group.

Jastrow, Pygmalion, and experimenter effects (Jastrow, 1900; Rosenthal & Rosnow, 2009) occur where the perception of the expectation of those in authority influence a person's performance. This is similar to the demand characteristics of a task in which the experimenters' expectancies create an implicit demand for the participants to perform as expected (Intons-Peterson, 1983). It is not necessarily the case that the participant will act in accordance to what the authority figure or experimenter wants; the participant might act to the contrary. For example, the client may not put much effort into the counselor's therapeutic agenda if the client perceives that counselor's expectations are too high, unreasonable, or exhibits some characteristics the client does not like.

The halo effect is the generalization from the perception of one outstanding personality trait to an overly favorable evaluation of the whole personality (Asch, 1946; Kelly, 1955; Nisbett & Wilson, 1977; Thorndike, 1920; Zebrowitz, Montepare, & Lee, 1993). This effect is applicable to situations in which an initial positive impression influences the tendency to evaluate subsequent events positively. One problem with this effect is the ignoring or minimizing of negative factors – thus an inaccurate evaluation can ensue. A variation of the halo effect is the effect of being in a novel situation – there is an improvement in the person's performance because the newness of the task increased enthusiasm and attentiveness.

The Pygmalion effect, or Rosenthal effect, or "expectancy advantage," refer to the effects of self-fulfilling prophecy. For example, if the client expects to be successful in therapy, the probability is increased that the client will succeed. If the client does not expect to be successful, the probability of success is decreased.

Forer effect, personal validation fallacy, and Barnum effect, refer to the tendency of people to think that vague general statements apply to them. For example, people will give high ratings of accuracy to descriptions of their personality that are supposedly tailored specifically to them, but the descriptions are in fact vague and general statements that apply to a wide range of people (Beins, 2010; Dickson & Kelly, 1985; Forer, 1949). This effect may account for the ability of those who appear to be able to predict and describe people. People such as astrologists and fortune-tellers make predictions that are often general and vague. Their predictions frequently are open to various interpretations and can be applicable to many situations. Similarly, when counselors use tests to describe a client, this effect might occur.

Subjective validation refers to the phenomena where unrelated random events are perceived to be related because the person expects there to be a relationship, e.g., clients expect a personality inventory to describe them, therefore they think it does. "Subjective validation is the process of validating words, initials, statements, or signs as accurate because one is able to find them personally meaningful and significant" (Carroll, 2009, para. 1).

These studies increase our awareness that interactions between the counselor and client convey multidimensional and multilayered messages. The following are some examples of how these effects can influence the counselor and client interactions. Clients might inordinately submerge their own thoughts and feelings because there is a halo effect in regard to the client's admiration of the counselor. The client's awareness that the counselor is observing may induce gains because of the Hawthorne effect – but improvements may diminish after the client leaves the auspices of the counselor. The client may accept the counselor's general statements as valid because of the Forer effect – and thus the counselor and client might not get an accurate impression of the matter at hand. A client may offer solutions to a problem, the counselor expresses doubts, then when the client tries the solutions there may be failure because of Rosenthal's self-fulfilling prophecy effect. These effects are garnered principally from studies in Western cultures. It is intriguing to consider what other effects, if any, might be found in other cultures.

The extra-therapeutic effects of expectancy are just a sample of many effects. The expectancy effects are mediated through parts of the brain (e.g., the cognitive area) that help interpret and define actions and reactions; therefore, they can influence such "mental" problems as depression and anxiety, as well as physical and chemical processes – such as reactions to pain (Wall, 1999), and fatigue (Harrington, 1997; Shapiro & Shapiro, 1997). It is highly likely that extra-therapeutic effects, in one form or another, are universal. Studies of the placebo effect have found it exists in other cultures – though there are variations in terms of reactions to the placebo and reactions to what the placebo is (Harrington, 1997; Moerman, 2000; Moerman & Jonas, 2002). Those extra-therapeutic effects that derive from anticipation and expectancy are based on psychological and neurological processes common to humans (McGuigan, 1993; Smith & Smith, 1966). However, other effects can occur that affect the therapeutic process.

The list of factors that transpire in counseling is extensive. The following are some of the typical ones the occur: the client may interpret the counselor's information differently than what the counselor intended to convey; the counselor's tone and intonation may convey unintended meaning; the client may take just a small bit of what the counselor conveyed and miss the counselor's intended message; the body language, attire, environment, and displayed items convey meanings that have an effect on the client. These effects occur because both the client and the counselor carry their experiences, histories, and perceptions with them into the therapeutic relationship.

Second-order Effects

Graziano and Fink (1973) wrote about "second-order effects" in mental health. These are effects that are external to therapy. There are a wide range of these effects and include problems associated with obtaining transportation, making babysitting arrangements, taking time away from work, therapeutic fees, the costs of self-help materials, family members needing to take on more tasks and responsibilities; family members, friends and the client experiencing embarrassment, shame, guilt, and the stigma of someone being in therapy and with a mental illness/disorder; and the allocation of the sick role diminishing of the authority and decisions of a parent with mental illness/disorder. These and other factors can impact clients' perception of the convenience and burden of therapy, the number of sessions they attend, and their attitude toward counseling.

It should be noted that the term "second-order change" has been used by some writers (e.g., Davey, Davey, Tubbs, Savla, & Anderson, 2010; Murray, 2002; Randy, 1987; Watzlawick, Weakland, & Fisch, 1974). This is different from "second-order effects." Authors who write about second-order change sometimes use the term in the same manner and others use the term differently. For example, Fraser and Solovey (2007) used the term to refer to the elements that unify effective treatments. As used by them, first-order changes can help stabilize or worsen a condition; second-order changes are the common factors that are effective across treatments and approaches. Other authors use the term first-order change to describe surface or superficial therapeutic changes, and second order to refer to changes that are in depth and longer lasting – to use an existential term: a phenomenological shift occurs with second-order changes. Ellis (1992; Lyddon, 1990) wrote that first-order change might occur with the correction of irrational thinking; second-order change occurs when the underlying patterns and overall irrational beliefs (cognitive schema) change. Dale and Lyddon (2000) refered to first-order change as the assimilation of knowledge into existing frameworks, and second-order change is the reorganization of cognitive frameworks. Bowman and Baylen (1994) characterized Western psychotherapy as focusing on changing the environment and conquering the ego (primarily a first-order focus). Whereas, Buddhism focuses on breaking free of the context that produces the problem and transcending the ego (a second-order process).

COUNSELOR AND CLIENT PROCESSES

There are many processes involved when the counselor and client interact. These are occurring between the two of them, within themselves, and extraneous to them. Among the many processes that occur are the following: values are influencing both the counselor and the client; the counselor and client are communicating with each other – and can do so with language, body, and facial expressions; and they are engaged in cognitive activities (thinking). These are explored next – along with neuroimaging and physiological measures that can monitor many of the processes.

Values

All societies have values that guide their members. These derive from such sources as customs, religions, laws, and traditions. Values are proscribed or endorsed by societies and can be a source of gratification or discord between the person and society and within the individual. Becker and McClintok (1967) wrote, "Human behavior is governed in large measure by values, i.e., by the attractiveness of alternatives" (p. 239). The client and counselor's values play an important role in therapy. Values can facilitate or hinder therapeutic goals. They can influence perceptions, feeling, and behaviors. They can help or encumber communications. Many values appear to be self-evident and acceptable to everyone; however, studies are not clear in regard to this assumption. The Union of International Associations (2009a) produces the *Encyclopedia of World Problems and Human Potential.* They have a section on human values. In terms of values, they wrote, "There are many definitions and innumerable studies. No definition has attracted widespread consensus" (Union of International Associations, 2009b, para. 1). They have compiled a list of 987 "constructive" or positive values (e.g., peace, love) and 1,990 "destructive" or negative values (e.g., war, hate). They cluster these into 230 "polarity" values; that is, paired opposite values, e.g., agreement-disagreement, freedom-restraint, and pleasure-displeasure (Union of International Associations, 2009c). They wrote that these values are not definitive and are subject to changes. There have been many attempts to obtain consensus of shared values and to cluster them (e.g., place them in groupings), but they have failed – buttressing a relativist view of values.

Another large scale, worldwide investigation is by the World Values Survey (2009a). The World Values Survey consists of a worldwide investigation of sociocultural and political change. Its purpose is to measure the impact of values and beliefs on political and social life, e.g., perception of life, environment, work, family, politics and society, religion and morality, and national identity. It consists of representative surveys of more than 80 countries, 97 societies; containing 85 percent to 90 percent of the world's population. Every ten years a network of social scientists at leading universities around the world conduct the survey. Face-to-face interviews are conducted using detailed questionnaires, consisting of about 250 questions, resulting in some 400 to 800 measurable variables. A number of variables are collapsed into two dimensions of cultural variation: "traditional versus secular-rational" and "survival versus self-expression" (Baker, 2006; Inglehart, 1997; Inglehart & Baker, 2001; Inglehart & Welzel, 2005). These account for more than 70 percent of the cross-national variance in a factor analysis of ten indicators (World Values Survey, 2009b). Concerning the traditional versus secular-rational values, traditional values include: importance of religion, family, country; absolute standards of morality (verse relative ones); respect for authority and conformity; and low tolerance for abortion and divorce. Secular-rational are on the other side of the spectrum. As to the survival versus self-expression values, people who are higher on survival values are characterized as having a preference for economic and physical security over self-expression and quality of life, being more likely to describe oneself as not very happy, being less likely to sign petitions, being against homosexuality, and being wary about trusting people. One main set of findings indicated that with increased industrialization, there were increases in self -expression, political activism, environmental concerns, and women's issues.

Schwartz and Bardi (2001) established what they considered ten comprehensive, universal values that are the core of all cultures. These values were derived from their analysis of other theorists, from responses to values questionnaires, and from the examination of the religious and philosophical values of the culture. They define values as "desirable, transsituational goals, varying in importance, that serve as guiding principles in people's lives" (p 269). They surveyed approximately 14,000 schoolteachers in 56 nations, and approximately 19,000 college students in 54 countries. The values they delineated were power, achievement, hedonism, stimulation, self-direction, universalism, benevolence, tradition, conformity, and security. Those answering the surveys rated the values of benevolence, self-direction, and universalism as most important. Least important were power, tradition, and stimulation (e.g., excitement, novelty, a varied and challenging life). In between the most and least important values were security, conformity, achievement, and hedonism.

In the United States, Gordon Allport is a writer often associated with the study of values. Kopelman and Rovenpor (2006) wrote that the *Allport-Vernon-Lindzey's Study of Values* had a substantial impact on practice and research for decades after its introduction in 1931 (Allport, 1931, 1977). They reported there was a period when it was the third most referenced nonprojective inventory. Then it went into abeyance. There have been updates to the inventory (Coffield & Buckalew, 1984). In their more recent review of the literature, Kopelman, Rovenpor, and Guanc (2003) found the inventory's validity and utility "impressive." The *Allport-Vernon Study of Values* (1931) categorizes values into six major types: (a) theoretical – interest in the discovery of truth through reasoning and systematic thinking; (b) economic – interest in usefulness and practicality, including the accumulation of wealth; (c) aesthetic – interest in beauty, form and artistic harmony; (d) social – interest in people and human relationships; (e) political – interest in gaining power and influencing other people; and (f) religious – interest in unity and understanding the cosmos as a whole. Values vary among and within individuals and societies. They can change, and a high preference for one can incur the expense of the other values.

Values can influence cognitive processes and logic. Kluckhorn and Strodtbeck (1961; Vogt & Albert, 1966) presented a model to examine cultural values which vary with cultures and individuals in (a) orientation to time – past, present, and future; (b) activity – doing, becoming, and being; (c) relations – individual (individuals are important), collateral (group orientation), and lineal (hierarchical orientation); (d) person-nature – humans dominant nature, or they are in harmony with nature; and (e) human nature – good, mixed, and evil. Variations in these can be one of the reasons why counselors and clients of different cultures view the other as not being logical.

An interesting aspect of values is that most of the literature seems to readily enumerate them. However, if submitted for consensus to other people in the world, as done by the Union of International Associations (2009a), then universal endorsement becomes a problem. This might be illustrative of features of categorizing universals – they seem self-evident; however, when we submit them to others in the world, there often is not consensus. Nuckolls (1998) presents the case that definitive values cannot be delineated because within each culture there are different degrees of the value, there are conflicting values, and values are engaged in a dialectic process. They change with circumstances, and they are reacting to each other. This might be said of trying to delineate universals in general.

Communications

Communications in therapy can take many forms. Therapy can be communicated through such physical expressions as theatrical performance, dance, singing, music, rituals, touching, gestures, signs, objects, and laying of hands. Other forms of communications in therapy could include massage, smells, and spatial distance. Facial expressions, writing and eye contact, and emotional expressions are options that can be used as well. Further approaches could be provided symbolically through paintings, pictures, symbols, prayers, dress, and attitude. Also, by such other means as divination, settings (e.g., providing therapy in an office can communicate something different than providing it on a bus), and timing (e.g., a therapist who arrives on time for therapeutic sessions conveys a different message than one who is habitually late). In the United States, and many other countries, counselors are trained to interact with clients through verbal language, to notice nonverbals, to monitor emotional expressions (e.g., through facial expressions), and to deal with thought content. These common practices are covered next.

Linguistics

Linguistics is the study of language. Language is one of the main tools that counselors use to provide treatment. Chomsky (1957, 1968) considered linguistics to be part of cognitive psychology. He wrote that linguistics provides an understanding of mental processes and human nature. Weiss (1925) considered language as a form of behavior that represents biological, physiological, and social conditions. Evolutionary psychologists (Kenneally, 2007) are interested in linguistics because language is a principle feature of humans. Therefore, understanding this feature provides valuable insight into humans. Even though counselors are trained to examine the emotional and verbal content of language, they may not be aware of the many aspects of language – as studied in linguistics. For example, linguistics can provide such information as language structure (grammar), meaning (semantics and pragmatics), how words are formed (morphology), the combinations of words (syntax), sounds of words (phonology), the evolution of language (evolutionary linguistic), the changes in language (historical linguistic), physical gestures (kinesics), the social context (sociolinguistics), the psychology of language (psycholinguistics), and the study of language and the brain (neurolinguistics).

Linguistic scholars have bantered around the question of universals and nonuniversals for a long time (Brown, 1976; Chomsky, 1957; Comrie, 1981; Enfield, Majid, & Van Staden, 2006; Goddard, 2002; Goddard & Wierzbicka, 1994; Goddard & Wierzbicka, 2002; Greenberg, Ferguson, & Moravcsik, 1978a; Greenberg, Ferguson, & Moravcsik, 1978b; Greenberg, Ferguson, & Moravcsik, 1978c; Greenberg, Ferguson, & Moravcsik, 1978d; Heine, 1997; Mairal & Gil, 2006; Majid, Enfield, & Van Staden, 2006; Pinxten, 1976; Rosch, Mervis, Gray, Johnson, & Boyes-Braem, 1976; Ross, 1992; Swoyer, 2003; Whorf, 1959; Wilkins, 1993). In terms of universals, there are a number of areas that can be explored – e.g., the neurological basis of language, the structure of language, and the content. Noam Chomsky (1957) wrote that humans have an innate set of linguistic principles underlying languages (universal grammar) that accounts for the linguistic variations. Levi-Strauss (1966), famous for structuralism and binary opposites, wrote that mental structures are universal; the contents are culturally specific. Advocates of linguistic relativism are often associated with the Sapir-Whorf hypothesis (Ross, 1992; Sapir, 1929; Swoyer, 2003; Whorf, 1956), which states that cultures influence the way people think and classify the world around them (linguistic structure), with each culture therefore having different effects. It should be noted that even though this book deals with linguistics and culture separately, these two categories are intertwined and theories in one category can readily be put in the other category.

Nonverbals

Counselors have long known that nonverbal communications play an important part of human and therapeutic interactions. There is a plethora of evidence indicating that there are individual and cultural variations in nonverbal expressions. There can also be gender differences. There are many aspects to nonverbal interactions, the following are some examples. Paralanguage (also referred to as paralinguistics) refers to the nonverbal elements of communication that modifies meaning and conveying of emotions, e.g., speech pitch, volume, and intonation. Sometimes this term is also used in the study of body language. Kinesics is the interpretation of body language such as facial expressions, gestures, and nonverbal movements. Semiotics, also called semiotic studies or semiology, is the study of signs and symbols that deals especially with their function in both artificially constructed and natural languages and comprises syntactics, semantics, and pragmatics (Semiotics, 2009). These areas of study are reminders that we may not be familiar or aware of the various manifestations of nonverbals; therefore, we should be careful with our interpretations of clients' expressions.

Facial and Emotional Expressions

Emotions are a fundamental part of humans. Emotions are part of the mammalian brain and the limbic system. There is evidence that emotional states occur not only with human, but also with other animals (Darwin, 1872; Ekman, 2003; Masson & McCarthy, 1995). In addition, emotional expressions are recognizable between humans and some other animals – such as dogs, and the great apes (Bekoff, 2007; Racca, Amadei, Ligout, Guo, Meints, & Mills, 2010). Darwin (1872/1998) observed that humans across cultures express the same emotions on their faces. He wrote that this is because emotions are part of the common genetic composition of humans. He also wrote that primates have the same expressions as humans, indicating a common heritage.

Facial expressions are one of the manifestations of emotions. Even though there are variations in the reasons and degree of manifestation of facial and emotional expressions, studies have indicated that people from different culture can usually recognize basic facial emotional expressions (Yrizarry, Matsumoto, Imai, Kooken, & Takeuchi, 2001). Studies have indicated that they can recognize facial expressions of anger, disgust, fear, happiness, sadness, and surprise (Ekman, 1972, 1973).

Three components of emotions are usually studied: the physiological, psychological, and behavioral. These have been the focus of studies in the fields of medicine, anthropology, and psychology. With the advent of neural imaging, e.g., positron emission tomography (PET) and functional magnetic resonance (fMRI), brain activity can be observed. These technological tools indicate that when people are in emotional states the amygdala and orbitofrontal cortex are more active. Damage to these areas can change emotional responses. In addition, chemicals are released under certain emotional conditions, e.g., the adrenal glands releases adrenaline (norepinephrine) when the fight or flight responses occur.

What purpose do emotions serve? Emotions serve an important motivational function (e.g., to protect offspring, to avoid exploitation, and to find a mate). Writers such as Nesse (1990), Fredrickson (1998), and Ekman (1994) categorize emotions as negative and positive. Negative emotions (e.g., fear, anger, guilt, anxiety, and sadness) are responses to aversive events. Fear and anger can focus attention and help induce action. There are writers (e.g., Fabrega, 2002; Nesse & Williams, 1995; Kring, Davison, Neale, & Johnson, 2007) who consider many psychological problems (e.g., anxiety, depression, paranoia, obsessive compulsive disorders, borderline, histrionic, and bipolar) to be the result of emotions. Positive emotions (love, happiness) may serve the function of facilitating social relationships. These emotions enable people to provide each other support and facilitate attachment (e.g., parent to child). Nesse (2005) wrote that there are twelve crucial points regarding emotions: (a) emotions are useful states shaped by natural selection; (b) no one aspect of emotions is primary; (c) each emotion is distinguished not by its function, but by the adaptive challenges of the situation in which it is useful; (d) the emotions and their subtypes have been partially differentiated from generic precursors into more specific emotions and subtypes to cope with specific kinds of situations; (e) the situations that arise in goal pursuit have shaped specific emotions; (f) the challenges associated with certain recurring social situations have shaped special social emotions; (g) emotions and affects have valence for good reason; (h) negative emotions are just as valuable as positive emotions; (i) negative emotions seem abnormal because of the "clinician's illusion"; (j) benign situations can produce overreactions because of the "smoke detector principle" (i.e., it is better to overreact because the cost of not reacting – such as not reacting to a snake – can be catastrophic); (k) there are large individual differences in emotional tendencies; and (l) most mental disorders are emotional disorders.

Workman and Reader (2008) summarized the research on emotions and evolution as: different cultures have the same basic emotional expressions under similar circumstance; primates have the same facial expressions under similar circumstances; and human have specific neural parts dedicated to recognizing and processing emotions.

Cognitive Processes

A number of factors and perspectives can be taken in the study of cognitive processes, e.g., the conscious and unconscious, mental representation, neuroimaging, learning, and artificial and natural operations. This section deals with cognitive process in terms of the influence of logic, cognitive distortions, and culture.

Logic

There are a number of definitions of logic. One set of definitions is that it is a science that deals with the principles and criteria of validity of inference and demonstration; another definition is that it is a particular mode of reasoning viewed as valid or faulty (Logic, 2010).

The study of logic, its illogical aspects, and its problems has a long history. Aristotle (Striker, 2009) divided logical fallacies into two types: linguistic (language based), and non linguistic (not language dependent). He dealt with such topics as the errors of logic of the Sophists as well as the problems of syllogism (a form of logic). Wittgenstein (1967, 1994; Kripke, 1982), among others (e.g., Kant), added to this rich history. Wittgenstein wrote about semantics, logic, and the mind, e.g., the dynamics of word games, the multiplicity of language, the meaninglessness in the use of words, and the private use of language; these can affect us in such a manner that we may not understand ourselves (not to mention that we may not be intelligible to others). He wrote that the forms of language we use can result in "illusions," "bewitchment," and "conjuring tricks" in our thinking. He wrote that the metaphysical use of language by philosophers does not reflect reality and results in contradictions and confusion – might the same be said of psychological theorists?

One way to categorize logic is to designate the thinking as logical, illogical, and nonlogical (Back, 1961; Simon, 1993; Zafirovski, 2003). There are numerous descriptions and definitions of these ways of thinking. A possible set of descriptions are that rational thinking is based on logic – there is a logical association between the ends and the means; irrational thinking is based on faulty reasoning; and nonrational thinking is not based on reason, e.g., based on intuition. Back (1961) wrote that rational models dominate decision-making theory in the behavioral sciences. These models are often used in game theory and statistical decision theory, where the optimal solution is to maximize payoff goals. He wrote that the irrational model is also used whereby decisions are made from psychodynamic factors or personal preferences, e.g., compulsions, prejudices, early childhood influences. He proposes the nonrational model reflects idiosyncratic thinking and that these decisions are unique and occur under conditions of either extreme or trivial importance, and when the client has limited information on the probabilities of the alternative options. One needs to see the choices from the client's perspective; determine why and how the client makes decisions; and fathom the client's perceptions of the alternatives, consequences, advantages, and disadvantages of decisions.

There is ample evidence that we often do not think in terms of classical logic or game theory (Basu, 2007; Loewenstein, 2008; Loewenstein & Thaler, 1989; Polski, 2008; Vohs, Baumeister, & Loewenstein, 2007) – that is, in a manner where the thought processes can be followed and which maximizes the goals of the person. Often emotions and other factors influence people to deviate from choices that would maximize benefits. Those of us in the mental health field are well aware of these phenomena. For example, Freud (1976) proposed that our actions are often the result of unconscious, suppressed, and repressed factors. Ellis (1957, 2001; Beck, 1970; Dryden & Neenan, 2004) pointed out that many of our problems are the result of faulty thinking and expectations. Gendlin (2007) reminded us that we often incorporate the mislabels and perceptions of others, and these may not accurately reflect our thoughts and feelings. In addition to the usual cognitive distortions that can occur, there is evidence that counselors' training and education may influence their perceptions in a manner that skews their perspective and interferes with a more valid view of phenomena (Hansen, 2007; Mischel, 1968).

Logical operations are the foundation of the interactions between the client and the counselor. It is the means by which they try to understand each other as well as convey problems and solutions. However, as indicated in the previous discussion, humans often behave in an irrational and nonrational manner. Further understanding of these aspects can be obtained by comprehending the values, perceptions, and cognitive operations of the client.

Cognitive Distortions

Cognitive biases and distortions influence our thinking, feelings, and perceptions (Baron, 2000; Bishop & Trout, 2004; Curtis, 2009; Engel, 1994a, 1994b; Gilovich, 1993; Gilovich, Griffin & Kahneman, 2002; Goldberg, 2003; Greenwald, 1980; Kahneman, Slovic, & Tversky, 1982; Kahane & Cavender, 2006; Kahneman, Knetsch, & Thaler, 1991; Pirie, 1985; Plous, 1993; Schacter, 1999; Tetlock, 2005; Virine & Trumper, 2007; Whyte, 2004). Mental health professionals have long observed that people have cognitive processes that are faulty and result in problems. There are many types of cognitive distortions, and there are numerous books and articles on the subject. Curtis (2009) lists 191 cognitive errors that distort communications. For example, words can be ambiguous or have multiple meanings; the intonations, accentuations of words can change meanings; people make inaccurate generalizations and mix correlations with cause and effect. Cognitive-behavioral therapists such as Beck (1970, 1976) and Burns (1980) have made this an important aspect of their therapy – that is, they consider many problems to be the result of faulty and inaccurate thinking. Therapy consists of helping clients see and correct thoughts that contribute to such problems as anxiety, depression, and guilt. Grohol (2009) presented Beck and Burns' cognitive distortions as filtering, polarized thinking, overgeneralization, jumping to conclusions, and catastrophizing. Other problematic thinking are personalization, control fallacies, fallacy of fairness, and blaming. Also, people can engage in faulty shoulds, emotional reasoning, and global labeling. Additionally, they might believe that they always have to be right, expect changes to occur, and expect they will be rewarded in heaven. Tagg (1996) divides cognitive biases into overgeneralization, mental filter, magnification and minimization, all-or-nothing thinking, disqualifying the positive, jumping to conclusions, labeling, mind reading, fortune-telling, emotional reasoning, shoulding yourself, shoulding others, personalization, and blame. StateMaster.com ("List of cognitive biases," 2010) provides a more extensive list. The site lists 28 decision-making and behavioral biases, 23 biases in probability and belief, 18 social biases, 4 memory errors, 33 memory biases, and 9 common theoretical causes of some cognitive biases. The site has a list of references to more information about cognitive biases. When working with someone with psychological problems, dysfunctional thinking can exacerbate communications and cognitive problems.

Culture

There have been numerous studies on the cultural aspects of cognitive processes. Hutchins (1980) wrote that the differences between cultures are not in logical operations or cognitive processes, rather the differences are in worldviews (p. 128). Piagetian operations (e.g., conservation, elementary logic, spatial thinking) have had a major influence on education and cognitive psychology. Piaget (Dasen & Heron, 1981) wrote that cultural factors affect the age of attaining of his stages. He stated that the stages are qualitatively different from each other, but the sequence should be the same across cultures. Studies have indicated that the degree of complexity of the culture correlates with Piaget's cognitive styles, and there is more support for the less advanced sensorimotor stages than the more advanced formal operations states. Those who study cognitive development are of two schools of thought: the nativists believe perception and cognition are innate, whereas the empiricists believe that they are obtained from their environment (culture). Results of studies across cultures are mixed. Some have found that the operations are universal. Others have found that they are not, while others have found there are differences in when they develop, e.g., earlier or later (Mishra, 1980). Hamill (1979) studied people in four cultures and found commonalities in the use of syllogistic reasoning. He wrote that all people are born with innate logical structures but have different logical patterns in different linguistic and cultural settings. The differences between groups can serve as indicators of the types of differences within members of each group. Therefore, general approaches to a particular group will not address the issues of individuals who depart from the group norms.

Even though people and cultures vary in their skills, ways of learning, perceptions of the world, and strategies to solve problems (Cole, 1988, 1992; Irvine & Berry 1988), there is evidence that they can learn other ways of thinking (Cole & Bruner, 1971, Cole, Gay, Click, & Sharp, 1971; Cole & Scribner, 1974; 1996; Dasen & Heron, 1981; Keats, 1985; Shea, 1985). Therefore, counselors can play a role in helping people change problematic behaviors.

George Kelly developed an approach that attempts to understand the way people think (Fransella, 1996; Kelly, 1955, 1970; Neimeyer & Neimeyer, 2002; Neimeyer & Raskin, 2001; Raskin & Bridges, 2002). He developed an interview technique to assess the client's perspective. With a technique called "The Repertory Grid Interview," he sought to help clients uncover their own "constructs" with minimal intervention or interpretation by the counselor. Kelly believed that anticipation and prediction are what direct us. We build constructs about how the world should work. Clients selectively perceive, maintain, and act on their constructs. The counselor should facilitate the process of clients understanding their own constructs.

It should be obvious that cognitive biases do not occur just with clients. Counselors are not immune to these very human phenomena. One type of counselor cognitive bias can be consequential. This is the bias that results from selective perceptions. We engage in selective perceptions to maintain our schemas. Selective perceptions (Hastorf & Cantril, 1954; Wilson & Abrams, 1977) occur when people selectively perceive information because the information reinforces their way of looking at phenomena – their schemas (Cohen, 1981; Kelley, 1972a; Weiner, 1979, 1986; Markus, 1977). We selectively perceive the client's behaviors that reinforce our diagnoses. We dismiss, diminish, and discount information that is not in keeping with our preconceived notions. In the process, we may miss important information that is helpful in obtaining a more accurate perception and diagnosis. Selective biases may increase the therapist's confidence, but accurate information might also be discounted. Other effects of therapist's cognitive biases can include the following: we tend to pathologize conditions, we tend to confabulate problems, and we tend to conceive the problem as requiring professional interventions (Jilek, 2001; Lee, 2002; Ndetei, 1988; Sam & Moreira, 2002; Watters, 2010; Westermeyer, 1987; Williamson, 1998).

Neuroimaging and Physiological Measures

Neuroimaging and physiological measures allow scientists to examine brain and body activities. Research has been conducted on the neurological changes that occur in psychotherapy (Anand, 2006; Bender, 2004; Beutel &

Huber, 2008). There is evidence that when counselors interact with clients there are neurological (Eberhart, 2005; Siegel, 1999), emotional, and cognitive changes (Nelson & Baumgarte, 2004; Steele, 1997). That is, their brain patterns are changed during their interactions with clients. Neuroimaging and physiological measures open vistas that can provide measures of conscious and unconscious processes. For example, Vanman, Paul, Ito, and Miller (1997) studied white and black college students enrolled in a psychology course. In their study, whites and blacks worked as partners on cooperative learning tasks. The researchers found whites rated black partners more favorably than white partners. However, the electromyographic (EMG) measures of the whites exhibited more responses known to indicate negative affect. Walker, Silvert, Hewstone, and Nobre (2007) found when people interact with those who are of similar ethnicity as themselves, there are fewer neurological changes. When they interact with people of a different ethnicity, there are greater changes. The more a person interacts with people of other ethnicities, the more the brain patterns are similar to reactions to the person's own ethnicity. Those with less experience with other ethnicities show greater disparity and disruption in the brain processing. Eberhart (2005) cited studies of black and white people interacting. There were differences on such measures as sweating of skin, pumping of heart, cortical voltage shifts, and facial muscles when they interacted. Not only have there been neurological studies indicating people react differently, there are also studies indicating that people process information differently. For example, Euro-Americans and U.S. Americans have been characterized as thinking more individualistically and independently, and those of Asian cultures as thinking in a more group oriented and interdependent manner (Kitayama, Duffy, Kawamura, & Larsen, 2003; Markus & Kitayama, 2003; Nisbett, Peng, Choi, & Norenzayan, 2001; Triandis, 1995). There is now neurological evidence that people from various cultures may process information differently. Using fMRI (functional magnetic resonance imaging) neuroimaging, Hedden, Ketay, Aron, Markus, and Gabrieli (2008) studied American students of European background and East Asian students. They found different areas of the brain were activated on visuospatial tasks, analyzing lines dependent and independent of context. They found Euro-American students perceived matters independent of context, whereas the East Asian students were influenced by the context. Even though these studies pertain to ethnic differences, it is worth considering that these differences could also occur with other types of people who are different from the counselor, e.g., the poor, the elderly, and those with handicaps – in general, people with whom the therapist has not had much contact.

Grawe (2007) wrote that instead of trying to determine which theory is better, we should look at the brain circuits for indications of the effects of therapy. The author states that effective psychotherapy produces changes in the brain that can be monitored through neuroimaging. The brain's plasticity allows for changes in the brain. He wrote that neural mechanisms function on consistency patterns and that the inconsistencies, that is, dissonance, produces tension and conflict. He defines inconsistency as "the incompatibility of simultaneously transpiring mental processes" (p. 283). Inconsistencies can be reduced through coping skills, defense mechanisms, emotional regulations, and stress reduction (Znoj & Grawe, 2000). In a similar vein, Cozolino (2002) stated that effective therapy helps normalize the person's brain. According to this view, when people are in distress or when they have disorders, their brains show different brain activities than what is normally seen. Therefore, the function of therapy is to bring brain activity to normal limits. It is posited that if the brain has faulty features to begin with, the plasticity of the brain will allow for corrections to be made (e.g., through learning new behaviors).

In closing this chapter, it should be noted that even though all humans share the same neurological mechanism, this does not necessarily mean that the "hardwiring" is immutable. For example, environmental factors such as poverty (Aber, Bennett, Conley, & Li, 1997; Bergen, 2008), diet (von Schenck, Bender-Götze, & Koletzko, 1997), and trauma can produce changes in the brain (Arehart-Treichel, 2001). Even though neuroimaging technology can be valuable tools, the results can be confounded. For example, conscious physiological manipulation can sometimes mask a person's true thoughts and feelings; correlation does not necessarily prove causation, and spurious information might be obtained if a person really believes in a faulty conviction. However, neuroimaging and physiological measures can help provide information on what transpires when the counselor interacts with the client. The advent of less expensive and better computers as well as communications makes the greater use of electronics in therapy more possible.

Chapter 3

CROSS-CULTURAL PERSPECTIVES OF HUMAN BEHAVIOR (AFRICAN, ARAB, CHINESE)

There are various ways to examine and explain human behavior, e.g., economists, philosophers, religious figures, anthropologists, historians, biologists, and many others have their views. Each field of study draws from other fields, and within each field there are a multitude of views, e.g., psychology alone has such views as systems theory, behavioral and social learning, psychodynamic, psychosocial, developmental, transpersonal, social exchange, social construction, symbolic interactions, conflict, contingency, spiritual, genetic, and species-essence (the latter is a term used by Marx, 1932/1959). Stevenson's (2000) book, The *Study of Human Nature*, depicts human behavior from the perspectives of the Hebrew Bible, Hinduism, Confucianism, Plato, Christianity, Islam, Descartes, Hobbes, Hume, Rousseau, Kant, Marx, Mill, Freud, Sartre, Skinner, Lorenz, Chomsky, Bracken, Wilson, Holmstrom, Rose, Lewontin, Kamin, and Ridley. Theories of human behavior are important because they guide people's views of themselves and others. They are what guide the counselor. They are what guide clients in terms their views of the cause of their problems and the solutions. Theories of human behavior can guide societies' responses to people's behaviors and to psychological services, e.g., if a society attributes mental illness/disorder to a person's own fault or because of transgressions in a previous life, they are less likely to be sympathetic and allocate funds to help.

Cultures throughout the world have explanations of human behaviors (Eysenck, 2004; Gielen, Fish, & Draguns, 2004; Kim, Yang, & Hwang, 2006; Mohan, 2000). One way to delineate cultural groups is by ethnicity. If we use this method of delineation, there are about 5,000 ethnic groups in the world (Doyle, 1998), and many of them have a variety of perspectives on human behavior. Within each group, there are also groups that have their own views.

For example, within the United States, people can provide a religious or secular explanation of phenomena, and within each of these perspectives there are different explanations – e.g., some Christian denominations believe in free will and others believe in predestination. In the secular communities, some believe that behavior is the result of environment and others believe it is the result of endogenous personality characteristics. Lillard (1997) made the distinction between the explanations offered by the folklore of people and by the explanations of the educated classes. The academic groups are more likely to be influenced by literature that exposes them to various theories outside their own culture. If they are influenced by European and U.S. American perspectives, they are more likely to have a scientific view. In terms of religious perspectives, according to Barrett, Kurian, and Johnson (2001) there are 19 major religions in the world. They are subdivided into 270 large religious groups which are in turn divided into many smaller ones. Those who identify themselves as Christians have 34,000 separate groups. Many of these groups can also have different explanations of human behavior. All of these views illustrate the point that there are many different perspectives of human behavior – and not just the ones depicted in psychology and counseling textbooks. It is not the purpose of this book to provide a comprehensive view of the different theories of human behaviors. However, a sampling of the literature on three major groups (African, Arabs, and Asian) will provide the reader with awareness that other groups in the world have different perspectives of human behavior. Reminder again: there are variations within groups and making ascriptions to entire groups would be inaccurate and invalid.

An ongoing problem in examining populations is how to classify people. All classification systems have their shortcomings and critics. There are problems of nomenclature as well as criteria to include and exclude group membership. The psychological and counseling literature often use the terms Asian, African, and European. If this system is used, there are data indicating that 60.2 percent of the people in the world live in Asia, 15.1 percent Africa, 10.6 percent Europe, 5.0 percent North America, 8.6 percent Latin America and the Caribbean, and 0.5 percent Oceania (Jannsen, Liu, & Badgett, 2012). One consequence of using figures such as these is to increase awareness that if the views of humans are represented by those held by the largest number of people, it would be the views of those in Asia.

AFRICAN PERSPECTIVES

In the literature on Africa, there are those who wrote that each African culture has unique environments that form distinct characteristics that differentiate them from others (Mazrui & Mazrui, 1995; Mbiti, 1969; Nyasani, 1997;

Osei, 1971; Wiredu, Karp, & Bird, 1996), e.g., in sub-Saharan Africa, there are 1,300 languages (Doyle, 1998). However, numerous writers have attributed certain characteristics to African people. Almost all of them attribute the affects of slavery, colonialism, and exploitation by Europeans and Caucasians as having a major lasting impact on African character, definition of self, and views of the world (Azibo, 1991; Belgrave & Allison, 2006; Carson, 1997; Grills, 2004; Khoapa, 1980; Lassiter, 1999; Mbiti, 1969; Minogue & Molloy, 1974; Nyasani, 1997; Osei, 1971; Wiredu, Karp, & Bird, 1996). Belgrave and Allison (2006) presented the characteristics of the African personality as spirituality, collectivism, time orientation, orality, sensitivity to affect and emotional cues, verve and rhythm (e.g., the way Africans present themselves through such dimensions as movement, posture, speech patterns, and behavior), balance and harmony with nature, and other aspects of Africentric psychology. Grills (2004) lists aspects of Africentricism as balance and cosmic order attained through such virtues as truth, justice, compassion, harmony, reciprocity, and order; dealing with the effects of European enslavement of Africans; veneration of all living things; spiritness which infuses mind, soul, energy, and passion; living an authentic life in which one is true to one's self; the use of affect and cognition as a means of knowing (and going beyond the five senses and logic); and examining the past when making progress. Azibo (1991) wrote that an analysis of theories of the African personality indicated that the minimum requirements for a metatheory of the African personality construct is that there must be an explanation of the nature of the underlying spiritual essence; the psychological effects of this spirituality; the interplay among the spiritual, mental, and physical dimensions on the person; and how this interplay impacts psychological functioning.

Traditional African medicine is practiced by diviners, midwives, and herbalists. They combined indigenous herbs and spirituality (Helwig, 2001; Kale, 1995) along with charms, incantations, and spells. Practitioners treat a wide variety of medical and psychological illnesses, e.g., cancers, acquired immunodeficiency syndrome (AIDS), psychiatric disorders, high blood pressure, cholera, infertility, most venereal diseases, epilepsy, asthma, eczema, hay fever, anxiety, depression, benign prostatic hypertrophy, urinary tract infections, gout, wounds, and burns (Helwig, 2001). Diviners try to determine the causes of illness, attributing causes to ancestral spirits and other influences. Midwives use indigenous plants to aid childbirth. Herbalists use plants to treat ailments. Illness is often attributed to a lack of balance between the patient and social environment or spiritual world, i.e., natural and supernatural causes. Healing plants were used to treat imbalances. The medicinal plants were also believed to have symbolic and spiritual significance. In African psychotherapy, the cause and healing of the problem are inextricably linked with the supernatural (Awanbor, 1982).

According to Kalipeni (1979), beliefs in the causes of problems can include harmful environmental agents, witchcraft and sorcery, disfavor of God, and the spirits of the dead. Suffering might be attributed to the patient or family incurring the displeasure of the supernatural in the omission or commission of some act. Witchcraft is often directed at those who have accomplished some economic success, e.g., laborers who return to the village with earned income. The cause of the illness affects the attitude of others toward the sufferer. The cure depends on the culture and can include a combination of such methods as exorcism, confession, atonement, appeasement, and restoration back into the family. It is not unusual for the community to believe an individual's illness is a reflection of something wrong with the community, and so collective fear and action might ensue.

The methods used by traditional African healers might help in alleviating some neurotic problems, but they are less successful with psychoses and severe depression. Some of the traditional techniques include restraints, flogging, starvation, and cautery ("At Home and Abroad," 1966). Many traditional healers are against medications (Okasha, 2002). Patel's (1995) studies in sub-Saharan Africa found that many African cultures believe the mind resides in the head, heart, or abdominal region; mental illnesses/disorders are often attributed to spiritual causes; the behavioral aspects of psychoses are often noticed rather than the delusions; and neuroses are often somatically expressed.

ARAB PERSPECTIVES

Who are the Arabs? They are diverse people, living in many parts of the world. According to the *Encyclopædia Britannica*, the term Arab: "In modern usage, it embraces any of the Arabic-speaking peoples living in the vast region from Mauritania, on the Atlantic coast of Africa, to southwestern Iran, including the entire Maghrib of North Africa, Egypt and The Sudan, the Arabian Peninsula, and Syria and Iraq" (Arab, 2010, para. 1).

Many Arabs are Muslims and believe in the Islamic Scriptures: the Qur'an (also spelled *Koran*). The language of the Qur'an is Arabic (though there are translations into many languages). Islam provides instructions in religious, social, legal, family, and individual matters. The personality traits advised by the Holy Qur'an (also spelled *Koran, Al-Coran, Coran, Kuran,* and *Al-Qur'an*) and the Prophet Muhammad (also spelled *Mohammad, Mohammed,* or *Muhammed*) are known as the "sunnah" (Khan, 2005). The Holy Qur'an points out nine behavioral categories of the believer's traits. These refer to belief, pray, social relationships, family relationships, morality, affect and emotions, mental and cognitive aspects, professional and occupational life, as well as physical traits.

The first two traits (belief and prayer) are the spiritual components, and they form the basis of guiding the other traits. It should be noted that not all Arabs are Muslims, and not all Muslims are Arabs (e.g., Indonesians are not Arabs, but Indonesia is the country with the largest population of Muslims). However, many Arabs have a common language (Arabic) and religion (Islam). The influence of these two factors is often mitigated by other sources (Barakat, 1978). Arabic views are influenced by regional and local customs, religious sectarianism, traditions, nationalism, secularisms (e.g., democracy, socialism, communism), and so on. Among the Arabs, there are different histories, languages, and effects of colonization. As an example of the diversity among Arabs, Barakat (1978) points out that Sudan alone has 572 tribes and 56 ethnic groups. Before the introduction of Islam (Muhammad, the founder of Islam, lived 570–632 C.E.), many regions had their own indigenous cultures, values, and beliefs. Some of these continued to influence them after the introduction of Islam. Religions such as Judaism, Christianity, Zoroastrianism, Sabi, and Hanafiyyah influenced the Arabs. Arab cultures are at the nexus of three continents: Africa, Asia, and Europe. As such, they are influenced by many sources.

There does not seem to be an agreement among Arab scholars as to a common Arab personality, or how it develops. Traditionally, views of personality are influenced by Hippocrates' humoral theory – excess or deficits in blood, phlegm, yellow bile, and black bile cause problems (Hammad, Kysia, Rabah, Hassoun, & Connelly, 1999).

Modern views are often influenced by Western theories. In term of mental illness/disorder, Hammad, Kysia, Rabah, Hassoun, and Connelly (1999) wrote:

> Mental illness and mental disorder are conditions that are highly shunned in the Middle East. While Islamic norms dictate kindness and care be given to the mentally ill/disordered, Arab social norms tend to approach mental illness/disorder with fear and social avoidance. It might be said of the ill person that he is touched by demons (jinn) or that God is punishing him. While it is acceptable to disclose mental stress, a breakdown is considered totally shameful and blameworthy for the individual, for his or her family, and in some instances, for his or her village. (p. 18)

Regarding personality development, Dwairy (1998) wrote that Arabic personality differs from Western society in two areas: the individuation process and self-control. Arab socialization entails enmeshing the person into interdependence and cooperation with the group – individualism and independent thinking are not encouraged. Control is external and is exercised by family and society rather than self-control. According to Dwairy, the superego is not differentiated from the social values of Arabic society. The author wrote that there is a continuum of acculturation in terms of influences on groups and individuals – some are more or less Westernized, bicultural, and traditional. Statements about Arab personality are probably more applicable to those who are more traditional.

Moughrabi (1978) reviewed the literature on Arab personality traits as an explanation of why Arab societies had not developed modern political and economic institutions. He rejected the common characterization of the Arab personality as consisting of free-floating hostility, rigidity, lacking in reality testing, and suspiciousness. He criticized the characterizations and research upon which these statements were made. He wrote that many of the statements about Arab personality were based on child-raising practices; however, child-raising practices were diverse and most of studies were based on anecdotal reports. The methodology and representativeness of the studies were criticized as flawed, and the characterizations of Arab personality were considered to be unscientific, demeaning, and consisting of categorical and sweeping generalizations. The point was also made that Arab cultures were changing. Therefore, generalizations of them were incorrect because they were static and not dynamic.

Various authors have written about Arabs and mental illness/disorder. The studies of El-Islam and Ahmed (1971), as well as Sayed (2003), provided good summaries of what has been written. El-Islam and Ahmed (1971) studied Arab psychiatric outpatient clinic patients in Cairo, Egypt. They described the patients in their study as illiterate, ritualistic, and traditional. These patients attributed mental illness/disorder more to supernatural mechanisms, e.g., spirits or envy, rather than to internal causes. El-Islam and Ahmed wrote that attribution to external causes elicited support from the community, and blame was projected onto spirits and unknown forces rather than on the person with the mental illness/disorder. Also, they found there was a tendency to present psychological problems in a somatic manner.

Sayed (2003) wrote about conceptualizations of mental illness/disorder within Arab cultures. He reported that seeking aid from a practitioner of psychological services was seen as a sign of weakness and shame (citing El-Islam, 1998; Okasha, 2000) that might bring disgrace to the family and the tribe. Sayed wrote that traditional healers in Arab cultures were the Sheikh or Matawaa. Their role was to drive the "evil spirit" and "evil eye" away. Family members may be present to keep family secrets from being revealed in session. The use of interpreters and translators might confuse clients because they are not sure of the role these people play in session, and it might also incur problems with issues of therapeutic alliance and transference. For Arab patients, there are no clear boundaries between the self and the body. These are woven into the person's cultural identity and have an effect on conceptualizations of health and mental health. Sayed wrote that Arab patients view medical doctors differently than they are viewed in the West. The doctor is viewed as powerful and mysterious (similar to traditional healers or religious Islamic figures). Patients conform to authority figures and perceive their role is to follow the doctor's orders. Because many Arabs readily seek help from religious figures, they may readily transfer this behavior toward those providing psychological help. Sayed cites studies and observations that indicate that patients are not comfortable with the idea of working collaboratively with the doctor – because of the power differential. If doctors want patients to work collaboratively with them, they will have to work against cultural expectations and put effort into role induction; that is, explain to the client the roles, functions, and behaviors to be expected of patient and doctor. The doctor will need to address clients' belief that self-disclosure means betrayal to the family, or that it is a weakness, a failure, or a sign of loss of religious faith. Sayed also cites studies indicating that somatization of emotional problems is common in Arab cultures – as it is in other Eastern cultures such as China, Korea, and Japan (citing Draguns, 1994). The most commonly accepted way of communicating distress was by playing the sick role. Having the sick role for a physical problem can relieve the family, tribal, or clan from obligations or from the stigma of being associated with someone with a mental illness or mental disorder. Psychological distress may be expressed in metaphors or idioms of distress, e.g., having a "sinking of the heart," or having a burning spleen or liver (to describe rage, sadness, anger, or anxiety). The author suggests that because metaphors are used so often, the study of the metaphors would be a good way to understand the patients' mental and physical states. Sayed adds the caveat that the use of metaphors and the lack of expressions of thoughts and feelings are not signs of inadequacy. Instead, they reflect cultural conceptualization and understanding of the mental processes. This is a lesson for all of us; the differences in the expressions, perceptions, and definitions of mental illness/disorder are not necessarily a reflection of inadequacy, deficit intelligence, or lack of understanding. Rather, the differences could be attributed to differences in the conceptualization and understanding of the behavior.

CHINESE PERSPECTIVES

China has 56 officially recognized ethnic groups, and there are 129 languages (Hongkai, 2008). Many of these groups have their own perceptions and explanations of human behavior and personality. However, 95 percent of the people are Han Chinese and their culture is the most common. They have various explanations for the causes of mental illness/disorder, including neurological factors, moral lapse, weak character, punishment for one's transgression in the present or previous life, failure to fulfill duties to ancestors, or eating foods that should be avoided. Stigma and shame are prominent features in Chinese folk views of mental illness/disorder, and there is often reluctance to obtain help. This view is shared by people in many cultures (Lam et al., 2010).

Many traditional Chinese do not view the mind, body, and spirit separately (Kuo & Kavanagh, 1994). Some may not differentiate illness from other problems of living. Traditional Chinese perspectives consider health and personality to be influences by five elements: wood, water, earth, metal, and fire (Ellis, Abrams, & Abrams 2009; Hsu, 2006). The Five Element Theory stems from Chinese medicine and philosophy, and there is a belief that it reflects primal forces in the universe, in nature, and in the body. Each element is associated with a personality type. For example, wood is associated with the aggressive personality type, water with resourceful and single-mindedness, earth with forgiving and compassion, metal with exceptional strength and endurance, and fire with warmth and good relationships.

Lam et al. (2010) wrote that Chinese core cultural values consist of harmony with nature, family as a central core of life, harmony in social relationships, and avoidance of extreme emotional expression. Confucianism, Taoism, and Buddhism have significant impact on the Chinese. Within each of these views there are different beliefs and practices. Unlike the monotheistic religions (Judaism, Christianity, and Islam) which differentiate themselves from each other, the Chinese do not make clear distinctions among Confucianism, Taoism, and Buddhism. In actual practice, various aspects of each of these are adopted and used by each group (Hui, Ng, & Tai, 2010).

Confucian thought stresses harmony in relationships. Harmonious interdependence is embodied by the Five Cardinal Relations (wu lun): between sovereign and subject, father and son, elder and younger brother, husband and wife, and friend and friend (King & Bond, 1985). Under this paradigm, humans do not exist alone but are conceptualized as relational beings. Mental illness/disorder is considered a result of a violation of interpersonal relationships. Therapy might consist of moralizing and telling the person how to behave (Kleinman & Lin 1981).

Taoism stresses harmony with nature and people. Illnesses such as mental disorders are viewed as disharmony within a person's body and soul. Healing consists of restoring balance. There are no boundaries between physical and psychological illness. Many mental health problems, such as depression, are commonly considered as "weakness" in spiritual strength. A Taoism's view of mental illness/disorder is that it is an "imbalance" of Yin and Yang (contrary forces) that need adjustment. Part of a Taoist's approach is to help the client realize that social attainments are untrustworthy and temporary; morality standards are unreliable; and self-image, self-evaluation, honor, disgrace, pride, as well as egocentrism get in the way of achieving a state of good mental health. A good state of mental health can be achieved through calm acceptance and letting go of thoughts and feelings that interfere with achieving harmony and balance (Yip, 2004).

Buddhism views the mind as the key to psychological and physical health. Yeung and Lee (1997) wrote that the Buddha said there are two kinds of illnesses: physical and mental. It is rare for anyone to be without mental illness (Rahula, 1978). Curing mental illness will free the person from physical illness and liberate the mind. The Buddha taught that people need to understand and realize that living entails suffering. Suffering comes from ignorance (e.g., ignorance of what is causing the suffering; ignorance of what is important), and ignorance leads to self-centered desires. Practicing Buddhist teachings will help extinguish various sufferings. This is accomplished through having the right view, right thinking, right speech, right action, right living, right endeavor, right memory, and right meditation. The Buddha taught that everyone is capable of achieving the goals of Buddhism. Because Buddhists believe in reincarnation, and that behaviors in previous lives affect each rebirth, a Buddhist's view is that disabilities are the result of punishment of one's wrongdoing in a past life – thus, stigma would be attached to the person with the disability. But compassion for those with disabilities, as well as for those who suffer, might lessen the effects of this view.

Folk religions (e.g., shamanism) continue to influence the less educated and more traditional. Many illnesses are believed to be supernatural in origin, and can occur for such reasons as lack of respect or failure to fulfill duties to ancestors. Shamans have significant influence (Tsoi, 1985) and serve to communicate with the spiritual world, help people settle their problems, and heal their illness. The mentally ill/disordered are often perceived as dangerous, disruptive, and unpredictable. Lay understandings of mental illness/disorder tend to consist of moralizing, and blaming the individual for the illness. People with mental illness/disorder are often judged to be responsible for their deviant behavior (Lam et al., 2010). There is a belief that modern drugs are not effective against the supernatural (Ferguson, Cheang, Dasananjali, Hawari, Peng, & Salzberg, 1998).

In terms of therapy, Lin (1983) reported that Western psychiatric treatments (e.g., medications) are generally accepted; however, psychotherapy (insight therapy) is not. There are a number of possible reasons why psychotherapy is not readily accepted. Chinese philosophy looks at relationship issues (and not internal factors) as an explanation of problems. There is the attitude that emotions and sex should be kept private. There is the belief that organic problems are the cause of psychological problems. In addition, there is the belief that verbal communications as a form of therapy is uncomfortable for many Chinese. They prefer nonverbal and symbolic communications. Lin noted that mental problems are frequently expressed somatically. Chen and

Mak (2008) suggested that counselors avoid threats to the client's self-worth and loss of face and attribute causes of problems to the environment and the hereditary – which the client has less control over, rather than attributing the problems to the client's personal shortcomings. Because the family plays a significant role in taking care of those with mental illness/disorder, Yip (2005) recommends more support be directed to families.

Yang (2006) wrote that most of the Chinese personality research is in the form of lexical or descriptive-term approaches (e.g., Cheung, Fan, To, 2008; Kim, Yang, & Hwang, 2006; Zhou, Saucier, Gao, & Liu, 2009). The studies of Yang and Wang (2000) as well as Zhou, Saucier, Gao, and Liu (2009) are examples of research that use these approaches. Yang and Wang (2000) gathered Chinese personality descriptors and found them to be the following: competence versus impotence, industriousness versus unindustriousness, other-orientedness versus self-centeredness, agreeableness versus disagreeableness, extraversion versus introversion, large-mindedness versus small-mindedness, and contentedness versus vaingloriousness. Zhou, Saucier, Gao, and Liu (2009) took 3,159 personality descriptors from the *Contemporary Chinese Dictionary* and through statistical and survey methods found the factors making up Chinese personality structure were extraversion, conscientiousness/diligence, unselfishness, negative valence, emotional volatility, intellect/positive valence, and dependency/fragility. Yang (1986) wrote that much of the psychological literature on Chinese views of personality is influenced by U.S. American perspectives. However, there are efforts to develop indigenous instruments and theories (Kim, Yang, & Hwang, 2006).

Cheung, van de Vijver, and Leong (2011) reviewed studies of culture and personality measures. They reported there were two types of studies. There were studies using etic approaches which focused on equivalence of cross-cultural imports of personality measures. There were also studies using emic approaches which examined personality in terms of specific cultures. They suggested a third approach that combines the methodological vigor of the etic approach with the cultural sensitivity of the emic approach.

Chapter 4

EUROPEAN AND U.S. PERSPECTIVES OF HUMAN BEHAVIOR

The humor theory was discussed earlier in this book (in the section on "Arab Perspectives"). Until modern science had more of an impact, around the latter part of the nineteenth century, the humor theory was significant in explaining human behavior and illnesses in Europe and the United States. This theory, which was interrelated with the seasons, cosmos, and a multitude of other phenomena, attributed health and character to the influence of black bile, yellow bile, phlegm, and blood (Arikha, 2007; Getz, 1998; Porter, 1997; Sudhoff, 1926; van Sertima, 1992). Some descriptors of the black bile personality are melancholic, introspective, sentimental, and irritable. Yellow bile (also known as Choleric) personalities can be short-tempered, ambitious, and easily angered. Phlegmatic types can be pallid, calm, and unemotional. Blood (Sanguine) types are amorous, happy, generous, and optimistic. One purpose of the physician is to have a balance of these humors. Even though Hippocrates (living about 460 to 370 B.C.) is often identified as the person who systemized and developed the humors into a medical theory, it may have origins in ancient Egypt (van Sertima, 1992) or Mesopotamia (Sudhoff, 1926). This theory, and variations of it, influenced ancient Greek, Roman, European, and Islamic physicians and philosophers. Other civilizations also had explanations of health and character in similar terms as those of humor theory. For example, the Yunani (also called Unani) school of Indian medicine (Dalrymple, 2003) still practiced in India, derived from Greco-Arabic traditions of humor theory. The Yunani's elements are fire, water, earth, and air. However, India had its own indigenous version, the Ayurveda, which lists the basic elements as earth, water, fire, air, and ether (Chopra, 2003).

Christianity also had a significant impact on European perspectives of mental illness/disorder. Christians have a history of viewing mental illness/disorder as the result of generational sin (e.g., origin sin of Adam and

Eve), demonic possession, or lack of faith (Alexander, 1902, Fink & Tasman, 1992; Kroll & Bachrach, 1984; Millon, 2004; O'Donnell, 1911; Stanford, 2008). Pinel (1745–1826) brought a different perspective (Shorter, 1997; Woodside & McClam, 2009). Instead of viewing mental illnesses/disorders as signs of possession by demons or as inflictions that are the result of sin, he campaigned for the treatment of mental illness/disorder as a disease requiring medical care. He advocated for the mentally ill/disordered to be treated humanely and with respect rather than as conditions to be persecuted and punished. His treatment was based on detailed examination and knowledge of the patient. However, secular, scientific views of mental illness/disorder are not accepted by everyone, and religious perspectives of mental illness/disorder still persist today. For example, recent research indicates that U.S. Christians are more likely to go to clergy with their psychological problems than to other professions (Chalfant, Heller, Roberts, Briones, Aguirre-Hochbaum, & Farr, 1990). Stanford (2007) surveyed 293 people diagnosed with mental illness/disorder who went to church pastors to be counseled. About a third of them reported such reactions as the church abandoning them, attributing the mental illness/disorder to the work of demons, or suggesting that the mental illness/disorder was caused by personal sin. Women were more likely than men to have their mental illness/disorder dismissed and to be told not to take their psychiatric medication. It should be noted that there is a wide range of views of mental illness/disorder among Christians.

Nowadays, mental health professionals view psychological problems from a number of different perspectives, e.g., it is the result of faulty learning, a chemical imbalance, trauma, hereditary factors, or disrupted psychosexual development. It is common practice for U.S. American counselors to view people via theories of personality. Yang (2006) wrote that personality research generally consists of personality genetics, personality development, personality structure and assessment, personality dynamics, and personality change. Among the issues that personality theorists have to contend with are the roles genetics and learning play in the development of personality. In the first case, implying that personality is heavily influenced by genes. In the second case, personality is viewed as mainly learned behavior. Plomin, DeFries, and McClellearn (1990) attributed about 30 percent to 50 percent of personality characteristics to genetics and 50 percent to 70 percent to environment. It is increasingly evident that genes, culture, and environment affect each other. Jacobson's (2009) summary of nature versus nurture studies concluded that each affects the other. She reported that genes affect environment and environment affects genes. She wrote that environmental factors account for over half the variation in individual behaviors and traits. Among the studies she cited are those that indicated (a) the environment can effect gene expression in future generations, (b) environmental stress can alter biological and genetic mechanisms associated with risky behaviors, (c) early rearing environments can disrupt psychobiological regulatory functions, and (d) interactions between genes and environment can affect the development and plasticity of the brain.

The categories and theorists presented in the next section of the book are derived from European and U.S. American literature. The psychological theories presented here are by no means comprehensive – or mutually exclusive. There are overlaps in the theories, and each theory has variations within them. The initiators of a particular theory might change their ideas over time, and their adherents might have different interpretations and stress different aspect of the original theory. These theories are very brief snapshots and serve as samples of various perspectives of human behavior. There are many other perspectives in the U.S. and elsewhere (Corsini & Wedding, 2005; Craighead, 2002; Kaslow, 2002). Almost all the theories have an explanation on the formation of personality. There are numerous definitions of personality, and there are often tests (inventories) developed to operationalize concepts. There are many ways to categorize these theories. Examples include theoretical and actuarial, clinical and nonclinical, culture-free and culturally biased, projectives and nonprojectives, and evidence-based and nonevidence-based. This book categorizes them as evolutionary, psychoanalytic, behavioral, social cognitive, humanistic, and biopsychological theories.

TRAITS (AND TYPES)

Early in history and up to the present times, people throughout the world have long ascribed patterns of behavior to individuals (and indeed to cultural groups). They have labeled these patterns as personality characteristics; that is, they ascribed certain characteristics to people, such as describing them as brave, friendly, generous, and so on. They ascribed these characteristics through various means. Observations of people is one method. They noticed people with certain characteristics and labeled them as such. Another method was to use astrology to define characteristics. The Chinese (Wu, 2005), Babylonians (Rochberg, 2010), Mayans (Scofield & Orr, 2007), and Europeans (Newman & Grafton, 2001) are among those who used astrological methods to categorize people's characteristics. Chinese and Western astrology characterized people into twelve types. The Chinese associate animals to the various personality types and traits: Rat, Ox, Tiger, Rabbit, Dragon, Snake, Horse, Goat, Monkey, Rooster, Dog, and Pig. In the West, these are associated with signs: Aries, Taurus, Gemini, Cancer, Leo, Virgo, Libra, Scorpio, Sagittarius, Capricorn, Aquarius, and Pisces. These types vary in the degree they have of their particular characteristic, and they are influenced by other types. Hippocrates (Hammad, Kysia, Rabah, Hassoun, & Connelly, 1999) characterized human behavior in terms of four temperaments, each associated with a different bodily fluid, or "humors" (previously discussed in this book).

More recently in the West, there was the question of whether personalities should be classified as traits and types. Trait theorists classify personalities in terms of characteristics on a continuum, e.g., a trait theorist might state that a person has aggressive characteristics. Type theorists classify personalities into distinct categories, e.g., a type theorist might label a person as aggressive. Cloninger (2009) wrote that characterizations of personalities into types, that is, as discrete categories, are spurious. Such characterizations of personalities are more a function of expediency and for descriptive purposes. Most writers agree that personality characteristics are a matter of degree rather than quantum differences. Also, even if a person has a distinct character, there are other characteristics that affect the person, e.g., an aggressive person might also be friendly. In addition, there are those, like behaviorists and social learning advocates, who believe that personality characteristics are shaped by the environment and can be changed through learning to behave differently, such as a nonviolent civilian in one environment being able to learn to be a violent soldier in another setting. Most writers view personality as a trait. In other words, they view personality as a matter of degree of a particular characteristic rather than as a distinct type.

Allport (1937, 1955; Evans, 1971; Lindzey, 1954, 1958; Murchison, 1935) has been described as a trait theorist. He developed his categories of traits by examining words that describe personality. He placed them in three categories: *Cardinal, Central,* and *Secondary* traits. *Cardinal* traits are single characteristics that direct a person's behavior, e.g., need for power and control. A *Cardinal* trait dominates, defines, and shapes a person's life. *Central* traits occur in all people, though they are manifested to different degrees, e.g., propensity to lie. *Central* traits help shape most of our behavior although they are not as overwhelming as cardinal traits. *Secondary* traits are characteristics that show under certain circumstances, like a preference for certain music or ice cream flavor. These traits are characteristics that are not obvious to the public, but close friends and family are often privy to them, e.g., personal likes and dislikes.

Cattell (1946, 1957) and his colleagues viewed personality structure as consisting of sixteen "primary factors" (16 Personality Factors). These 16 factors group into five "secondary factors." The 16PF Questionnaire (Conn, Rieke, 1994; Russell & Karol, 2002) was developed to assess basic traits of human personality. The "primary" factors are as follows: *Warmth, Reasoning, Emotional Stability, Dominance, Liveliness, Rule-Consciousness, Social Boldness, Sensitivity, Vigilance, Abstractedness, Privateness, Apprehension, Openness to Change, Self-Re-*

liance, Perfectionism, and *Tension.* These are grouped into five factors (referred to as Global Factors or the "Big Five"): *Extraversion, Anxiety, Tough-Mindedness, Independence,* and *Self-Control.*

Eysenck (1998; Eysenck & Eysenck, 1969) believed three traits defined personality: *Extraversion, Neuroticism,* and *Psychoticism.* He, along with colleagues, developed a number of tests. He referred to *Extraversion* as tendencies to respond in social situations. People high on extraversion are comfortable in social situations – people on the other end of the scale are not as comfortable. *Neuroticism* refers to tendencies to experience negative emotions. Those high on neuroticism have emotionally unstable characteristics. Those low on neuroticism are more emotionally stable. *Psychoticism* refers to vulnerability to psychoses. Those high on psychoticism are often egocentric, insensitivity, unconcerned for others, and socially inept. Those low on psychoticism are not as likely to show these characteristics.

Murray (1938, 2008; Ruitenbeek, 1964) and his colleagues studied personality and needs. Edwards (1954, 1959) popularized Murray's ideas through the Edwards Personal Preference Schedule (EPPS; Helms, 1982). Jackson (1997) developed the Personality Research Form (PRF). This is also based on Murray's ideas and is similar to the EPPS. There are various versions of the PRF, the Form E version scales are: *Abasement, Achievement, Affiliation, Aggression, Autonomy, Change, Cognitive Structure, Defendence, Desirability, Dominance, Endurance, Exhibition, Harmavoidance, Impulsivity, Infrequency, Nurturance, Order, Play, Sentience, Social Recognition, Succorance,* and *Understanding.*

Holland (Hogan & Blake, 1999; Holland, 1973; Holland, 1997) considered the role of personality in making vocational choices. He delineated personalities and vocational types into six categories: *Realistic* – these people like tangible things; they are practical, hands-on, and tool-oriented. *Investigative* – they like solving problems and scientific activities; they are curious, analytical, and intellectual. *Artistic* – they like self-expression and artistic activities. *Social* – they like dealing with people. *Enterprising* – these people like influencing people; power, control, and status. *Conventional* – they prefer order and structure.

The Five-Factor model has received considerable attention these days (e.g., Diaz-Guerrero, Diaz-Loving, & Rodriguez de Diaz, 2001). The Five-Factor model developed from the study of words that are used to describe people. This approach has been referred to by various terms, e.g., a lexical, actuarial, empirical, or data-based approach. Descriptive words, e.g., adjectives, in English and other languages were grouped together (factor analyzed) and resulted in five factors being delineated (Cattell, 1946; Cheung, Leung, Zhang, Sun, Gan, Song, & Xie, 2001; Costa & McCrae, 1992; Digman, 1990; Digman, 1996; Digman & Takemoto-Chock, 1981; Goldberg, 1992, 1993; Hendriks et al., 2003; John, 1989; John, 1990; John, Angleitner, & Ostendorf, 1988; Mc-

Crae, 2002; McCrae & Allik, 2002; McCrae & Costa, 1990; Norman, 1963; Rolland, 2002; Trull & Geary, 1997; Wiggins & Trapnell, 1997). The NEO-PI-R was developed by Costa and McCrae (1992) and based on the Five-Factor model. This is a personality test that refers to the five factors as "domains." The NEO PI-R five domains of personality and the six facets that comprise each domains are as follows:

1. *Openness* – being open to experiences and ideas. The facets are *Fantasy, Aesthetics, Feelings, Actions, Ideas,* and *Values.*
2. *Conscientiousness* – good at staying on tasks and achieving goals. The facets are *Competence, Order, Dutifulness, Achievement Striving, Self Discipline,* and *Deliberation.*
3. *Extraversion* – being sociable, liking being in groups and interacting with people. The facets are *Warmth, Gregariousness, Assertiveness, Activity, Excitement Seeking,* and *Positive Emotion.*
4. *Agreeableness* – wanting to be kind and cooperative and to help others. The facets are *Trust, Straightforwardness, Altruism, Compliance, Modesty,* and *Tender Mindedness.*
5. *Neuroticism* – tendency to easily experience negative feelings; emotional instability. The facets are *Anxiety, Angry Hostility, Depression, Self Consciousness, Impulsiveness,* and *Vulnerability.*

There are many writers who have provided categories of human types. Sheldon (1940, 1954) classified personality by body types (somatotypes): the *Endomorph* (heavy and easy-going), the *Mesomorph* (muscular and aggressive), and the *Ectomorph* (thin and intellectual or artistic). Marston (1979) developed the DISC system that categorized human behavior into four key areas: *Dominance, Influencing, Steadiness,* and *Compliance.* Every individual was thought to be a combination of these four categories, with one dominant style. Keirsey's (1998, Keirsey & Bates, 1984) description of personality parallels the Myers-Briggs' 16 types. He lists four personality types: *Artisan, Guardian, Idealist,* and *Rational.* These four temperaments are divided into two categories (roles), each with two types (role variants). Friedman (1996) helped bring attention to *Type A* and *Type B* personalities. *Type A* personalities are achievement oriented, irritable, and impatient. *Type B's* are less competitive and more easygoing than type *A's.*

At the present time, Jung is the main person associated with type theory. He is the founder of analytical psychology, also known as Jungian psychology. A popular implementation of some of Jung's ideas is the Myers-Briggs Type Indicator inventory. Even though the validity, reliability, and degree to which it reflects Jung's concepts and ideas are questionable (Pittenger, 2005), it is nevertheless widespread. The Myers-Briggs Type Indicator (Cox, 1968; Fordham, 1978; Hall & Nordby, 1973; Homans, 1979; Samuels, 1985) provides 16 personality types that are a combination of four scales: *Extraversion (E)* or *Introversion (I), Sensing (S)* or *Intuition (N), Thinking (T)* or *Feeling (F),* and *Judging (J)* or *Perceiving (P). Extraversion* indicates a preference to focus on the outer world of people or things; *Introversion* indicates a preference to focus on the inner world of ideas and thoughts. *Sensing* indicates a preference to focus in the here and now, the use of senses, and dealing with concrete information; *Intuition* indicates a preference to look at the future and to look at patterns and possibilities. *Thinking* indicates a preference to base decisions on logic as well as cause and effect; *Feeling* indicates a preference to base decisions on subjective factors. *Judging* indicates a preference to plan and organize as well as to have structure; *Perceiving* indicates a preference for flexibility and spontaneity.

It should be noted that most of the type theorists recognize that a person can have varying degrees of a particular type of characteristic and that there are other factors that modify a particular characteristic. For example, Jung believed people have a dominant function (type) supported by an auxiliary (2nd) function, tertiary (3rd) function, and inferior (4th) function. Cattell (1950) considered broad surface traits as types. "Eysenck used the term 'type' to refer to second-order factors which are organizations of traits based on observed correlations" (Cattell, 1950, p. 132).

Modern-day scholars frequently attempt to delineate personality traits by such methods as examining the use of personality descriptors in the language. Because language is believed to be based on neurological mechanisms and structures (Chomsky, 1957, 1968), one reasonable corollary would be that the personality characteristics described by words reflect some "hardwiring" in the brain – keeping in mind that hardwiring can be changed by environment and learning.

BEHAVIORIST THEORIES

Behaviorists (Baum, 1994; Lattal & Chase, 2003; Mills, 2000; Pavlov, 1957, 1994; Rachlin, 1991; Skinner, 1938, 1945, 1969, 1991; Staddon, 2001; Watson, 1913; Zuriff, 1985) explain personality in terms of the effects of stimulus, response, and consequences of behavior. Herrnstein (Brown & Herrnstein, 1975) extended this theory and applied it to attitudes and traits. An attitude is a stable (it happens repeatedly) response to a group of stimuli. Most behaviorists today recognize the role genetics and biology play in traits. Personality is mainly shaped and conditioned by the environment. Therapy consists of applying principles of learning, e.g., the use of rewards, punishment, desensitization, aversion therapy, and modeling. Abnormal behavior is the result of faulty learning, which can be remedied by learning new and different behaviors. The unconscious, hidden, and underlying reasons for disorders are rele-gated subordinate roles. Behaviorists often use experimental methods to vali-date what they use. They focus on what can observed, measured, and ma-nipulated.

BIOPSYCHOLOGICAL THEORIES

Proponents of these perspectives of personality and behaviors study neur-al mechanisms, structures, functions, and chemistry of the brain. Biopsycho-logical theories have been referred to as biological psychology, behavioral neuroscience, biopsychology, and psychobiology. Livesley (2001) wrote that biopsychological structures rest on environmental influences on genetic dis-positions. These influence the way people behave, how they interpret their surroundings, and the choices they make. An example of the environment in-fluencing genetic predisposition is that of phenylalanine – deficiencies of this amino acid can cause mental retardation.

Studies of the brain involvement in personality and behavior come from multiple sources. For example, there have been studies (Davidson, 2001, 2001a, 2003; Davidson, Pizzagalli, Nitschke, & Putnam, 2002; Johnstone, van Reekum, Urry, Kalin, & Davidson, 2007) of the prefrontal cortex and amyg-dala as well as of prefrontal-subcortical circuitry areas of the brain in relation-ship to emotion and affective disorders, e.g., anxiety and depression. David-son (2003) found that those with nonverbal learning disorders have hemi-spheric asymmetry, which can affect personality; they often have problems interpreting nonverbal cues and thus have problems in social situations. They can also have problems with gross motor skills and visual-spatial relations. Studies have found that damage to certain areas of the brain can cause changes in language, information processing, memory, cognition, emotions, and mood. There is an association between frontolimbic dysfunction and bor-derline personality disorder (Minzenberg, Fan, New, Tang, Siever, 2008). Al-cohol is found to affect many brain functions and structures (Alterman & Cac-ciola, 1991; Chelune & Parker, 1981; Horton & Wedding, 2008; Malloy, Noel, Longabaugn, & Beattie, 1990; Miller, 1990; Parsons, Butters, & Nathan (1987). It can affect the brain in a number of ways, including the processing infor-mation, abstract concept formation, set-maintenance, set-shifting, behavioral control, cognitive flexibility, verbal skills, and language functioning. Person-ality studies of alcoholics and addicts have found drugs affect such character-istics as field dependency, external locus of control, attenuated time exten-sion, poor ego strength, disturbed object relations, and regulation of affect and behavior.

Pinel (2007) wrote the divisions of biopsychology are physiological psychology, psychopharmacology, neuropsychological, psychophysiology, cognitive neuroscience, and comparative psychology. The outline – with slight modifications on my part – of Breedlove, Rosenzweig, and Watson's (2007) book, *Biological Psychology*, provides a good overview of this area of study: biological foundations of behavior, evolution and development of the nervous system, evolution of the brain and behavior, perception and action, regulation and behavior, emotions and mental disorders, and cognitive neuroscience. Biological psychologists examine hormones, sensory processing (touch, pain, hearing, vestibular perception, taste, smell, vision), motor control and plasticity, sex (evolutionary, hormonal, and neural bases), homeostasis, biological rhythms, sleep, dreaming, emotions, aggression, stress, psychopathology, learning, memory, language, and cognition.

EVOLUTIONARY THEORIES

The evolutionary perspectives have demonstrated the ability to explain behaviors across time, place, and species. It has been able to analyze and explain behaviors from people in Alaska to people in New Guinea, from microbes to whales. Even though there are numerous problems with the evolutionary perspective (for example, many behaviors can have a variety of explanations to account for them), it has nevertheless proven to be a useful and productive approach. In terms of the "nature" versus "nurture" debate, Buss (2001) wrote from an evolutionary perspective and rejected the "dichotomy of culture versus biology, acknowledging a universal human nature, and recognizing that the human mind contains many complex psychological mechanisms that are selectively activated, depending on cultural contexts" (Buss, 2001, p. 955).

The evolutionary model provides a view to help determine which behaviors and perspectives are common to all cultures. Those behaviors that are observed across cultures and in animals are more likely to be more fundamental and thus more universal. From this perspective, the needs on the lower rung of Maslow's (1954, 1968, 1971) hierarchy are more universal. Maslow has refined and added to his hierarchy of needs, which consist of (a) physiological needs – these are basic biological needs, e.g., eating, sleeping, sex, avoidance of pain; (b) safety and security needs – need to be safe from harm and loss, e.g., loss of social and economic security; (c) love and belonging – the need to be part of a group, e.g., family, friends, community; (d) esteem needs – need to be held in positive regard by self and others; and (e) self-actualization – need to feel fulfilled, to have reached one's potential.

Those who study human evolution (e.g., Symons, 1992) reported that many of the behaviors and problems we encounter today have their origins during the Pleistocene period, which started around 1.8 million years ago and ended about 12,000 years ago. During this time, our neural mechanisms and behavioral patterns developed for survival in those environments. Generally, evolutionary psychology is focused more on explaining group variation instead of individual variation. The focus is usually on species-typical psychological mechanisms. Individual differences are the result of heritable and nonheritable factors (Buss, 2001). They attribute cultural differences to shared group mechanisms developed in response to environmental conditions; this information is transmitted from one generation to the next. Even though Darwin had applied his works to human behavior (Darwin, 1998/1872; Ekman, 1973), and influenced Freud as well as others in the area of psychology (Kennair, 2002), the concerted application of Darwinian and evolutionary models to psychology and psychopathology is relatively new, starting about 25 years ago (Hendrick, 2005; Palmer & Palmer, 2002).

In general, there is agreement that the evolutionary model is applicable to psychology, but there has yet to be consensus as to the interpretation of the reasons for behaviors and the treatment of disorders. Writers on evolutionary psychology, as well as writers in other fields, often use the term "mechanism" in their expositions of behavior. This term is defined and used differently by writers. One definition, from the perspective of evolution and psychology, is that provided by Buss and Malamuth (1996), they define psychological mechanisms as information-processing algorithms or decision rules. They wrote that these mechanisms guide our reactions to the environment (p. 272).

The prevailing perspective among evolutionary psychologists is that the mind is composed of specific domains rather than general mechanisms that respond to various specific domains (Buss, 1995; Cosmides & Tooby, 1987). Each species is unique, and each species differs from others by its unique adaptation to survive in its environment (over time). The mind is the result of specific adaptations to solve the specific problems of survival.

Persistence of Mental Illness Theories

Why do we have mental problems? From an evolutionary perspective, there are a number of theories and ideas as to why we have mental problems and why they have persisted (Buss, 1999; Nesse,1999; Nesse & Williams, 1995; Workman & Reader, 2008). This is an interesting question because one would surmise that over time there would be culling of undesirable characteristics from human gene and behavioral pools.

Buss (1999) wrote that mental illness and dysfunctional behaviors might still be occurring because there is (a) activation failure – the mechanism fails to activate in a present relevant environment, e.g., a person is warned to be careful when going into a dangerous area, and responds in a lackadaisical manner that jeopardizes safety; (b) context failure – the mechanism activates inappropriately in its present environment, e.g., the person is anxious in a benign situation; and (c) coordination failure – there is a mismatch or lack of coordination between various evolved mechanisms, e.g., whether to engage in fight or flight, or whether to act in self-interest or in the interest of the group. He wrote that the causes of these failures could be the result of genetic factors (for instance, genetic variations, mutations, and defects) and developmental problems (like autistic disorder). In addition, he wrote that the dynamics of living with others provides an explanation for some human behavior and problems. For example, people engage in behaviors because they want to belong to certain groups, because they are in competition for resources, or because they are dealing with social hierarchies.

Workman and Reader (2008) provided a number of explanations for the existence of psychiatric problems, including the following. They could occur as a function of trait variation. That is, traits follow the normal distribution curve, and too much or too little of a certain characteristic (e.g., emotional lability, and extroversion) could induce problems in certain situations. Another explanation is that physical and mental problems are engaged in an adaptation and counter-adaptation syndrome. This is much like the relationship between microbial pathogens and a host; the host develops adaptations to a pathogen, the pathogen develops ways to counter the host's adaptation, the host counters these adaptations, and so on.

Other explanations of psychiatric symptoms have been attributed to: (a) adjustments to contemporary life; (b) compromises to other competing traits; (c) genes that are predisposed to mental illness share the same gene pool as other genes that have beneficial effects that outweigh the negative ones; (d) natural selection and genetic changes are not prepared to deal with the factors presented in the environment in which the person is having problems; (e) the problematic symptoms are the expression of defenses against harm, e.g., the feeling of pain is a warning to look at the injured body part; a fever is to raise the body temperature to make it inhospitable for invasive bacteria; fear of the dark may serve as protection against predators in the dark; and (f) the biological and behavioral foundations of humans extend back to the simplest single-celled organisms; therefore, humans have aspects in them that may be maladaptive and dysfunctional for present needs; for example, there are the effects of the "reptilian," triune brain (MacLean, 1990; Patton, 2008). This is similar to Freud's (1976) id which consists of the more basic emotional, instinctual, pleasure-seeking, and pain avoidance behaviors. These might be in conflict when living and interacting with others.

Evolutionary theories conveniently combine psychology and biology. They integrate many human behaviors with those of other animals.

HUMANISTIC/EXISTENTIAL THEORIES

Whether or not existential and humanistic approaches to therapy should be lumped together is debatable (Burston, 2003; Hoffman, 2004–2009; "Existential psychotherapy," 2010). In the United States they are depicted together, and in the United Kingdom and Europe they are not (Burston, 2003). The two terms have been used differently by different authors at different times. The terms are so broad and encompass such diverse views and applications that delineations between the two result in exceptions and disagreement. Existential psychotherapy in Europe preceded U.S. humanistic psychology. Both draw more heavily from philosophical literature. Both askew mechanistic approaches. Both psychotherapies focus on the current experience of the patient in resolving problems ("Existential psychotherapy," 2010). The Association for Humanistic Counseling (n.d.) website states as written:

> Humanistic theories attempt to describe the phenomenologically constructed world of the client by exploring the potential of humanity through the nature and experience of values, spirituality, meaning, emotions, transcendence, intentionality, healthy relationships, the self, self-actualization, creativity, mortality, holism, intuition, and responsibility (among other topics) (para. 2).

American Psychological Association's Society for Humanistic Psychology (2012) website states as follows:

> Humanistic psychology aims to be faithful to the full range of human experience. Its foundations include philosophical humanism, existentialism and phenomenology. In the science and profession of psychology, humanistic psychology seeks to develop systematic and rigorous methods of studying human beings, and to heal the fragmentary character of contemporary psychology through an ever more comprehensive and integrative approach (para. 3).

Existential and humanistic therapies are diverse and are more philosophical perspectives rather than common techniques (Cain & Seeman, 2002; Cooper, 2003; Kaslow & Massey, 2004; Mendelowitz & Schneider, 2008; Rowan, 1998; Schneider, Bugental, & Pierson, 2001; Schneider & Krug, 2010; Yalom, 1980). Humanistics approaches (and those associated with them) include bioenergetics (Wilhem Reich, Alexander Lowen), sensory awareness through movement (Moshe Feldenkreis), focusing (Eugene Gendin), authentic movement (Mary Whitehouse), encounter (Carl Rogers, Will Schultz), rational-emotive therapy (Albert Ellis), reality therapy (William Glasser), analytical and archetypal psychology (C. G. Jung, James Hillman), psychosynthesis (Roberto Assagioli), gestalt art therapy (Janie Rhyne), existential analysis (Rollo May, James F. T. Bugental), logotherapy (Viktor Frankl), self-disclosure (Sidney Jourard), conjoint family therapy (Virginia Satir), and neuro-linguistic programming (Richard Bandler and John Grinder).

PSYCHOANALYTIC THEORIES

Psychoanalytic theories (de Mijolla, 2005; Erwin, 2002; Mitchell & Black, 1995; Thompson, 1950) were initiated by Freud and his followers. They emphasized the role the unconscious plays in personality development and behavior. Freud wrote that human personality consists of the dynamics among the id, superego, and ego. The id wants pleasure and immediate gratification. The superego consists of ideals, moral codes, and what a "good" person should be. And the ego negotiates between the two and tries to accommodate them realistically. Therapy consists of helping the client understand and interpret these dynamics. As with all the other theorists and models, there are differences among the adherents of psychoanalytic theories. They might differ in their emphasis in such areas as social factors, psychosexual development, interpersonal relations, culture, or explanations of the cause of neuroses. Freud influenced such people as Alfred Adler, Erik Erikson, Erik Fromm, Frieda Fromm-Reichmann, Karen Horney, Carl Jung, Abram Kardiner, Otto Rank, Harry Stack Sullivan, and Clara Thompson. Freud's ideas have permeated European and U.S. American cultures. He has had an impact in such areas as the arts, anthropology, medicine, psychology, and philosophy. Many people have drawn from him and his influence has been widespread

SOCIAL LEARNING THEORIES

Social-learning theorists (Bandura, 1977, 1986; Krasner & Ullman, 1965; Miller & Dollard, 1941) emphasize environmental and cognitive processes. These are considered to influence the development and maintenance of personality. Social learning studies have been conducted in a number of areas.

A great deal of research has been conducted on cognitive styles (Baron, 1985; Collis & Messick, 2001; Guilford, 1980; Kagan & Kogan, 1970; Perkins & Salomon, 1987). Cognitive styles are patterns of attitudes, thinking, judging, and processing of information. The concepts and theorists associated with so-

cial cognitive and cognitive styles theories include those who subscribe to attributional style theory (Abramson, Seligman, & Teasdale, 1978; Metalsky &
Alloy, 1989). This theory focuses on the way people explain what happens to
them. People can attribute themselves as the control agent or they can attribute it to others; effects are viewed as permanent or temporary; and events
are considered as pervasive or situational.

Another area studied is that of field dependency (Witkin, Moore, Goodenough, & Cox, 1977). These studies investigate field dependent and field independent learning styles. Field dependent learners process information globally. They pay less attention to detail and analysis. Field independent people
engage in analytical thinking. They break the field down into its component
parts and are not as influenced by the application of general ways of perceiving information.

Investigators have also engaged in categorical thinking studies (Fryer &
Jackson 2003). They examine the way people categorize the world around
them. For example, people consistently have a certain number of categories
in which they put heterogeneous objects.

Self-efficacy studies examine people's belief in whether they are capable of
performing certain tasks. Bandura (1997) worked in this area. Among the findings of self-efficacy research are that people will be more likely to take on
tasks they believe they can succeed in, and they are more likely to avoid tasks
they think they will not be successful at. Part of the counselor's job is to have
clients believe they are capable of accomplishing goals. This can take the
form of modeling, encouragement, providing skills, etc.

Researchers have also engaged in locus of control studies (Rotter, 1966).
These studies examined how people view who controls their lives – do they
think they are in control, or do they think external factors control them?

Walter Mischel (1968, 1973; Mischel & Shoda, 1995; Mischel, Shoda, & Ayduk, 2008) considered factors such as how the person encodes and categorizes
stimuli, affect responses, goals and values, beliefs and expectations, and competencies and self-regulatory practices. According to Mischel, to comprehend
behavior there needs to be understanding of the person, the situation, and the
dynamics between the two.

ANIMAL STUDIES.

Many studies of animals have shed light into human behaviors (Blaney &
Millon, 2009; Boulton, Baker, & Martin-Iverson, 1991a, 1991b; Fisch, 2009;
Overmier & Murison, 2002; Pawlak, Ho, Rainer, & Schwarting, 2008; Seligman, 1975; Suomi, 2000). One of the foundations of modern-day learning theories rests on Pavlov's studies of animals (Rokhin, Pavlov, & Popov, 1963;

Spence, 1956; Todes, 2000). Animal studies have been used to study social withdrawal and gambling (Adriani et al., 2010); attention deficit/ hyperactivity disorder (Cockbrun & Holroyd, 2010); sleep-wake patterns and plasma cortisol levels (Barrett et al., 2009); methamphetamine behaviors (Carson et al., 2010); maternal separation, cognitive performance, stress sensitivity and anxiety (Hulshof, Novati, Sgoifo, Luiten, den Boer, & Meerlo, 2011); anxiety (Maximino et al., 2010); schizophrenia (O'Tuathaigh & Waddington, 2010); impulsivity and amphetamine use (Rivalan, Grégoire, & Dellu-Hagedorn, 2007); helplessness (Seligman & Beagley, 1975); fear and anxiety (Sylvers, Lilienfeld, & LaPrairie, 2011); sensitization, drug addiction and psychopathology (Vezina, 2007); and many, many other problems and behaviors. Madden (1991) studied invertebrates, vertebrates, and primates. He studied the neurobiology of learning and affect; the biological, neural, chemical, behavioral, and affective responses to stress; and the impact of these on motivation, emotions, anxiety, depression, personality, and psychopathology. Nelson and Winslow (2009) studied primates. Primates (e.g., monkeys) and humans have comparable development, brain structures and processes, as well as cognitive skills, social systems, and emotions. They examined the animals by such methods as changing their environments, inducing behavioral change with drugs, and brain surgery. Their studies of primates provided information about the interactions between genes, environment, and development – which affected psychopathology.

There are those who take the position that there is a quantum difference between humans and animals; therefore, animal studies cannot be applied to humans. They claim humans are more complicated. The behaviors that are seen in animals are inappropriately ascribed to human characteristics (anthropomorphize). Also, culture differentiates humans from other animals. Humans learn more and many different things, and there are more variable behaviors among humans – because among other animals, anomalous behaviors will be culled by predators or will be exorcised or not supported by the group (and thus the animal would perish).

Whether or not animal studies can be generalized to humans may be debatable, but there is little doubt that many areas of behavior, medicine, biochemistry, neurology, learning, memory, and psychopathology have studied animals to provide information about humans. Both the supporters and distracters of animal studies agree that animals should not be treated in a cruel fashion, and animals should not be submitted to unnecessary suffering. Animal studies should follow ethical guidelines such as those provided by the American Psychological Association (Committee on Animal Research and Ethics, n.d.), the International Society for Applied Ethology (2010), and National Institutes of Health (Morrison, Evans, Ator, & Nakamura, 2002).

NEUROIMAGING AND PERSONALITY

The use of neuroimaging to study the brain structures and biochemicals involved in human and nonhumans personality characteristics is a relatively new area of research. These involve the study of personality and emotional traits in such areas and activities as frontal serotonin-1A receptor distribution, monoamine oxidase, dopamine D2 receptors in the insular cortex, frontolimbic serotonin 2A receptor binding, the striatal 6-(18F) fluoro-L-dopa uptake, cerebral blood flow, anterior cingulate gyrus, and the amygdala (Adelstein, et al., 2011; DeYoung, 2010; Solis, 2012; Stelmack, 2004). This is an ongoing area of study that needs further research to provide information on the brain correlates with personality. It is interesting to note that when researchers attempt to find neurological evidence for their particular theory of personality, they find it, e.g., DeYoung (2010) found neurological evidence for the Five-Factor model, Nardi (2011) for the Myers Briggs perspective, and Johnson (2008) for the psychoanalytic.

NOTES ON CROSS-CULTURAL ASPECTS OF THEORIES

Theories are valuable in helping to organize concepts and data. The large number of theories reflect both the diverse aspects of people and the many different ways to view them. The next expositions are by no means exhaustive or comprehensive; they are comments on the various theories. It is interesting to note that when different (out of the norm) behaviors are noticed within a culture, they are often viewed in a negative manner – and therapist might attach a diagnostic label to the behavior. When people notice different behaviors exhibited by those from other cultures, there is more of a tendency to attribute the behaviors to cultural differences. Perhaps one lesson to be learned here is that all too often people are likely to pass judgment and attach detrimental labels to behaviors that are not in keeping with their social, religious, and political norms – rather than recognize many behaviors as benign variations of the different ways humans can act, think, and feel.

In terms of therapeutic approaches, despite the fact that approaches are delineated into different theories of personality, most counselors do not use a single approach to counseling. It is more common for them to use eclectic approaches (Lebow, 2002). This flexibility allows counselors to choose approaches and techniques that they are comfortable with and enables them to provide therapy that suits the client. Even though psychological theories are viewed as different from each other, they are not mutually exclusive. For example, humanistic psychologists and counselors can use rational-emotive therapy, reality therapy, and psychoanalysis (Association for Humanistic Psychology, 2001).

Traits (and Types)

Research with such inventories as the Myers-Briggs (Myers & McCaulley, 1985), NEO-PI-R (Costa & McCrae, 1992), and Personality Research Form (Jackson, 1997) are attempts to determine the degree to which traits vary in different populations. Findings indicate both similarities and differences (Albright, et al., 1997; Church & Lonner, 1998; Illovsky et al., 2008; Rossier, 2005). There is general agreement that many cultures facilitate or hinder the expression of characteristics they deem desirable or undesirable. It is evident that biology and environment play a role in traits, and they both influence each other. Corr and Matthews (2009) wrote, "The attribution of around 50 per cent of the variance in major personality traits to heritability is uncontroversial" (p. xxxi).

African, Arab, and Chinese

Non-Europeans and non-North Americans comprise most of the world, and their views constitute the views of the majority. Europe and North America comprise approximately 17.3 percent of the world population: Europe has 12.2 percent and North America has 5.1 percent (United Nations Population Division, 2010). Traditional African, Arab, and Chinese views of human behavior and mental illness are examples of perceptions of people in other cultures. They demonstrate similarities and differences among themselves and with European and U.S. American views. The comments and observations of some of the writers of particular cultures are also relevant to other cultures, e.g., Moughrabi (1978) has criticized studies of Arab personality traits. He wrote that the studies are inadequate because they use static models which do not reflect the dynamic changes that are occurring. His criticisms can be applied to many studies of other cultures and not just those of Arabs. In addition, many of the studies of cultures present profiles that may not be applicable to numerous groups and individuals within the culture, e.g., there may be differences between the educated and uneducated and males and females, as well as there may be generational, ethnic, and religious differences. Sayed's (2003) comment about traditional Arab views is important to keep in mind about other cultural groups. That is, their beliefs about mental illness/disorder are not indicative of inadequacy but rather reflect cultural perceptions.

Biosocial

Biosocial processes can differ among cultures. For example, food and environment can determine what and how much people eat, and this can affect the body and its chemistry, e.g., affecting such characteristics as height and weight (Bogin, 1999). People can experience and express pain differently across cultures because of different cultural expressions and biochemical processes. Epigenetic studies (Epigenetics, 2011; Pembrey et al., 2006) suggest that the environment (e.g., famine) can influence the expression of genes in later generations. Medications can have different effects across cultures. The U.S. Surgeon General's report (United States Public Health Service, 1999a) illustrate the connection between biological and social factors:

> There is wide racial and ethnic variation in drug metabolism. This is due to genetic variations in drug-metabolizing enzymes (which are responsible for breaking down drugs in the liver). These genetic variations alter the activity of several drug-metabolizing enzymes. Each drug-metabolizing enzyme normally breaks down not just one type of pharmacotherapy, but usually several types. Since most of the ethnic variation comes in the form of inactivation or reduction in activity in the enzymes, the result is higher amounts of medication in the blood, triggering untoward side effects (para. 42).

Humanistic/Existential

Many view existential approaches as well suited for multicultural work (e.g., Corey, 2009; Deurzen, 2002a). Because of their broad conceptual perspectives, humanistic and existential views can be both universal and relativistic. For example, an existential view would consider all people to have problems of living (a universal perspective), and all people are a unique confluence of biology and environment (a relativistic perspective). Vontress' (1999) views the existential approach as appropriate for all cultures because it deals with issues encountered by all people. Dealing with such issues as finding meaning and harmony in life and dealing with love, anxiety, suffering, and death. Vontress' (1996) wrote that all people are composites of many cultures; therefore, cross-cultural interactions can be familiar to most people. Vontress (1979) wrote that three concepts are of concern to counselors in cross-cultural counseling: the physical environment (Umwelt), the interpersonal world (Milwelt), and one's inner world (Eigenwelt). He wrote that such perspectives demonstrate that people are more alike than they are different. Corey (2009) wrote that one of the strengths of the existential approach is that people examine their behaviors in the context of social and cultural conditioning, and that everyone has to deal with themselves as individuals.

Humanistic and existential counselors often take the view that the complexity, depth, and breadth of human existence cannot be fully measured. Therefore, tests are often considered inadequate, and the full effects of therapy cannot be validly assessed.

Psychoanalytic

Cross-cultural studies have found variations in Freudian psychodynamic theories. For example, Segall, Dasen, Berry, and Poortinga (1999) wrote that Freud's oral, anal, Oedipal, and genital personality traits were found in cross-cultural studies. But they were not found as child development stages. In addition, later adult traits were not confirmed to be the result of early childhood experience. In his study of the Trobriands, Malinowski (1927) found Oedipal fears in dreams were associated with the power of uncles and not with sexual jealousy directed at fathers. He attributed this to the role that uncles (the mother's brother) played in their culture: uncles disciplined the boys – and not the boy's biological father.

Psychoanalytic approaches often use interpretations of thoughts, feelings, and behaviors as a form of therapy. The client may express these symbolically because they are not socially sanctioned. Among the factors to consider in applying psychoanalytic approaches is the impact of culture. Culture mediates thoughts, feelings, and behaviors. Culture affects what people think, how they express themselves, and how they behave. Therefore, a psychoanalytic application across cultures carries with it caveats in terms of symbolic interpretations. The importance and meaning of interpretations and symbols can differ among cultures (Minturn, 1965), e.g., the color black is a sign of mourning in European cultures, whereas the color white is associated with mourning in China, Korea, and other Asian cultures (Byrne, 2003). Because culture and individual idiosyncratic experiences and perceptions can influence symbolic expressions, it would behoove the counselor to ask clients what the symbol means to them. This is good practice anyway, regardless of culture.

Social Learning

Social learning theories lend themselves well in cross-cultural applications. Anthropologists have long observed that information, customs, attributes, rituals, and perceptions of phenomena are passed from one generation to the next through such processes as imitation, reinforcement, punishment, rewards, expectations, modeling, observation, approval, and disapproval. These are the foundations of learning theories.

Verbal, Behavioral, Cognitive Therapies

The main characteristic of U.S. American counseling is the use of verbal language as a means of providing treatment. This can be a significant handicap when providing counseling to people who do not speak the same language as the counselor, or who do not feel comfortable in interacting with the counselor in this manner. There are many possible reasons as to why a client might be reticent to engage in verbally based forms of therapy. For example, the client may not be adept in the use of language. Another possibility is that the client might be less willing to talk because of the perceived power differential between the client and the counselor: the counselor is often more proficient in the use of therapeutic language; therefore, the client may feel at a disadvantage. There have been criticisms of verbally based therapists by such proponents as those who use behavioral approaches. The behavioral approach places more emphasis on changing the behavior of people as a form of treatment rather than resolving problems through verbal insight. Of course, behavioral therapies also have critics (Chomsky, 1967; Nudler, 1975; Wolpe, 1976). Among the criticisms are that behavioral approaches neglect the importance of relational factors, they focus on behavioral changes and not on providing insight, they treat symptoms and not causes; additionally, suppressing the undesirable behavior can result in other problem behaviors occurring (symptom substitution). Criticisms have also been directed at an affiliate of behavioral therapies: cognitive-behavioral therapy (Beidel & Turner, 1986). The sections of this book on "Cognitive Processes" and "Client Characteristics" deal with some of the problems that affect cognitive processes. In addition to individuals and cultures having different cognitive processes and engaging in cognitive distortions, the reasons for making behavioral changes can also vary; people might make changes for religious reasons or reasons of tradition. Other inspirations for change could be related to community values, or they might also make changes based on economics, ideas of fairness, gender equality, and concepts of freedom and independence (Berger, Hardenberg, Kattner, & Prager, 2010; Graeber, 2001; Haviland, Prins, Walrath, & McBride, 2008; Patka, 1964).

Animal Studies

Humans have long recognized a relationship between themselves and animals. The Chinese use animals in their Zodiac to depict human characteristics. Native peoples have often associated themselves with animal-like qualities. Societies have looked at animal entrails (hepatomancy) and animal bones (osteomancy) to predict human behavior. Most people recognize animals and the qualities associated with them. The study of animals has been going on for millenniums. Animal studies can provide information on human behaviors that preceded recorded history. They can also provide information on human behaviors that are of animal origin but which are expressed through human culture (e.g., mating rituals, and aggressive behaviors).

Animal studies in and of themselves are important. The study of them and their pathologies can be of value in learning about them and in helping them, and if the studies do not provide direct evidence that is of value to understanding humans, then they can provide circumstantial information. For example, animal studies indicate that stressful environments can affect them; there are neurological, biochemical, and behavioral changes. Such finding can indicate that humans under stressful environments (e.g., poverty, abuse, prolonged exposure to war, and food deprivation) can also be affected.

Comments

Collectivistic and Individualistic Perspectives

Even though there are some who are critical of the constructs of collectivism and individualism to delineate cultures (e.g., Fiske, 2002), most authors subscribe to the characterization of cultures in this manner (Hofstede, 2001; Kim, Triandis, Kağitçibaşi, Choi, & Yoon, 1994). Accordingly, the general view is that Western cultures and psychology focuses primarily on the individual, and most other cultures focus on the group. Triandis (1989) wrote that approximately 70 percent of the world's cultures are collectivistic as compared to individualistic. This has important implications for counselors, not only when dealing with people from collectivistic societies but also when dealing with people in European and U.S. American cultures who have strong ties to their family, group, and community.

Studies have indicated some differences between collective and individualistic cultures. Individualistic cultures tend to focus more on the individual's independence from the group and subordinating the group's needs to that of the individual (McCarthy, 2005). The terms "idiocentric" is sometimes used to describe individualistic cultures and "allocentric" to describe collectivistic cultures. Idiocentric refers to focusing on the personal and private. Allocentric refers to focusing on others. Collectivistic cultures are often found in Asia, South America, and the Pacific (Triandis, Brislin, & Hui, 1991). Dwairy (2002) wrote that collective and individualistic peoples differ in their degree of individuation from the family. In the West, individuals form an independent personality (or self) that is different from others. Their personality is predictive of behavior. Psychopathology is attributed to intrapsychic problems within the person. For people socialized in collective social systems, there is less development of independent personality. Social norms, roles, and family expectations are more predictive of behavior than personality; psychopathology is attributed more to interpersonal problems with others. Compared to individualistic cultures, collectivistic cultures tend to have lower rates of suicide, psychopathology, and loneliness, and higher rates of marital satisfaction (Antill, 1983; Cobb, 1976; Narol, 1983). In addition, harmony and respect for authority are often associated with the effects of living in collectivistic cultures; and personal responsibility is often associated with individualistic ones.

One of the effects of having an individualistic orientation is to treat clients in the privacy of one-to-one interactions; the client is treated as an individual. From a collectivistic perspective, the isolated interaction between the client and counselor is an unusual and unnatural one: treatment is occurring under conditions that are artificial and disassociates the individual from the natural environment in which there are interactions with people. The segregation of the client from the community might induce the stigma of the client having a problem that warrants special attention, and the client may feel isolated and differentiated from the group. Similarly, group therapy can also induce some of the same problems of isolation that can occur with individual therapy; group therapy consists of people with a common problem that separates them from others. In the individualistic approach, the healing agent is not the individual or the community. Rather, it is attributed to the client and counselor interactions – under the auspices of the skills of the counselor.

It is evident that European and U.S. American approaches are not strictly individualistic in their approaches. Many European and U.S. American sociologists and social psychologists recognize the importance of the group on the individual. There are European and U.S. American psychological treatments that incorporate group and community approaches to therapy (Bion, 1961; Montgomery, 2002; Yalom, 1970). These illustrate that the wide range of experiences, problems, and solutions within one society can be applied to other societies. In this case, even though the focus of European and U.S. American therapies are individualistic, there are approaches that emphasize the group, and these can be used with cultures and individuals who view therapy from a collectivistic perspective.

In terms of the influence of collectivistic and individualistic cultures on seeking therapeutic services, both types of cultures have elements that may affect the utilization of services. There is evidence that people influenced by collectivistic cultures use mental health services less (Tata & Leong, 1994). Those influenced by individualistic cultures may value self-sufficiency and want to solve problems on their own. Those from collectivistic cultures may feel uncomfortable obtaining help outside the group. People from individualistic cultures tend to have briefer relationships and move in and out of them more often. One implication of this is that they may prefer shorter-term therapy and more limited relationships with counselors. People from individualistic cultures may tend to attribute problems and solutions to aspects of themselves (e.g., lack of coping skills), and those influenced by collectivistic cultures might tend to attribute their problems to external factors (e.g., lack of support, and loneliness). People from collectivistic cultures may also want to keep therapy brief because of the strain of talking to someone (the counselor) outside the group; however, some of them might feel comfortable talking to others because they have done so within their community and therefore can more easily transfer these behaviors to those outside the group. However, some members of both individualistic and collectivistic groups may like the privacy, confidentiality, and attention provided by many European and U.S. American therapeutic approaches.

Treatment Success

It is probably the case that many of the Western and non-Western practices and theories are relatively successful with the less severe disorders. The success of the effective therapies may share common factors, universal, and extra-therapeutic features. However, the challenge is in treating the more severe cases – most of the treatment methods are stymied in regard to this.

Political and Social Aspects

We should bear in mind that there are political and social aspects to theories of human behavior (Barbu, 1956/2002; Bertalanffy, 1968; Cottam, Dietz-Uhler, Mastors, Preston, 2010; Sears, Huddy, & Jervis, 2003). Whichever group controls a society can influence definitions of problems and allocation of resources. It is important that therapists be aware of the effects of the systems they are under. It would be specious to think they function under objective, professional standards. The services they offer, the people they can treat, their fees, and many other factors are determined by whoever controls society. Awareness of the pitfalls and benefits of their role and function in society will allow them to determine when their personal values, ethics, professional ideals, and contributions as citizens and humans are being facilitated or compromised.

Chapter 5

COUNSELOR CHARACTERISTICS

Counselors are products of their cultural milieu, and as such, share many of the same characteristics as their society. They also engage in many of the same activities as other professions (e.g., research, ethical standards, and methods of classifying problems – such as methods of diagnosing disorders). It is important to be aware of characteristics of counselors because the more information we have about them – or anybody else, the better we are able to examine the factors that influence their values, perceptions, and behaviors. There are numerous sources that provide information about counselors as well as other occupations. The U.S. government produces the *Occupational Outlook Handbook* (Bureau of Labor Statistics, 2009), and the Occupational Information Network (O*NET, n.d.). These provide information about occupations. O*NET lists 239 occupations that have the term "therapist," 118 occupations with the term "counselor," and 50 under "psychologist." Tests and inventories such as the Strong Interest Inventory (Strong, Donnay, Morris, Schaubhut, & Thompson, 2004), the Personality Research Form (Jackson, 1997), and the Myers Briggs (Myers & McCaulley, 1985) often have data on characteristics of people in various occupations – including therapists and counselors.

How many mental health practitioners are there? There are different ways to count them. The number depends on which types of practitioners are counted and the source from which the figures are obtained. For example, the American Counseling Association reported they have 42,594 members (Yep, 2010). The United States Department of Labor (2009) reported that there were 665,500 counselors. It lists the types of counselors as the following: elementary school counselors, high school counselors, vocational counselors (also called employment counselors or career counselors), rehabilitation counselors, mental health counselors, substance abuse and behavioral disorder counselors, and marriage and family therapists. The American Psychological Association's Center for Workforce Studies estimates from a set of 2004 figures that there are 93,000 practicing psychologists in the United States, about 85,000 are licensed (American Psychological Association, 2012). The *Occupational Outlook Handbook* states there are 174,000 employed psychologists: 154,300 clinical psychologists, counseling and school psychologists; 2,200 industrial-organizational psychologists; and 17,500 other psychologists (Bureau of Labor Statistics, 2012). Among the enormous amount of data provided by the United States Department of Health and Human Services (Manderscheid & Berry, 2006) are the number and percentage of clinically trained mental health personnel. They are delineated into psychiatry, psychology, social work, advanced psychiatric nurse, counseling, marriage and family therapy, psychosocial rehabilitation, school psychology, and pastoral counseling. There are 422,527 clinically trained mental health professionals: 282,333 females (67%), 137,985 males (33%); most are Caucasian (85%), and the others, in decreasing frequency, are Blacks (4%), Hispanics (2.8%), Asians/Pacific Islander (2.4%), and Native Americans/Alaska Native (0.5%). The percentages are very rough estimates (from Manderscheid & Berry, 2006, Table 22. 2, page 261). Problems in calculations included inexactness because of the use of rounding off figures; lack of figures in some categories; and figures in the categories "Not specified," "NA," and "Other" were not used.

In addition to demographic information, there have also been studies of other characteristics of counselors, psychologists, and others. For the interested reader, many studies have examined their characteristics as therapists, as well as their effectiveness and competence (Ackerman & Hilsenroth, 2003; Hiebert, 1984; Hogan, 1980; Mozelle & Thompson, 1971; Rowe, Murphy, & Csipkes, 1975; Vacc & Loesch, 2000; Wiggins & Weslander, 1979).

MAJOR U.S. CULTURAL INFLUENCES

What are some of the main cultural influences on U.S. therapists? What are these influences that are so ingrained in their personal and professional lives that they may not be aware of them (Sue, 2004)? Awareness of these influences on therapists and on their theories, approaches, and techniques will enable them (and their clients) to be aware of some of their strengths, weaknesses, and characteristics.

Europeans and Their Influence

Even though a therapist may not be of European heritage, the effects of Europeans permeate the United States (Allen, 1997; Anderson & Middleton,

2005; Dorrien, 2009; Du Bois, 1998; Feagin, 2006; Hall, 2006; Hays & Chang, 2003; Hill & Jones, 1992; Lipsitz, 1995; Lucal, 1996; Manglitz, 2003; Massey & Denton, 1993; Pence & Fields, 1999; Powell, Branscombe, & Schmitt, 2005; Rothenberg, 2005; Steinhorn & Diggs-Brown, 1999; Williams, 2003; Wildman, Armstrong, Davis, & Grillo, 1996). Europeans have influenced many parts of the world. Who are the Europeans from whom so many U.S. Americans derive? What are some of their influences on U.S. trained therapists? What are some other influences? What follows is not an exhaustive analysis of U.S. counselors' characteristics and cultural influences, but are samples of factors that are often affecting them.

The Europeans are the people who have historically inhabited the continent of Europe. Europeans constitute heterogeneous people of different traditions, languages, histories, and cultures. A look at European ethnicity, nationality, and language can illustrate their diversity. According to Pan, Pfeil, and Geistlinger (2004), there are about 87 distinct "peoples of Europe" and there numerous linguistic groups (Harding & Sokal, 1988). Europe has 47 countries that are officially recognized (WorldAtlas, 2010). The European Union, which consists of 27 members, recognizes 23 official languages; not included in the count are 60 or so regional/minority languages, and languages spoken by people from other parts of the world (Europa, 2009). It should be noted that these data are presented with caveats: defining ethnicity and determining the number of linguistic groups in Europe is problematic; for example, there are various definitions of "ethnic," and languages can be counted by what is spoken at the present time, or in the past. If we count languages spoken in the past, what time period should be selected – what was spoken a hundred years ago, two hundred years ago, or when? Do we count those languages only spoken by large numbers of people – what criteria should be used to define large and small? There are similar time and size criteria problems with counting ethnic groups.

Europeans have influenced and been influenced by many cultures. They have not lived in isolation from the rest of the world. Interactions occurred through such vectors as commerce, scholarship, pilgrimages, and a myriad of other exchanges. They invaded others and others invaded them, e.g., Attila the Hun (apparently from the northern Eurasia area) invaded Russia, Germany, France, Italy, and other parts of Europe. Muslim invasions from the Middle East and North Africa extended to France and Austria. And, of course, the Europeans themselves have gone to the far corners of the earth.

Europeans often attribute much of their intellectual, scientific, and philosophical foundations to the Greeks (Connolly & Solway, 2002). The Greeks in turn were influenced by the Egyptians (Freeman, 2004; Gadalla, 2009). One of the contributions of the ancient Greeks was the focus on reason and logic (e.g., the use of the Socratic Method to answer questions). The Greeks influenced the Romans whose cultural and military power spread throughout the Mediterranean and many parts of Europe. After the fall of the Roman Empire, the Catholic Church controlled much of Europe, resulting in features that many Europeans share: the influences of Christianity. Religion lost some of its hold on Europe with the advent of the Renaissance. The Renaissance stimulated science and European expansion throughout the world – increasing exploration, mercantilism, colonialism, migrations, evangelization, imperialism, and other forms of interactions with different cultures.

Linear and Dualistic Thinking

Greek philosophers and Christianity produced characteristics that influenced much of European behavior and attitude; that is, linear and dualistic thinking. "The linear worldview finds its roots in Western European and U.S. American thought. It is logical, time oriented, and systematic, and has at its core the cause-and-effect relationship" (Cross, 2010, para. 5). Linear thinking played a significant role in European problem-solving and expansion. Linear thinking was conducive to science, rationalism, pragmatism, and the industrial revolution.

Dualistic thinking is the other characteristic of Europeans (Alford, 2000; Collins, 2005; Cross, 2010; Oster & Rice; 2004; Rorty, 1999; Landheer, 1973; Nicotera, Clinkscales, & Walker, 2008). "It was the Greeks who invented Europe. The Greeks were given to dichotomous thinking – that is, the penchant to dividing things into two mutually exclusive groups" (Ostergren & Rice, 2004, p. 5). Rorty (1999) wrote that in Plato's *Dialogues* there are such philosophical distinctions as appearance-reality, matter-mind, made-found, sensible-intellectual, and so on. Rorty wrote, "These dualisms dominate the history of Western philosophy. . ." (p. xii). The philosopher and mathematician Renes Decartes had considerable influence in the West. One of the main tenants of his ideas was dualism, e.g., the mind consists of a nonphysical substance – in contrast to the physical brain. However, it should be noted that another influential figure, Spinoza, offered the double-aspect theory which proposed the mind and body stem from the same substance: God.

Christianity also made clear delineations. There were such distinctions as between body and soul, sinful humans and sinless Christ, good and evil, Christians and non-Christians, Protestants and Catholics, and the saved and unsaved. They cite numerous places in the Bible that state that the only way to be saved is through Christ, e.g., "Jesus said to him, I am the way, and the truth, and the life: no one comes to the Father, but by me" (John 14:6, *Oxford Annotated Bible – Revised Standard Version*). There are many other such statements that the Christian way is the only way, e.g., Acts 4:12; 1 Timothy 2:5; Ephesians 4:4; John 14:6: John 3:36; and 1 John 5:11.

The dualistic thinking of the Europeans and the Christians provided them with the certainty that their views were correct and other views are incorrect. This gave them the confidence and energy to explore the world and share and impose their values, religion, customs, and ideas on to others. In regard to the West, Chakrabarty (2000) wrote: "For generations now, philosophers and thinkers who shape the nature of the social science have produced theories that embrace the entirety of humanity. As we well know, these statements have been produced in relative, and sometimes absolute, ignorance of the majority of humanity – that is, those living in non-Western cultures" (p. 29).

It should be noted that linear and dualistic thinking are not unique to Europeans and U.S. Americans. Many people in other cultures engage in dualistic thinking. They believe their views are the correct ones and other people's views are erroneous. Also, people in other cultures are fully capable of linear thinking. However, they have not facilitated the development and expansion of the infrastructure, technology, institutions, values, and intellects to the extent it has been done in the West, resulting in its influence in much of the world.

U.S. Americans

The United States consists of diverse populations – thirty-one ancestry groups have more than a million members. White Americans are the largest ethnic group, consisting mostly of German Americans, Irish Americans, and English Americans (Brittingham & de la Cruz, 2004). The ethnic composition of the United States is 79.96 percent white, 12.85 percent black, 4.43 percent Asian, 0.97 percent Amerindian and Alaska native, 0.18 percent native Hawaiian and other Pacific islander, 1.61 percent two or more races (July 2007 estimate). Of these different ethnic groups, about 15.1 percent of the total were Hispanic. European languages dominate in the United States: 82.1 percent speak English, 10.7 percent Spanish, 3.8 percent other Indo-European, 2.7 percent Asian and Pacific island, 0.7 percent other (World Fact Book, 2009). In terms of the religions of the United States, 78.4 percent are Christian, 4.7 percent other religions, and 16.1 percent are unaffiliated (Pew Forum on Religion & Public Life, 2010).

Even though Europeans have had significant influence on the United States, it is also clear that non-Europeans have contributed enormously to the United States (Adams & Strother-Adams, 2001; Bak, 1993; Brown & Roucek, 1945; Carnes & Garraty, 2007; Levinson & Ember, 1997; McClain, 1993; Mc-Donogh, Gregg, & Wong, 2002; Santa Barbara County Board of Education, 1972; Thompson & Hickey, 2005; United States Congress Senate Committee on Small Business, 1982). Their list of contributions is vast. They have contributed to such areas as science, literature, food, music, sports, agriculture, the military, the arts, and education

There have been a number of portrayals of U.S. Americans. Spindler and Spindler (1983) reviewed Mead, Kluckhohn, Gorer, Ruesch and Bateson, Hsu, Spindler, Gillin, and other anthropologists for their common characterizations of U.S. Americans. Spindler and Spindler characterized these beliefs and values as "cultural ideology" and grouped them as factors indicating individualism, achievement orientation, equality, conformity, sociability, honesty, competence, optimism, work, and authority. Their studies of U.S. Americans, over a period of 30 years, indicated high consistency in the values of honesty, work with clear goals, self-reliance, and sociability (getting along with others). They found the trend of the data were toward greater tolerance for nonconformity, more interest in self-development rather than individualism, more concern for others, more relativists views of morality, less certainty that work is best for all, and more suspicion of authority. Pre and post studies indicated the values of work, success, achievement, and individuality were unchanged. Longitudinal studies such as Spindler and Spindler's indicate that some values change and others can remain relatively stable. If these studies can be generalized, then they illustrate that societies and individuals can change, and therefore statements about them should be made tentatively, especially during times of transition

Other characteristics include that the U.S. is one of the most religious among the developed countries (Pew Global Attitudes Project, 2002). Canadians and U.S. citizens are the most satisfied people in the world (Pew Global Attitudes Project, 2004). They are most satisfied with their family lives, less satisfied with their jobs and incomes, and despite having higher per-capita incomes, often complain more about economic problems compared to Europeans. According to Hofstede and Hofstede (2005), the United States has the highest individualism score of any country studied. One of the remarkable aspects of those living in the United States are the number of groups that feel a need to organize, to engage in political action, and to educate the public of their issues. These groups include African Americans, Arab-Americans, the disabled, immigrants; lesbians, gays, bisexuals, and transgender people; older people, men, overweight people, poor people, religious people, Spanish Americans, and women ("Political advocacy groups," 2010; Fountain, 2008; Rate it all, 2008; University of Dayton School of Law, 2001).

Psychological profiles of various U.S. Americans groups (e.g., Euro-American, and African-Americans) can often be obtained through the normative data provided by such psychological tests and inventories as the Millon Clinical Multiaxial Inventory (Millon, Millon, & Grossman, 2006), the Minnesota Multiphasic Personality Inventory (Butcher, Dahlstrom, Graham, Tellegen, & Kaemmer, 1989), the NEO PI-R (Costa & McCrae, 1992), the Personality Assessment Inventory (Morey, 1991a), and the Personality Research Form (Jackson, 1997). These often provide data and comparisons among and between groups, e.g., by ethnicity and gender.

EXPERIENCES AND EXPOSURE TO DIVERSITY

One of the characteristics of modern-day counselors is that they often have exposure to diverse people and ideas. This is not to deny that counselors can be limited in their interactions and experiences. Their relationships might be confined to a selected group of acquaintances, and to particular communities. They may have limited knowledge of others, and their views of others may be in the form of stereotypes and categories. Also, the information they get of others, whether it is in the form of books, movies, or the news and documentaries, does not capture the full dimension of individuals and societies. However, we should not lose sight of the other side of the coin: counselors often have exposure to diversity. This is brought about through various vectors. The increased access to massive amounts of electronic media exposes them to the lives of others. Our schools, society, and professional associations provide information about other people. Discrimination laws remind us that there are people who are different in terms of ethnicity, color, national origin, religion, sex, age, disability, marital status, political affiliation, and sexual orientation. Numerous writers (many of them mentioned in this book) have called our attention to cross-cultural issues. Whatever their experience and knowledge of diversity, counselors have a responsibility to continue learning. The following elaborates further on some of the aspects of counselors that expose them to diversity.

Intra-Populations as Samples of Human Cultures

Within many countries, there are often groups and individuals who have a wide array of different perceptions, feeling, values, languages, religions, classes, and so on. In the United States, there are diverse groups that provide opportunities to learn about other cultures. The Gale Encyclopedia of Multicultural America (2000) contains profiles of 152 ethnic, ethnoreligious, and Native American cultures in the United States. The Harvard Encyclopedia of American Ethnic Groups (1980) has listings of about 106 ethnic groups. Fischetti's (1997) book compiles information about more than 100 ethnic groups in the United States. The Human Relations Area Files (eHRAF World Cultures (2009) list 42 cultural groups in North America.

It should be noted that the definition of ethnicity and the determination of the number of people in each other group varies. There are many aspects and confounding factors in these endeavors (Illovsky, 2003). For example, there is little agreement as to which categories to use to classify people. There are differences in how to define ethnicity. There are differences in who should define ethnicity (e.g., self, the state government, the national government, members of the ethnic community, members outside the community, sociologists, anthropologists, or geneticists?). There is the question of how to classify those who are in multiple ethnic categories. A number of classification schemes have been used to classify ethnic groups. The U.S. census has changed its criteria and categories over the years. Recently, it has used six categories: American Indian or Alaska Native, Asian, black or African American, Native Hawaiian or Other Pacific Islander, white, and Some Other Race. There was 63 possible combinations of the six basic racial categories: six categories for those who report exactly one race, and 57 categories for those who report two or more races (United States Census Bureau, 2008). The 2010 census questionnaire (Population Reference Bureau, 2009) has 15 racial (sic) categories: White; Black, African American, Negro; American Indian or Alaska Native; Asian Indian; Chinese; Filipino; Japanese; Korean; Vietnamese; Native Hawaiian; Guamanian or Chamorro; Samoan; Other Pacific Islander, e.g., Fijian, Tongan; Other Asian, e.g., Hmong, Laotian, Pakistani, Cambodian; and Some other race. Hispanics are considered separately (they can identify with any race) and are grouped into: Mexican, Mexican American, Chicano; Puerto Rican; Cuban; and Other Hispanic, Latino, or Spanish origin – e.g., Argentinean, Colombian, Dominican, Nicaraguan, Salvadoran, Spanish. The questionnaires are in English, Spanish, Chinese (Simplified), Korean, Vietnamese, and Russian, as well as language guides in 59 languages (United States Census Bureau, 2009).

There are many groups that offer opportunities to study and have interactions. There are visitors from other countries (such as students and business people – Cole, 2009). There are newly arrived immigrants who still retain their previous cultural values and perceptions. There are individuals and groups with different degrees of acculturation in the United States. Some are immersed in the country's culture. Others retain their previous culture or develop their own.

Counselors can also gain experience in diversity by dealing with those who define themselves, or are defined by others, as different. These include women, veterans, gays, lesbians, transsexuals, conservatives, socialists, those with handicaps, the uneducated, the educated, the old, the poor, those with mental illness, those with disabilities, those from rural areas, and those with various degrees of religiosity, and so on. Definitions and perceptions of who are considered different are psychological, social, and political constructs; therefore, there are many possible people who can be defined as different.

Personality Types as Samples of Human Types

As part of their training, mental health therapists learn about personality types and theories. Familiarity with these theories and experience in working with a variety of personality types can provide experience in dealing with a wide array of human types. For example, familiarity with the Five-Factor model (Costa & McCrae, 1992; Diaz-Guerrero, Diaz-Loving & Rodriguez de Diaz, 2001) provides counselors with a view of people with characteristics of openness, conscientiousness, extraversion, agreeableness, and neuroticism. Similarly, the personality types presented by Allport (1937, 1955), Eysenck (1998), Cattell (1946, 1957), Jackson (1997), Holland (1973; 1997), and by the psychoanalytic, behavioral, social cognitive, learning, humanistic, existential, and biopsychological schools, are among the many perspectives that provide samples of human types encountered throughout the world.

"Disorders" as Samples of Human Behavior

Mental health professionals are trained to treat many problems. This training can provide the basis for dealing with various types of people. Most U.S. counselors are trained to use the *Diagnostic and Statistical Manual of Mental Disorders* (American Psychiatric Association, 2000). People in other parts of the world are often trained in the *International Statistical Classification of Diseases and Related Health Problems* (World Health Organization, 2008), and the Chinese use the *Chinese Classification of Mental Disorders* (Chinese Medical Association, 1990). The symptoms and behaviors described by the various classification schemes can provide counselors with information about a wide variety of behaviors and personalities.

Another perspective is that the less problematic forms of clinical disorders can familiarize counselors with the many different types of behaviors that are encountered in the community, e.g., knowledge of paranoid schizophrenic features, can help counselors understand nonclinical individuals who have suspicious thoughts and who do not subscribe to social norms; or knowledge of how to treat people with attention deficit/hyperactivity disorder can help the counselor counsel nonclinical people with problems paying attention and sitting still. Thus, knowledge of clinical behaviors can provide familiarity with how to deal with the more benign forms of the behavior.

Commonalities With Clients

Living in and of itself can entail commonalities with other humans. Even though history and contemporary life can readily present evidence of differences among people, such as gender, ethnic, political, social, and religious differences, it is also equally apparent that people have a great deal in common. There are many ways a counselor can have commonalities with clients:

- Many of the behaviors, thoughts, and feelings seen in one set of people (e.g., Europeans) are common to those who appear to be dissimilar. For example, people throughout the world have similar needs for food and security. They have an understanding of such emotions as fear, humiliation, joy, love, hate, anger, concern for others, and group pressure. Thoreau (an Euro-American), writing about his experiences in an isolated cabin in Concord, Massachusetts, influenced people in other times and places, e.g., he influenced Tolstoy in Russia and Gandhi in India. The ideas and values of Buddha, Christ, and Muhammad struck a chord with many people throughout the world. Marxism and democracy influence people outside the confines of the originating authors and cultures.

- Counselors' personal encounters can expose them to different people. In their communities, and among their friends, family, and co-workers, there can be people of different ethnicity, religion, disability, personality, sexual orientation, and so on.

- Even though counselors have their professional roles and functions to adhere to, they also share many of the same experiences and emotions as their clients, like anger, love, sadness, joy, anxiety, loneliness, abandonment, and depression. Of course, these experiences can also entangle them (e.g., through countertransference) in their client's issues.

- Counselors and clients can have common interests and characteristics that compensate or overcome such barriers as ethnicity and gender (Cole, 2009). For example, the counselor and client might be able to interact through such commonalities as both being parents, athletes, hunters, gardeners, veterans, hobbyists, and so on.

There is evidence that commonalities are not necessarily a source of cohesion, and differences are not necessarily the cause of barriers. People who share a lot in common may be in conflict with each other. Families often have more in common with each other than with others, yet they often have more problems with each other. It is not unusual for clients to be in counseling because of problems with peers. Within groups that share some similar characteristics there can be friction for a number of reasons, e.g., because of socioeconomic, educational, place of origin, occupational, religious, political, personality, and other reasons. Therefore, to assume compatibility because of a particular shared characteristic may be spurious. Differences can be a source of facilitating interactions. People may associate with those who are different for a multitude of reasons. For example, they may be dissatisfied with their own cohorts, or they are curious and want to learn from others. Another possibility could be that they share mutual interests and values. Therefore, to assume that differences are a source of alienation, friction, and lack of understanding may be incorrect. For some people, differences might function to promote interchanges.

ACTIVITIES

There are rapid changes in the world and in the United States. These changes call attention to the need of counselors and their organizations to evaluate their roles and functions. Counselors need to determine which aspects of counseling they want to retain and which new and different ones they want to engage in. In the *Star Wars* movie *Return of the Jedi*, there were cute, warm, furry, primitive creatures called Ewoks. They lived amidst a flurry of advanced technology swirling around them. Are counselors the Ewoks of the modern world? Should they remain Ewoks? Which activities should they retain, change, or abandon? Which of their decisions are the result of thoughtful, rationale, and efficacious thinking, and which are the result of myopic perspectives, self interests, inertia, lack of creative, fear of the unknown, or inadequate educational training?

Whether U.S. counselors like it or not, their influence is spreading around the world. Therefore, they need to consider the consequences of what they are doing. They also need to consider whether there are activities in other parts of the world that they would like to emulate. Counselors should be of a caliber to be able to think and explore behaviors and values that are conducive to helping them learn and to help others. The following are some of the many activities counselors engage in. It is hoped that these comments will induce further thought.

Ethics

Ethics encompass counselors' activities. It is the counselor's responsibility to act ethnically (Corey, Schneider Corey, & Callahan, 2007; LaFollette, 2002). When counselors offer their services, they have a responsibility to consider the implications and effects of their presence and interventions. Ethics are important because they help counselors keep in good stead with the public, and they help counselors adhere to their personal, social, and professional values. Ethical interactions are not abstract, philosophical, and pedantic activities. Ethical behaviors are functional, useful, practical, and of great therapeutic value. Unethical interactions can have dire consequences for counselors and those they represent. Counselors can lose their license or have lawsuits against them if they engage in unethical behaviors. Clients might lose their confidence or be distrustful and suspicious of unethical counselors. Unethical behaviors can have long-lasting impact on the memory of people in a community (Cohen, 2007). Counselors have to consider their own professional ethics, as well as those of the client and community. Knowledge of clients' values and those of the clients' culture can provide guidelines as to perceptions of ethical and unethical behavior.

Orr, Marshall, and Osborn (1995) wrote about resolving ethical dilemmas between physicians and patients of other cultures. Among their suggestions are to allocate time to learn and deal with ethical issues; have effective communications; do not respond to stereotypes; ask questions; find out more about the ethics of the client, family, and community; identify who and what is guiding the ethics of the client; obtain views of the cause and solutions to problems; consult with others; examine your own values and biases; respect the client's views and be willing to consider that other people's views can be as valid as yours; and be willing to engage in discussion until a resolution or compromise is reached.

Research

Research is one of the main pillars that justifies what counselors do. Research provides information on what works and what does not work. Interventions based on research can increase the client's confidence in what the counselor does, and helps distinguish legitimate providers from charlatans. Research contributes to our knowledge and allows data to be evaluated and improved upon. It is the method for testing hypotheses and determining the best way to help people. However, it should be done in a responsible manner. Governments, professional organizations, and many groups and organizations (e.g., universities) provide guidelines for doing research. In the minds of many people, researchers could be representatives of science or academia, or the researchers' agency, ethnicity, class, etc. High ethical standards are important when doing research in communities. Doing research in ethnic communities engender extra issues or accentuate the problems that are typically involved with research in general (Liamputtong, 2008; Marshall & Batten, 2004).

Cross-Cultural Research

Research can be of great value for a community or it can be exploitive and damaging. Researchers have to be alert to the effects of what they are doing and how they are perceived by the community.

Much has been written on the problems and aspects of doing cross-cultural research. The reader is encouraged to read the many authors who have written on this subject, e.g., Berry, Poortinga, Segall, & Dasen, 1992; Georgas & Berry, 1995; Helfrich, 1999; Segall, Lonner, & Berry, 1998; Spering, 2001; Whiting, 1974. An example of the material written on this topic is that by Marshall and Batten (2003). Their guidelines and suggestions are of value not only for cross-cultural research but also for research in general. They recommend that the researcher consider such issues as values and worldviews, definitions, research design, informed consent, entry into the field, confidentiality, approaches to data collection, participant roles, ownership of data, and the writing, representation, and dissemination of results. They suggest better use of informational meetings, detailed letters of consent, and that prospective participants need to understand the purposes and consequences of involvement in the research. Having many community perspectives can provide information on the community's ethics and moral views. There needs to be an accurate depiction of the group members and their views. Respect for cultural values is important, and the results need to improve the conditions of the community. According to them, participants and researchers need to work together in such areas as sharing the conception and definition of the research. Even though the latter statements are addressed to communities and ethnic groups, there are valid points that can be applied to individuals and groups in general.

There is an ongoing dialogue as the degree to which any research can be generalized. There are those who have the view that samples, using good statistical methods, can be generalized to other groups (Arnett, 2008; Erard, 2009; Haeffel, Thiessen, Campbell, Kaschak, & McNeil, 2009; Kim, Sherman, & Taylor, 2009; LoSchiavo & Shatz, 2009; Stroebe & Nijstad, 2009; Webster, Nichols, & Schember, 2009). There are many confounding variables that make generalizations tenuous, for example, there can be age, gender, regional, and class characteristics that are not accurately depicted in the sample. It is readily recognized that there are limitations of findings based on samples and that generalizations are often unwarranted and inappropriate. However, the results of some studies can provide possible applications to apparently dissimilar groups. For example, a study can find that Euro-Americans college students who are rewarded for a behavior will increase the probability of that behavior occurring again, and if the behavior is not rewarded it will decrease the probability of it occurring. A study based on such a limited sample could also be applicable to other groups; that is, reinforcement theory can be applied to other groups and situations – and even if it is not, it is worthwhile for the counselor and client to know about this phenomenon in order to add this to their repertoire of ways to change and motivate people. Consider another example: if it is found from a small sample that there are beneficial effects in providing support to people who are raped, this finding may be applicable to people in other cultures. Therefore, research and samples of limited design and sample size can be relevant to other groups.

There are a number of possible ways to determine whether a finding is applicable across populations. Findings based on basic biological and physiological processes are more likely to have some degree of generalizability to people of other cultures, e.g., if breathing exercises are effective for stress management for a group of Inuit hunters, it might also be effective for Algerian youths. Another possible indicator of whether a finding is applicable to others not represented in the sample is the degree to which it is based on basic human processes. Consider the capacity to engage in cognitive processing, if it assumed that people in other cultures have this capacity, then game theory might be applicable, e.g., cross-cultural studies have indicated that game theory can be applied to the Shiwiar of Ecuadorian Amazonia based on their capacity for cognitive specialization (Sugiyama, Tooby, & Cosmides, 2002). Also, if the finding can be applied to animals then it increases the probability that it can be applied across human populations, e.g., if food can entice an animal into a trap, it might also attract humans to attend a meeting. However, it is obvious that samples cannot fully characterize a group, and findings may not be applicable to all members of the sample or to all members of other samples and populations. Using the previous example, food may not be much an enticement for a well-fed animal or person.

Some Critiques of Psychological Research

Much of psychological research is criticized. The shortcomings of the statistical and design aspects of research are often readily noticed and discussed (Campbell & Boruch, 1975; Cook & Campbell, 1979; Cronbach, Freedman, Collier, Sekhon, & Stark, 2010; Ernst, Pittler, & White, 1999; Harris, Reeder & Hyun, 2009; Schneider, Carnoy, Kilpatrick, Schmidt, & Shavelson, 2007; Shadish, Cook, & Campbell, 2002; Trochim & Land, 1982). However, there are other aspects of research that have not received much attention. A few of them are discussed next; that is, the fragmentation of knowledge, the use of concepts, problems in identifying the causal variable, the possible limitations of dealing with multiple factors, the mutable nature of the observed and observer, the tendency to publish politically correct views, and the inclination to publish research with positive results.

FRAGMENTATION OF KNOWLEDGE. Psychological research and knowledge is often scattered among different sources. The American Psychological Association has 56 divisions, 146 international organizations, 54 state and territorial associations, and six Canadian associations. The American Counseling Association has 19 chartered divisions, four regions, and 56 branches. For political, economic, personal, professional, and other reasons, many of these groups have their own publications. PSYCline (http://www.psycline.org/) contains an index of over 2,000 psychology and social science journals. The Psychology Virtual Library (http://www.vl-site.org/psychology/journals.html) has over 130 electronic and print psychology journals. The large number and the scattered amount of information result in fragmentation of knowledge in psychology, making it difficult to determine what is generally known of a particular factor or in a particular field. Recently, the American Psychological Association announced the launching of a new journal that covers the entire discipline of psychology: "Archives of Scientific Psychology" ("APA Launches Archives of Scientific Psychology," 2012). According to their web site this is its "first open methodology, open data, open access journal." This journal is designed to cover the entire discipline of psychology, rather than just focusing on a particular area, and it is accessible to the public. Journals such as these can help provide a more intergrated view of the state of knowledge in the profession and it offers a more complete view of the factors the influence people.

USE OF CONCEPTS. Another aspect of research that can be problematic is the use of concepts. Of course, there is no practical way to avoid using them, but therapists should at least be aware of the effects of their use. Merriam-Webster defines "concept" (2012) as (a) something conceived in the mind – thought, notion, and (b) an abstract or generic idea generalized from particular instances. Even if it can be said that everything is based on concepts, compared to such fields as the mathematical, biological, and physical sciences, psychology and counseling are governed more by concepts. Recently, in an attempt to use more measureable, empirical approaches, psychology has resorted to evidence-based research. However, evidence-based research has received such criticisms as the narrow definition of evidence, the lack of efficacy evidence, and the limited usefulness for individual cases (Cohen, Stavri, & Hersh, 2004; Iglehart, 2005). In the mathematical, biological, and physical sciences, there is some degree of acceptance of concepts and objects of analysis. For example, in viewing a hand, there is usually general agreement that a hand is being viewed and it should be viewed as a hand. Such is not the case with psychology and counseling. There is often disagreement on how to define the object of our analysis: Is alcoholism a medical problem or a psychological one? Is it an addiction or an obsession? Is depression a pathological response or a healthy one?

IDENTIFICATION OF "CASUAL" VARIABLE. In general, researchers investigating a variable of human behavior may not be identifying the main variable or may incorrectly identify it, and then the findings of the effect of the variable might be generalized to the entire sample and population. The same problem exists in medicine and drugs in terms of confounders: "Confounders are hidden connections that make it harder to tell whether a drug really works or if the results of a study are correct" (Zeeberg, 2012). The following is an example of a researcher investigating a mislabeled behavior and the dynamics that can ensue: a couple might engage in counseling because one member of dyad consistently asks the other where the person is going, with whom, and when is the anticipated time of return. A researcher might investigate this behavior under the rubrics of control or jealousy issues; however, the behavior could be the result of another factor: the person asking the questions does not like ambiguity. If statistical significance was found, it would be reported as a function of jealousy or control factors. Even if the researcher was careful and reported the limitations of the study, many readers might ascribe the individual or group studied as having control or jealousy issues.

MULTIPLE REASONS FOR BEHAVIORS. The attempt to isolate the causal variable is certainly a hallmark of the scientific approach. However, a multitude of factors may induce a behavior. Multivariate statistical methods allow us to examine many variables. However, are we psychologically willing, and cognitively able, to process multiple factors? Often, it is tedious to accept results in terms of "there are many complicated factors." It is easier to process results that identify a single or a few variables.

THE MUTABLE NATURE OF THE OBSERVED AND OBSERVER. Both the person who is studied (the observed person) and the person who is observing (the researcher or clinician) can change. This is illustrated in various parts of this book that discuss the problems in physics in perceiving and measuring phenomena. People are multidimensional, they can change, they can present only certain aspects of themselves, our views of them can be selective and can change. For example, therapists' views of a divorce might be influenced by a book that was read recently, or if they recently went through a difficult divorce. Therapists are trained to view clients through the *Diagnostic and Statistical Manual of Mental Disorders* – which is routinely changing (American Psychiatric Association Development, 2010). The *International Classification of Diseases* was supposed to be revised every ten years but it is now revised every year (World Health Organization, 2010c). An existential and humanistic view might be that our diagnoses, perceptions, and attempts to categorize people are inadequate because people are too complex and our perceptions and methods of assessing them are limited (Association for Humanistic Counseling, n.d.; Society for Humanistic Psychology, 2012).

PUBLICATION BIAS. Politically correct results, that is, results that affirm generally endorsed values and views, are more likely to be accepted (Cummings & O'Donohue, 2012; Hunter, 2005; MD Anonymous, 2006; Michalko, 2012; Wright & Cummings, 2005; Tierney, 2008). In reporting about medical journals, Tierney (2008) wrote "The boundary between scientific research and activism have become blurred, to the detriment of scientific standards" (para.

4). He quoted Sara Johnsdotter and Birgitta Essen: "One of the hazards of science is when politically correct results are uncritically welcomed, readily published and repeatedly cited; while politically embarrassing results are ignored or marginalized" (para. 2).

Also, studies that report positive results are more likely to be published than those that do not (Fanelli, 2010; Scherer, 2012; Simmons, 2011; Yong, 2012). Fanelli (2010) found this:

> When correcting for the confounding effect of presence/absence of multiple hypotheses, the odds of reporting a positive result were around five times higher for papers published in Psychology and Psychiatry and Economics and Business than in Space Science. . . . When correcting for the confounding effect of pure/applied discipline and presence/absence of multiple hypotheses, the odds of reporting a positive results were about 2.3 times significantly higher for papers in the social sciences compared to the physical sciences. . . , and about 3.4 times significantly higher for behavioral and social studies on people compared to physical-chemical studies. (p. 4)

Yong (2012) reviewed articles published in psychology journals. He reported there was pervasive bias toward the publication of research that had positive findings. There were seldom attempts to replicate studies, and when replications were attempted, the results often did not confirm the positive results of the initial studies. He quoted Eric-Jan Waganmakers: "Positive results in psychology can behave like rumors: easy to release but hard to dispel. They dominate most journals, which strive to present new, exciting research. Meanwhile, attempts to replicate those studies, especially when the findings are negative, go unpublished, languishing in personal file drawers or circulating in conversations around the water cooler" (Yong, 2012, para. 3).

These are just a few of the many critiques of research in psychology. They are challenges. They alert us to keep ourselves informed. They can encourage us not to let the veneer of science, research, and publications in professional journals lull us into complacency.

Classifications of Mental Illness

There are various classification schemes for mental illness (Mezzich, Honda, & Kastrup, 1994; Patel & Stein, 2007). The two main ones in the West are the *International Classification of Diseases-10*, Chapter V: "Classification of Mental and Behavioral Disorders" (World Health Organization, 2008, 2010a), and the *Diagnostic and Statistical Manual of Mental Disorders* (*DSM;* American Psychiatric Association, 2000). China also has its own classification of mental illness, the *Chinese Classification of Mental Disorders* (Chinese Medical Association, 1990). Both the Chinese and Americans are working to have their classification systems coincide with the World Health Organization's. The "Classification of Mental and Behavioural Disorders" section of the *International Classification of Diseases-10* (*ICD*) was developed in consultation with mental health professionals throughout the world. It provides a common scheme to view mental disorders. One of the problems in classifying mental problems is to have common terms and definitions (Ameen, 2002). To help with this situation, the World Health Organization (1997) produced the *Lexicon of Cross-Cultural Terms in Mental Health*. This provides definition of terms with the purpose of improving reliability in the diagnoses of disorders.

Examples of Past and Present Critiques of DSM and ICD

In general, with every revision of the *DSM* (and *ICD*) there have been criticisms. Usually, the criticisms from psychologists and counselors are that they want a greater role in its development and in the provision of services.

The fifth edition of the *Diagnostic and Statistical Manual of Mental Disorders* (*DSM-V*) is planned for publication on May 2013 (American Psychiatric Association Development, 2010). This has already encountered criticism (Chapman, n.d.; Livesley, 2010; British Psychological Association, 2010; Young, 2010). Among the criticisms by Livesley (2010) are that it is confusing, inconsistent, lacking in coherence, and unsupported by empirical evidence in places. Bradshaw (2012) complains that lowering the threshold of mental disorders will classify nonclinical problems as clinical disorders, and many mental disorders will be viewed as biological conditions needing medication. Frances (2012) briefly summarized some of the criticisms: expansion of the diagnostic system includes untested new diagnoses with reduction of thresholds of the old ones, there is lack of scientific rigor and independent review, and the dimensional proposals are too complex.

The *DSM* has received a plethora of criticisms from its inception. Among the criticisms were of its validity and reliability: it did not measure what it is suppose to measure, and therapists may see the same symptom and give different diagnoses (Kirk & Kutchins, 1994; McLaren, 2009; Rosenhan, 1973). Another criticism was that the number and types of disorders are so numerous that it was possible to pathologize every conceivable behavior (Wakefield, 1992, 1997, 1999). Beutler (1989) made the case that psychiatric diagnoses were of limited value in the development of therapeutic plans and in predicting therapeutic outcome. Wahl (1999) criticized the *DSM* for following the medical model – which induces a view that attaches a social stigma to mental illness. Ellis, Abrams, and Abrams (2009) reported that the symptom based approach resulted in a cumbersome catalog of mental problems. They preferred explanations for the problem or that the theoretical basis be provided. They stated that the *DSM* did not distinguish between poor adaptations to ordinary problems from pathological disorders, and it was insufficient and limited in dealing with anger, hostility, and aggression. They also criticized the *DSM* because it gave the impression that medications were the solution to many problems. Gadit (2010) wrote "Critics view the *DSM-IV* as somewhat biased, less culturally sensitive, opinionated, political, and drug-industry driven" (para. 3). Zur and Nordmarken (2010) contributed to the criticisms of the *DSM* by writing as follows:

> The current criterion focuses on medication management of behavioral symptomology over psychotherapy. The primary elements that have survived all revisions are the intrapsychic focus and the power of political and economic agendas. Many clinicians are unaware that the DSM is more political than scientific, that there is little agreement among professionals regarding the meaning of vaguely defined terms and that it includes only scant empirical data. (para. 1)

In terms of the *ICD*, it has gone through numerous revisions, just as the *DSM* has, and they will both continue to change. *ICD* (and *DSM*) made changes to address criticisms and to incorporate information provided by new data. The *ICD* had its origins in the 1850s and the recent *ICD-10* was endorsed by the World Health Assembly in 1990 (World Health Organization, 2010a). "It had been realized that the great expansion in the use of the *ICD* necessitated a thorough rethinking of its structure and an effort to devise a stable and flexible classification, which should not require fundamental revision for many years to come" (World Health Organization, 2010b, p. 8). The plan had been to revise the *ICD* every ten years, but it was decided that the interval between revisions was too long and revisions were needed at shorter intervals. The *ICD* is updated and revised annually (World Health Organization, 2010c). A beta version of the *ICD-11* was anticipated for 2010 and a final version by 2014. The fact that so many revisions are needed suggests that the *ICD* is a changing document and that the statements and criteria should be considered tentative.

Various criticisms have been directed at the *ICD* at different times. Some of the criticisms have been addressed, others have not, and still others are waiting for further research and inputs. A sample of past, present, and future criticisms include the following. The criteria-based diagnoses was been criticized as giving the illusion that the criteria were objective and the guidelines were accurate, when actually they were neither (Mombour et al., 1990). Furthermore, the differences in the time criteria for diagnosing symptoms of schizophrenia (six months in *DSM-III-R* and one month in *ICD-10*) could result in a "worldwide diagnostic dichotomy; statistics, treatment and outcome evaluation of schizophrenia will be split – a deplorable future prospect" (Mombour et al., 1990, p. 198). Section 2. 6 F5: *behavioral syndromes and mental disorders associated with physiological dysfunction and hormonal disturbances of ICD-10*, was criticized as too long and verbose. Some of the critics called for better and more uniform arrangement of the text. There was also criticism that it was oriented more toward the clinician instead of serving more of a didactic function and did not have a multiaxial diagnosis (which the *DSM* has). "The *ICD-10* also has faced criticism mainly because of its limited scope in countless clinical situations" (Gadit, 2010, para. 3). In general, the structure of the *ICD* was criticized as "tediously formulated and poorly arranged" (p. 199). Those who reviewed the 1987 draft also recognized some of the of the positive aspects of the *ICD-10*. They reported that they liked the descriptive approach: the discarding of many theoretical concepts, the further operationalization of descriptions of diagnoses, and the synchronization of its structure and terms with the *DSM-III-R*. Just as there are attempts to synchronize the *DSM* with the *ICD*, so too there are various efforts to synchronize the *ICD* with the *DSM* (Mombour et al., 1990).

In their critique of the *ICD-10*, Cooper and Hassiotis (2009) found the criteria were difficult to apply for adults with intellectual disabilities. Among the many problems they noted were the specifiers did not clarify whether a behavior was adaptive or a problem – or whether a problem occurred because of a psychiatric disorder or was the expression of another disorder (e.g., a symptom of depression could be the result of depression or a toothache); and the specifiers were not operationalized, which could result in varied diagnoses among diagnosticians.

In addition to criticisms and caveats directed at the *DSM* and *ICD* diagnostic classification systems (Cooper & Hassiotis, 2009; Frances & Spitzer, 2010; Gadit, 2010; Livesley, 2001), the entire process of diagnosing has been challenged. Farmer and Adwa (2007) wrote about nosological and diagnostic practices of the *DSM* and the *ICD*. Among their criticisms were that the diagnostic categories are hypotheses that have been reified (that is, they are abstractions that are considered concrete or real), and they are social constructs and are not actual diseases. Psychiatric conditions are poorly delineated, and their conceptual bases are vague. Also, they seldom have demonstrable evidence, such as lab tests, to substantiate the diagnoses. Furthermore, there are disorders that are severe and dysfunctional but defy the diagnostic categories, and many mental disorders are syndromes and dimensions rather than categories. There are differences in the diagnostic practices among therapists, and there can be different operational definitions to a disorder. The operational definitions can leave out relevant factors. With some conditions, the majority of the diagnoses do not fit the standard categories and are relegated to the "atypical" or "not otherwise specified" categories. Also, with some symptoms, it is difficult to rate the client on certain items.

Stirling and Hellewell (1999) criticized both the *DSM* and the *ICD*. The reliability and validity, especially of subtypes of the major categories, of both were questioned, as well as the use categorical (discrete) rather than dimensional (on a continuum) approaches. They warned that therapists should be aware that they are treating people and not diagnostic labels.

Comments

Mental illness classification systems are the expression of controversial scientific and theoretical views and values that are continuously changing. They are the products of personalities, and political, social, and economic influences, e.g., insurance companies and government agencies have their views of what constitutes a mental problem – and which problems are reimbursable.

Each version and revision of the *ICD* and *DSM* have raised criticisms. With all the shortcomings of the *ICD* and the *DSM*, they are nevertheless needed. They provide a common method to categorize behaviors. They provide a common language for therapists in the United States and the world to communicate with each other. They provide a basis upon which to add, delete, and modify information. They provide the groundwork upon which a scientific approach can be developed. Responsible therapists should be aware of the strengths and weaknesses as well as appropriate and inappropriate uses of these classification and labeling systems.

Are U.S. Approaches the Most Appropriate?

There have been a number of critics of psychology and psychotherapy (Lilienfeld, 2002; Norsworthy, Heppner, Aegisdottir, Gerstein, & Pedersen, 2009; Szasz, 1961, 1970; Teo, 2005). For example, Lilienfeld's (2002) criticisms of psychology included the following: it is a soft science (it does not have agreement on any basic theory – which the sciences of chemistry and physics have). Also, practitioners do not use the findings of science and research – most of what they do is untested – and sometimes harmful. Finally, what is used is controversial and utilizes poorly studied diagnostic labels, e.g., codependency. There have been criticisms of the statistics upon which psychology justifies as evidence and data of therapeutic effectiveness (McBurney & White, 2009; Ziliak & McCloskey, 2008). There are those who claim psychotherapy is effective (e.g., McNeilly & Howard, 1991), and there are those who question its effectiveness (e.g., Bentall, 2009; Eysenck, 1952; Truax & Carkhuff, 2008). Dawes (1994) assets that psychology and psychotherapy are based on myths.

We need to consider the implications of what we are doing. In 1918, the American-Medico Psychological Association (the forerunner of the American Psychiatric Association) helped publish the predecessor to the *Diagnostic and Statistical Manual* (*DSM*): the "Statistical Manual for the Use of Institutions for the Insane" (American Medico-Psychological Association..., 1918). It had 22 diagnoses and 40 pages. The more recent *DSM-IV* (American Psychiatric Association, 1994) had 297 disorders and 886 pages. On the one hand, we can attribute this dramatic increase to better diagnostic skills and data. On the other hand, questions can be raised as to whether there are other factors that contribute to the increase – and what are the mental health professionals' responsibilities? Are there professional, economic, and political interests involved? If the increases reflect greater incidences of mental illness, why is there such a large increase? Does our society induce the development of certain problems (Watters, 2010)? Are these increases in mental health problems a necessary sacrifice that accompany economic and material improvement? Are there detrimental aspects to therapists' interactions with people? Do therapeutic services have equal benefits and consequences for everyone? Does simply diagnosing a problem take the place of examining the effects of our culture? Do therapists have an obligation to inform clients of the benefits and disadvantages of our culture and services? For example, U.S. Americans value the material accumulation of goods (Barber, 2008; Cross, 2000; Friedman, 1985; Kasser, 2002; Kasser & Kanner, 2004; Lankford, 2006; Twitchell, 1999). However, even though U.S. Americans have more material benefits and live under better economic conditions than their predecessors – and many other people in the world – their mental health is not necessarily better (Inglehart, Welzel, & Foa, 2006; Kessler, & Ustun, 2008; WHO World Mental Health Survey Consortium, 2004; World Values Survey, 2006). Studies have found suicide, depression, obesity, diabetes, mental illness, bulimia, and anorexia often increase in developed countries (Kessler & Ustun, 2008). What role do counselors play in light of this information? In the United States, a common solution to mental health problems is greater funding and the use of more professional mental health services. However, there is some evidence that this might not be the complete answer. Bickman et al. (1995) conducted the Fort Bragg Child and Adolescent Mental Health Demonstration experiment. The effectiveness of system-of-care services to children with emotional disorders was tested. Funding was generous. The program offered full continuum of children's mental health services to military dependents. The goal was to avoid restrictions to treatments and to be responsive to the needs of children and families. The program consisted of such services as in-home crisis stabilization, after-school group treatment, and therapeutic foster care. Crisis management helped to fill the gap between outpatient psychotherapy and institutional treatment. Results indicated that both the demonstration group (the treatment group) and the comparison groups (groups that did not received full spectrum of care) had the same clinical outcomes – but the treatment group was more expensive. One conclusion of these studies is that the expenditure of more resources and money does not necessarily improve treatment outcome and that there are other factors involved in effective treatment. What role can counselors play in light of studies such as these – besides criticizing the research and researchers? Do counselors have any ethical and social responsibility to find solutions that do not aggrandize their pocketbooks?

Another aspect of counseling is the influence of increased economic development and the accompanying rise of specializations. In addition to the benefits obtained by having specialists, there are other effects that are often not addressed, e.g., fragmentation of the person. The distinction between the mind and body is not made in many other cultures. Other cultures consider the two to be intertwined. Kirmayer and Young (1998) wrote that the interpretation of the symptoms, perceived mechanisms, and functions often differ among cultures, but the physical manifestation of psychological conditions (somatization) is ubiquitous. Many cultures also believe the metaphysical (e.g., beyond the immediate senses, such as the spiritual and ancestral) is intertwined with "psychological" conditions. Most counselors trained in the European and U.S. American traditions work with the "psyche" from a cognitive and affective perspective. When we deal with just the mind, i.e., thoughts and feelings, are we ignoring other important aspects of treatment? Are we involved in the fragmentation of the individual? Is counseling part of the reductionist pattern whereby we separate people from themselves and from each other? Counseling consists of a special relationship with the client; it is confidential, removed from others, and clients are viewed as relatively autonomous individuals. Increases in economic development are often accompanied by increases in counseling services and such problems as social anomie, loneliness, and disengagement of individuals from families and communities. Counselors help people with these problems, but the question might be asked if some aspects of what they do are unintentionally contributing to the problem. Fragmentation and separateness might also occur when groups (e.g., women, African-Americans, and those with handicaps) promote distinctions between themselves and others. What role should counselors play in facilitating and hindering these distinctions? For example, in group counseling, do we draw people closer to each other in one group and isolate them from other groups? Do we buttress and validate that there are barriers between people? It might be beneficial for people to feel special because they are part of a group. They may get satisfaction in having a particular group that advocates for them. They may be part of networks that commiserate, support, and encourage each other. On the other hand, there are those who oppose reductionist views. They view people are more than their parts (Adler, 1998; Aristotle, 1907; Bohm, 1980; Durkheim, 1974; Perls, Hefferline, & Goodman, 1951). Whatever the effects of reductionistic processes – if indeed this is happening – at the very least, therapists should be aware of their possible role in treatment.

Watters (2010) wrote of the enormous influence of U.S. American views of mental illness in the world, and he questioned if these views provided effective and better treatment. He cited research of anthropologists and cross-cultural psychiatrists. There was convincing evidence that mental illness takes different forms, and culture significantly determines features, treatment, and prognosis. Some of the treatments provided by other cultures were more effective than European and U.S. American psychological treatments. Some disorders had greater recovery rates and did not last as long as in the developed countries. For example, McGruder (2010) had a chapter in Watters' book in which she reported on studies of Zanzibar families with members who had schizophrenia. Indigenous treatments and beliefs resulted in those with schizophrenia having less of a stigma and integrating quicker and better into the community compared to European and U.S. American societies. Watters wrote that despite our overwhelming resources, our treatments were not necessarily better and were often detrimental. We view ourselves as benevolent, kind, supportive, and empathetic toward those with mental illness, but he cited research showing that European and U.S. American approaches resulted in increased distance between society and those with mental illness. There was harsher treatment, greater stigma, and more fearful reactions toward those with psychological disorders. He showed our core values and assumptions are culturally based. Not every culture shares our definitions of self, human nature, time, pain, and suffering. Cultures differ in their definitions of trauma and its effects. They vary in their perception of the venting of emotions as therapeutic, and they do not all necessarily subscribe to the view that many emotional and mental problems require professional intervention. Watters (2010a) wrote that we are homogenizing mental illness. We are teaching the world how to view mental illnesses/disorders and treat problems. In doing so, we are losing the diversity of treatments, some of which, using our own scientific measures, are more effective than the ones we are using. He also wrote the following:

> Offering the latest Western mental-health theories, treatments and categories in an attempt to ameliorate the psychological stress sparked by modernization and globalization is not a solution; it may be part of the problem. When we undermine local conceptions of the self and modes of healing, we may be speeding along the disorienting changes that are at the very heart of much of the world's mental distress. (p. 6)

Sartorius (2008) comments were in the same vein as Watters'. Sartorius is the former Director of the Division of Mental Health of the World Health Organization. He wrote, "The outcome of schizophrenia was, on the whole, better in the developing than in the developed countries" (para. 5), and "the percentage of people with severe or persisting symptoms and chronic disability was much smaller in Third World countries than in the centres in the industrialized countries" (para. 6). MindFreedom International (2008) wrote of Sartorius's studies, "The World Health Organization (WHO) sponsored major studies comparing how people recover in poor and more developed nations. The people in the poorer developing nations, on average, recovered at a far higher rate" (para. 1).

We need to determine if we are involved in Kafkaesque and iatrogenic endeavors where we are the vectors of aspects of our culture and services that induce more problems than we are trying to solve. We need to determine how to better deal with the increases in suicide, depression, anxiety, eating problems, and other illnesses as cultures become economically developed. We need to determine whether our services are justified under the rational that the net benefits of what we do outweigh the negative impact. We need to consider if our approaches are the most appropriate for all economic, social, and political systems. Most of our treatments entail relatively long-term interactions, reliance on counselors (even though we assert otherwise), and great expense. We need to find better ways to provide treatment. Research into how other societies treat social and psychological problems might contribute to helping us improve the way we help people. We need to determine how such factors as capitalism, entrepreneurship, and politics influence what we do. We need to determine where technology and other ways of providing services can augment or improve counseling services.

Counselors have a lot to offer as humans and as professionals. Greater awareness of what they have to offer, the ramifications of their activities, and knowledge of their strengths and weaknesses will be of great contribution to the art and science of counseling. They need to determine if the self-serving, political, economic, and striving for power aspects of their activities do not sabotage and blind their efforts to explore new and better ways to help people – and themselves.

Chapter 6

CLIENT CHARACTERISTICS

When counselors interact with clients, they are contending with a vast number of characteristics. Some of these are presented in the next sections on the influences of culture, styles or patterns of thinking, sources of information, and characteristics unique to the individual.

CULTURE

We all live under the influence of various cultures, e.g., there are the family, group, community, corporate, national, and religious cultures. Writers have offered information on the factors that comprise culture (e.g., Jandt, 2009). Knowledge of these, and other factors, can help the counselor be aware of some of the social and psychological influences on the person. Zakour (2004) provided a summary of the most common factors (referred to as dimensions) presented by authors that constitute culture: power distance, individualism/collectivism, masculinity/femininity, uncertainty avoidance, long-term orientation (citing Hofstede, 1997); conservatism, intellectual autonomy, affective autonomy, hierarchy, egalitarianism, mastery, and harmony (citing Schwartz, 1994a, 1994b, 2004); universalism/particularism, individualism/communitarianism, neutral/emotional, specific/diffuse, achievement/ascription, attitudes to time, attitudes to environment (citing Trompenaars, Hampden-Turner, 1998); communication context, perception of space, monochronic and polychronic time (citing Hall, 1989; Hall & Hall, 1987); and nature of people, person's relationship to nature, person's relationship to other people, primary mode of activity, conception of space, and person's temporal orientation (citing Kluckhohn, & Strodtbeck, 1961). Thus, there are writers offering a variety of factors that comprise culture, so the counselor can determine which are the relevant ones for a particular setting.

STYLES OF THINKING

Style of thinking can differ among cultures and individuals. These are patterns of thinking that are characteristic of people in the manner in which they process information and make decisions. These are mentioned in sections of this book, e.g., in the sections on theories of personality. Styles of thinking are influenced by personality, beliefs, traditions, religion, and norms, and have such characteristics as thinking that are processed mainly in a linear fashion compared to holistically (Smith, 1953); sensory based compared to pattern based (Myers & McCaulley, 1985); guided mainly by the group compared to guided by self (Triandis, 1989); and by emotions compared to logic (Loewenstein & Lerner, 2003). It should be noted that in addition to the process of thinking, there are other factors that are part of it, e.g., the manner in which information is obtained, decisions are made, and implemented (Myers & McCaulley, 1985).

There are a number of possible ways to deal with people whose styles of thinking differ from the therapist's or whose problems are exacerbated because of it.

- Styles of thinking often occur automatically; therefore, people (this includes counselors) may not be aware of the ways they are thinking. The counselor and client can explore their styles of thinking and determine the ramifications.
- The counselor and client can accept the differences.
- The counselor can inform the client that there are alternative views. For example, a person may be confused because of contradictions that are the result of viewing a problem from dualistic and linear thinking (e.g., why would a smart person do stupid things?). The counselor can inform the client that there are other ways to view this apparent contradiction; that is, we are multidimensional – each of us has elements that are smart and stupid, good and bad, rational and irrational, and so on. For a person who believes that people have many aspects to their being, the intermingling of apparent dualistic elements is not as great a cause of cognitive dissonance.
- The counselor can encourage clients to interpret the problematic behavior differently. For example, the client could think positively, take an objective view of the problem, or define the problem in a less negative manner.

Many forms of therapy consist of changing the client's manner of thinking. This can be done through such methods as providing insight into why people behave the way that they do (e.g., psychoanalytic and existential therapy), or by pointing out how their thinking might be contributing to the problem (e.g., cognitive-behavioral therapy).

Attribution

Attribution theory endeavors to explain behaviors. It has been the focus of many studies (e.g., Jones & McGillis, 1976; Kelley, 1972b). Heider (1958) was one of the first in the psychological literature to draw attention to attribution theory (Folkes, 1988). He presented the view that people often attribute what happens to them and to others as either the result of personal causes (the result of one's actions) or external causes (environmental, situational causes). Jones and Nisbett (1972) are among the many who have investigated aspects of attribution. Among their findings are that the observer and the observed (the actor) can have different explanations for the actor's behavior. The observer is likely to attribute the actor's behavior to personal characteristics and the actor is likely to explain the behavior as a reaction to the situation. Weiner (1986) called attention to such factors as locus of control, effort, and ability to play a role in explaining why people engage in behaviors. In their expositions, many writers call attention to attribution errors and biases; that is, people make attributions that are inaccurate or they make attributions that are skewed, e.g., heavily influenced by emotions. Fiske and Taylor wrote (1991) that Weiner's attribution theory has exerted considerable influence in other countries and there is substantial cross-culture support for it. However, the attributional traditions among cultures differ (Berry, Segall, & Kağitçibaşi, 1997; Herve Kuendig, Plant, Plant, Miller, Kuntsche, & Gmel, 2008; Hsiao, Klimidis, Minas, & Tan, 2006; Suthahar & Elliott, 2004). For instance, Eastern cultures might be more likely to attribute the situation as an explanation of behavior, whereas Western cultures are more likely to attribute behaviors to personality characteristics (Choi, Nisbett, & Norenzayan, 1999). Manusov and Spitzberg (2008) wrote that although there are cultural and personal differences in attribution (citing Lawrence, Murray, Banerjee, Turner, Sangha, Byng et al., 2006; Maddux & Yuki, 2006), the underlying processes are basically the same. For example, people might attribute behavior to be the result of karma, fate, genes, God, personality, tradition, and so on; however, these different attributions can be analyzed from the perspective of internal or external attributions.

It is important to consider these attributional traditions and to be aware that there are many similarities between "modern" practices and beliefs and those of other cultures. Such awareness can help the counselor view other people's views in a more benign fashion – and not as ignorance or backwardness. For example, some cultures might attribute present problems and behaviors to what their ancestors did or did not do; a "modern" society might attribute present problems to the inheritance of ancestral genetics, past abuse, or epigenetics. Some societies might attribute a problem to a person having sinful thoughts; a modern society might attribute problems to faulty thinking (e.g., catastrophizing). The traditional belief that many problems were caused by an imbalance in the body fluids (humor theory) has its parallel in modern medicine's belief that many problems are caused by the excess or deficits of certain biochemicals – therefore, drugs and medications are needed. One society may attribute problems to not performing the correct rituals, and another might attribute problems to not taking medications or not exercising. One culture might attribute problems to spirits and the supernatural; another might attribute problems to the psyche and mental illness. Reminder: even though the beliefs and practices of people in other cultures may seem strange to a counselor, people in other cultures may view the counselor's thoughts and behaviors to be strange as well.

INFLUENCES OF SOURCES OF INFORMATION

There are many influences on the person (Bronfenbrenner, 1979, 2005; Gibson & Pick, 2003). These influences contribute to the uniqueness of the individual (Conyne & Cook, 2004; Fuchs, 2007). When counselors interact with clients, they have to consider the influences of such sources as those of religion, politics, radio, TV, internet, family, friends, advertisements, and education. These sources influence peoples' perceptions, values, criteria and definitions – as illustrated by the following. There are many in the U.S. who are persuaded by sources that consider such values as independence, economic success, equal rights, and democracy to be critical aspects of a person's wellbeing. They may view Western women as liberated and Islamic women as oppressed. They may view Islamic law (the Sharia) and Islamic men as harsh and unjust. A 2005 Gallup Poll (Mogahed, 2010) of Muslim views was conducted in eight predominantly Muslim countries: Egypt, Iran, Jordan, Lebanon, Morocco, Pakistan, Saudi Arabia, and Turkey. The responses of the Muslim women indicated that they perceived Western women as having a degraded status because they were treated as exploited sexual objects and did not wear veils. Muslim women preferred the Sharia to other forms of guidance of public policy. Muslim women were not as likely to cite gender inequality as an aspect of Islamic societies they did not like. Surveys of Muslim men indicated that they believed women should have the same basic rights as men. They also believe Muslim women should be allowed to vote without influence, and they should work at any job for which they are qualified.

There are many other examples of the diversity of views among people (Baumeister, Zhang, & Vohs, 2004; DiFonzo & Bordia, 2007; Burgess & Maiese, 2004; Kapferer, 1990; Kimmel, 2004; Rosnow, 1988, 2001; Rosnow, Yost, & Esposito, 1986). The variety of views can be the result of exposure to different sources of information, or they can be the result of different interpretations of the same source. For example, there are those who rely on prayer rather than science and medicine as healing agents (Eddy, 1991). Some people reject the H1N1 vaccine because they believe it hurts rather than helps (Specter, 2009). Some people believe yellow corn causes sterility (Jaynes, 2009). There are those who believe genetically modified foods can be harmful (Whitman, 2000). Some people question the use of prophylactics as a means to prevent STDs ("Family Values vs. Safe Sex," 1999). There were concerns that Hepatitis B and AIDS programs were conspiracies against gays (Cantwell, 1993). Cervarix vaccine for the human papillomavirus (HPV) is believed by some to cause death and brain damage (Adams, 2009). Some believe crack cocaine is part of a government plan to destroy the African-American community (United States Department of Justice, 1997). Books have been written denouncing many modern mental health treatments as bogus (Bobgan & Bobgan, 1987; Campbell, 1994; Dawes, 1994; Dineen, 1999). There are those who claim that many pharmaceutical drugs are detrimental forms of treatment (Cohen, 1990; Colbert, 1996; Tracy & Shephard, 1994). The list of sources of information and perspectives is extensive.

Religion and Paranormal Beliefs

Many people in the world have religious beliefs, and many believe in paranormal phenomena. These beliefs can have an impact on therapy. Paranormal has been defined as "not understandable in terms of known scientific laws and phenomena" (Paranormal, 2012). Religious beliefs may differ from paranormal beliefs in that religious beliefs often have more moral and spiritual components as well as greater social legitimacy and institutional support. However, the two may be similar because they involve the metaphysical and phenomena that are not readily scientifically substantiated. About 87.3 percent of the people in the world are religious; 12.7 percent are nonreligious (Congress of World and Traditional Religions, 2005-2012). In the U.S. about 84 percent have religious beliefs, 12.1 percent are unaffiliated, and 4 percent have no religion (Central Intelligence Agency, n.d.). In studies of the paranormal, a Gallup Poll (Moore, 2005) of American beliefs found 55 percent believed in the healing powers of the mind. Many in the Christian community also believe that religious activities, such as prayer, can heal (Dossey, 1993; Hunter, 2009; Koenig, 1999; MacNutt, 2001). The belief in the mind's capacity to bring about cure may have relevance in its relationship to placebos. It appears that the beliefs in the mind's capacity to heal and the belief in the capacity of prayer to heal are both related to expectancy effects. There have been many studies investigating the relationship between psychological factors, paranormal beliefs, and religion (Irwin, 2009; Jahoda, 1969; Musch & Ehrenberg, 2002; Roig, Bridges, Renner, & Jackson, 1997; Tobacyk & Mil-

ford, 1983; Wiseman & Watt, 2004). The results do not show clear patterns –
some studies indicate associations and characteristics, and others do not. Similarly, results of studies in the U.S. and other countries investigating who is influenced by paranormal beliefs, and the degree to which they are affected, are
often unclear or contradictory (Aanio & Lindeman, 2005; Callaghan & Irwin,
2003; Coll, Lay, & Taylor, 2008; Dudley, 2002; Duncan, Donnelly, Nicholson, & Hees, 1992; Ellis, 1988; El-Islam & Malasi, 1985; Endler & Parker,
1994; George & Sreedhar, 2006; Holahan & Moos, 1987; Irwin, 1992;
Olorundare, 1998; Ozkan, 2004; Peltzer, 2003; Rogers, Qualter, Phelps, &
Gardner, 2006; Russell & Jones, 1980; Sachs, 2004; Sadler-Smith, 2011;
Singer & Benassi, 1981; Williams, Francis, Lewis, 2009; Zeidner & Beit-Hallahmi, 1998). Vyse (2000) found that irrational beliefs are common among all
occupations, incomes, and educational levels. Moore (2005) reported no sta-
tistically significant differences in belief in the paranormal because of age,
gender, education, race, or region of the country. Seventy-five percent of
Christians had some paranormal beliefs, and 66 percent of non-Christians
had such beliefs. Authors report different figures for the previous figures and
groups; for example, Jacobson, Foxx, and Mulick (2005) reported studies indicating 90 percent of Americans believed in the paranormal, and women
were more likely to believe in various paranormal phenomena.

It is likely that the impact of religion and paranormal on counseling depends on the individual, culture, and religion. For example, in some Islam
cultures, they may transfer to the therapist the relationship they have with authoritative religious figures (Sayed, 2003); in some U.S. Christian groups, they
are likely to go to pastors with their mental health problems (Chalfant, Heller,
Roberts, Briones, Aguirre-Hochbaum, & Farr, 1990), and some are likely to
attribute mental disorders to the work of demons and personal sin (Stanford,
2007). It is evident that religion can play a role in many people's perceptions
and interactions with therapists. If there are questions about therapists' roles
and functions in reference to religious matters, perhaps one approach to take
is for therapists to explain what they do and what therapists have to offer and
let clients choose what they want.

Counselors who are aware of influences of sources of information on the
client can increase the probability of therapeutic effectiveness (Campinha-Bacote, 2003; Godlas, n.d.; Hodge, 2002, 2005; Huda, 2006; Pollitt, 2009;
Rashidi & Rajaram, 2001; Rassool, 2000). Awareness of these influences can
come from a variety of sources. For example, asking or observing the client
can provide information. Often, there are people who are familiar with important influences on the person. They can serve as cultural or information
brokers. If the counselor participates in the client's group and communal activities, these interactions might reveal perspectives, concerns, and sources of
influence. There is no single or best way to deal with these various influences,

but a sample of possible responses are the following:

- The counselor discusses with the client the influences on the client. With this approach, the counselor engages in dialogue about what the client has heard; the client's concerns, expectations, and so on.
- Ignore the problem. Usually, counselors feel uncomfortable with this approach. If there is an issue, or a hidden agenda (e.g., the counselor knows that the client has been told something negative about therapy and the counselor), counselors usually want to deal with it and get it out of the way so that the focus would be on the therapy.
- Provide information. In this case, the counselor provides information about what the counselor has to offer and what the alternative perspectives have to offer – and lets the client choose.
- Challenge the validity and credibility of the source. This is a classic approach. The counselor challenges the client's information source and points out the discrepancies, faulty argument, and biases of the other views.
- Deal with the client's interpretation of the information or influence. The counselor may believe, or induce in the client the belief, that the client's perspective is naive, ignorant, incomplete, and faulty; and the counselor can provide better or more complete information.
- Use neutral intermediaries or credible allies to counter the other views. Third parties may be able to provide perspectives and information that lend support to the counselor. The third party's "objectivity" can help the client believe that personal biases are not involved in promoting the decision to engage in therapy or to make changes.
- If it is anticipated that the client will be influenced by other views, the counselor can deal with them before they occur. This approach prepares the client for counterarguments before encountering the other views – it helps "inoculate" the client to deal with other views.
- We also need to consider that the counselor might need to change. The counselor might be influenced by sources that are inaccurate, ignorant, or biased.

It should not be ignored that governments and political agendas can also influence clients (and control their access to services). They can legitimize or discredit psychological services. For example, the former president of Latvia, Vaira Vike-Freiberga, who was also an experimental psychologist, said of the Soviet Union's attitude toward psychology: "The Soviet system didn't believe in psychology – it was considered too bourgeois and too individualistic, and thus unwelcome and even dangerous in a totalitarian state. In a socialist state, there shouldn't be any place for it – there is no need for soul searching in a worker's 'paradise'" (Dingfelder, 2010, p. 36).

IDIOSYNCRATIC ASPECTS

We know from personality research that there are differences among individuals because of genetic variations, environmental influences, and life experiences. Clients from both domestic and other cultures may vary in such characteristics as verbal expression of emotions, openness and intimacy, insight, competition and cooperation, linear-static time emphasis, nuclear and extended family experience, locus of control, awareness and use of scientific empiricism, learning styles, sense and attitude regarding free will, self-esteem, cognitive development, stressors, perceptions, self-disclosure, conflict resolution style, life experiences, religion, socioeconomic background, victimization, and many other factors (Illovsky, 2003). These contribute to unique individual characteristics that guide the client's views and behaviors (Cliaborn, 1986; Fischer, Jome, & Atkinson, 1998; Frank & Frank, 1991; Hutchins, 1980; Prince, 1980; Trevifio, 1996). Clients often have their own idiosyncratic criteria by which they evaluate themselves and the world around them. They can have their own views of what makes them happy or sad, successful or unsuccessful, depressed or not depressed, worthy or not, and so on. Even though knowledge of a person's culture is important, the client's idiosyncratic experiences and views can determine receptivity to the counselor's interventions.

Chapter 7

APPROACHES AND TECHNIQUES

Just as it would be beneficial for clients to be open to change and to try new and different activities, so too can counselors and therapists benefit by being open to other approaches to mental health. Other approaches can add to their therapeutic repertoire. In terms of learning from others, consider some Native American views of disabilities. U.S. American therapists usually define a physical disability as a limitation, a deficit, a problem, or a handicap that hinders a person in areas of functioning; however, Johnson (n.d.) wrote this:

> Native Americans honor and respect them. They believe that a person weak in body is often blessed by the Creator as being especially strong in mind and spirit. By reducing our emphasis on the physical, which promotes our view of separation from our fellow man and all that is, a greater sense of connection with the whole is created, the ultimate source of strength. (para. 16–17)

Here is another example from Native Americans: in many cultures (e.g., European and U.S. American) the view is that there are two genders. However, in many Native-American cultures it is believed that there are three or four genders; these genders are often viewed in a positive manner (Fledman, 2012; Jacobs, Thomas, & Lang, 1997).

It is of value for therapists to recognize that there are other views and to respect them. The two Native American views just presented are benign views. However, therapists should also recognize that there are views, both domestic and foreign, that can be faulty and hurtful. With all their faults, contemporary Western treatments are most often more benign in their approaches to mental illness/disorder than many other cultures.

COMMON ASSUMPTIONS IN COUNSELING

There are some approaches and techniques that counselors assume to be universally applicable that need to be examined. The evidence supporting the notion that these behaviors are necessary for improvements in therapy is still a moot point (Elliott, Greenberg, & Lietaer, 2004); nevertheless, they are often considered necessary core conditions for therapeutic improvement. This section of the book provides examples of approaches commonly used by U.S. trained counselors and some caveats in their application. It should be noted that a considerable amount has been written on using these approaches in culturally sensitive ways, and the reader is encouraged to examine the literature (Pedersen, Draguns, Lonner, & Trimble, 1996, 2002). The next exposition should not be construed as counselors are not to exhibit these behaviors or are not to have these feelings. They are presented here as examples of questioning basic assumptions – the assumptions could be correct or they may need to changed – but they certainly need to be examined.

Caring

Caring is a fundamental aspect of counseling. However, the definition of caring and the expressions of caring might not be shared by the client. Individuals and cultures define caring differently, e.g., providing food or direct advice might be signs of caring in some cultures; other cultures might consider it inappropriate for the counselor to engage in these behaviors. In some cultures listening and empathy might be indicative of caring, whereas in other cultures it might be indicative that the counselor is not dealing with the issues. People living under different economic conditions may have different perceptions of what constitutes caring. People in danger and without food might perceive caring in terms of their safety and whether or not they have food; whereas those who have their security and biological needs met might perceive caring as someone who will listen to them. In more affluent developed countries, clients might define good and caring services based on counselors' characteristics such as their sexual orientation, ethnicity, disabilities, veteran status, gender, religion, and drug and alcohol experience. They might also define caring in terms of whether the service is provided by a doctoral or master level counselor or psychologist, or by a psychiatrist, social worker, psychiatric nurse, child specialist, AIDS specialist, family specialist, and so on. In summary, definitions of caring and counseling can differ with individuals, cultures, and circumstances.

Empathy

Empathy is often considered crucial for counselors to exhibit (Gladstein, 1987; Goldstein & Michaels, 1985; Hackney, 1978; Marangoni, Garcia, Ickes, & Teng, 1995; Parloff, Waskow, & Wolfe, 1978). There are studies indicating the therapeutic effectiveness of empathy (Neumann, Bensing, Mercer, Ernstmann, Ommen, & Pfaff, 2009). Other studies call to question its effectiveness as well as that of the other core conditions espoused by Rogerians and person-centered therapists (Mitchell, Bozarth, and Krauft, 1977; Lambert & Bergin, 1994). Parloff, Waskow, and Wolfe (1978), and Duan and Hill, (1996) reported the results of studies on empathy are mixed and inconsistent.

Authors have also written about some of the problems with the use of empathy in psychotherapy (Gladstein, 1987; Goldstein & Michaels, 1985). Even though empathy can be a desirable quality for a counselor to have, there can be differences between counselors and clients in their definitions and perceptions, and the effects it has on clients can differ (Bachelor, 1988). Also, the counselor's empathic feelings could be based on an inaccurate reflection of the client's experience and feelings (Hollan, 2008; Kirmayer, 2008), and some clients may view it as intrusive and as an attack (Groark, 2008; Hollan, 2008). It is the client's perception rather than the counselor intentions or behaviors that matter in terms of what is considered empathetic and what constitutes a therapeutic relationship (Bachelor, 1995). There are studies that indicated that empathy and other facilitative conditions are not sufficient unless under specific conditions (Bergin & Suinn, 1975). Lambert and Bergin (1992) reported that it might be relevant for milder problems rather than for the severe ones.

Feelings

In many forms of counseling, getting the client to express and deal with feelings and emotions is considered critical (Brems, 2000; Carkhuff, 1987; Egan, 2002; Hackney, 2008; Haney & Leibsohn, 1999; McHenry, 2006; Meier & Davis, 2004; Phillipsen, 2004; Reiter, 2007; Seligman, 2008). Clients are encouraged to fathom their feelings during counseling. People who do not emote are often considered to have deficits in this area, especially men, who have been characterized as lacking in their expression of emotions (Fanning & McKay, 1993; Levant & Kopecky, 1995; Osherson, 1986; Pasick, 1992; Pittman, 1993; Pollack, 1998; Real, 1997). People who inadequately express their feelings might be considered to be ignorant of what they are suppose to do in counseling, lacking in basic human skills, or resistant to counseling. However, Sommers and Satel (2005) wrote, "recent findings suggest that reticence and suppression of feelings, far from compromising one's psychological well-being, can be healthy and adaptive" (p. 7). They stated that one of the effects of the work of psychologists is to decrease clients' self-reliance and de-crease self-control. They wrote that therapism (their term) has increased dependence on therapists, increased self-centeredness, and pathologized trauma. They stated that schools and others are involved in facilitating and perpetuating this process and that whole industries have been developed over trauma. The authors recommend that therapists develop the client's strengths and resilience rather than developing emotionality and vulnerabilities; working on vulnerabilities and deficits can lead to pessimism and negative views.

Therapists should keep in mind that one of the main functions of therapy is to use elements that are of treatment value. The exploration of feeling in and of itself may or may not be of therapeutic value. However, some approaches to counseling routinely consider this as one of the goals of therapy rather than considering it to be one of the tools in their repertoire.

In addition to the problems revolving around emoting, there are the problems of the expression, interpretation, and function of feelings. The counselor cannot assume these are similar to the counselor's. The counselor cannot assume that the investigation and catharsis of feelings is of equal therapeutic value for everyone. There has to be awareness that its effects are dependent on the individual rather than on whether or not the individual can emote and whether the counselor can elicit expressions of feelings. The studies of cultural variations in the function, roles, and expressions of feelings show that these vary (Eid & Diener, 2001; Markus & Kitayama, 1991; Mesquita & Frijda, 1992; Suh, Diener, Oishi, & Triandis, 1998). For example, there is evidence that people in Western and Asian cultures may react differently to happiness. Leu, Wang, and Koo (2011) studied a mix of Asian immigrants, Asian American, and European American college students. They found positive emotions helped the European American students deal with stress and depression. However, they found no such relationships with Asian students. In many Asian cultures, feelings of happiness may not correlate directly with depression because of concerns it could lead to subsequent feelings of jealousy and disharmony with friends and family. It is likely that there are individuals in Western cultures whose happiness is muted by concerns that these feeling will incur jealousy and resentment in others, and there are those in Eastern cultures whose happiness does indeed lessen the effects of depression.

Even though the experiencing of emotions is universal, counselors cannot assume that emoting is necessary, that they understand and correctly interpret the various expressions, or that it serves the same function for all individuals. It would be beneficial for counselors to be aware that the role emotions play in counseling is an expression of their own personality, culture, and society.

Insight and Nondirectiveness

Insight and nondirectiveness are the cornerstones of many Western psychological techniques. However, it cannot be assumed that these are necessary and sufficient for therapy to be effective with everyone. Prince (2004) worked with Yoruba (a Nigerian cultural group) patients and found the psychotherapeutic techniques – such as insight and nondirectiveness – he had been taught in Canada were culturally-bound and of limited therapeutic value. He found the client's insight of earlier childhood experiences was not helpful in treating the presenting problems. The client's explanation of the problem and the client's remedy had more of a therapeutic effect than nondirective, insight techniques. Cao (2009) studied the psychological reactance of Chinese students' impression of directive and nondirective approaches. Findings suggested that brief, solution-focused, and directive therapy was most effective.

The possibility that insight and nondirectiveness may not be universally applicable is common knowledge among some psychological schools of thought. In North America and Europe, there are therapists, e.g., Behaviorists, who do not consider insight and nondirectiveness as a necessary condition for therapeutic change. They focus on changing behaviors that are presented and on using direct communications with the client. The variations seen in the different schools of psychology could reflect variations in individuals and societies; therefore, some individuals and societies may do better with insight and nondirective approaches, and others may not.

Intentions

One basic aspect of counseling is the role intentions play: it is generally accepted that counselors should have *good* intentions when they engage in counseling. This is certainly commendable and valued. If they do not act in "good faith," there are undesirable professional, ethical, and legal ramifications. It is understood that when the client perceives that the counselor has good intentions, rapport is more likely to develop, and the client is more likely to accept interventions. However, this approach also has its problems. A considerable amount of human interactions occur under the auspices of good intentions and benevolence – often with dire consequences (Freire, 1972). For example, the Europeans introduced the inquisition to China and South America (Green, 2009) and had other intended and unintended effects such as the destruction of endogenous systems, the spread of disease, and the introduction of unhealthy life styles (Bullock & Bell, 2005; Robertson, 2001; Watts, 1999). When countries invade other countries, it is often under the guise of benevolence, e.g., liberation for the invaded country. When products are sold, it is often under such rationale of introducing modernity, or making life easier for the buyer, though it often brings more income to the seller. Writing as an economist, Moyo (2009) wrote that foreign aid to Africa has perpetuated the cycle of poverty and dependency, fostered corruption, hindered economic growth, fueled inflation, increased debt burdens, and inhibited entrepreneurship. She is not against aid to Africa, but she wrote that it should be short-term and it should serve the function of the development of self-sustaining economic development. She wrote that African countries do not need pity and sympathy. What they need is economic development, the building of infrastructure, and job opportunities. If we applied her ideas to mental health services, counselors might be of greater value if they developed indigenous self-help skills and systems to replace the counselor rather than foster dependence.

Therapists have a lot to contribute. However, they may not be aware of the detrimental effects of what they are doing. They may not be aware of the detrimental effects of a diagnosis. They may not be aware that they could be eroding the client's problem-solving skills. They may not be aware that they may be increasing alienation between the client and the community. They may not be aware that they are introducing the client into a psychological and drug industry. They may not be aware of the flaws of the psychotherapy they are providing, e.g., the research upon which the therapy is provided is based on questionable statistics and on samples that may be different from the client's.

It is also possible that the therapist's benevolent intentions have benign and helpful effects. Nevertheless, the client might still view the counselor and the counselor' services with suspicion and avoidance. They are many possible reasons for this, e.g., the client may view the expressions of good intentions as a false façade, or it takes time it takes time to develop a trusting relationship with some people. Therefore, whatever the counselor's good and commendable intentions, it warrants to be aware that it may not be perceived as such.

Listening

Listening seems to be an innocuous, universal, positive approach to use. It obviously should be done. It is a significant method of obtaining information and having the client feel the counselor is attending to what is being conveyed. However, some cultures may vary in the amount of listening that the counselor is expected to engage in. Not only might there be variation in the amount of listening, but there can be differences in what to expect after that listening – e.g., the client may expect to be told what to do (Jo, 2005). Uzoka (1983) studied Nigerian students and staff at a university psychological service center. Therapy was provided by either an active or passive counselor: highly verbal and directive compared to minimal verbal and directive interactions. Results indicated that participants with the active counselor had significantly greater verbalization, attended significantly more therapy sessions, and showed greater self-disclosure than those with the passive counselor. Individuals in all cultures can have different expectations in terms of the amount of listening that is consider productive and what to expect after the listening.

Number of Sessions

Clients differ in their expectations of the number of sessions needed for therapeutic effectiveness (Owen, Smith, & Rodolfa, 2009). Some domestic clients and people in various cultures expect quick answers because they view the counselor as the expert and therefore can readily provide answers. The client might consider long-term therapy as a ploy for the therapist to make more money or as an indication of the counselor's inaptitude. A cliché among therapists is that it took at long time for the client to learn the dysfunctional behavior; therefore, it will take a long time to learn new and different ways of thinking and feeling. However, there are indications that more sessions does not necessarily mean greater improvement (Barkham et al., 2006; Fiorentine, 2001). The best predictor of how many sessions clients will attend is the client's expectation of the length of therapy (Mueller & Pekarik, 2000). Most U.S. clients attend between eight and ten sessions (Lowry & Ross, 1997). About 35–40 percent do not return by the third session, and 70 percent do not return by the tenth session (Mueller & Pekarik, 2000). Therapeutic effectiveness also varies. Some studies indicate therapy can be effective after three sessions (Davidson & Horvath, 1997), and other studies indicate it can be effective after five and a half hours. Couples and family therapy research indicated that the rate of improvement and number of sessions needed for therapeutic gains depended on the type of problems, characteristics of partners, and focus of treatment (Barkham et al., 2006; Lowry & Ross, 1997). The same can be said of therapeutic effectiveness in general: the number of counseling sessions needed to make therapeutic changes varies based on the type of problem, client characteristics, and therapeutic approach.

Resistance

Counselors should be aware of their reactions to clients who are not receptive or who exhibit reticence to engage in counseling and therapy. The mental health professional might attribute these behaviors to shortcomings or negative qualities of the client, e.g., the client has deficits in social, relational, or communication skills – or the client might be perceived as being resistant, or defensive. U.S. males are often said to have deficits in these areas and to be more resistant to counseling (Allen, 1993; Bar-Levav, 1988; Carlson, 1980; Flood, 2008; Frey, 1997; Gray, 1992; Kindlon & Thompson, 2000; Kundtz, 2004; Oliver, 1993; Shields, 2002; Sieverding, 2009; Ussher, 2010). Unwillingness or inability to engage in counseling could reflect variability in human responses; not everyone has to like or have the same ability to engage in counseling. Resistance may be influenced by clients having different values in terms of self-disclosure and help-seeking. It may reflect negative experiences with previous counselors, transference issues, or discomfort because of the counselor's gender, ethnicity, or sexual orientation. There can be other factors: clients may be reluctant to relinquish the control that is entailed in counseling; they may not like the prospect of the counselor evaluating them; they might not like to engage in activities in which the counselor is more skilled at performing; they are involved in a process that takes effort, expenditure of time – and often money; there could be discomfort and uncertainly as to how counselors will react to information that is divulged (for example, the counselor might be judgmental or report to others of what has been revealed); clients may be resistant because of lack of confidence in what a counselor can do – for example, many people who commit suicide have seen therapists, and clients with anxiety, depression, addiction, and other disorders have had treatment but have not been cured.

What can be done with reticent clients? It may be of value to hold judgment in abeyance, gain a better understanding of the client, and work with the client to determine what role the counselor can play. We could also consider resistance as a topic that both the client and counselor can engage in to induce further counseling interactions. One way to start such an interaction would be to view resistance as a healthy sign, at least for some individuals. Resistance could indicate good ego-strength as well as desire to problem-solve and work independently.

Effectiveness

The preceding are just some of the many examples of factors to consider in counseling. Similar issues can be raised concerning the effectiveness of ameliorating problems that counselors deal with. As with many areas of counseling and psychology, there are differences in opinion and interpretation of data, concepts, and results. Prout, Chard, Nowak-Drabik, and Johnson (2000) stated "The effectiveness of psychotherapy has been a controversial issue among mental health professionals for many years" (para. 1). Truax and Carkhuff (2008) wrote, "A considerable amount of evidence also seems to suggest that counseling or psychotherapy is not superior to 'no treatment'" (p. 5).

An editorial review of Truax and Carkhuff's *Toward Effective Counseling and Psychotherapy* (2008) stated this:

> The field of counseling and psychotherapy has for years presented the puzzling spectacle of unabating enthusiasm for forms of treatment whose effectiveness cannot be objectively demonstrated. With few exceptions, statistical studies have consistently failed to show that any form of psychotherapy is followed by significantly more improvement than would be caused by the mere passage of an equivalent period of time (Aldine Transaction, 2008).

Many statements about the effectiveness of psychotherapy in general can be said about specific disorders. Cutler and Fishbain (2005) reviewed the studies on Project MATCH (Matching Alcoholism Treatments to Client Heterogeneity). This was the largest and most expensive alcoholism treatment trial ever conducted. It was sponsored by the National Institute on Alcohol Abuse and Alcoholism, conducted over eight years on multiple sites. They found psychosocial treatments for alcoholism were not notably effective. In another area of treatment, grief counseling, Konigsberg (2011) presented extensive research indicating there is no evidence that counseling is any more effective than the passage of time in dealing with grief. The findings of these lines of research are surprising because society and counselors usually accept as a truisms that alcohol and grief counseling are effective. For alcohol and grief, it is commonly believed that counseling will improve recovery, and for grief therapy, it is believed that counseling might decrease posttraumatic stress. For alcohol, it is believed that counseling might decrease relapse. These studies call to question some of our assumptions of the effectiveness of counseling.

The concerns about the effectiveness of therapy, along with the issues mentioned in the section of this book titled "Are U.S. Approaches the Most Appropriate?", are reminders that despite the fact that we have more specialists, books, articles, research, data, sophisticated statistical techniques, and mental health professionals, this should not misguide us to believe that we are correspondingly more effective; in some areas we are more effective, in other areas we are not. The issues raised about the effectiveness of therapy provide challenges to continue to explore and be open to ideas.

Barriers

In addition to the usual barriers to counseling services such as costs, availability of services, and reluctance to use services, there are other barriers. Counseling is oriented by and for the U.S. middle-class (Balmforth, 2009; Estrella, 2010; Graff, Kenig, & Radoff, 1971; Liu, Soleck, Hopps, Dunston, & Pickett, 2004; Lott, 2002; Moskowitz, 1996; Nelson, Englar-Carlson, Tierney,

& Hau, 2006; Newton, 2010; Smith, 2010; Strupp & Bloxom, 1973; Thompson, 1989; Trevithick, 1998). Sue and Sue (1977) wrote about generic characteristics of counseling third-world groups. They found three variables that hinder counseling with third-world groups: language variables, class-bound values, and culture-bound values. These variables are also relevant to counseling many groups and individuals in the U.S.

1. Language variables. Counselors are trained to use "white," middle-class standard English and verbal communication. This may impede interactions with those of the lower class and of different ethnicity.
2. Class-bound values. Counselors work with strict time schedules, ambiguity, and long-range solutions. Those of other classes and ethnicity might not place as much emphasis on schedules; in sessions they may expect clarity and immediate solutions.
3. Culture-bound values. Counselors are individual centered, and expect verbal/emotional/behavioral expressiveness, client to counselor communication, openness and intimacy, cause-effect orientation, and mental and physical well-being distinction. Those of other classes and ethnicity might be more oriented toward the family and community; they may not feel comfortable with verbal, emotional, intimate expressions; they may differ in their perceptions of what are the causes and effects of problems; and they may feel the mental and physical are more intertwined than what the counselor believes.

Change

Getting people to change is one of the cornerstones of therapy. It is also of interest to many other groups, e.g., business groups want consumers to buy their products, religious groups want converts, politicians want citizens to accept their views, and agricultural agents want farmers to change their farming methods. These and other groups have a plethora of methods to bring about change – e.g., through advertisements, education, propaganda, publicity, demonstrations, and literature. One group that has substantial experience trying to bring about behavioral changes is the religious community. Their experiences provide an illustration of the dynamics of why people change. Barro and Hwang's (2007) investigated religious conversions in 40 countries and found that people are likely to convert to another religion where there is religious pluralism and where there are no government restrictions to conversions. They also found conversions were more likely among those with more education. The potential convert looked at such factors as what are the advantages of converting – the "payoffs"? How much nurturance and guidance will the convert receive? And will there be support for the new behaviors? A possible application of these ideas to therapy would be to educate clients about the problem, let clients know the advantages of changing the behavior, determine the obstacles to therapeutic changes, help clients as they make the changes, and provide support for the new behaviors.

Rambo (1995) is another author who examined religious conversations. The author interviewed converts and researched the psychological, sociological, anthropological, historical, theological, and missiological literature. He found personal, cultural, social, and religious factors were involved when making changes. Rambo presented the stages of changes as opening oneself to new options; wanting a resolution to a problem that makes change seem attractive; meeting the agent who embodies the religious vision; learning new roles, rituals, and rhetoric; and committing oneself to a new way of life.

Prochaska and his colleagues (Prochaska & DiClemente, 2005; Prochaska, Norcross, & DiClemente, 1994; Prochaska, Redding, & Evers, 2008) developed a transtheoretical model of behavioral change (for a critique, see Bridle et al., 2005). They wrote that people go through the following stages when making changes: precontemplation stage – people are not thinking about changing; contemplation stage – they recognize there is a problem and weigh the pros and cons of their behaviors; preparation stage – they intend to change; action stage – they make efforts to change; maintenance stage – they try to prevent relapse; and termination stage – they have been successful in making the changes permanent.

Castonguay and Beutler (2005) reported the findings of the Joint Presidential Task Force of the Society of Clinical Psychology (Division 12 of APA) and of the North American Society for Psychotherapy Research. The mandate of the task force was to examine the empirical data on treatments that work. They delineated over 61 principles for applying treatments to four problem areas: dysphoric disorders, anxiety disorders, personality disorders, and substance abuse disorders. The joint task force identified aspects of patients, counselors, relationships, and treatments that contribute to successful outcomes. Among the principles that facilitate successful counselor and client therapeutic change were the following: flexibility, ability to tolerate ambiguity, and tolerance of negative responses to others. Detrimental indices for client recovery included the negative effects of those with personality disorders, lack of adequate social support, and chaotic history of severe problems. Principles that facilitated therapeutic change consisted of the counselor and client working collaboratively as well as the counselor's skill in forming a therapeutic alliance. The interventions that are more successful were the ones that adjusted to the unique qualities of the client and the client's environment.

Concerning therapeutic change, Trevifio (1996) researched anthropological and counseling studies and found the common mechanisms of change in all counseling and therapy. Citing Cliaborn (1986) and Frank and Frank (1991), she offered two principles. First, she wrote that worldviews mediate therapeutic changes. Often, the client's problems are the result of ineffective aspects of a worldview. The resolution to the problems is not limited to any particular approach to therapy, e.g., it does not matter whether it is a cognitive, behavioral, or affective approach. The second principle involves congruence; that is, when there is incongruence between the counselor and the client, therapeutic changes can occur because the client will make changes to be congruent with the counselor (e.g., counselor's attitude, style, locus of control; perceptions of problems and solutions). Congruency (also known as consistency) theory proposes that people are uncomfortable with cognitive dissonance. For example, they like their values, attitudes, beliefs, and behaviors to be consistent. If they are inconsistent (different), then they try to change, or rationalize, their inconsistencies. The model for change entails the following. The client forms a worldview from personal experiences that are made of shared cultural and unique experiences. General levels of abstraction and specific views differentiate worldviews. There is congruence between the various levels; one affects the other. Change is facilitated when the counselor and client are congruent at the general level and incongruent at the specific level. When there is congruence at the general level, then good communication, empathy, and understanding may be in effect. When there is incongruence on a specific level, e.g., a problematic behavior, then this may facilitate the client to change to the counselor's perspectives and solutions. Trevifio (1996) wrote that therapeutic changes occur when the client's specific perception of the problematic behavior is changed, but the general cultural worldviews are not changed. The counselor does not impose on the client's cultural views but provides alternative views and solutions to the client's problem. One of the examples Trevifio provided was of a student who was upset and depressed. The student was overextended in helping others (specific problem) and as a result was failing in school and experiencing health problems. The student's general view (worldview) was that the self and group are interdependent. Instead of framing the solution as the student had to withdraw from group activities to deal with the stress, the counselor presented the perspective that in order for the student to help the group, the student had to take care of self. In this case, the counselor did not change the student's worldview (the group and self are intertwined) but offered another view that was incongruent with the student's perspective: taking care of self also takes care of the group. To minimize the incongruence, the student might then assume the counselor's perspective – and take care of self.

There is abundant literature, especially in the cross-cultural area, about the difficult issues involved in helping people change, acculturate, adapt, and adjust (Berry & Sam, 1997; Brislin, 1981; Furukawa & Shibayama, 1995; Gao & Gudykunst, 1990; Matsumoto, Hirayama, & LeRoux, 2006; Matsumoto, Yoo,

& LeRoux, 2010; Pederson, 1995; Stone & Ward, 1990; Ward, 2001; Yoo, Matsumoto, & LeRoux, 2006). These concerns and problems are well-founded. However, changing and adapting does not necessarily have to be traumatic. We should be cautious that we are not defining natural phenomena, such as change, as necessarily traumatic. The experience of change is not foreign to most peoples and cultures of the world. Change is a part of the human condition. Changes occur in a number of different ways and for many reasons. For example, outsiders can come into communities and introduce ideas that bring about changes; people can leave their communities and return with new ideas; and they can learn from education, the Internet, friends, and relatives in other places. From these interactions people learn new religions and perspectives as well as hunting, agricultural, and pottery techniques. People also experience changes in vegetation, temperature, and activity with the seasons. People experience changes when they leave and enter families and communities, e.g., through marriage. They experience change as they go through the developmental stages; there are biological, physical, psychological, and physical changes. People's roles and functions change as they go through life – from a child who is looked after, to an adult who looks after others. Those around them are also changing; children grow to be adolescents, significant life partners enter and leave their lives, friends and relatives change, and people get old. If we expect change to be difficult and we convey this to the client, then we may be making change more difficult. Of course, reactions to change are predicated on the client's characteristics and the type of change entailed. It is clear that within societies there are those who are open to change; some are ambivalent and some are resistant. Change can entail new and better experiences. It can add to one's quilt of life. It can entail learning better or different ways to deal with problems.

Even though the previous discussion focused mainly on the psychological and social aspect of change, it should be noted that the initiation and maintenance of behavioral changes also involve neurological and chemical factors. Environmental factors (such as drugs and stress) facilitate neurochemical changes and neurochemical factors (such as dopamine) facilitate behavioral changes. The types of changes that occur in the brain depend on what changes are being made, e.g., perceptual, motor, and cognitive changes effect the corresponding areas of the brain. Part of the process in inducing change is to modify patterns of thinking, feeling, and behaving; in other words, changing habits. Studies in the areas of habit formation (Duhigg, 2012; Wickens, Horvitz, Costa, & Killcross, 2007; Wood & Neal, 2007; Yin & Knowlton, 2006), addictions (Chou & Narasimhan, 2005; Everitt, Belin, Economidou, Pelloux, Dalley, & Robbins, 2008), and obsessive-compulsive disorders and other neurological disorders (Berthier, Kulisevsky, Gironell, & Heras, 1996; Bloom, Beal, & Kupfer, 2008) help provide information on the brain structures and activities involved in behavioral changes. The cortical areas of the brain, the basal ganglia, and the dopaminergic system are among the many neurological aspects of the brain involved in behavior. Many of our beliefs, actions and reactions, and ways of perceiving are habitual and thus we may not be aware that they are automatically occurring. Duhigg (2012) wrote that there are three aspects to habit formation – stimulus, response, and reward; changing any of these can bring about changes.

TESTS

The uses and definitions of tests are multiple and diverse. Among the definitions of the word "test" (Merriam-Webster, 2010) are the following: a critical examination, observation, or evaluation; specifically, the procedure of submitting a statement to such conditions or operations as will lead to its proof or disproof or to its acceptance or rejection a test of a statistical hypothesis; also: something, as a series of questions or exercises, for measuring the skill, knowledge, intelligence, capacities, or aptitudes of an individual or group. The term "assess" is one of the synonyms for "test." Among the definitions for "assess" (Merriam-Webster, 2010) are the following: to determine the importance, size, or value of a problem.

Tests have long played a role in human history. In mythology, many cultures have heroes who undergo tests of strengths, loyalty, worthiness, determination, and courage (Campbell, 1959). Societies often have tests in the form of rites of passages when people move from one stage of their lives to another (Frazer, 1922). The use of tests has a long tradition in preparing, evaluating, and predicting behavior, e.g., in 551 B.C.–478 B.C., China had civil service exams to determine who would work for the government (Han, 1946). Cultures often have apprenticeships in which there is the teaching of skills at different stages of development, and there is an assessment of the apprentice's skills to determine suitability for the next stage of training. Tests are prevalent in many areas of society and for varied purposes, e.g., there are pregnancy, metallurgy, rocket, employment, lab, paternity, soil, drug, and genetic tests. Almost all fields have methods of testing products, services, and materials. Tests are a means to operationalize concepts and values. They are a method to obtain feedback of whether goals are met.

Tests have also been used to interpret and predict behaviors, e.g., projective and aptitude tests. The interpretation and prediction of phenomena has a long history across many cultures, e.g., Chrisomalis (2007) lists 163 ways people in many cultures, at various times have used to divine phenomena, from acultomancy, aeromancy, ailuromancy, alectormancy, alectryomancy, aleuromancy, and alomancy, to tyromancy, uranomancy, urimancy, xenomancy, xylomancy, and zoomancy.

The start of modern psychological tests is often associated with Francis Galton and Alfred Binet (Neill, 2005). Galton, in the late 1800s, studied individual differences. Binet developed an IQ test in the early 1900s to determine which students needed special help. Most proponents of theories of personality have inventories, tests, surveys, forms, assessments, etc. to operationalize their concepts. There are many psychological and personality tests in this country and in the world, e.g., typing the term "personality test" in an Internet search engine (Google) resulted in 46,100,000 hits. There are many kinds and uses of tests in psychology and counseling, e.g., there are tests of personality, IQ, mental disorders, career exploration, and learning. They are used to measure accountability. As an example: are the teachers and counselors effective? They are used to assessment progress. For instance, how much are clients learning, and is the treatment working? They are used for comparisons, e.g., how do the client's symptoms, interests, values, and abilities compare with others and to self? They can provide algorithms as a method to insure fairness, e.g., is everyone being evaluated the same way?

There are beneficial and detrimental aspects to the use of tests in therapy. The abuse of tests has a long history, and there are continuous calls bringing this to our attention (Eyde, Robertson, & Krug, 2009; Gould, 1981; Groth-Marnat, 2009; Kaplan & Saccuzzo, 2009; McIntire & Miller, 2007; Paul, 2004; Vassaf, 1982; Watkins & Campbell, 2000). Hopefully, the history of abuse makes counselors more sensitive to the misuse of tests and will provide information on how to use them in an ethical and beneficial fashion.

Tests can serve useful functions in therapy. For those who are uncomfortable with ambiguity, tests can provide figures, charts, and statements. They can provide data that can be analyzed and critiqued. They can serve as a means to view people, e.g., the NEO PI-R provides information from the perspective of the Five-Factor theory (Costa & McCrae, 1992). The Personality Research Form provides information about the person's traits and behaviors (Jackson, 1997), and the Wechsler Intelligence Scale for Children (Wechsler, 2003) provides information about memory and comprehension. These provide information on similarities and differences among people. They provide the client with information about their strengths and weakness and how their characteristics compare with others. Tests normed on one culture when applied to another culture can indicate areas of similarities and differences. Projective tests can be a way to access the client's perceptions, e.g., the Rorschach inkblot test has the client respond to what they see on inkblot plates. If people in one culture see a tree on an inkblot and people of another culture see a kangaroo, this can provide information on differences in perceptions. With the Thematic Apperception Test, the client is asked to tell a story of pictures that are shown to them. Such a test can provide information about what people think and feel in certain situations. Similarly, if a client answers "true" to a test question such as: "I see things others do not see," this could provide a basis for a follow-up inquiry about the client perspectives.

Many problems are associated with applications of tests across cultures (e.g., Butcher, 2009; Eshun & Gurung, 2009; Fernandez-Ballesteros, 2003; Ferraro, 2001; Geisinger, 2003; Hambleton, Merenda, & Spielberger, 2005; Hays, 2008; Lee, Blando, Mizelle, & Orozco, 2007; Lim, 2006; Loue & Sajatovic, 2008; Moskowitz & Stephens, 2004; Paniagua, 2005). For example, there are problems associated with translations, and differences in concepts and terms.

In terms of mental illness, even though there is general agreement that people in all cultures have mental illness (Mezzich, Honda, & Kastrup, 1994; Sartorius & Ustun, 1995; World Health Organization, 2005), there is less agreement on how to measure it. In addition to the usual problems of applying tests developed in one culture to other cultures – such as problems in using comparable terms and concepts, clinical tests run into such problems as differing definitions of normality and psychopathology.

There are a number of ways to help promote the constructive and beneficial use of tests. One way is to educate clients in their use. Another way is to enlist the help of the public in the development and use of tests. The enhanced transparency as to why and how tests are used might increase the public's acceptance of tests. Tests can provide a means for analyzing, critiquing, modifying, and building subsequent information.

DIAGNOSTIC PRACTICES

In a previous section of this book on "Classifications of Mental Illness," the problems associated with the use of classification systems such as the *DSM* was mentioned. In addition, there are other problems that can occur when making diagnoses (Corning, 1986; Davis, 1979; Dawes, 1994, 2001; Dumont & LeComte, 1987; Farber, 1975; Faust, 1986; Frances et al., 1991; Gilovich, 1991; Goodyear & Parish, 1978; Gove, 1982; Hays, McLeod, & Prosek, 2009; Kendell, 1975; Langer & Abelson, 1974; Lehmann, Joy, Kreisman & Simmens, 1976; Link & Cullen, 1990; Link, Cullen, Struening, Shrout, & Dohrenwend, 1989; Lopez, 1989; Millon, 1991; Morey, 1991b; Murphy, 1976; Nisbett, Borgida, Crandall, & Reed, 1976; Nisbett & Ross, 1980; Ruscio, 2004; Scheff, 1974; Skinner, Berry, Griffith, & Byers, 1995; Spitzer, 1975; 1976; Sushinsky & Wener, 1975; Swets, Dawes, & Monahan, 2000; Szasz, 1961; Temerlin, 1968; Trierweiler, Muroff, Jackson, Neighbors, & Munday, 2005).

Some aspects and problems in making diagnoses include the following.

Counselors may define behaviors as aberrant based on the limited paradigms of their profession and culture (Kuhn, 1962). They may be so embedded in their culture that they may not realize that many of their perceptions are based on the time period they are in, as well as the values of their society – and if these are changed, definitions and perceptions can change. For example, cocaine use (other than through prescription) is considered unacceptable behavior in the United States. But in some South American Indian cultures, cocaine was considered a gift from the gods, and it is still being used as an energizer and to ward off feelings of hunger (Karch, 1997). Epilepsy was considered a spiritual ailment or a gift of the gods in some cultures (e.g., Fadiman, 1997; Temkin, 1971), but now it is considered a neurological problem. Not being able to sleep for eight hours at a time is considered a problem in developed countries. People who live in other cultures might consider it normal to have intermittent sleep during the night (Bower, 1999; Buijs et al., 1996; Jones et al., 1999; Travis, 1999; Worthman & Melby, 2002). At night they may need to attend to fires, take care of babies and animals, and engage in other activities such as maintaining vigilance against predators and lurking enemies. At one time in the United States shyness, social withdrawal, anxiousness, anger, fear of snakes, emotionality, and a myriad of other problems were considered personality characteristics or eccentricities. Nowadays, we view these as clinical symptoms of social phobia, depression, anxiety, impulse control, specific phobia, and histrionic personality disorders that require treatment by specialists (Caplan, 1995; Dawes, 1997; Dineen, 2001; Horwitz, 2002; Kutchins & Kirk, 1997; Lane, 2007; Rosenhan, 1973, 1975; Szasz, 1997). These differences indicate that definitions of problems can vary with time and culture. It is understandable and natural for therapists to cater to the definitions and behaviors endorsed by their profession and society. Some authors discuss this in terms of the role of therapists as agents of social control (Krasner & Ullman, 1965; Schorr, 1985, 1987; Stolz, 1978). However, therapists need to distinguish between behaviors that are pathological forms of mental illness from those that are dysfunctional in the context of society.

There is evidence that mental health professionals can differ in their approaches and diagnoses of the same problem. For example, in diagnosing Attention Deficit/Hyperactivity Disorder, Handler and DuPaul (2005) found clinical, counseling, and school psychologists differed in their use of the *Diagnostic and Statistical Manual of Mental Disorders*, diagnostic criteria, use of clinical interviews, and behaviors that are observed to make a diagnosis. Similar diagnostic differences have been found when physicians make diagnoses. In addition, regional differences have been found (Song et al. 2010).

Not only can there be diagnostic differences, there is also the phenomenon where the counselor's diagnoses could have an iatrogenic effect; that is, the counselor's inaccurate diagnoses inadvertently produces an adverse effect. The counselor could be involved in confabulation and could be inducing false memories (Koss, Tromp, & Tharan, 1995; Loftus & Ketcham, 1994; Loftus & Pickrell, 1995; Pezdek, Finger & Hodge, 1997). For example, in terms of post-traumatic stress disorder (PTSD), some counselors might assume that being exposed to combat induces psychological problems and if a client exhibits problems, the counselor might attribute it to PTSD, or if the client does not exhibit problems, then the counselor might attribute the absence of problems to repression, suppression, and denial when in fact the person's problems could be attributed to factors other than PTSD. Another possibility is that the person's lack of problems might be attributed to the client being able to successfully deal with the trauma of combat and therefore not experience PTSD. This is evidenced in the considerable research indicating people in other countries might be affected by PTSD differently (Baggaley, Piper, Cumming, & Murphy, 1999; Creamer, Burgess, & McFarlane, 2001; Department of Veterans Affairs, 2001; Greenberg, Iversen, Hull, Bland, & Wessely, 2008; Litz, Orsillo, Friedman, Ehlich, & Batres, 1997; Richardson, Frueh, & Acierno, 2010; Sandweiss et al., 2011; Pearn, 2000; Shigemura & Nomura, 2002). In situations such as these, counselors should be careful that they are not prompting the client to define as a problem a condition that is not a problem.

Studies indicate that mental health professionals often diagnose clients on factors other than clinical characteristics. For example, Schwartz, Perlman, Paris, Schmidt, and Thornton (1980) found diagnoses were sometimes based on where the diagnoses were being sent and how they were to be used. This resulted in unreliability and differential diagnoses. Strickland, Jenkins, Myers, and Adams (1988) found white therapists tended to underrate pathology of black clients, and black therapists tended to overrate pathology of white clients. Results were mixed for black therapists' ratings of black clients. Baskin, Bluestone, and Nelson (1981) studied patients in psychiatric outpatient clinics. They found black patients were more often diagnosed as schizophrenic and were given more severe diagnoses, and Hispanic-American patients were more likely to be diagnosed with depression. Li-Repac (1980) had Chinese-American and white therapists score the same Chinese and white clients. Results indicated white therapists rated Chinese clients as having more depression and inhibition, and lower on social poise and interpersonal capacity. Chinese-American therapists rated white clients as more severely disturbed. This tendency to diagnose clients differentially based on characteristics other than clinical symptoms has been found with other groups as well. For example, Caplan and Cosgrove's (2004) studies indicated there was bias in therapists' diagnoses because of the clients' gender, ethnicity, age, mental retardation, income, and learning disability. They also found bias against children and against women from rural areas.

These are just some of the many problems associated with the *DSM* and those who diagnose (Bayer, 1981; Breggin, 1994; Caplan, 1995; Caplan & Cosgrove, 2004; Cockerham, 2010; Colby, 1983; Coryell, Lowery, & Wasek, 1980; Foucault, 1988; Kaplan, 1971; Kim & Ahn, 2002; Kirk & Kutchins, 1992; Laing, 1986; Moore, Stunkard, & Srole, 1962; Muntaner, Borrell, & Chung, 2007; Plous, 1993; Poland, Von Eckardt, & Spaulding, 1994; Rosenhan, 1975; Ross, 1977; Rothblum, Solomon, & Albee, 1994; Rubinstein, 1995; Russell, 1986; Sarbin & Mancuso, 1980; Spitzer, 1975; Szasz, 2001; Whitaker, 2002; Wylie, 1995). The problems serve as caveats for therapists to be aware of the influences on them and the consequences of their diagnostic practices. Despite the enormous criticisms, diagnostic practices allow professionals to have a common method to categorize mental problems, to expedite the use of common terms in the perception and exchange of mental health information, and to facilitate the development of a systematize approach to mental problems that promote the accumulation, exchange, and modification of data. They are works in process.

WHY DOES A CLIENT INTERACT WITH THE COUNSELOR?

Many groups have persons who comfort, interpret, cure, mediate, provide herbs, and perform rituals to relieve discomfort (Bromberg, 1975). Exposure to these experiences can occur in the family setting and in the community. Therefore, clients may be familiar with aspects of counseling and have experienced helping and supportive behaviors prior to interactions with the counselor. However, it is not unusual for people to be suspicious, distrustful, and feel uncomfortable with therapists (Amada, 2001; Baptiste, Hardy, & Lewis, 1997; Gilman, King, Porter, Rousseau, & Showalter, 1993; Wittkower & Warms, 1974). Cultures vary in their perceptions of shamans, therapists, counselors, and people in similar roles. These people can be viewed as special people with special skills (Kehoe, 2000; Lee & Armstrong, 1995; Yeh, Hunter, Madan-Bahel, Chiang, & Arora, 2004), or as ordinary people with ordinary skills (Paper, 2007; Szimhart, 2008).

Knowledge of the reasons clients are in counseling can provide valuable information. Many factors can induce clients to engage in counseling, e.g., clients might seek counseling because society has defined certain behaviors as problems that need professional help – such as defining divorce as traumatic and something that needs counseling; clients may be in distress and interact with the counselor because the counselor is viewed as someone who specializes in dealing with the problem; clients may be referred by others because of perceived problems; clients may engage in counseling because they have been unsuccessful in treating themselves or with resources in their community. They also may seek services out of curiosity or because they want to learn or improve themselves. In terms of the latter factors, there is ample evidence that many people are interested in learning new and different treatment methods. For example, in Europe and the United States there are people interested in Eastern yoga and meditation. The opportunity to learn and explore appears to be a very basic aspect of many animals (Hayes, 1994). Montgomery (1954) found that the opportunity for rats to explore an unfamiliar area, with no food as a reward, could serve as a reward. Butler (1954) found that rhesus monkeys preferred to look at anything new rather than looking at familiar scenes. Harlow, Harlow, and Meyer (1950) found the opportunity to touch and manipulate objects could serve as a reward for rhesus monkeys. Exploration enables us to find better or alternative patterns of behavior. Therefore, seeking new therapies, with unfamiliar counselors, is within the behavioral repertoire of many people.

It would be desirable for counselor to understand the circumstances under which they are meeting with the client. Expectations and boundaries can be established. Concerns can be addressed; hindrances can be explored. Treatment can be directed to fit the client's needs.

POSSIBLE WAYS TO FRAME THE RELATIONSHIP

There are various roles and functions a counselor can play in a therapeutic relationship (Hou & Zhang, 2007). Counselors can consider which is the most efficacious framework to interact with the client. Counselors may assume the view that: (a) they are experts in providing help and information in regard to the presenting problem; (b) the client is temporarily in need of help in a particular area of life, and the counselor is a fellow human who is presently in a position to be able to help the client; (c) the client and counselor are engaged in an interaction to learn from each other; (d) the client has a deficit in an area, and the counselor is the provider of information and skills; (e) the client has a problem, and the counselor is a problem-solver; (f) the counselor's role and job is to help – that is, it is the counselor's professional role, or the counselor's agency function, to provide services for the client's problem; (g) the counselor has access to resources, e.g., the counselor can provide support for the obtaining of medications from a physician; (h) the counselor is a partner, consultant, or coach, (i) the counselor is a paid friend; and (j) and there are numerous other roles and functions that a counselor can assume. The framing of the relationship can help facilitate or hinder the therapeutic relationship. For example, if one is working with university students, and there is a stigma to receiving therapeutic services because there is an association with "mental illness," the relationship could be framed as the counselor is part of a problem-solving collage. That is, the student is being educated in school to be a problem-solver, as part of good problem-solving one has to gather information and consult with authorities on the problem. The counselor is an authority on the subject and can provide information; therefore, consult with a counselor. Counselors need to consider the framework within which they provide their services. They need to consider such factors as these: are they presenting treatment framed in a manner that benefits the counselor or the client; or what are the beneficial and detrimental aspects of using a particular framework?

THERAPEUTIC COMPLIANCE
(CONCORDANCE AND ADHERENCE)

Nowadays, the terms "concordance" and "adherence" (to what the counselor says) are preferred to the term "compliance." Compliance implies a power differential with the client complying to the therapist, whereas the term "concordance" has connotations of working together. The term "adherence" implies abiding to treatment plans. However, even though there are differences among the terms, they are often used interchangeably (Jin, Sklar, Oh, & Li, 2008). For the most part, the terms refer to the patient's behaviors coinciding with care providers' recommendations.

Therapeutic compliance has been an ongoing issue in the counseling, medicine, and psychology (Adler, 1999; Baune, Aljeesh, & Bender, 2005; Benfari, Eaker, & Stoll, 1981; Bezie, Molina, Hernandez, Batista, Niang, & Huet, 2006; Blackwell, 1997; Bosley, Fosbury, & Cochrane, 1995; Boudes, 1998; Cameron, 2008; Harris Interactive, 2005; Jung, Nam, Kam, Yeh, & Park, 2003; Jin, Sklar, Oh, & Li, 2008; Lee & Son, 1998; Loeb et al., 2005; Muller-Oerlinghausen, 1982; Pina-Lopze, & Sanchez-Sosa, 2007; Razali & Yahya, 1995; Russo, 2005; Sperry, 2006). Jin, Sklar, Oh, and Li (2008) reviewed compliance studies in biomedicine and health journals published in Medline: the United States National Library of Medicine's (2010) bibliographic database. They examined studies from 1970 to 2005, covering different diseases, population settings, and countries. They identified the following compliance factors that had wide generalizability. Compliance was more likely if the treatment was not invasive and simple. Long-term treatment and side effects might compromise compliance. Providers should work with the client to consider the barriers to compliance. Ready accessibility to services and satisfaction with services increased compliance. There was more compliance with problems that were acute and short in duration, whereas problems that were chronic, fluctuated, or had an absence of symptoms were less likely to have compliance. The financial cost of services could threaten compliance. They also discussed psychosocial factors such as patient's beliefs, attitude towards therapy, and motivation to engage in therapy as affecting compliance. Those with chronic problems would weigh the cost-benefits of engaging in therapy. They would consider such factors as how much compliance constrained their daily lives, the side effects of compliance, and the time and effort involved. Sometimes compliance would be mitigated because the client had erroneous or inadequate information, or the client had a negative relationship with the provider. The client's beliefs, knowledge, and relationship with the healthcare provider seemed to be factors involved in compliance. Therefore, it was important to provide good information, have a good relationship with the client, and have good communication.

Cialdini and others (2001a, 2001b; Cialdini & Goldstein, 2004) investigated compliance behaviors in such areas as business, advertising, public relations, and sales. If their findings were adapted to counseling, compliance is more likely to occur:

- If the person for whom the compliance is being made is credible.
- The person doing the complying feels there should be reciprocity, e.g., the counselor is being nice to the client; therefore, the client feels inclined to be nice to the counselor in return, such as by complying with the therapeutic regime.
- The client likes the counselor. People are more likely to comply with those they like – as compared to people they do not like.
- The services of the counselor are valued and perceived as limited; therefore, the client would want to avail themselves to the scarce, limited resource which other people value.
- Other people are using the services, and this validates its usefulness.
- If people comply with an initial smaller request, they are more likely to comply with a subsequence greater request.
- If an initial great request is made and rejected, the client is more likely to comply with a subsequent smaller or lesser request.

There are many factors to consider in working with the client to attain a common goal. Drawing on the aforementioned writers and others, the following suggestions are possible ways to increase compliance:

- Work with the client to establish a viable therapeutic program. If the counselor unilaterally presents a therapeutic plan, there might be less of likelihood that the client will be implementing it. However, if the program is developed in conjunction with the client, there may be less resistance, the client will be more invested, and the client may be more likely to implement either the client's plan or their mutual plan rather than just the counselor's plan alone. Of course, even though working with the client might be more democratic, there are individuals who respond better to authority figures.

- Work with the client to deal with possible factors that might inhibit compliance. The client may be able to provide feedback in terms of problems in the implementation of the program; the client may have a better understanding of family and community and be able to strategize on how to overcome possible impediments.
- Have a manageable therapeutic program – from the client's perspective. Therapeutic programs that are too ambitious may discourage the client, and if they experience failure they may have less confidence in themselves and in the counselor; therefore, this would decrease the likelihood of success. On the other hand, if therapeutic tasks are within the client's capabilities and chances for success are optimal, then the client is more likely to try to implement the program and continue to try and make it successful.
- Enlist the environment, e.g., involve family, influential individuals, and friends to remind and facilitate implementation and maintenance of therapeutic goals. If people in the client's environment are willing to help promote therapeutic goals, then this can increase the likelihood of attaining therapeutic goals. People in the client's environment can remind the client to practice behavioral changes. They can provide transportation to sessions. They can assume some of the client's responsibilities at home and at work.
- Establish a therapeutic program that is syntonic (in keeping) with the client's values and culture. Therapeutic programs that are not in sync with the client's values and cultural patterns can decrease the likelihood of success.
- Counselor should consider the *second-order effects* (mentioned in another section of this book), e.g., the problem of fees, transportation, when sessions are held, time away from family and work, and stigma associated with seeing a counselor.

PSYCHOTHERAPEUTIC INTEGRATION

In regard to which therapeutic approach to use, there are a number of possibilities (Messer, 1992; Stricker & Gold, 1993; Weinberger, 1995). In addition to using one's usual approach and techniques, there is also the option of integrating therapeutic approaches. Stricker (2007–2008) offers the following in terms of integrating psychotherapies: (a) the counselor can use the common factors that have been found in effective therapies; (b) the counselor can use the Assimilative Integration approach in which the counselor adheres to one approach and uses other therapeutic approaches; (c) the counselor can use the Technical Eclecticism in which the counselor uses various techniques – unlike the Assimilative Integration approach, there is no unifying theory that guides the work; and (d) the counselor can use the Theoretical Integration approach – this does not exist. The Theoretical Integration approach integrates the various theoretical concepts and philosophies of psychology into a unified theory from which to provide therapy.

No matter which orientation therapists take, they have to abide by standards of treatment. All the main professional associations have information on ethics and standards of care.

OVERCOMING BARRIERS

To overcome some of the barriers that might hinder counseling and to facilitate therapeutic interactions, here are some suggestions:

1. Examine the client's perception of the problem(s), e.g., does the client believe the problem is the result of chemical imbalance, the omission or commission of a certain act, God's disfavor, fate/karma, personal action or that of others, personal weakness, the result of family dynamics and child-raising practices, early developmental problems, sexual abuse, trauma to the brain, or the consequence of activities in a previous life? People have different explanations for problems. The counselor can ask such questions as, "Why do you think you have this problem?" "Why do you think this happens to people?" And so on. This provides more insight into the client's phenomenological perspective. The counselor can listen and be respectful of the client's perceptions and definitions, but that does not mean that the counselor has to agree.

2. Examine the client's perception of how the problem can be resolved. This step would be a logical extension of the previous step. Understanding the client's perception of the problem can shed light on possible resolutions. Does the client believe that certain rituals need to be performed? Is there a belief that amends need to be made? Is medication the solution? Or does the client believe explorations of earlier experiences and feelings are solutions to the problem? The counselor can ask such questions as, "Do you know how to get rid of the problem?" or "How do other people become better when they have this

problem?"

3. Examine the client's perspective of the role the counselor is to play in the process. The counselor can ask such questions as, "What can I do?" or "What do people usually do that can help?"

4. If therapists expect certain behaviors from the client, these expectations should be expressed. The client is informed of what therapy entails. The client and counselor roles are defined. Expected behaviors are delineated. It is well known that there are differences among cultures and individuals in what kind of information is conveyed and to whom. Sometimes information is not conveyed because of shyness or because of family and community customs not to talk about issues to others. Information might also not be conveyed out of politeness or from not wanting to contradict the counselor, and for a myriad of other reasons. If therapists express to the client behaviors that are expected, they should do so with careful consideration. On the one hand, the counselor is defining what counseling consists of and is presenting counseling as it is done in the U.S.; on the other hand, the counselor can withhold their expectations and allow the client to define what the session consists of, e.g., by the client expressing this verbally or by what transpires in their interactions.

5. Examine the client's perception of the counselor. No matter what is in the counselor's heart and no matter what the counselor's intentions are, the client has certain perceptions about the counselor's values, religion, ethics, behaviors, and so on. The counselor needs to consider if any of the client's perceptions are hindering treatment. Counselors might be able to influence perceptions by defining who they are and what their purpose is, e.g., "I am here to help." "I was sent by my agency to help people in this community." "I came here because I want to serve you however I can." "I am here to learn about people who have problems with their families." And so on.

6. If there is initial discomfort in the therapeutic relationship, a relationship can develop based on commonalities (such as common interests, values, experiences, socioeconomic similarities).

7. Another method to expedite the development of a relationship is for the counselor to take on the role of a learner. Many people throughout the world often want to help others. For example, the counselor might ask the client's help to learn more about the client's community, family, work, religion, and interests. If the counselor takes on the role of someone who wants to learn, then the client may be more apt to engage the counselor in conversation. This method allows the client to talk about familiar matters. The client may feel more in control, may feel like a contributor in the relationship, and may feel re-

spected for having knowledge.

8. Know the client's culture (that is, the influences on the client). One of the reasons culture is important for therapy is because of its role in the definition, interpretation, and management of illness. Sussman (2004) and Helman (1994) wrote that culture provides the lens through which actions, reactions, perceptions, and ways to categorize are learned.

9. Know your cultural influences. This is the other mantra of those who write on cross-cultural therapy. Counselors are the product of a society. They are influenced by their training, education, personality, community, religion, and a myriad of other factors. These can have enormous impact on the counselor's perception of the client and the client's problems.

10. Be aware that therapists enter therapy with their own paradigms. They incorporate information into their own categories. Information that is not congruent with these categories are squeezed into them, or are minimized or rejected – and thus, limiting, distorting, or eliminating information that could be of value.

11. Know the client's place in the community. For example, is the person considered a pariah? Does the client have social support? Are the client's personality, values, and behaviors in harmony with the community's norms? Is the client part of a subgroup – and what is the relationship of the subgroup with the larger community?

12. Know your basic assumptions. One of the exciting and burdensome parts of counseling is the need to question the most basic assumptions. Even though this is advice for cross-cultural work, it is also relevance when working with domestic groups. Counselors need to consider if there are aspects of their basic assumptions that are interfering with accurate perceptions and treatment.

13. The therapist should be aware of the implications and repercussions for the client interacting with the therapist. How will the community act and react to the client interacting with the counselor? What aspects of the community will maintain therapeutic gains, and which will sabotage efforts? If the counselor provides treatment only in the context of their relationship and the therapeutic setting, the counselor may have helped the client adapt to the counselor's environment, but the learned behavior might not function as well in the client's own environment.

People who provide counseling should be aware that what they think they know, and their practices and beliefs, are likely to change (Asch, 1955; Bermúdez, 1998; Chalmers, 2002; Clark, 2000; Dawes, 1994; Fodor, 2011; Frances, 2010; Gardner, 1957; Goldberg, 2003; Heil, 2003; Hergenhahn,

2009; Hintzman, 2011; Hoffmann & Bailey, 1992; Jacobson, Foxx, Mulick, 2005; Masson, 1988; Moss & Francis, 2007; Murphy, 2006; Paris, 2012; Schreck & Miller, 2010; Peacocke, 1992; Rosenthal, 1991; Sherif, 1936; Sorensen, 2004; Sternberg & Lubart, 1995; Szasz, 1978, 1988). This keeps the field exciting and can be an indication that they are open to new ideas and exploration.

Chapter 8

IMPROVING COUNSELING

There are rapid changes in the world and in the United States. This provides opportunities for counselors to keep their profession effective, viable, and relevant. There are many possible activities to engage in. New generations of counselors, public input, suggestions from other professions, and feedback from people from other cultures can open many vistas for counselors. The following are some activities to consider.

ETHICS

As U.S. American views of mental health spread to other parts of the world, counselors need to consider ethics from a domestic and cross-cultural perspective. Are ethical standards a matter determined by each country, or are there principles that transcend borders? Are the ethical standards of the counseling and psychological professions in the United States apropos globally, or do we need to resort to international organizations such as the United Nations to provide protocols? Would it be beneficial to have people outside the profession and outside the culture to evaluate professional ethics? Such an approach might provide different perspectives and insights, e.g., greater awareness of political, religious, social, economic, and self-interest influences that are affecting ethical values.

PUBLIC INVOLVEMENT

A number of factors, such as the following, are involved in attitudes toward the use of noncounselors in dealing with mental health issues. The concern for the confidentiality that is involved in counseling can be generalized to other aspects of mental health; that is, therapists are so used to dealing with confidentiality issues in counseling that they are uncomfortable with public involvement in other aspects of mental health. There is a belief that counseling entails a certain set of skills that are required for effective counseling, and there is concern that the irresponsible use of counseling can do harm. These are genuine concerns which have to be accorded serious attention. However, these concerns should not eliminate some of the beneficial aspects of involving the public in various areas of mental health.

Use of Volunteers

Increasing the role of the public in counseling affairs can provide the profession with new ideas. There is often little public involvement in counseling organizations and in the planning of mental health services; often, public involvement is in the form of advocacy groups trying to make their voices heard, e.g., Learning Disabilities Association of America as well as the National Alliance on Mental Illness. Fresh perspectives might open with increased public participation in mental health areas. The use of people from outside a profession is not unusual – it has been mentioned by such groups and writers as the Institute for Family-Centered Care (2010), Mental Health America (2011), National Working Group on Evidence-Based Health Care (2008), Lasker and Weiss (2003), Shkolyar (2009), and Simpson and House (2003). The use of volunteers is encouraged in such fields as archeology (National Trust, 2010; Polasky, 2002), meteorology (Senerdem, 2010; Bureau of Meteorology, 2001), ornithology (British Trust for Ornithology, n.d.; Ornithological Societies of North America, 2010), and police work (Virginia State Police, 2009; Volunteers in Police Service, n.d.). The United Nations coordinates the Online Volunteering service (United Nations Volunteers, n.d.) in which volunteers – both professionals and nonprofessionals – work with organizations over the Internet. In 2009, individuals from 182 countries participated and provided services to 1,347 nonprofit development organizations. According to their website, they provided such help as advice on waste disposal, contract drafting, project planning, volunteer management, data collection, database development, newsletters production and translation, and moderation of online discussion groups. In astronomy, there are about 500,000 volunteers worldwide working with professional astronomers (Shkolyar, 2009). They contribute to such activities as data gathering, cataloging, and computation. "We live in a world where cutting-edge technical research can be done at home. Now, with nothing but a computer with an Internet connection, any user can participate in . . . projects around the world" (Shkolyar, 2009, para. 2). Shkolyar (2009) wrote that the volunteers are amateur astronomers, ordinary people, groups of volunteers, and anonymous participants. There are many possible areas of counseling where members of the public can be of service. For example, they can monitor the community's needs and provide feedback to counselors. They can help with surveys, data collecting, cataloging, and analyses. They can serve on committees and add their insights and problem-solving skills – and perhaps generate more supporters, resources, and network connections for the counseling field. They can be trained in counseling techniques that they can teach others.

Learning from Communities

Presently, our therapeutic approaches are based on what therapists have read, been taught, or learned from colleges and other professionals. Another possible approach is to observe and survey groups in the community to delineate what actually works – rather than simply providing services with preset approaches and techniques. Observing and discovering what actually works follows the tradition of pragmatism (Galileo [Claveli, 1974]; Biagioli, 1993; Peirce, 1958; James, 1907; Dewey [McDermott, 1981]). Such an approach would enable therapists to accumulate more information about what works and with whom.

Teaching Research and Statistics

Instead of just training graduate students in research and statistics, another possible approach is to also train community members in these skills. This is feasible because (a) research is possible without sophisticated statistics, (b) good statistical software (e.g., freeware) is available to everyone, and (c) those trained in statistics can make themselves available to serve as consultants.

Working in Communities

Counselors are trained to work with individuals and with therapeutic groups. However, they might also consider expanding their services and work with communities, groups, schools, clubs, and other aggregates of people. Many models and approaches are available in the provision of services (Barrera, González Castro, & Holleran Steiker, 2011; Bechtel & Ts'erts'man, 2002; Gullotta & Bloom, 2003; Gumucio-Dragon & Tufte, 2006; Herzfeld, 2001; Meade, Menard, Martinez, & Calvo, 2007). The following are some ways to provide services to communities: (a) the counselor visits the community, provides services, and then leaves; (b) the counselor immerses in the community and delivers services; (c) the counselor teaches the community counseling skills, and the community is involved in providing treatment; (d) the counselor trains indigenous individuals to provide counseling and has them provide treatment to the community; (e) the counselor integrates their particular counseling approaches with those of the indigenous group; (f) the counselor teaches indigenous individuals and communities to integrate and modify what they have been taught in order for them to meet the needs of the community; (g) the counselor develops new or modified approaches, or expedites the indigenous approaches; (h) the counselor explores approaches used in other communities and selects, or has the indigenous community select, what they want; and (i) the counselor facilitates communications between the indigenous group with other communities and has them share their thoughts and ideas as well as develop their own approaches. Functionally, it is likely that some combination of these approaches would be most effective.

Empowering and Educating the Public

Psychologists are engaged in many beneficial public activities. For example, they are involved in HIV and AIDS prevention (Clay, 2012), teaching mindfulness (Davis & Hayes, 2012), helping to overcome barriers to Medicaid (Nordal, 2012), reminding us that money does not necessarily bring happiness (Novotney, 2012), helping to reduce health disparities (Puryear Keita, 2012), helping to build peace (Willyard, 2012), informing us of environmental factors that are damaging to cognitive functions (Wier, 2012), and educating the public of important issues in psychology (Winerman, 2012). These are commendable activities. In terms of counseling, it is obvious that among the assets professionals have to offer are confidentiality, ethical standards, attestment of skills (e.g., through education, certification, or licensure), and recourse for unsatisfactory services (e.g., appeal to a credentialing or regulatory group).

To meaningfully fulfill their roles as professionals, citizens, and humans with a sense of social responsibility, mental health workers have to take into consideration the effects of the values and systems under which they are working. For example, societies that focus on individuals should be aware this might have an effect of estranging them from the group, and societies that focus on the group should be aware of the needs of the individual. Mental health workers who work under capitalistic systems might consider the effects this has on them; similarly, those who work under socialistic, communistic, and other systems should also consider the effects of working under these systems. Most systems will assert that what they do takes care of the group and individual, and most professional associations will assert similarly. However, mental health workers have to look at the effects of their actions – and inactions. For example, those who make a living under capitalism are working under a money-oriented, competitive system. All occupations under such systems are competing with each other and with other occupations for economic, social, and political power. They have a tendency to try to monopolize their services as well as discredit and disparage those who engage in the activities of their occupation.

Nevertheless, mental health professionals should not be dismissive of non-professional attempts to engage in therapeutic activities. For example, in the area of pain management, studies indicated that some "alternative" approaches have been helpful – and some have been found to be ineffective (Cloud, 2011). Similarly, there are many activities most people can engage in that can improve their mental health. These include the use of breath (Meuret, Rosenfield, Seidel, Bhaskara, & Hofmann, 2010), diet (Werbach, 1999; Pfeiffer, 1988), exercise (Smits & Otto, 2009), herbs (Schreck, 2008), imagery (Utay & Miller, 2006), laughter (Goodheart, 1994), massage (Fritz, Chaitow, & Hymel, 2007), meditation (McKay, Wood, & Brantley, 2007), relaxation (Arias, Steinberg, Banga, & Trestman, 2006), smiling (Bernstein, Clarke-Stewart, Penner, Roy, & Wickens, 2000; Davis & Palladino, 2000), and thinking (Beck, 1970, 1976; Burns, 1980). Both professional and nonprofessional services should be evaluated by such standards as effectiveness of the treatment and avoidance of harm.

Increasing the role of the public in helping themselves might help lessen the pattern where increased economic development is accompanied by increases in mental illness/disorder (Inglehart, Welzel, & Foa, 2006; Kessler & Ustun, 2008; Watters, 2010; WHO World Mental Health Survey Consortium, 2004; World Values Survey, 2006), even though mental health services are also increased. There are many possible reasons why increased economic development is accompanied by increases in mental illness/disorder, e.g., there are more stressors and there are fewer traditional support systems. Also, there are many possible reasons why increase in mental health services do not decrease in rates of mental illness/disorder, e.g., the rate of mental illness/disorder increases faster than the number of mental health services, there are better services to diagnose problems, and more services does not necessarily mean more effective services. However, empowering and teaching people skills to deal their problems, and with the problems of others, might have an impact on the rates of mental illness/disorder.

ELECTRONIC DELIVERY OF SERVICES

The advent of modern communications exponentially facilitates communications and the sharing of ideas (and training) among communities. The electronic delivery of services has been used in many areas of counseling (Kraus, Zack, & Stricker, 2004; Rollins, 2011a, 2011b). Ritterband, Andersson, Christensen, Carlbring, and Cuijpers (2006) have written of the success of the Internet in treating a wide range of medical and mental health problems and predicted that it will play a prominent role in global health in the future. Barak (2011) listed sites dealing with the Internet and psychology into the following categories: net behavior and usage; children, adolescents, and the Internet; the Internet and the elderly; net addiction, crime, pathological use; the Internet and suicide; online information-seeking behavior; online gaming and gambling behavior; online dating and romance; virtual communities, online groups, and social networks; online shopping behavior; Internet-assisted therapy and counseling; online support groups and self-help; online testing and assessment; the Internet and sexuality; the Internet, work, and career behavior; online learning; Internet research methodology and ethics; books; and free, relevant online books and journals. The technology and skills have been available for years to use artificial intelligence and expert systems in counseling. Artificial intelligence computer programs can determine the client's language, learning styles, psychological needs, and any other relevant factors and provide counseling tailored to the client characteristics. Expert systems programs can provide counseling as an expert would (Illovsky, 1994). It behooves counselors to be skilled in technology and for them to develop ways to provide services to populations that do not have ready geographic and economic access to counseling.

EVALUATION OF LANGUAGE-BASED COUNSELING

As illustrated in the "Communications" section of this book, there are many forms of communications. In counseling, the verbal form constitutes the foundation of counseling. It is a natural modality to use. However, there are problems associated with providing therapy in this manner: the limitations of its use with people who are not proficient in the use of the language used by the counselor. Much has been written on this subject (Berardo, 2007; Faubert & Gonzalez, 2008; Hornberger et al., 1996; Ivey & Ivey, 2007; Kim, Liang, & Li, 2003; Lee, 1997; Piya, 2007; Stefferud & Bolton, 1981; Sue & Sue, 1977). If U.S. counselors are to offer models in the provision of counseling to people in other cultures, and if they are to make their services more accessible to a wider range of domestic groups, they will need to evaluate hindrances to providing verbally based therapies to clients who do not speak the counselor's language. Obviously, the use of intermediaries, interpreters, and the training of local providers are possible options. Hornberger, Gibson, Wood,

Dequeldre, Corso, Palla, and Bloch (1996) wrote of the use of remote-simultaneous interpretation; that is, someone at another site is electronically connected to the client and provider and serves as an interpreter and facilitator. However, the question remains: can therapists provide services that rely less on verbal language? This is an exciting area to investigate. There is evidence that verbal forms of therapy may not be effective even for those who speak the same language as the therapist. For example, Barber, Barrett, Gallop, Rynn, and Rickels (2012) found, for some people, antidepressants and talk therapy are no better than placebos. It is worth considering the possibility that nonverbal forms of therapy could be of similar or better effectiveness and can add to the repertoire of the therapist's mode of providing services; nonverbal therapeutic modes can also be used with those who share the same language as the therapist. Possible approaches that do not rely heavily on verbal therapy include the use of art and music; relaxation, breathing; kinesthetic activities; reinforcement and modeling; and the use of materials, activities, and resources that are in the client's environment. Perhaps there are ideas to be gained from Straus' (1999) *No-Talk Therapy – for Children and Adolescents.* She presented approaches and activities to provide therapy without relying on talk therapy. She found therapy could be provided by developing a relationship with the client and facilitating the client's sense of accomplishment through activities. She used empathy, games, community involvement and resources, and support from others. In her appendix, she provided "Gimmicks, Gadgets, and Games," "to help get unstuck in a session and can serve as a springboard for new ideas" (p. 194). Lin (1983) also wrote about the use of nonverbal communication and treatment. Because most people in the world express their psychological problems somatically (Kirmayer & Young, 1998), Lin's studies in treating Chinese clients might have particular relevance: He wrote that many Chinese believe organic problems are the cause of psychological problems and they are uncomfortable with verbal communications in treatment. They prefer nonverbal and symbolic communications. Considerable research is needed to determine effective modalities of delivering services – and to whom. Also, studies are needed to determine effective ways to induce counselors to make changes to meet the needs of their clients. The language barrier in the provision of psychotherapeutic services may be one reason why "Western" medications are more accepted as treatment in Chinese society (Lin, 1983) – there is less of a language barrier. It may be that counseling, by definition, means the delivery of services through the verbal mode. Another possibility may be that as therapists expand their services to a wider spectrum of people, their definition of counseling and of counseling activities is expanded.

NEW AND DIFFERENT APPROACHES AND TECHNIQUES

Presently, therapeutic approaches and techniques are based on (a) what has been taught in schools and (b) what the counselor has obtained through various media and presentations – which usually consist of other counselors' experiences and thoughts. These are highly commendable approaches. Another possible approach is to engage in experimental psychotherapy. That is, in educational programs, experiment with different ways of providing psychotherapy. Many fields of science and the arts do experimental work. It would be interesting – and maybe eventually productive – for psychotherapists to engage in experimental activities. If nothing else, it might energize and get the creative juices flowing in the field of psychotherapy and counseling. For example, students can try what has been done in other cultures. They can explore ways of providing services to clients who do not speak the language of the counselor. In regard to this, is there anything to be learned from providers of services to those with limited verbal language, like animals, babies, and those with language and communication disabilities? Neuroimaging could be used to determine which aspects of counseling are therapeutic: does touching, being present, or showing empathy help – and if so, under what conditions and with whom? Does counseling with graphs, pictures, and computers help? Studies have been done with these modes of providing therapy, but they have not been studied as modes of therapy without verbal language. In the West, they have found that psychotherapy in conjunction with medicine has been found to be helpful with various disorders. Does this suggest that psychotherapy in conjunction with other forms of treatment (such as those provided by endogenous providers) might be helpful when dealing with those who do not speak the language? The main point here is that there are opportunities to explore and try other ways of providing counseling; it could be done through experimental psychotherapy or it could be done by many other means.

DATA GATHERING, CATALOGING, AND DISTRIBUTION

Counselors in the United States are in a unique position to contribute to counseling on a worldwide basis. They have the infrastructure and resources to gather and catalog counseling material. The present systems are antiquated and reflect conditions that existed centuries ago: a few scholars presenting their thoughts through a few main journals. Nowadays, there are more people trained to be scholars, and they produce massive amounts of material. Yet, our professional publications still reflect the views of a limited, selected few authors. There needs to be better methods to reflect the works and thoughts of members of the profession; modern-day methods are available to make greater amounts of information available to the profession. For example, editors can increase the publications of meta-analyses (e.g., Whiston, Tai, Rahardja, & Eder, 2011) as well as summaries of the material that is submitted to them (e.g., Erford, Miller, Schein, McDonald, Ludwig, & Leishear, 2011). This will enable members of the profession to be aware of the state of knowledge in their field. More effort needs to be directed at informing the profession of material produced on a global level by such groups as the Association of German Professional Psychologists, Chinese Psychological Society, Israel Psychological Association, Japanese Psychological Association, Max Planck Institute, Singapore Psychological Society, Societe Francaise de Psychologie, and the Turkish Psychological Association. The studies conducted by groups such as these have little presence in U.S. counseling literature.

Within the United States counselors have opportunities to study a wide spectrum of cultures to test and gather data on the robustness of theories, approaches, and techniques. For example, Zane, Nagayama Hall, Sue, Young and Nunez (2004) wrote about studies of African Americans, American Indians, Asian Americans, and Latino/a Americans in the United States. Immigrants from other countries can be studied as samples of the cultures they came from. Many U. S. Americans have connections with their countries of origin; therefore, counselors and psychologists can avail themselves to these avenues for obtaining data. Students and visitors from other countries also provide opportunities to study other cultures and the efficacy of U.S. models and approaches. For example, Singaravelu and Pope (2007) studied international students in the United States from Latin American and the Caribbean, East Asia, Africa, Middle East, Europe, Australia, New Zealand, and former USSR. Professional counseling and psychological associations often have relationships with colleagues in various countries. These connections can be used. Scholars in the counseling and psychological professions can draw from anthropological, medical, religious, political, business, and numerous other sources. There are many opportunities in this country to learn about general and specific relevant principles to counseling people. Such studies can increase our understanding of the ranges of human behavior.

In addition to gathering information, there needs to be effective methods to categorize and retrieve information. The depiction of data as presented in *Bergin and Garfield's Handbook of Psychotherapy and Behavior Change* (Lambert, 2004) can serve as a template of how to structure and categorize the data. Another example of how to collect and organize data comes from anthropologists. Anthropologists have the Human Relations Area Files (HRAF). This serves as a repository of cultural anthropology data from throughout the world. The counseling professions can have a similar repository for counseling data. The counseling profession can work with World Health Organization in gathering data. The International Classification of Diseases provides one standardized set of lexicons. Both the World Health Organization and the International Classification of Diseases provide algorithms for gathering, measuring, and reporting data. A world counseling data repository can serve as a nexus for the gathering of information on approaches and techniques. The data can result in the delineation of patterns that can provide insight into counseling and clients.

ROLE OF SCIENCE

One area therapists can improve on is to increase the role of science. There are many who assert that psychological treatment is based on dubious premises, questionable methods, and ineffective treatment (Baker, McFall, & Shoham, 2008; Begley, 2009; Psychology: A Reality Check, 2009; Levenson, 2010; McFall, 2006, 2010; Mischel, 2008; Rickman, 2012). Feltham (1996) wrote the counseling profession "has its share of unconvincing theories, terminological obstacles, unnecessary rituals and institutionalized opinions masquerading as knowledge"; the "counselling profession creates an illusion that sanctioned counsellors know more about human nature and are necessarily more skilful listeners and helpers than others" (p. 297). He compares counseling to religions and states they both create myth and superstition. There is enough evidence to question the effectiveness of counseling (Bentall, 2009; Dawes, 1994; Jaffe, 2010; Leventhal & Martell, 2006; Scott, Lilienfeld, Lynn, & Lohr, 2003). There certainly is a place in psychology and science to go beyond the data, to extrapolate, to consider alternatives, and to be open to other ideas. However, there are many reasons for advocating the use of science, logic, and empirical evidence. These provide the grounds for accumulating and modifying information in a systematic fashion. They form a common language for people throughout the world. Scientific approaches have made significant contributions to humanity, such as areas in medicine, biology, and technology. It would be reasonable for therapists to try to emulate these fields to try to improve the human condition.

Publishers, editors, and writers also have responsibilities. It is their responsibility to provide information in a manner that is understandable and concise – if readers want more, follow-up information which can be provided by authors. Presently, studies are directed at readers in particular fields. If the language and methods used in specialized fields were readily understandable and accessible to a wider range of readership, then research and data might be used more by practitioners.

STANDARDS

As with ethics, professional standards are important. The question arises as to whether universal standards are applicable or whether standards should be determined on a more local and regional basis. Usually, when standards are proposed they are under the auspices of serving and protecting the interests of the public and to insure the competent delivery of services. However, there should be constant vigilance that the standards do not put the profession's interests before those of the public. To help provide competent and ethical services the president of the American Psychological Association, S. B. Johnson (2012), supported the efforts of APA to follow the clinical practice guidelines provided by the Institute of Medicine (2011) for those in the medical field. She reports the guidelines as "standards for developing rigorous, trustworthy guidelines: establishing transparency; managing conflict of interest; selecting a multidisciplinary guideline – developing group with patient and public input; articulating the link between guideline development and systemic review of the literature; establishing evidence foundation for and rating of the strength of recommendations, conducting external reviews of the guidelines; and updating the guidelines" (p. 5). It is hoped that standards such as these are implemented and are not rhetorical.

GLOBALIZING COUNSELING

A number of authors have called to attention global perspectives of counseling and psychology (Arnett, 2002; Leong, 2008; Leung, 2003; Paredes et al., 2008; Ponterotto, Suzuki, Casas, & Alexander, 2010; Stevens & Uwe, 2007). A global perspective can be of value to this country as well as to other countries (Gerstein, Heppner, Aegisdóttir, Seung-Ming, Norsworthy, 2009b; Gerstein, Heppner, Aegisdóttir, Seung-Ming, Norsworthy, 2009c; Seung-Ming, Clawson, Norsworthy, Tena, Szilagyi, & Rogers, 2009). A global perspective might enable therapists to be more aware of human responses that are "normal," as well as those that are culturally influenced. A global perspective might provide better insight into dysfunctional and pathological behaviors and help delineate which concepts, approaches, and techniques are common to most people of the world. Problems and solutions can be shared. As the U.S. interacts more with the rest of the world, there are opportunities to learn from others and contribute to the world community.

Chapter 9

CONCLUDING REMARKS

The literature reviewed in this book indicated a number of patterns. It is evident that helping behaviors have a long history in both our species as well as in other species. In terms of psychotherapy, when examined on a worldwide basis, it is evident that people in many cultures express their psychological problems somatically. People in many cultures are reluctant to seek help for psychological issues, e.g., because of cultural norms, desire to solve problems on their own, or because of shame, embarrassment, or stigma. Many of them view themselves as part of communities, and not just as individuals. They often view themselves and their problems as consisting of interactions among mind, body, and transcendentals (for example, the supernatural, ancestors, and previous lives). Also, extra-therapeutic effects most likely occur with all treatment.

It is obvious that biology and environment play significant roles in human behavior. The mind contains many aspects that can be activated. There are numerous perspectives of human behavior. These reflect human variability and their multiple dimensions; therefore, therapists have many perspectives to choose from.

The assumptions of counseling should be questioned. Necessary or sufficient factors for effective therapy differ with individuals and groups. The differences may be attributed to experiential, genetic, cultural, economic, political, and other reasons. In counseling, clients may differ in their definitions of needs and what constitutes counseling. This is reflected in the schools of psychological theories in Europe and the United States: they are diverse. Some advocate therapy that is focused on the here and now; others advocate extensive investigations into thoughts, feelings, behaviors, family background, and developmental history. People in some cultures define therapy as short-term – with clear directions and goals. Others define therapy as long-term, with relatively little structure. Whether or not there are universals and whether or not therapy is effective, competent counselors will learn as much as possible about the group and individuals they are dealing with. Ethical and competent counselors are aware that their culture and values affect their services. They seek ways to improve the lives of those they serve.

Nowadays, there are more interactions among people of different cultures (Choucri & Mistree, 2009). International trade has increased exponentially. Electronics enable people to communicate at an unprecedented level. There are many opportunities to interact, learn, and contribute to others. The cross-fertilization of perspectives among cultures provides fuller insight into human behavior. Our present theories of behavior are a product of our times, conditions, and personalities. There are aspects of them that are applicable to all people, and there are aspects that have limited application. Counselors can help define the healthy and conducive aspects of interactions, and not just focus on the problems. In an age of increasing globalization, there are factors that pull people away from others. For example, with increased values of individuality, people can feel culled from the group; subgroups can focus on their differences, needs, perspectives, and issues. Perhaps one of the main functions counselors can serve is to remind people that we have more in common with each other than what draws us apart. In counseling, counselors draw together couples and group members who have differences. Perhaps we can use some of these skills and learn new ones to help draw communities and people together.

This book contains many critiques. The purpose of bringing attention to flaws and critiques is not to discourage or present a gloomy picture; rather, the purpose is to increase awareness and encourage further investigation. Also, critiques are made because one of the functions of psychologists, counselors, scientists, scholars, and responsible people is not to accept information uncritically.

Counselors have played a role in societies for millenniums. It is highly likely that they will have a place in the future. Many factors exist to induce problems that counselors can attend to, including the following. Living entails dealing with problems. With each circumstance, there arise problems to deal with. The human mind is constantly active and evaluating people and situations – with concomitant cognitive and affective reactions that can be problematic. Humans exist in complex systems within themselves and their environment – which are often changing and can be confusing and conflicting. Not only are there bona fide, genuine problems that have to be contended with, there are also many problems that are concocted; these are not real problems but have been defined as such. Counselors can help clients delineate pertinent problems from reified ones. Counselors can help people deal with the stressors of living in the modern world, such as those that are the result of family, work, and mental illness/disorder. Counselors can help people deal with the increases in social and technological complexity. They can help people encountering problems with the rapid changes in norms, expectations, roles, and values. Counselors can teach resiliency skills and how to deal with anticipated problems. Additionally, they can interpret and apply to therapy the massive amount of data that accumulates in the literature. They can provide human, face-to-face contact as clients encounter problems. Counselors also have a responsibility to examine the costs and benefits of their activities. They need to develop approaches that do not increase and exacerbate clients' problems. Finally, they need to determine effective ways to provide services.

When the counselor interacts with clients, it is an interaction between parties with their own unique characteristics, stereotypes, narratives, scripts, generalizations, and perceptions. Lambert, Garfield, and Bergin (2004) wrote about micro theories and macro theories. They wrote that the question to ask is what works with this particular person rather than the nature of personality and other broader perspectives. In therapy, both client and counselor bring internal and external factors that affect the relationship and treatment – some are under the control of counselors, and others are not. We are composites of common factors and unique configurations that make up the individual. Knowledge of common factors can be of value in understanding general influences, and personal interactions can be of value in delineating unique aspects of the individual. In therapy, counselors bring to bear their skills. They also bring those aspects of their being that treat others with respect, compassion, and kindness. Such an approach is not only an expression of therapists' personal values, it is also probably an effective way to accompany whatever treatment is provided. The best advice is to learn as much as possible about the client and about one's self, to have an open mind, and to question basic assumptions.

BIBLIOGRAPHY

Aanio, K., & Lindeman, M. (2005). Paranormal beliefs, education, and thinking styles. *Personality and Individual Differences, 39*(7), 1227–1236. doi:10.1016/j.paid.2005.04.009

Aber, J. L., Bennett, N. G., Conley, D. C., & Li, J. (1997). The effects of poverty on child health and development. *Annual Review of Public Health, 18,* 463–83. doi:10.1146/annurev.publhealth.18.1.463

Abramson, L. Y., Metalsky, F. I., & Alloy, L. B. (1989). Hopelessness depression: A theory based subtype of depression. *Psychological Review, 96*(2), 358–372. doi:10.1037/0033-295X.96.2.358

Abramson, L. Y., Seligman, M. E., & Teasdale, J. D. (1978). Learned helplessness in humans: Critique and reformulation. *Abnormal Psychology, 87*(1), 49–74. doi:10.1037/0021-843X.87.1.49

Ackerman, S., & Hilsenroth, M. (2003). A review of counselor characteristics and techniques positively impacting the therapeutic alliance. *Clinical Psychology Review, 23,* 1–33. doi:10.1016/S0272-7358(02)00146-0

Adams, J. Q., & Strother-Adams, P. (2001). *Dealing with diversity.* Chicago, IL: Kendall/Hunt.

Adams, M. (2009, October 11). Consumer health group calls for scientific inquiry into safety of cervical cancer vaccines. *Natural News.* Retrieved from http://www.naturalnews.com/027218_vaccine_health_vaccines.html.

Adams, R. B., Ambady, N., Nakayama, K., & Shimojo, S. (Eds.). (2011). *The science of social vision.* New York: Oxford University Press.

Adelson, J. (1991). Politically correct psychology. *American Scholar, 60*(4), 580–83.

Adelstein, J. S., Shehzad, Z., Mennes, M., DeYoung, C. G., Zuo, X-N., Kelly, C., Margulies, D. S., Bloomfield, A., Gray, J. R., Castellanos, F. X., & Milham, M. P. (2011). Personality is reflected in the brain's intrinsic functional architecture. *PLoS ONE, 6*(11): e27633. doi:10.1371/journal.pone.0027633

Adler, A. (1998). *Understanding human nature* (C. Brett, Trans.). Center City, MN: Hazelden Publishers. (Original work published 1927)

Adriani, W., Boyer, F., Leo, D., Canese, R., Podo, F., Perrone-Capano, C.,Dreyer, J-L., & Laviola, G. (2010). Social withdrawal and gambling-like profile after lentiviral manipulation of DAT expression in the rat accumbens. *International Journal of Neuropsychopharmacology, 13*(10), 1329–1342. doi:10.1017/S1461145709991210

Ahmed, A. S. (1984). Al-Beruni: The first anthropologist. *RAIN (Royal Anthropological News,* name changed to *Anthropology Today* in 1985), *6,* 9–10.

Albright, L., Malloy, T. E., Dong, Q., Kenny, D. A., Fang, X., Winquist, L., & Yu, D. (1997). Cross-cultural consensus in personality judgments. *Journal of Personality and Social Psychology, 72*(3), 558–569. doi:10.1037/0022-3514.72.3.558

Alder, B. (1999). *Psychology of health: Applications of psychology for health professionals.* Amsterdam, Netherlands: Harwood Academic Publishers.

Aldine Transaction. (2008). [Editorial review of *Toward effective counseling and psychotherapy: Training and practice,* by C. Truax, & R. R. Carkhuff]. Retrieved from http://www.transactionpub.com/title/Toward-Effective-Counseling-and-Psychotherapy-978-0-202-30988-0.html.

Alexander, W. M. (1902). *Demonic possession in the new testament.* Edinburgh, UK: Clark & Street.

Alford, D. M. (2000, September 12). *Linguistics & nominalising languages.* [Hilgartner & Associates Research Group]. Retrieved from http://hilgart.org/enformy/ll02.htm.

Allen, M. (1993). *In the company of men: A new approach to healing for husbands, fathers & friends.* New York: Random House.

Allen, T. (1997). *The invention of the White race: The origin of racial oppression in Anglo-America.* New York: Verso.

Allport, G. W. (1931; 1977, Revised). *A study of values: A scale of measuring the dominant interests in personality – Manual of directions.* Boston: Houghton Mifflin Company.

Allport, G. W. (1937). *Personality: A psychological interpretation.* New York: H. Holt.

Allport, G. W. (1955). *Becoming: Basic considerations for a psychology of personality.* New Haven, Yale University Press.

Alper, J. (2003, June). Rethinking Neanderthal. *Smithsonian Magazine, 34,* 82.

Alterman, A. I., & Cacciola, J. S. (1991). The antisocial personality disorder diagnosis in substance abusers: Problems and issues. *Journal of Nervous and Mental Disease, 179*(7), 401–9. doi:10.1097/00005053-199107000-00003

Altruism. (2010). In *Merriam-Webster online dictionary.* Retrieved from http://www.merriam-webster.com/dictionary/altruistic.

Amada, G. (2001). *Mental health and student conduct issues on the college campus: A reading.* Saint Johns, FL: College Administration Publications.

Ameen, S. (2002) Transcultural psychiatry: A critical review. *Mental Health Reviews.* Retrieved from http://www.psyplexus.com/excl/transcultural_psych.html.

American Counseling Association. (2005). *2005 ACA code of ethics.* Retrieved from http://www.counseling.org/Resources/CodeOfEthics/TP/Home/CT2.aspx.

American Counseling Association. (2010). *Resources – Definition of counseling.* Retrieved from http://www.counseling.org/Resources/.

American Counseling Association. (2011). *Our history.* Retrieved from http://www.counseling.org/AboutUs/OurHistory/TP/Home/CT2.aspx.

American Medico-Psychological Association and National Committee on Mental Hygiene. (1918). *Statistical manual for the use of institutions for the insane.* New York: National Committee for Mental Hygiene.

American Psychiatric Association. (1994). *Diagnostic and statistical manual of mental disorders.* Washington, DC: Author.

American Psychiatric Association. (2000). *Diagnostic and statistical manual of mental disorders* (Rev. 4th ed.). Washington, DC: Author.

American Psychiatric Association Development. (2010). *DSM-5: The future of psychiatric diagnosis.* American Psychiatric Association, Arlington, VA. Retrieved from http://www.dsm5.org/Pages/Default.aspx.

American Psychiatric Association. (2012). *The principles of medical ethics with annotations especially applicable to psychiatry.* Retrieved from http://psychiatry.org/practice/ethics/resources-standards/ethics-resources-and-standards.

American Psychological Association. (2002a). *American Psychological Association ethical principles of psychologists and code of conduct.* Retrieved from http://www.apa.org/ethics/code/code.pdf.

American Psychological Association. (2002b). *Guidelines for multicultural education and training, research, practice, and organizational change for psychologists.* Washington, DC: Author.

American Psychological Association. (2010). *Ethical principles of psychologists and code of conduct.* Retrieved from http://www.apa.org/ethics/code/index.aspx.

American Psychological Association. (2012). *Support center.* Retrieved from http://www.apa.org/support/about/psych/numbers-us.aspx#answer.

Anand, R. (2006). Exploring emotion: An essay on the neurology of emotion and the theory of karma. *The Internet Journal of Mental Health, 3*(1). Retrieved from http://www.ispub.com/ostia/index.php?xmlFilePath=journals/ijmh/vol3n1/karma.xml.

Anderson, S. K., & Middleton, V. A. (Eds.). (2005). *Explorations in privilege, oppression, and diversity.* Belmont, CA: Thomson-Brooks/Cole.

Antill, J. K. (1983). Sex role complementarity versus similarity in married couples. *Journal of Personality and Social Psychology, 45,* 145–155. doi:10.1037/0022-3514.45.1.145

APA launches archives of scientific psychology, its first open methodology, open data, open access. (2012). *APA Access, 1*(15). Retrieved from http://www.apa.org/pubs/newsletters/access/2012/08-21/first-journal.aspx.

Arab. (2010). In *Encyclopædia Britannica online.* Retrieved from http://www.britannica.com/EBchecked/topic/31348/Arab.

Arias, A. J., Steinberg, K., Banga, A., & Trestman, R. L. (2006). Systematic review of the efficacy of meditation techniques as treatments for medical illness. *Journal of Alternative and Complementary Medicine, 12*(8), 817–32. doi:10.1089/acm.2006.12.817

Ardrey, R. (1961). *African genesis; A personal investigation into the animal origins and nature of man.* New York: Atheneum.

Arehart-Treichel, J. (2001). Psychological abuse may cause changes in brain. *Psychiatric News, 36*(5), 36.

Arikha, N. (2007). *Passions and tempers: A history of the humours.* New York: Ecco/Harper Collins Publishers.

Armstrong, D. (1989). *Universals.* Boulder, CO: Westview Press.

Aristotle. (1907). *The metaphysics* (J. H. McMahon, Trans.). New York: Cosimo.

Arnett, J. J. (2002). The psychology of globalization. *American Psychologist, 57*(10), 774–783. doi:10.1037//0003-066X.57.10.774

Arnett, J. J. (2008). The neglected 95%: Why American psychology needs to become less American. *American Psychologist, 63,* 602–614. doi:10.1037/0003-066X.63.7.602

Arredondo, P., Toporek, M. S., Brown, S., Jones, J., Locke, D. C., Sanchez, J., & Stadler, H. (1996). *Operationalization of the multicultural counseling competencies.* AMCD. Alexandria, VA. Retrieved from http://www.amcdaca.org/amcd/competencies.pdf.

Asay, T. P., & Lambert, M. J. (1999). The empirical case for the common factors in therapy: Quantitative findings. In B. L. Duncan, M. A. Hubble, & S. D. Miller (Eds.), *The heart and soul of change* (pp. 23–55). Washington, DC: American Psychological Association.

Asay, T. P., & Lambert, M. J. (2004). The empirical case for the common factors in therapy: Quantitative findings. In M. A. Hubble, B. L. Duncan & S. Miller (Eds.), *The heart and soul of change: What works in therapy* (pp. 23–55). Washington, DC: American Psychological Association. doi:10.1037/11132-001

Asch, S. E. (1946). Forming impressions of personality. *Journal of Abnormal and Social Psychology, 41,* 258–290. doi:10.1037/h0055756

Asch, S. E. (1955). Opinions and social pressure. *Scientific American, 193,* 31–35. doi:10.1038/scientificamerican1155-31

Assess. (2010). In *Merriam-Webster's online dictionary.* Retrieved from http://www.merriam-webster.com/dictionary/assessing.

Association for Humanistic Psychology. (n.d.). *What defines humanistic theories?* Retrieved from http://afhc.camp9.org/Default.aspx?pageId=1242938.

At home and abroad: Mental illness in Africa. (1966, April 16). *British Medical Journal, 1*(5493), 975. doi:10.1136/bmj.1.5493.975

Avari, B. (2007). *India, the ancient past: A history of the Indian sub-continent from c. 7000 to AD 1200.* New York: Routledge.

Awanbor, D. (1982). The healing process in African psychotherapy. *American Journal of Psychotherapy, 36*(2), 206–13.

Axelrod, R., & Hamilton, W. D. (1981). The evolution of cooperation. *Science, 211,* 1390–1396. doi:10.1126/science.7466396

Azibo, D. A. (1991). Towards a meta-theory of the African personality. *The Journal of Black Psychology, 17*(2), 37–45. doi:10.1177/00957984910172004

Bachelor, A. (1988). How clients perceive counselor empathy: A content analysis of received empathy. *Psychotherapy: Theory, Research and Practice, 25,* 227–40.

Bachelor, A. (1995). Clients' perception of the therapeutic alliance: A qualitative analysis. *Journal of Counseling Psychology, 42,* 323–37. doi:10.1037/0022-0167.42.3.323

Bachelor, A., & Horvath, A. (2004). The therapeutic relationship. In M. Hubble, B. L. Duncan & S. Miller (Eds.), *The heart and soul of change: What works in therapy* (pp. 133–178). Washington, DC: American Psychological Association.

Back, K. W. (1961). Decisions under uncertainty rational, irrational, and non-rational. *American Behavioral Scientist, 4*(6), 14–19. doi:10.1177/000276426100400604

Baggaley, M., Piper, M., Cumming, P., & Murphy, G. (1999). Trauma related symptoms in British soldiers 36 months following a tour in the former Yugoslavia. *Journal of the Royal Army Medical Corps, 145,* 13–4.

Bailey, K. G. (1987). *Human paleopsychology: Applications to aggression and pathological processes.* Hillsdale, NJ: L. Erlbaum Associates.

Bak, H. (Ed.). (1993). *Multiculturalism and the canon of American culture.* Amsterdam: VU University Press.

Baker, D. B. (Ed.). (1993). *Explorers and discovers of the world.* Detroit/Washington, DC/London: Gale Research.

Baker, T. B., McFall, R. M., & Shoham, V. (2008). Current status and future prospects of clinical psychology: Toward a scientifically principled approach to mental and behavioral health care. *Psychological Science in the Public Interest, 9*(2), 67–103.

Baker, W. E. (2006). *America's crisis of values: Reality and perception.* Princeton, NJ: Princeton University Press.

Balcazar, F. E., Suarez-Balcazar, Y., & Taylor-Ritzler, T. (2009). Cultural competence: Development of a conceptual framework. *Disability & Rehabilitation, 31*(14), 1153–1160.

Balmforth, J. (2009). "The weight of class": Clients' experiences of how perceived differences in social class between counsellor and client affect the therapeutic relationship. *British Journal of Guidance & Counselling, 37*(3), 375–386. doi:10.1080/03069880902956942

Bandura, A. (1977). *Social learning theory.* Englewood Cliffs, NJ: Prentice-Hall.

Bandura, A. (1986). *Social foundations of thought and action: A social cognitive theory.* Englewood Cliffs, NJ: Prentice-Hall.

Bandura, A. (1997). *Self-efficacy: The exercise of control.* New York: Freeman.

Baptiste, D. A., Hardy, K. V., & Lewis, L. (1997). Family therapy with English Caribbean immigrant families in the United States: Issues of emigration, immigration, culture, and race. *Contemporary Family Therapy, 19*(3), 337–359. doi:10.1023/A:1026112126048

Barak, A. (2011). *References related to the internet & psychology.* Retrieved from http://construct.haifa.ac.il/~azy/refindx.htm.

Barakat, H. (1993). *The Arab world: Society, culture, and state.* Berkeley & Los Angeles, CA: University of California Press.

Barber, B. R. (2008). *Consumed: How markets corrupt children, infantilize adults, and swallow citizens whole.* New York: W. W. Norton.

Barber, J. P., Barrett, M. S., Gallop, R., Rynn, M. A., & Rickels, K. (2012). Short-term dynamic psychotherapy versus pharmacotherapy for major depressive disorder: A randomized, placebo-controlled trial. *Journal of Clinical Psychiatry, 73*(1), 66–73. doi:10.4088/JCP.11m06831

Barbu, Z. (1956/2002). *Democracy and dictatorship.* London: Routledge.

Bareket, E. (2002). Rādhānites. In N. Roth (Ed.), *Jewish civilization: An encyclopedia* (pp. 558–561). New York: Routledge.

Barkham, M., Connell, J., Stiles, W. B., Miles, J. N. V., Margison, F., Evans, C., & Mellor-Clark, J. (2006). Dose-effect relations and responsive regulation of treatment duration: The good enough level. *Journal of Consulting and Clinical Psychology, 74*, 160–167. doi:10.1037/0022-006X.74.1.160

Barker, R., & Gump, P. (1964). *Big school, small school: High school size and student behavior.* Stanford, CA: Stanford University Press.

Barkow, J., Cosmides, L., & Tooby, J. (Eds.). (1992). *The adapted mind: Evolutionary psychology and the generation of culture.* New York/Oxford: Oxford University Press.

Bar-Levav, R. (1988). *Thinking in the shadow of feelings: A new understanding of the hidden forces that shape individuals and societies.* New York: Simon & Schuster.

Baron, J. (1985). What kinds of intelligence are fundamental? In S. F. Chipman, J. W. Segal, & R. Glaser (Eds.), *Thinking and learning skills: Research and open questions* (Vol. 2, pp. 365–390). Hillsdale, NJ: Lawrence Erlbaum Associates.

Baron, J. (2000). *Thinking and deciding* (3rd. ed.). New York: Cambridge University Press.

Baron-Cohen, S. (Ed.). (1997). *The maladapted mind: Classic readings in evolutionary psychopathology.* Hove, East Sussex, UK: Psychology Press.

Barrera, M., González Castro, F., & Holleran Steiker, L. K. (2011). A critical analysis of approaches to the development of preventive interventions for subcultural groups. *American Journal of Community Psychology* [On-line], *48*(3–4), 439–454. doi: 10.1007/s10464-010-9422-x. Retrieved from http://www.springerlink.com/content/np65243575k08577/.

Barrett, C. E., Noble, P., Hanson, E., Pine, D. S., Winslow, J. T., & Nelson, E. E. (2009). Early adverse rearing experiences alter sleep-wake patterns and plasma cortisol levels in juvenile rhesus monkeys. *Psychoneuroendocrinology, 34*(7), 1029–40. doi:10.1016/j.psyneuen.2009.02.002

Barrett, D. B., Kurian, G. T., & Johnson, T. M. (2001). *World Christian encyclopedia: A comparative survey of churches and religions – AD 30 to 2200.* Oxford: Oxford University Press.

Barrett, S. (2009). *Anthropology: A student's guide to theory and method.* Toronto/Buffalo/London: University of Toronto Press.

Barro, R. J., & Hwang, J. (2007). *Religious conversion in 40 countries.* Cambridge, MA: National Bureau of Economic Research (NBER Working Paper No. W13689).

Baskin, D., Bluestone, H., & Nelson, M. (1981). Ethnicity and psychiatric diagnosis. *Journal of Clinical Psychology, 37*(3), 529–537. doi:10.1002/1097-4679(198107) 37:3<529::AID-JCLP2270370315>3.0.CO;2-3

Basu, K. (2007, June). The traveler's dilemma. *Scientific American Magazine, 296*(6), 68–73.

Batson, C. D., & Shaw, L. L. (1991, April). Evidence for altruism: Toward a pluralism of prosocial motives. *Psychological Inquiry, 2*(2), 107–122. doi:10.1207/s15327965 pli0202_1

Baum, W. M. (1994). *Understanding behaviorism: Science, behavior, and culture.* New York: HarperCollins.

Baumeister, R. F., Zhang, L., & Vohs, K. D. (2004). Gossip as cultural learning. *Review of General Psychology, 8,* 111–121. doi:10.1037/1089-2680.8.2.111

Baune, B. Th., Aljeesh, Y., & Bender, R. (2005). Factors of non-compliance with the therapeutic regimen among hypertensive men and women: A case-control study to investigate risk factors of stroke. *Journal European Journal of Epidemiology, 20*(5), 411–419. doi:10.1007/s10654-005-0675-x

Bayer, R. (1981). *Homosexuality and American psychiatry.* New York: Basic.

Beaglehole, J. C. (1974). *The life of captain James Cook.* Stanford, CA: Stanford University Press.

Bechtel, R. B., & Ts'erts'man, A. (2002). *Handbook of environmental psychology*. New York: John Wiley & Sons.

Beck, A. T. (1970). Cognitive therapy: Nature and relation to behavior therapy. *Behavior Therapy, 1*(2), 184–200. doi:10.1016/S0005-7894(70)80030-2

Beck, A. T. (1976). *Cognitive therapy and the emotional disorders*. Madison, CT: International Universities Press.

Becker, G. M., & McClintock, C. G. (1967). Value: Behavioral decision theory. Annual *Review of Psychology, 18,* 239–286. doi:10.1146/annurev.ps.18.020167.001323

Beecher, H. K. (1955). Powerful placebo. *Journal of the American Medical Association, 159*(17), 1602–1606.

Begley, S. (2009, October 1). *Ignoring the evidence – Why do psychologists reject science?* [Newsweek]. Retrieved from http://www.thedailybeast.com/newsweek/2009/10/01/ignoring-the-evidence.html.

Beidel, D. C., & Turner, S. M. (1986). A critique of the theoretical bases of cognitive-behavioral theories and therapy. *Clinical Psychology Review, 6*(2), 177–197. doi:10 1016/0272-7358(86)90011-5

Beins, B. C. (2010). The Barnum effect. In I. B. Weiner and W. E. Craighead (Eds.), *Corsini's encyclopedia of psychology* (4th ed., pp. 203–204). New York: Wiley.

Bekoff, M. (2007). *Animals matter: A biologist explains why we should treat animals with compassion and respect.* Boston/London: Shambhala.

Belgrave, F. Z., & Allison, K. W. (2006). *African American psychology: From Africa to America.* Thousand Oaks, CA: Sage Publications.

Bender, E. (2004, May 7). Brain data reveal why psychotherapy works. *Psychiatric News, 39*(9), 34.

Benedetti, F., Mayberg, H. S., Wager, T. D., Stohler, C. S., & Zubieta, J-K. (2005). Neurobiological mechanisms of the placebo effect. *The Journal of Neuroscience, 25*(45), 10390–10402. doi:10.1523/JNEUROSCI.3458-05.2005

Benenson, J. F., Pascoe, J., & Radmore, N. (2007). Children's altruistic behavior in the dictator game. *Evolution and Human Behavior, 28*(3), 168–175. doi:10.1016/j.evol humbehav.2006.10.003

Benfari, R. C., Eaker, E., & Stoll, J. G. (1981). Behavioral interventions and compliance to treatment regimes. *Annual Review of Public Health, 2,* 431–471. doi:10.1146/annurev.pu. 02.050181.002243

Benner, D. G. (Ed.). (1985). *Baker encyclopedia of psychology.* Grand Rapids, MI: Baker Book House.

Bentall, R. P. (2009). *Doctoring the mind: Is our current treatment of mental illness really any good?* New York: New York University Press.

Berardo, K. (2007). *10 Strategies for overcoming language barriers.* [Culturosity.com]. Retrieved from http://www.culturosity.com/pdfs/10%20Strategies%20for%20Overcoming%20Language%20Barriers.pdf.

Bergen, D. C. (2008). Effects of poverty on cognitive function: A hidden neurologic epidemic. *Neurology, 71,* 447–451. doi:10.1212/01.wnl.0000324420.03960.36

Berger, P., Hardenberg, R., Kattner, E., & Prager, M. (Eds.). (2010). *The anthropology of values.* Nioda, India: Pearson Education India.

Bergin, A. E., & Suinn, R. M. (1975). Individual psychotherapy and behavior therapy. In M. R. Rosenzweig & L. W. Porter (Eds.), *Annual review of psychology* (pp. 509–556). Palo Alto, CA: Annual Reviews.

Bermúdez, J. L. (1998). *The paradox of self-consciousness*. Cambridge, MA: MIT Press.

Bernstein, D. A., Clarke-Stewart, A., Penner, L. A., Roy, E. J., & Wickens, C. D. (2000). *Psychology* (5th ed.). Boston, MA: Houghton Mifflin Company.

Berry, J. W., Poortinga, Y. H., Segall, M. H., & Dasen, P. R. (1992). *Cross-cultural psychology: Research and applications*. Cambridge: Cambridge University Press.

Berry, J. W., & Sam, D. L. (1997). Acculturation and adaptation. In J. W. Berry, M. H. Segall & Ç. Kağitçibaşi (Eds.), *Handbook of cross-cultural psychology: Social and behavioral applications* (Vol. 3). Boston, MA: Allyn and Bacon.

Berry, J. W., Segall, M. H., & Kağitçibaşi, Ç. (Eds.). (1997). *Handbook of cross-cultural psychology: Social behavior and applications* (2nd ed., Vol. 3). Boston, MA: Allyn and Bacon.

Bertalanffy, L. V. (1968). *General system theory: Foundations, development, applications*. New York: George Braziller.

Berthier, M. L., Kulisevsky, J., Gironell, A., & Heras, J. A. (1996). Obsessive-compulsive disorder associated with brain lesions. Clinical phenomenology, cognitive function, and anatomic correlates. *Neurology, 47*(2), 353–361. doi:10.1212/WNL.47.2.353

Beutler, L. E. (1989). Differential treatment selection: The role of diagnosis in psychotherapy. *Psychotherapy: Theory, research, practice, training, 26*(3), 271–281. doi:10.1037/h0085436

Beutel, M. E., & Huber, M. (2008). Functional neuroimaging – Can it contribute to our understanding of processes of change? *Neuro-Psychoanalysis, 10*(1), 5–16.

Bezanson, B. J., & James, S. (2007, October). Culture-general and culture-specific approaches to counseling: Complementary stances. *International Journal for the Advancement of Counselling, 29*(3–4), 159–171. doi:10.1007/s10447-007-9036-7

Bezie, Y., Molina, M., Hernandez, N., Batista, R., Niang, S., & Huet, D. (2006). Therapeutic compliance: A prospective analysis of various factors involved in the adherence rate in type 2 diabetes. *Diabetes & Metabolism, 32*(6), 611–616. doi:10.1016/S1262-3636(07)70316-6

Bion, W. R. (1961). *Experiences in groups*. London: Tavistock/Routledge.

Biagioli, M. (1993). *Galileo, courtier: The practice of science in the culture of absolutism*. Chicago, IL: University of Chicago Press.

Bickman, L., Guthrie, P. R., Foster, E. M., Lambert, E. W., Summerfelt, W. T., Breda, C. S., & Heflinger, C. A. (1995). *Evaluating managed mental health services: The Fort Bragg experiment*. New York: Plenum.

Bishop, M. A., & Trout, J. D. (2004). *Epistemology and the psychology of human judgment*. New York: Oxford University Press.

Blackwell, B. (Ed.). (1997). *Treatment compliance and the therapeutic alliance*. Amsterdam, Netherlands: Harwood Academic Publishers.

Blaney, P. H., & Millon, T. (2009). *Oxford textbook of psychopathology* (2nd ed.). New York: Oxford University Press.

Bloom, F. A., Beal, M. F., & Kupfer, D. J. (Eds.). (2003). *The Dana guide to brain health*. New York: Dana Press.

Bobgan, M., & Bobgan, D. (1987). *Psychoheresy: The psychological seduction of Christianity*. Santa Barbara, CA: EastGate Publishers.

Boesch, C. (1992). New elements of a theory of mind in wild chimpanzees. *Brain and Behavioral Sciences, 15*(1), 149–150.

Bogin, B. (1999). *Patterns of human growth*. Cambridge, UK: Cambridge University Press.

Bohannan, P. (1969). *Social anthropology*. New York: Holt, Rinehart & Winston.

Bohm, D. (1980). *Wholeness and the implicate order*. London: Routledge.

Bolles, R. C. (1993). *The story of psychology*. California: Brookes/Cole.

Bordin, E. S. (1979). The generalizability of the psychoanalytic concept of the working alliance. *Psychotherapy: Theory, Research and Practice, 16*, 252–260.

Bosley, C. M., Fosbury, J. A., & Cochrane, G. M. (1995). The psychological factors associated with poor compliance with treatment in asthma. *European Respiratory Journal, 8*(6), 899–904.

Boudes, P. (1998). Drug compliance in therapeutic trials: A review. *Contemporary Clinical Trials, 19*(3), 257–268. doi:10.1016/S0197-2456(98)00005-1

Boulton, A. A., Baker, G. B., & Martin-Iverson, M. T. (Eds.). (1991a). *Animal models in psychiatry, I. Neuromethods, 18*. doi:10.1385/0896031985

Boulton, A. A., Baker, G. B., & Martin-Iverson, M. T. (Eds.). (1991b). *Animal models in psychiatry, II: v. 2*. Clifton, NJ: Humana Press.

Bower, B. (1999). Slumber's unexplored landscape. *Science News, 156*(13), 205. doi:10.2307/4011789

Bowles, S., & Gintis, H. (2004). The evolution of strong reciprocity: Cooperation in heterogeneous environments. *Theoretical Population Biology, 65*, 17–28. doi:10.1016/j.tpb.2003.07.001

Bowman, R., & Baylen, D. (1994). Buddhism as a second-order change psychotherapy. *International Journal for the Advancement of Counselling, 17*(2), 101–108. doi:10.1007/BF01407966

Bradshaw, J. (2012, January 16). APA leading the charge against 'medicalizing' dsm-5. [*The National Psychologist*]. Retrieved from http://nationalpsychologist.com/2012/01/apa-leading-the-charge-against-medicalizing-dsm-5/101594.html.

Breedlove, S. M., Rosenzweig, M. R., & Watson, N. V. (2007). *Biological psychology: An introduction to behavioral, cognitive, and clinical neuroscience* (5th ed.). Sunderland, MA: Sinauer Associates.

Breggin, P. (1994). *Toxic psychiatry: Why therapy, empathy, and love must replace the drugs, electroshock, and biochemical theories of the new psychiatry*. New York: St. Martin's Press.

Brems, C. (2000). *Basic skills in psychotherapy and counseling*. Pacific Grove, CA: Thomson-Brooks/Cole.

Brent, P. (1976). *The Mongol empire: Genghis Khan: His triumph and his legacy*. London: Weidenfeld & Nicholson.

Bridle, C., Riemsma, R. P., Pattenden, J., Sowden, A. J., Mather, L., Watt, I. S., & Walker A. (2009). Systematic review of the effectiveness of health behavior interventions based on the transtheoretical model. *Psychological Health, 20*, 283–301.

Brislin, R. W. (1981). *Cross-cultural encounters*. Elmsford, NY: Pergamon.

British Psychological Society. (2011). *Response to the American Psychiatric Association: DSM-5 development.* Retrieved from http://apps.bps.org.uk/_publicationfiles/consultation-responses/DSM-5%202011%20-%20BPS%20response.pdf.

British Trust for Ornithology. (n.d.). *BTO – Looking out for birds.* Retrieved from http://www.bto.org/.

Brittingham, A., & de la Cruz, P. (2004). *Ancestry: 2000-census 2000 brief.* U.S. Census Bureau. Retrieved from http://www.census.gov/prod/2004pubs/c2kbr-35.pdf.

Broad, K. D., Curley, J. P., & Keverne, E. B. (2006). Mother-infant bonding and the evolution of mammalian social relationships. *Philosophical Transactions of the Royal Society B: Biological Sciences, 361*(1476), 2199–2214. doi:10.1098/rstb.2006.1940

Bromberg, W. (1975). *From shaman to psychotherapist.* Chicago: Regnery.

Bronfenbrenner, U. (1979). *The ecology of human development: Experiments by nature and design.* Cambridge, MA: Harvard University Press.

Bronfenbrenner, U. (Ed.). (2005). *Making human beings human: Bioecological perspectives on human development.* Thousand Oaks, CA: Sage.

Broude, G. J. (1995). *Growing up: A cross-cultural encyclopedia.* Santa Barbara, CA: ABC-CLIO.

Brown, C. H. (1976). General principles of human anatomical partonomy and speculations on the growth of partonomic nomenclature. *American Ethnologist, 3*(3), [Folk Biology], 400–424.

Brown, D. (1991). *Human universals.* Philadelphia, PA: Temple University Press.

Brown, F. J., & Roucek, J. S. (1945). *One America: The history, contributions, and present problems of our racial and national minorities.* New York: Prentice-Hall.

Brown, G. S., Cameron, J., & Brown, L. (2008). In search of the active ingredient: What really works in mental health care? *Perspectives on Fluency and Fluency Disorders, 18,* 53–59. doi:10.1044/ffd18.2.53

Brown, R., & Herrnstein, R. J. (1975). *Psychology.* Boston: Little, Brown and Company.

Bruner, J. (1990). *Acts of meaning.* Cambridge, MA: Harvard University Press.

Buckser, A., & Glazier, S. D. (2003). *The anthropology of religious conversion.* Lanham, MD: Rowman & Littlefield Publishers.

Buijs, R. M., Kalsbeek, A., Romijn, H. J., Pennartz, C. M. A., & Mirmiran, M. (Eds.). (1996). *Hypothalamic integration of circadian rhythms.* Amsterdam: Elsevier.

Bureau of Labor Statistics. (2009). *Occupational outlook handbook, 2010–11: Counselors.* Retrieved from http://www.bls.gov/oco/ocos067.htm.

Bureau of Labor Statistics. (2012). *Psychologists.* Retrieved from http://www.bls.gov/ooh/Life-Physical-and-Social-Science/Psychologists.htm#tab-6.

Bureau of Meteorology. (2001, March, 22). *Weather volunteers honoured on World Meteorological Day.* [Press release] [Commonwealth of Australia]. Retrieved from http://www.bom.gov.au/announcements/media_releases/ho/010322.shtml.

Burgess, H., & Maiese, M. (2004). Rumor control. *Peace and Conflict Studies.* Retrieved from http://www.beyondintractability.org/essay/rumor_control/.

Burkart, J. M., Fehr, E., Efferson, C., & van Schaik, C. P. (2007). Other-regarding preferences in a non-human primate: Common marmosets provision food altruistically. *PNAS, 104*(50), 19762–19766. doi:10.1073/pnas.0710310104

Burns, C. D. (1913). William of Ockham on universals. *Proceedings of the Aristotelian Society, 14,* 76–99.

Burns, D. D. (1980). *Feeling good: The new mood therapy.* New York: New American Library.

Burston, D. (2003). Existentialism, humanism & psychotherapy. *Journal of the Society for Existential Analysis, 14*(2), 309–319.

Burtsev, M., & Turchin P. (2006). Evolution of cooperative strategies from first principles. *Nature, 440,* 1041–1044. doi:10.1038/nature04470

Buss, D. M. (1995). Evolutionary psychology: A new paradigm for psychological science. *Psychological Inquiry, 6,* 1–30. doi:10.1207/s15327965pli0601_1

Buss, D. M. (1999). *Evolutionary psychology: The new science of the mind.* New York: Allyn and Bacon.

Buss, D. M. (2001). Human nature and culture: An evolutionary psychological perspective. *Journal of Personality, 69*(6), 955–78. doi:10.1111/1467-6494.696171

Buss, D. M. (Ed.). (2005). *Handbook of evolutionary psychology.* Hoboken, NJ: Wiley.

Buss, D. M., & Malamuth, N. (Eds.). (1996). *Sex, power, conflict: Evolutionary and feminist perspectives.* Oxford: Oxford University Press.

Butcher, J. N. (Ed.). (2009). *Oxford handbook of personality assessment.* Oxford/New York: Oxford University Press.

Butcher, J. N., Dahlstrom, W. G., Graham, J. R., Tellegen, A., & Kaemmer, B. (1989). *The Minnesota Multiphasic Personality Inventory-2 (MMPI-2): Manual for administration and scoring.* Minneapolis, MN: University of Minnesota Press.

Butler, R. A. (1954). Incentive conditions which influence visual exploration. *Journal of Experimental Psychology, 48,* 19–23. doi:10.1037/h0063578

Byrne, M. (2003). Culture & communications: Similarities of color meanings among diverse cultures. [Bibliotheque: World Wide Society]. Retrieved from http://www.bwwsociety.org/feature/color.htm.

Cabeza de Vaca, A. N. (1993). *The account: Álvar Núñez Cabeza de Vaca's Relacíon* (M. Favata & J. Fernández, Trans.). Houston, TX: Arte Público Press.

Cain, D. J., & Seeman, J. (Eds.). (2002). *Humanistic psychotherapies: Handbook of research and practice.* Washington, DC: American Psychological Association.

Callaghan, A., & Irwin, H. J. (2003). Paranormal belief as a psychological coping mechanism. *Journal of the Society for Psychical Research, 67,* 200–207.

Cameron, C. (2008). Patient compliance: Recognition of factors involved and suggestions for promoting compliance with therapeutic regimens. *Journal of Advanced Nursing, 24*(2), 244–250. doi:10.1046/j.1365-2648.1996.01993.x

Campbell, D. T., & Boruch, R. F. (1975). Making the case for randomized assignment of treatments by considering the alternatives: Six ways in which quasi-experimental evaluations tend to underestimate effects. In C. A. Bennet and A. A. Lumsdaine (Eds.), *Evaluation and experience: Some critical issues in assessing social programs.* New York: Academic Press.

Campbell, D. T., & Stanley, J. C. (1966). *Experimental and quasi-experimental designs for research.* Chicago: Rand McNally.

Campbell, J. (1959-[68]). *The masks of God.* New York, Viking Press.

Campbell, T. W. (1994). *Beware the talking cure: Psychotherapy may be hazardous to your mental health.* Boca Raton, FL: Upton Books.

Campinha-Bacote, J. (2003). Many faces: Addressing diversity in health care. *Online Journal of Issues in Nursing, 8*(1), 3.

Canadian Mental Health Association. (2010). *History of mental illness treatment: A brief history of psychotherapy.* Ottawa, ON: Author. Retrieved from http://www.manito ba.cmha.ca/data/1/rec_docs/953_a%20brief%20history%20of%20psychothera py.pdf.

Cangelosi, A., & Harnad, S. (2001). The adaptive advantage of symbolic theft over sensorimotor toil: Grounding language in perceptual categories. *Evolution of Communication, 4*(1), 117–142. doi:10.1075/eoc.4.1.07can

Cantwell, A. (1993). *Queer blood: The secret AIDS genocide plot.* Los Angeles, CA: ARIES Rising Press.

Cao, J. (2009). The credibility of psychotherapy: Psychological reactance and Chinese students' impressions of directive and nondirective approaches. *Dissertation Abstracts International: Section B: The Sciences and Engineering, 69*(9-B), pp. 5769. [Dissertation].

Caplan, P. J. (1995). *They say you're crazy: How the world's most powerful psychiatrists decide who's normal.* Reading, MA: Addison Wesley.

Caplan, P. J., & Cosgrove, L. (Eds.). (2004). *Bias in psychiatric diagnosis.* Lanham, MD: Rowman & Littlefield.

Carkhuff, R. R. (1987). *The art of helping* (6th ed.). Amherst, MA: Human Resource Development Press.

Carlson, D. (1980). *Boys have feelings too: Growing up male for boys.* New York: Scribner/ Simon & Schuster.

Carnes, M. C., & Garraty, J. A. (2007). *The American nation: A history of the United States* [combined volume]. New York: Longman Publishing Group.

Carroll, R. T. (2009). Subjective validation. The skeptic's dictionary. Retrieved from http://www.skepdic.com/subjectivevalidation.html.

Carson, D. S., Cornish, J. L., Guastella, A. J., Hunt, G. E., & McGregor, I. S. (2010). Oxytocin decreases methamphetamine self-administration, methamphetamine hyperactivity, and relapse to methamphetamine-seeking behavior in rats. *Neuropharmacology, 58*(1), 38–43. doi:10.1016/j.neuropharm.2009.06.018

Carson, N. J. (1997). Ethnopsychiatry and theories of "the African Mind": A historical and comparative study. *McGill Journal of Medicine, 3*(1). Retrieved from http://www. medicine.mcgill.ca/mjm/v03n01/.

Carter, C. S., Ahnert, L., Grossmann, K. E., Hrdy, S. B., Lamb, M. E., Porges, S. W., & Sachser, N. (Eds.). (2006). *Attachment and bonding: A new synthesis.* Cambridge, MA: MIT Press.

Carter, J. A. (2006). Theoretical pluralism and technical eclecticism. In C. D. Goodheart, A. E. Kazdin, & R. J. Sternberg (Eds.), *Evidence-based psychotherapy: Where practice and research meet* (pp. 63–80). Washington, DC: American Psychological Association. doi:10.1037/11423-003

Castonguay, L. G., & Beutler, L. E. (Eds.). (2005). *Principles of therapeutic change that work.* New York: Oxford University Press.

Cattell, R. B. (1946). *The description and measurement of personality.* Yonkers-on-Hudson, NY: World Book Company.

Cattell, R. B. (1950). *Personality: A systematic theoretical and factual study.* New York, McGraw-Hill.

Cattell, R. B. (1957). *Personality and motivation structure and measurement.* New York: World Book.

Central Intelligence Agency. (n.d.). *The world factbook* (United States). Retrieved from https://www.cia.gov/library/publications/the-world-factbook/geos/us.html.

Charness, G., & Rabin, M. (2002). Understanding social preferences with simple tests. *Quarterly Journal of Economics, 117,* 817–869. doi:10.1162/003355302760193904

Cehner, U. (2008). *European year of intercultural dialogue 2008: Together in cross-cultural learning diversity on a small Mediterranean island – Malta case study.* (Final Thesis, Univerza V Ljubljani, 2008). Retrieved http://dk.fdv.uni-lj.si/diplomska/pdfs/cehner-urska.pdf.

Chakrabarty, D. (2000). *Provincializing Europe: Postcolonial thought and historical difference.* Princeton, NJ: Princeton University Press.

Chalfant, H. P., Heller, P. L., Roberts, A., Briones, D., Aguirre Hochbaum, S., & Fan, W. (1990). The clergy as a resource for those encountering psychological distress. *Review of Religious Research, 31,* 305–313. doi:10.2307/3511620

Chalmers, D. J. (Ed.). (2002). *Philosophy of mind: Classical and contemporary readings.* Oxford/New York: Oxford University Press.

Chapman, S. (n.d.). *DSM-5 and ICD-11 Watch: Monitoring the development of DSM-5, ICD-11, ICD-10-CM.* WordPress.com. Retrieved from http://dsm5watch.word press.com/category/criticism-of-dsm-v-dsm-5/.

Chelune, G. J., & Parker, J. B. (1981). Neuropsychological deficits associated with chronic alcohol abuse. *Clinical Psychology Review, 1*(2), 181–195. doi:10.1016/0272-7358(81)90002-7

Chemero, A. (2009). *Radical embodied cognitive science.* Cambridge, MA: MIT Press.

Chen, S. X., & Mak, W. W. S. (2008). Seeking professional help: Etiology beliefs about mental illness across cultures. *Journal of Counseling Psychology, 55,* 442–450. doi: 10.1037/ a0012898

Cheung, F. M., Fan, W., & To, C. (2008). The Chinese personality assessment inventory as a culturally relevant personality measure in applied settings. *Social and Personality Psychology Compass, 2*(1), 74–89. doi:10.1111/j.1751-9004.2007.00045.x

Cheung, F. M., Leung, K., Zhang, J.-X., Sun, H.-F., Gan, Y.-Q., Song, W.-Z., & Xie, D. (2001). Indigenous Chinese personality constructs: Is the five-factor model complete? *Journal of Cross-Cultural Psychology, 32*(4), 407–33. doi:10.1177/0022022 101032004003

Cheung, F. M., van de Vijver, F. J. R., & Leong, F. T. L. (2011). Toward a new approach to the study of personality in culture. *American Psychologist, 66*(7), 593–603. doi:10.1037/a0022389

Child, I. L. (1973). *Humanistic psychology and the research tradition: Their several virtues.* New York: Wiley.

Chinese Medical Association. (1990). *Chinese classification of mental disorders* (2nd ed.). Changsha, China: Hunan Medical University.

Choi, I., Nisbett, R. E., & Norenzayan, A. (1999). Causal attribution across cultures: Variation and universality. *Psychological Bulletin, 125,* 47–63. doi:10.1037/0033-2909.125.1.47

Chomsky, N. (1957). *Syntactic structures.* The Hague/Paris: Mouton.

Chomsky, N. (1967). A review of B. F. Skinner's verbal behavior. In L. A. Jakobovits & M. S. Miron (Eds.), *Readings in the psychology of language* (pp. 142–143). Upper Saddle River, NJ: Prentice-Hall.

Chomsky, N. (1968). *Language and mind.* New York: Harcourt, Brace & World.

Chopra, Ananda S. (2003). Åyurveda. In H. Selin, *Medicine across cultures: History and practice of medicine in non-western cultures.* Norwell, MA: Kluwer Academic Publishers. pp. 75–83.

Chou, I-h., & Narasimhan, K. (Eds.). (2005). Focus on neurobiology of addiction [Special issue]. *Nature Neuroscience, 8*(11), 1413–1626. doi:10.1038/nn1105-142

Choucri, N., & Mistree, D. (2009). Globalization, migration, and new challenges to governance. *Current History, 108*(717), 173–179. Retrieved from http://web.mit. edu/polisci/research/choucri/Choucri_Mistree_Globalization_ Migration_New_ Challenges_Governance.pdf.

Christmas, D. (2010). *Cross-cultural psychiatry.* Retrieved from http://www.trickcyclists. co.uk/pdf/Culture_Specific_Disorders.PDF.

Chrisomalis, S. (2007). *Divination and fortune-telling.* The phrontistery. Retrieved from http://phrontistery.info/divine.html.

Church, A. T., & Lonner, W. J. (1998). The cross-cultural perspective in the study of personality. *Journal of Cross-Cultural Psychology, 29*(1), 32–62. doi:10.1177/0022022 198291003

Cialdini, R. B. (2001a). *Influence: Science and practice* (4th ed.). Boston: Allyn & Bacon.

Cialdini, R. B. (2001b). The science of persuasion. *Scientific American, 284,* 76–81.

Cialdini, R. B., & Goldstein, N. J. (2004). Social influence: Compliance and conformity. *Annual Review of Psychology, 55,* 591–621. doi:10.1146/annurev.psych.55. 090902.142015

Cliaborn, C. D. (1986). Social influence: Toward a general theory of change. In F. J Dorn (Ed.), *Social influence processes in counseling and psychotherapy* (pp. 65–74). Springfield, IL: Charles C Thomas.

Clark, A. (2000). *Mindware: An introduction to the philosophy of cognitive science.* Oxford/ New York: Oxford University Press.

Clark, A. J. (2010). Empathy: An integral model in the counseling process. *Journal of Counseling & Development, 88*(3), 348–356.

Clauss-Ehlers, C. S. (Ed.). (2009). *Encyclopedia of cross-cultural school psychology.* New York: Springer.

Clavelin, M. (1974). *The natural philosophy of Galileo.* Cambridge, MA: MIT Press.

Clay, R. A. (2012, July/August). The psychology of hiv/aids prevention. *Monitor on Psychology, 43*(7), 38–40.

Cloninger, S. (2009). Conceptual issues in personality theory. In P. J. Corr & G. Matthews (Eds.), *The Cambridge handbook of personality psychology* (pp. 3–26). Cambridge, UK: Cambridge University Press.

Cloud, J. (2011, March 7). Beyond drugs: How alternative treatments can ease pain. *Time, 177*(9), 80–4, 86, 88.

Cobb, S. (1976). Social support as a moderator of life stress. *Psychosomatic Medicine, 38,* 300–314.

Cockburn, J., & Holroyd, C. B. (2010). Focus on the positive: Computational simulations implicate asymmetrical reward prediction error signals in childhood attention-deficit/hyperactivity disorder. *Brain Research, 1365,* 18–34. doi:10.1016/j.brainres.2010.09.065

Cockerham, W. C. (2010). *Sociology of mental illness* (8th ed.). Upper Saddle River, NJ: Pearson/Prentice-Hall.

Coffield, K. E., & Buckalew, L. W. (1984). The study of values: Toward revised norms and changing values. *Counseling and Values, 28*(2), 72–75.

Cohen, A. B. (2009). Many forms of culture. *American Psychologist, 64*(3), 194–204. doi: 10.1037/a0015308

Cohen, A. M., Stavri, P. Z., & Hersh, W. R. (2004). A categorisation and analysis of the criticisms of evidence-based medicine. *International Journal of Medical Informatics, 73*(1), 35–43. doi:10.1016/j.ijmcdinf.2003.11.002

Cohen, C. E. (1981). Person categories and social perception: Testing some boundary conditions of the processing effects of prior knowledge. *Journal of Personality and Social Psychology, 40,* 441–452. doi:10.1037/0022-3514.40.3.441

Cohen, D. (Ed.). (1990). Challenging the therapeutic state: Critical perspectives on psychiatry and the mental health system. *The Journal of Mind and Behavior, 11*(3 & 4).

Cohen, E. (2007, February 26,). Tuskegee's ghosts: Fear hinders black marrow donation. *CNN.com.* Retrieved from http://www.cnn.com/2007/HEALTH/02/07/bone.marrow/index.html.

Colbert, T. C. (1996). *Broken brains or wounded hearts: What causes mental illness.* Santa Ana, CA: Kevco Publishing.

Colby, K. M. (1983). *Fundamental crisis in psychiatry: Unreliability of diagnosis.* Springfield, IL: Charles C Thomas.

Cole, E. R. (2009). Intersectionality and research in psychology. *American Psychologist, 64*(3), 170–180. doi:10.1037/a0014564

Cole, M. (1988). Cross-cultural research in socio-historical tradition. *Human development, 31,* 137–157.

Cole, M. (1992). Context, modularity and cultural constitution of development. In L. T. Winegar & J. Valsiner (Eds.), *Children's development within social context* (Vol. 2, pp. 5–31). Hillsdale, NJ: Lawrence Erlbaum.

Cole, M. (1996). *Cultural psychology: A once and future discipline?* Cambridge, MA: Harvard University Press.

Cole, M., & Bruner, J. S. (1971). Cultural differences and inferences about psychological processes. *American Psychologist, 26,* 867–76. doi:10.1037/h0032240

Cole, M., Gay, J. H., Click, J. A., & Sharp, D. (1971). *The cultural context of learning and thinking.* London: Methuen.

Cole, M., & Scribner, S. (1974). *Culture and thought: A psychological introduction.* New York: Wiley.

Coll, R. K., Lay, M. C., & Taylor, N. (2008). Scientists and scientific thinking: Understanding scientific thinking through an investigation of scientists views about superstitions and religious beliefs. *Eurasia Journal of Mathematics, Science & Technology Education, 4*(3), 197–214.

Collins, M. D. (2005). Transcending dualistic thinking in conflict resolution. *Negotiation Journal, 21*(2), 263–280. doi:10.1111/j.1571-9979.2005.00063.x

Collis, J. M., & Messick, S. (Eds.). (2001). I*ntelligence and personality: Bridging the gap in theory and measurement.* Mahwah, NJ: Lawrence Erlbaum Associates.

Committee on Animal Research and Ethics. (n.d.). *Guidelines for ethical conduct in the care and use of animals.* [American Psychological Association]. Retrieved from http://www.apa.org/science/leadership/care/guidelines.aspx.

Comrie, B. (1981). *Language universals and linguistic typology.* Chicago: University of Chicago Press.

Congress of World and Traditional Religions. (2005–2012). *Dynamics of religions in the world.* Retrieved from http://www.religions-congress.org/content/view/130/35/lang,english/.

Conn, S. R., & Rieke, M. L. (1994a). *The 16PF fifth edition technical manual.* Champaign, IL: Institute for Personality and Ability Testing.

Connelly, R. J. (1987). Deception and the placebo effect in biomedical research. *IRB: Review of Human Subjects Research, 9*(4), 5–7.

Connolly, P., & Solway, A. (2002). *Ancient Greece.* New York: Oxford University Press.

Constable, G. (1973). *The Neanderthals* (pp. 38–58). New York: Time-Life Books.

Constantine, M. G., & Sue, D. W. (Eds.). (2005). *Strategies for building multicultural competence in mental health and educational settings.* Somerset, NJ: John Wiley and Sons.

Conyne, R. K., & Cook, E. P. (Eds.). (2004). *Ecological counseling: An innovative approach to conceptualizing person-environment interaction.* Alexandria, VA: American Counseling Association.

Cook, T. D., & Campbell, D. T. (1979). *Quasi-experimentation: Design and analysis issues for field settings.* Boston, MA: Houghton Mifflin Company.

Cooper, A., & Hassiotis, A. (2009). Appendix A: Critique of the ICD 10 and DSM IV based classification of mental disorders in intellectual disability. In A. Hassiotis, D. A. Barron & I. Hall (Eds.), *Intellectual disability psychiatry: A practical handbook.* Chichester, UK: John Wiley & Sons. doi:10.1002/9780470682968.app1

Cooper, M. (2003). *Existential therapies.* London: Sage.

Corey, G. (2009). *Theory and practice of counseling and psychotherapy.* Belmont, CA: Thomson-Brooks/Cole.

Corey, G., Schneider Corey, M., & Callahan, P. (2007). *Issues and ethics in the helping professions* (7th ed.). Belmont, CA: Thomson-Brooks/Cole.

Corning, W. C. (1986). Bootstrapping toward a classification system. In T. Millon & G. L. Klerman (Eds.), *Contemporary directions in psychopathology: Toward the DSM-IV* (pp. 279–303). New York: Guilford.

Corr, P. J., & Matthews, G. (2009). (Eds.). *The Cambridge handbook of personality psychology.* Cambridge, UK: Cambridge University Press.

Corsini, R. J., & Wedding, D. (Eds.). (2005). *Current psychotherapies.* Belmont, CA: Thomson-Brooks/Cole.

Coryell, W., Lowry, M., & Wasek, P. (1980). Diagnostic instability and depression. *American Journal of Psychiatry, 137,* 48–51.

Cosmides, L. (1989). The logic of social exchange: Has natural selection shaped how humans reason? Studies with the Wason selection task. *Cognition, 31,* 187–276. doi:10.1016/0010-0277(89)90023-1

Cosmides, L., & Tooby, J. (1987). From evolution to behavior: Evolutionary psychology as the missing link. In J. Dupre (Ed.), *The latest on the best: Essays on evolution and optimality*. Cambridge, MA: The MIT Press.

Costa, P. T., Jr., & McCrae, R. R. (1992). *Revised NEO personality inventory (NEO-PI-R) and NEO five-factor inventory (NEO-FFI) professional manual*. Odessa, FL: Psychological Assessment Resources.

Cottam, M. L., Dietz-Uhler, B., Mastors, E., & Preston, T. (2010). *Introduction to political psychology*. New York: Psychology Press.

Counsel. (2011). In *Merriam-Webster dictionary online* [Medical]. Retrieved from http://www.merriam-webster.com/medical/counselling.

Counseling. (2011). In *Merriam-Webster dictionary online*. Retrieved from http://www.merriam-webster.com/dictionary/counseling.

Counselor. (2011). In *Merriam-Webster dictionary online*. Retrieved from http://www.merriam-webster.com/thesaurus/counselor.

Cox, D. (1968). *Modern psychology, the teachings of Carl Gustav Jung*. New York: Barnes & Noble.

Cozolino, L. (2002). *The neuroscience of psychotherapy: Building and rebuilding the human brain*. New York: W. W. Norton & Company.

Craighead, W. E. (Ed.). (2002). *The Corsini encyclopedia of psychology and behavioral science* (3rd ed.). Chichester, NY: Wiley.

Craighead, W. E., & Nemeroff, C. B. (Eds.). (2004). *The concise Corsini encyclopedia of psychology and behavioral science* (3rd ed.). Hoboken, NJ: John Wiley & Sons.

Creamer, M., Burgess, P., & McFarlane, A. C. (2001). Post-traumatic stress disorder: Findings from the Australian national survey of mental health and well-being. *Psychological Medicine, 31,* 1237–47.

Critelli, J. W., & Neumann. K. F. (1984). The placebo. Conceptual analysis of a construct in transition. *American Psychology, 39*(1), 32–39. doi:10.1037/0003-066X.39.1.32.

Cronbach, L. (1982). *Designing evaluations of educational and social programs*. San Francisco: Jossey-Bass.

Crosby, A. W. (1987). *The Columbian voyages, the Columbian exchange, and their historians*. Washington, DC: American Historical Association.

Cross, G. (2000). *An all-consuming century: Why commercialism won in modern America*. New York: Columbia University Press.

Cross, T. L. (2010). *Relational worldview model*. National Indian Child Welfare Association (NICWA). Retrieved from http://www.nicwa.org/Relational_Worldview/.

Cudd, A. E. (2006). *Analyzing oppression*. Oxford: Oxford University Press. doi:10.1093/0195187431.001.0001.

Culture. (2012a). In *Merriam-Webster's online dictionary*. Retrieved from http://www.merriam-webster.com/dictionary/culture.

Culture. (2012b). In *Merriam-Webster's online dictionary*. Retrieved from http://www.merriam-webster.com/concise/culture.

Cummings, N. A., & O'Donohue, W. T. (2008). *Eleven blunders that cripple psychotherapy in America: A remedial unblundering*. New York: Routledge/Taylor & Francis Group.

Curtin, P. D. (1998). *Cross-cultural trade in world history.* Cambridge, UK: Cambridge University Press.

Curtis, G. N. (2001–2009). *The fallacy files.* Retrieved from http://www.fallacyfiles.org/index.html.

Cutler, R. B., & Fishbain, D. A. (2005). Are alcoholism treatments effective? The Project MATCH data. *BMC Public Health, 5,* 75. doi:10.1186/1471-2458-5-75

Dale, M. A., & Lyddon, W. J. (2000). Sandplay: A constructivist strategy for assessment and change. *Journal of Constructivist Psychology, 13,* 135–154.

Dalrymple, W. (2003). *City of Djinns: A year in Delhi.* Flamingo. Harmondsworth, Middlesex, England: Penguin.

Damper, R. I., & Harnad, S. (2000). Neural network modeling of categorical perception. *Perception and Psychophysics, 62*(4), 843–867. doi:10.3758/BF03206927

Danziger, N., Faillenot, I., & Peyron, R. (2009, January). Can we share a pain we never felt? Neural correlates of empathy in patients with congenital insensitivity to pain. *Neuron, 61*(2), 203–212. doi:10.1016/j.neuron.2008.11.023

Dart, R. A. (1953). The predatory transition from ape to man. *International Anthropological and Linguistic Review, 1,* 201–217.

Darwin, C. (1872/1998). *The expression of the emotions in man and animals* (3rd ed.). New York: Oxford University Press.

Dasen, P. R., & Heron, A. (1981). Cross-cultural tests of Piaget's theory. In H. C. Triandis & A. Heron (Eds.), *Handbook of cross-cultural psychology* (Vol. 4, pp. 295–342). Boston: Allyn and Bacon.

Davey, M. P., Davey, A., Tubbs, C., Savla, J., & Anderson, S. (2010). Second order change and evidence-based practice. *Journal of Family Therapy, 32*(4), 1–19. doi:10.1111/j.1467-6427.2010.00499.x

Davidson, G., & Horvath, A. (1997). Three sessions of brief couples therapy: A clinical trial. *Journal of Family Psychology, 11,* 422–435. doi:10.1037/0893-3200.11.4.422-435

Davidson, R. J. (2001). The neural circuitry of emotion and affective style: Prefrontal cortex and amygdala contributions. *Social Science Information, 40*(1), 11–37. doi:10.1177/053901801040001002

Davidson, R. J. (2001a). Toward a biology of personality and emotion. *Annals of the New York Academy of Sciences, 935,* 191–207.

Davidson, R. J. (2003). Affective neuroscience and psychophysiology: Toward a synthesis. *Psychophysiology, 40,* 655–665. doi:10.1111/1469-8986.00067

Davidson, R. J., Pizzagalli, D., Nitschke, J. B., & Putnam, K. M. (2002). Depression: Perspectives from affective neuroscience. *Annual Review of Psychology, 53,* 545–574. doi:10.1146/annurev.psych.53.100901.135148

Davis, D. A. (1979). What's in a name? A Bayesian rethinking of attributional biases in clinical judgment. *Journal of Consulting and Clinical Psychology, 47,* 1109–1114. doi:10.1037/0022-006X.47.6.1109

Davis, D. M., & Hayes, J. A. (2012, July/August). What are the benefits of mindfulness? *Monitor on Psychology, 43*(7), 64–70.

Dawes, R. M. (1994). *House of cards: Psychology and psychotherapy built on myth.* New York: The Free Press.

Davis, S. F., & Palladino, J. J. (2000). *Psychology* (3rd ed.). Upper Saddle River, NJ: Prentice-Hall, Inc.

Dawes, R. M. (2001). *Everyday irrationality: How pseudo-scientists, lunatics, and the rest of us systematically fail to think rationally.* Boulder, CO: Westview Press.

Dawes, R. M. (2008). Psychotherapy: The myth of expertise. In S. O. Lilienfeld, J. Ruscio & S. J. Lynn (Eds.), *Navigating the mindfield: A user's guide to distinguishing science from pseudoscience in mental health* (pp. 311–344). Amherst, NY: Prometheus Books.

Dawkins, R. (1976). *The selfish gene.* Oxford: Oxford University Press.

DeCarvalho, R. J. (1991). *The founders of humanistic psychology.* New York: Praeger.

Decety, J., & Jackson, P. L. (2006). A social-neuroscience perspective on empathy. *Current directions in psychological science, 15*(2), 54–58. doi:10.1111/j.0963-7214.2006.00406.x

de Mijolla, A. (Ed.). (2005). *International dictionary of psychoanalysis.* Detroit: Macmillan Reference.

Department of Veterans Affairs. (2001, April). *Annual report to congress – 1999: Research on Gulf war veterans' illnesses.* Retrieved from http://www.research.va.gov/resources/pubs/docs/1999_Gulf_War_Illnesses.doc.

De Raad, B. (2009). Structural models of personality. In P. J. Corr & G. Matthews (Eds.), *The Cambridge handbook of personality psychology* (pp. 127–147). Cambridge, UK: Cambridge University Press.

deWaal, F. D. (1996). *Good natured: The origins of right and wrong in humans and other animals.* Cambridge: MA: Harvard University Press.

De Waal, F. (2009). *The age of empathy – Nature's lessons for a kinder society.* New York: Crown/Random.

DeYoung, C. G. (2010). Personality neuroscience and the biology of traits. *Social and Personality Psychology Compass, 4*(12), 1165–1180. doi:10.1111/j.1751-9004.2010.00327.x

Dhammika, V. S. (1993). *The edicts of king Asoka: An English rendering.* Kandy, Sri Lanka: The Wheel Publication No. 386/387 [Buddhist Publication Society].

Diaz-Guerrero, R., Diaz-Loving, R., & Rodriguez de Diaz, M. L. (2001). Personality across cultures. In L. L. Adler & U. P. Gielen, *Cross-cultural topics in psychology* (2nd ed.). Santa Barbara, CA: Greenwood Publishing Group.

Dickson, D. H., & Kelly, I. W. (1985). The 'Barnum Effect' in personality assessment: A review of the literature. *Psychological Reports, 57*(1), 367–382.

DiFonzo, N., & Bordia, P. (2007). *Rumor psychology: Social and organizational approaches.* Washington, DC: American Psychological Association. doi:10.1037/11503-000

Digman, J. M. (1990). Personality structure: Emergence of the five-factor model. *Annual Review of Psychology, 41,* 417–440.

Digman, J. M. (1996). The curious history of the five-factor model. In J. S. Wiggins (Ed.), *The five-factor model of personality: Theoretical perspectives.* New York: Guilford.

Digman, J. M., & Takemoto-Chock, N. K. (1981). Factors in the natural language of personality: Re-analysis, comparison, and interpretation of six major studies. *Multivariate Behavioral Research, 16,* 149–170. doi:10.1207/s15327906mbr1602_2

Dineen, T. (1999). *Manufacturing victims: What the psychology industry is doing to people.* London: Constable & Robinson Limited.

Dingfelder, S. F. (2010). From psychologist to president. *Monitor on Psychology, 41*(1), 36–39.

DiSalvo, D. (2009). Forget survival of the fittest: It is kindness that counts. *Scientific American Mind, 20*(5), 18–19.

Dobbs, L. (2006). *War on the middle class: How the government, big business, and special interest groups are waging war on the American dream and how to fight back.* New York: Penguin Books.

Donner, F. (1981). *The early Islamic conquests.* Princeton, NJ: Princeton University Press.

Doongaji, D. R., Vahia, V. N., & Bharucha, M. P. (1978). On placebos, placebo responses and placebo responders – A review of psychological, psychopharmacological and psychophysiological factors. *Journal of Postgraduate Medicine, 24*(2), 91–7.

Dorrien, G. (2009). *Social ethics in the making: Interpreting an American tradition.* Chicester, UK: Wiley & Sons.

Dossey, L. (1993). *Healing words: The power of prayer and the practice of medicine.* San Francisco, CA: Harper.

Dovidio, J. F., Schroeder, D. A., Penner, L. A., & Piliavin, J. A. (2006). *The social psychology of prosocial behavior.* London: Taylor & Francis (Psychology Press – formerly published by Lawrence Erlbaum Associates).

Doyle, R. (1998, September). By the numbers: Ethnic groups in the world. *Scientific American Magazine, 279*(3), 30.

Draguns, J. G. (1994). Pathological and clinical aspects. In L. Adler & U. Gielen (Eds.), *Cross-cultural topics in psychology* (pp. 164–177). Westport, CT: Greenwood Publishing Group.

Draguns, J. G. (1995). Cultural influences upon psychopathology: Clinical and practical implications. *Journal of Social Distress and the Homeless, 4*(2), 79–103. doi:79-103.10.1007/BF02094611

Draguns, J. G., Gielen, U. P., & Fish, J. M. (2004). Approaches to culture, healing, and psychotherapy. In U. P. Gielen, J. M. Fish, & J. G. Draguns (Eds.), *Handbook of culture, therapy, and healing* (pp. 1–11). Mahwah, NJ: Lawrence Erlbaum.

Draper, S. W. (2008). *The Hawthorne, Pygmalion, placebo and other effects of expectation: Some notes* [WWW document]. Retrieved from http://www.psy.gla.ac.uk/~steve/hawth.html.

Dreyer, E. L. (2006). *Zheng He: China and the oceans in the early Ming, 1405–1433.* London: Longman.

Dryden, W., & Neenan, N. (2004). *The rational emotive behavioural approach to therapeutic change.* London: Sage Publications.

Duan, C., & Hill, C. E. (1996). The current state of empathy research. *Journal of Counseling Psychology, 43*(3), 261–274. doi:10.1037/0022-0167.43.3.261

Du Bois, W. E. B. (1998). *Black reconstruction in America, 1860–1880.* New York: Free Press/Simon & Schuster.

Dudley, R. T. (2002). Order effects in research on paranormal belief. *Psychological Reports, 90,* 665–666. doi:10.2466/pr0.2002.90.2.665

Duhigg, C. (2012). *The power of habit.* New York: Random House.

Dumont, F., & LeComte, C. (1987). Inferential processes in clinical work: Inquiry into logical errors that affect diagnostic judgments. *Professional Psychology: Research and Practice, 18,* 433–438. doi:10.1037/0735-7028.18.5.433

Duncan, D. F., Donnelly, J. W., Nicholson, T., & Hees, A. J. (1992). Cultural diversity, superstitions, and pseudoscientific beliefs among allied health students. *College Student Journal, 26*(4), 525–530.

Dundas, P. (2002). *The Jains.* New York: Taylor & Francis.

Dunn, R. E. (2005). *The adventures of Ibn Battuta.* University of California Press.

Durkheim, E. (1974). *Sociology and philosophy.* Glencoe, IL.: The Free Press.

Duska, R., & Whelen, M. (1975). *Moral development: A guide to Piaget and Kohlberg.* New York: Paulist.

Dwairy, M. A. (1998). *Cross-cultural counseling: the Arab-Palestinian case.* [Chapter 4: Arabic personality development, structure, and dynamics]. Binghamton, NY. Haworth Press.

Dwairy, M. (2002). Foundations of psychosocial dynamic personality theory of collective people. *Clinical Psychology Review, 22*(3), 343–360. doi:10.1016/S0272-7358(01)00100-3

Eaton, R. M. (1990). *Islamic history as global history.* American Historical Association.

Eberhardt, J. L. (2005). Imaging race. *American Psychologist, 60,* 181–190. doi:10.1037/0003-066X.60.2.181

Eddy, M. B. (1991). *Science and health: With key to the scriptures.* Boston, MA: First Church of Christ, Scientist.

Edwards, A. L. (1954). *Edwards Personal Preference Schedule.* New York: Psychological Corporation.

Edwards, A. L. (1959). *Manual for the Edwards Personal Preference Schedule.* New York: Psychological Corporation.

Egan, G. (2002). *The skilled helper* (7th ed.). Pacific Grove, CA: Brooks/Cole.

eHRAF World Cultures. (2009). *Results per culture.* [Human Relations Area Files, Inc]. Retrieved from http://ehrafworldcultures.yale.edu/ehrafe/lookup.do?method=lookupIndexTerm.

Eid, M., & Diener, E. (2001). Norms for experiencing emotions in different cultures: Inter- and intranational differences. *Journal of Personality and Social Psychology, 81*(5), 869–885. doi:10.1037/0022-3514.81.5.869

Eisenberg, N., Fabes, R. A., & Spinrad, T. L. (2006). Prosocial development. In N. Eisenberg, W. Damon, & L. M. Lerner (Eds.), *Handbook of child psychology: Vol. 3. Chpt. 11, Social, Emotional, and Personality Development* (6th ed., pp. 646–702). New York: John Wiley & Sons.

Ekman, P. (1972). Universal and cultural differences in facial expression of emotion. In J. R. Cole (Ed.), *Nebraska symposium on motivation, 1971* (pp. 207–283). Lincoln, NE: Nebraska University Press.

Ekman, P. (1973). Cross-cultural studies of facial expressions. In P. Ekman (Ed.), *Darwin and facial expression: A century of research in review* (pp. 169–222). New York: Academic Press.

Ekman, P. (1994). Are there basic emotions? In P. Ekman & R. Davidson (Eds.), *The nature of emotions: Functional questions* (pp. 15–19). Oxford: Oxford University Press.

El-Islam, M. F. (1998). Clinical applications of cultural psychiatry in Arabian Gulf communities. In S. O. Okpaku (Ed.), *Clinical methods in transcultural psychiatry* (pp. 155–170). Washington, DC: American Psychiatric Press.

El-Islam, M. F., & Ahmed, S. A. (1971). Traditional interpretation and treatment of mental illness in an Arab psychiatric clinic. *Journal of Cross-Cultural Psychology, 2*(3), 301–308. doi:10.1177/002202217100200308

El-Islam, M. F., & Malasi, T. H. (1985). Delusions and education. *Journal of Operational Psychiatry, 16,* 29–31.

Elliott, R., Greenberg, L. S., & Lietaer, G. (2004). Research on experiential psychotherapies. In M. J. Lambert's, *Bergin and Garfield's handbook of psychotherapy and behavior change* (5th ed., pp. 493–539). New York: John Wiley & Sons.

Elisseeff, V. (Ed.). (2000). *The silk roads: Highways of culture and commerce.* UNESCO/ Berghahn Books.

Elkes, A., & Thorpe, J. G. (1967). *A summary of psychiatry.* London: Faber & Faber.

Ellis, A. (1957). Rational psychotherapy and individual psychology. *Journal of Individual Psychology, 13,* 38–44.

Ellis, A. (1992). First-order and second-order change in rational-emotive therapy: A reply to Lyddon. *Journal of Counseling & Development, 70*(3), 449–451.

Ellis, A. (2001). *Overcoming destructive beliefs, feelings, and behaviors: New directions for rational emotive behavior therapy.* Amherst, NY: Promotheus Books.

Ellis, A., Abrams, M., & Abrams, L. D. (2009). *Personality theories: Critical perspectives.* Thousand Oaks, CA: Sage.

Ellis, L. (1988). Religiosity and superstition: Are they related or separate phenomena? *Psychology: A Journal of Human Behavior, 25*(2), 12–13.

Ember, M. (1997). Evolution of the human relations area files. *Cross-cultural research, 31,* 3–15.

Ember, C. R., & Ember, M. (1998). Cross-cultural research. In H. R. Bernard (Ed.), *Handbook of methods in cultural anthropology* (pp. 647–90). Walnut Creek, CA: AltaMira Press.

Ember, C. R., & Ember, M. (2001). *Cross-cultural research methods.* Lanham, MD: AltaMira Press.

Encyclopedia of Mental Disorders. (2009). *Person-centered therapy.* Retrieved from http://www.minddisorders.com/Ob-Ps/Person-centered-therapy.html.

Endler, N. S., & Parker, J. D. A. (1994). Assessment of multidimensional coping: Task emotion and avoidance strategies. *Psychological Assessment, 6,* 50–60. doi:10.1037/1040-3590.6.1.50

Enfield, N. J., Majid, A., & Van Staden, M. (2006). Cross-linguistic categorisation of the body: Introduction. *Language Sciences, 28*(2-3), 137–147.

Engel, S. M. (1994a). *Fallacies and pitfalls of language: The language trap.* New York: Prentice-Hall.

Engel. S. M. (1994b). *With good reason: An introduction to informal fallacies* (5th ed.). New York: St. Martin's Press.

Epigenetics [theme issue]. (2011). *The scientist – magazine of the life sciences, 25*(3).

Erard, R. E. (2009). The paradox of indiscriminate multiculturalism. *American Psychologist, 64*(6), 564. doi:10.1037/a0016089

Erford, B. T., Miller, E. M., Schein, H., McDonald, A., Ludwig, L., & Leishear, K. (2011). Journal of counseling & development publication patterns: Author and article characteristics from 1994–2009. *Journal of Counseling & Development, 89*(1), 73–80.

Ernst, E., Pittler, M. H., & White, A. R. (1999). Efficacy and effectiveness. *Focus on Alternative and Complementary Therapy, 4,* 109–10.

Erwin, E. (Ed.). (2002). *The Freud encyclopedia: Theory, therapy, and culture.* New York: Routledge.

Eshun, S., & Gurung, R. A. R. (Eds.). (2009). *Culture and mental health: Sociocultural influences, theory, and practice.* Chichester, U.K.; Malden, MA: Wiley-Blackwell.

Esposito, J. L. (Ed.). (2010). *The Oxford encyclopedia of the Islamic world* [Oxford Islamic studies online]. Retrieved from http://www.oxfordislamicstudies.com/Public/book_oeiw.html.

Estrella, K. (2010). Class in context: A narrative inquiry into the impact of social class mobility and identity on class consciousness in the practice of psychotherapy. *Dissertation Abstracts International: Section B: The Sciences and Engineering, 70*(9-B), 5816.

Europa. (2009). *European day of languages.* Retrieved from http://ec.europa.eu/education/languages/orphans/doc3302_en.htm.

Evans, R. I. (1971). *Gordon Allport, the man and his ideas.* New York: Dutton.

Everitt, B. J., Belin, D., Economidou, D., Pelloux, Y., Dalley, J. W., & Robbins, T. W. (2008). Neural mechanisms underlying the vulnerability to develop compulsive drug-seeking habits and addiction. *Philosophical Transactions of the Royal Society – B: Biological Sciences, 363*(1507), 3125–3135. doi:10.1098/rstb.2008.0089

Existential psychotherapy. (2010). In *Encyclopædia Britannica.* Retrieved December 22, 2010, from Encyclopædia Britannica Online: http://www.britannica.com/EBchecked/topic/689536/existential-psychotherapy.

Eyde, L. D., Robertson, G. J., & Krug, S. E. (2009). *Responsible test use: Case studies for assessing human behavior.* Washington, DC: American Psychological Association.

Eysenck, H. J. (1952). The effects of psychotherapy: An evaluation. *Journal of Consulting and Clinical Psychology, 16,* 319–24.

Eysenck, H. J. (1998). *Dimensions of personality.* New Brunswick, NJ: Transaction Publishers.

Eysenck, H. J., & Eysenck, S. B. G. (1969). *Personality structure and measurement.* London: Routledge.

Eysenck, H. J., & Eysenck, S. B. G. (1976). *Psychoticism as a dimension of personality.* London: Hodder and Stoughton.

Fabrega, H., Jr. (2002). *Origins of psychopathology: The phylogenetic and cultural basis of mental illness.* New Brunswick, NJ: Rutgers University Press.

Fabrega, H., Jr. (2004). Culture and the origins of psychopathology. In U. P. Gielen, J. M. Fish, & J. G. Draguns, (Eds.). *Handbook of culture, therapy, and healing.* Mahwah, NJ: Lawrence Erlbaum Associates.

Fadiman, A. (1997). *The spirit catches you and you fall down.* New York: Farrar, Straus, & Giroux.

Fagan, B. (1987). *The great journey.* London: Thames and Hudson.

"Family Values vs. Safe Sex" (1999, November 22). Population Research Institute. Retrieved from http://www.pop.org/00000000207/family-values-vs-safe-sex.

Fanelli, D. (2010). "Positive" results increase down the hierarchy of the sciences. *PLoS ONE, 5*(4), e10068. doi:10.1371/journal.pone.0010068

Fanning, P., & McKay, M. (1993). *Being a man: A guide to the new masculinity.* Oakland, CA: New Harbinger Publ.

Farber, I. E. (1975). Sane and insane: Constructions and misconstructions. *Journal of Abnormal Psychology, 84,* 589–620. doi:10.1037/h0092969

Farmer, A., & Adwa, M. (2007). Principles of nosology [Chap. 28]. In G. Stein & G. Wilkinson (Eds.), *Seminars in general adult psychiatry* (pp. 711–723). [Royal College of Psychiatrists]. London: RCPsych Publications.

Farwell, B. (1988). *Burton: A biography of Sir Richard Francis Burton.* Middlesex, England; New York: Viking.

Faubert, M., & Gonzalez, E. (2008). What counselors need to know about language and language acquisition to enhance their effectiveness with clients. [Counseling Outfitters] *VISTAS08.* Retrieved from http://counselingoutfitters.com/vistas/vistas08/Faubert.htm.

Faust, D. (1986). Research on human judgment and its application to clinical practice. *Professional Psychology: Research and Practice, 17,* 420–430. doi:10.1037/0735-7028.17.5.420

Feagin, J. R. (2006). *Systemic racism: A theory of oppression.* New York: Taylor & Francis/CRC Press.

Feldman, S. (2012). *The two-spirit tradition.* Retrieved from http://androgyne.0catch.com/2spiritx.htm.

Fell, B. (1984). *America b.c.: Ancient settlers in the new world.* New York: Simon & Schuster.

Feltham, C. (1996). Beyond denial, myth and superstition in the counselling profession. In R. Bayne, I. Horton, & J. Bimrose (Eds.), *New directions in counseling* (pp. 297–308). Florence, KY: Taylor & Frances/Routledge.

Ferguson, C. A. (1978). Historical background of universals research. In J. H. Greenberg, C.A. Ferguson, & E. Moravcsik (Eds.), *Universals of human languages* (pp. 7–31). Stanford, CA: Stanford University Press.

Ferguson, G., Cheang, M., Dasananjali, T., Hawari, D., Peng, K. L., & Salzberg, S. (1998). Legal regulation of mental disorder: Looking east and west. In D. M. Johnston & G. Ferguson (Eds.), *Asia-Pacific legal development.* Vancouver, BC: UBC Press.

Fernandez-Ballesteros, R. (Ed.). (2003). *Encyclopedia of psychological assessment.* London; Thousand Oaks, CA: Sage.

Ferraro, F. R. (Ed.). (2001). *Minority and cross-cultural aspects of neuropsychological assessment.* Lisse; Exton, PA: Swets & Zeitlinger.

Filesi, T. (1972). *China and Africa in the Middle Ages* (D. Morison, Trans.). London: Frank Cass.

Fink, P. J., & Tasman, A. (Eds.). (1992). *Stigma and mental illness.* Washington, DC: American Psychiatric Press.

Fiorentine, R. (2001). Counseling frequency and the effectiveness of outpatient drug treatment: Revisiting the conclusion that 'more is better'. *American Journal of Drug and Alcohol Abuse, 27*(4), 617–631. doi:10.1081/ADA-100107659

Fisch, G. S. (2009). Models of human behavior: Talking to the animals. In Y-K. Kim (Ed.), *Handbook of behavior genetics* (pp. 61–77). New York: Springer Science + Business Media. doi:10.1007/978-0-387-76727-7_5

Fischer, A. R., Jome, L. M., & Atkinson, D. R. (1998). Reconceptualizing multicultural counseling: Universal healing conditions in a culturally specific context. *The Counseling Psychologist, 26*(4), 525–588. doi:10.1177/0011000098264001

Fischetti, P. R. (1997). *The ethnic cultures of America: A reference for teachers, librarians and administrators.* Washington, DC: Educational Extension Systems.

Fish, J. M. (2004). Cross-cultural commonalities in therapy and healing: Theoretical issues and psychological and sociocultural principles. In U. P. Gielen, J. M. Fish, & J. G. Draguns (Eds.), *Handbook of culture, therapy, and healing* (pp. 67–81). Mahwah, NJ: Lawrence Erlbaum Associates.

Fiske, A. P., Kitayama, S., Markus, H. R., & Nisbett, R. E. (1998). The cultural matrix of social psychology. In D. Gilbert, S. Fiske & G. Lindzey (Eds.), *The handbook of social psychology* (4th ed., pp. 915–981). San Francisco: McGraw-Hill.

Fiske, A. P. (2002). Using individualism and collectivism to compare cultures: A critique of the validity and measurement of the constructs: Comment on Oyserman et al. (2002). *Psychological Bulletin, 128*(1), 78–88. doi:10.1037/0033-2909.128.1.78

Fiske, S. T., & Taylor, S. E. (1991). *Social cognition* (2nd ed.). New York: McGraw Hill.

Flood, M. (2008). *Men's bibliography* (On-line). http://mensbiblio.xyonline.net/.

Fodor, J. (1983). *The modularity of mind.* Cambridge, MA: MIT Press.

Fodor, J. (2011). *In critical condition: Polemical essays on cognitive science and the philosophy of mind.* Cambridge, MA: MIT Press.

Folkes, V. S. (1988). Recent attribution research in consumer behavior: A review and new directions. *Journal of Consumer Research, 14,* 548–565. doi:10.1086/209135

Foltz, R. C. (2010). *Religions of the silk road: Overland trade and cultural exchange.* New York: Palgrave Macmillan.

Fordham, M. (1978). *Jungian psychotherapy: A study in analytical psychology.* Chichester, Eng.; New York: Wiley.

Forer, B. R. (1949). The fallacy of personal validation: A classroom demonstration of gullibility. *Journal of Abnormal and Social Psychology, 44,* 118–123. doi:10.1037/h0059240

Foucault, M. (1988). *Madness and civilization: A history of insanity in the age of reason.* New York: Vintage Books (Random House).

Fountain, K. C. (2008). *Political advocacy groups.* Washington State University Vancouver Library. Retrieved from http://www.vancouver.wsu.edu/fac/kfountain/about.html.

Fox, A. S., Oakes, T. R., Shelton, S. E., Converse, A. K., Davidson, R. J., & Kalin, N. H. (2005). Calling for help is independently modulated by brain systems underlying goal-directed behavior and threat perception. *The Proceedings of the National Academy of Sciences Online (US), 102*(11), 4176–4179. doi:10.1073/pnas.0409470102

Frances, A. J. (2012). DSM5 in distress. [Psychology Today]. Retrieved from http://www.psychologytoday.com/blog/dsm5-in-distress/201110/psychologists-start-petition-against-dsm-5.

Frances, A. J., First, M. B., Widiger, T. A., Miele, G. M., Tilly, S. M., Davis, W. W., & Pincus, H. A. (1991). An A to Z guide to DSM–IV conundrums. *Journal of Abnormal Psychology, 100,* 407–412. doi:10.1037/0021-843X.100.3.407

Frances, A. J., & Spitzer, R. (2010). *Allen Frances and Robert Spitzer on DSM-5 scientific review work group and DSM-5 field trials and deadlines* [DSM-5 and ICD-11 Watch]. Retrieved from http://dsm5watch.wordpress.com/.

Frances, A. J. (2010). Normality is an endangered species: Psychiatric fads and over-diagnosis. *Psychiatric Times.* Retrieved from http://www.psychiatrictimes.com/dsm-5/content/article/10168/1598676?CID=rss.

Frank, J. D. (1961). *Persuasion and healing: A comparative study of psychotherapy.* Baltimore: Johns Hopkins University Press.

Frank, J. D. (1974). Psychotherapy: The restoration of moral. *American Journal of Psychiatry, 131,* 271–274.

Frank, J. D., & Frank, J. B. (1991). *Persuasion and healing: A comparative study of psychotherapy* (3rd ed.). Baltimore: Johns Hopkins University Press.

Frank, S. A. (1998). *Foundations of social evolution.* Princeton: Princeton University Press.

Fransella, F. (1996). *George Kelly.* Thousand Oaks, CA; London: Sage.

Fraser, J. S., & Solovey, A. (2007). *Second-order change in psychotherapy: The golden thread that unifies effective treatments.* Washington, DC: American Psychological Association. doi:10.1037/11499-000

Frazer, J. G. (1922). *The golden bough.* New York: Macmillan.

Fredrickson, B. L. (1998). What good are positive emotions? *Review of General Psychology, 2,* 300–319. doi:10.1037/1089-2680.2.3.300

Freedman, D. A., Collier, D., Sekhon, J. S., & Stark, P. B. (Eds.). (2010). *Statistical models and causal inference: A dialogue with the social sciences.* Cambridge/New York: Cambridge University Press.

Freedman, D. H. (2010, July/August). The streetlight effect. *Discover Magazine – Science, Technology, and the Future,* 55–57.

Freeman, C. (2004). *Egypt, Greece and Rome: Civilizations of the ancient Mediterranean.* New York: Oxford University Press.

Freire, P. (1972). *Pedagogy of the oppressed.* London: Penguin.

Freud, S. (1976). *The standard edition of the complete psychological works of Sigmund Freud.* New York: W. W. Norton & Co.

Freud, S. (2000). *Totem and taboo: Resemblances between the psychic lives of savages and neurotics/Sigmund Freud* (A. A. Brill, Trans.). Amherst, NY: Prometheus Books. (Original work published 1913)

Frey, C. (1997). *Men at work: An action guide to masculine healing.* Dubuque, IA: Islewest.

Friedman, M. (1985). Are Americans becoming more materialistic? A look at changes in expressions of materialism in the popular literature of the post-world war II era. *Advances in Consumer Research, 12,* 385–387.

Friedman, M. (1996). *Type A behavior: Its diagnosis and treatment.* New York: Plenum Press (Kluwer Academic Press).

Friedman, R. A. (2002, August 27). Like drugs, talk therapy can change brain chemistry. *New York Times.* Retrieved from http://www.nytimes.com/2002/08/27/health/psychology/27BEHA.html.

Fries, S. (2002). *Cultural, multicultural, cross-cultural, intercultural: A moderator's proposal.* [TESOL France]. Retrieved http://www.tesol-france.org/articles/fries.pdf.

Frith, C. (1992). *The cognitive neuropsychology of schizophrenia.* Mahwah, NJ: Lawrence Erlbaum Associates.

Fritz, S., Chaitow, L., & Hymel, G. M. (2007). *Clinical massage in the healthcare setting.* New York: Elsevier Health Sciences.

Fryer, R. G., & Jackson, M. O. (2003). *Categorical cognition: A psychological model of categories and identification in decision making.* (NBER Working Paper 9579). Cambridge, MA: National Bureau of Economic Research. Retrieved http://www.nber.org/papers/w9579.pdf.

Fuchs, T. (2007). Psychotherapy of the lived space: A phenomenological and ecological concept. *American Journal of Psychotherapy, 61*(4), 423–439.

Fujita, C. (1986). *Morita therapy.* New York & Tokyo: Igaku-Shoin Medical Publishers.

Fukuyama, M. A. (1990, September). Taking a universal approach to multicultural counseling. *Counselor Education & Supervision, 30*(1), 6–17. doi:10.1002/j.1556-6978.1990.tb01174.x

Furukawa, T., & Shibayama, T. (1995). Factors including adjustment of high school students in an international exchange program. *Journal of Nervous and Mental Disease, 182*(12), 709–714. doi:10.1097/00005053-199412000-00006.

Gabrieli, F., & Costello, E. J. (1984). *Arab historians of the crusades.* London: Routledge and Kegan Paul.

Gadalla, M. (2009). *The ancient Egyptian culture revealed.* Greensboro, NC: Tehuti Research Foundation.

Gadit, A. A. M. (2010). Both DSM and ICD systems are needed. *Clinical psychiatry news.* Retrieved from http://findarticles.com/p/articles/mi_hb4345/is_7_38/ai_n54876762/.

Gale Encyclopedia of Multicultural America (2nd ed.). (2000). Detroit, MI: The Gale Group.

Galens, J., Sheets, A., & Young, R. V. (Eds.). (1995). *Gale encyclopedia of multicultural America.* Detroit, MI: Gale Research.

Gallese, V. (2003). The roots of empathy: The shared manifold hypothesis and the neural basis of intersubjectivity. *Psychopathology, 36,* 171–180. doi:10.1159/000072786

Gao, G., & Gudykunst, W. B. (1990). Uncertainty, anxiety, and adaptation. *International Journal of Intercultural Relations, 14*(3), 301–317. doi:10.1016/0147-1767(90)90017-Q

Gardner, A., West, S. A., & Barton, N. H. (2007). The relation between multilocus population genetics and social evolution theory. *The American Naturalist, 169*(2), 207–226. doi:10.1086/510602

Gardner, M. (1957). *Fads and fallacies in the name of science.* New York: Dover Press.

Garfield, S. L. (1973). Basic ingredients or common factors in psychotherapy? *Journal of Consulting and Clinical Psychology, 41*(1), 9–12. doi:10.1037/h0035618

Geisinger, K. F. (2003). Testing and assessment in cross-cultural psychology. In I. B. Weiner, A. F. Healy, & R. W. Protor, *Handbook of psychology* (pp. 95–118). New York: Wiley.

Gendlin, E. T. (2007). *Focusing.* New York: Bantam Books.

Gillespie, R. (1991). *Manufacturing knowledge: A history of the Hawthorne experiments.* Cambridge: Cambridge University Press.

Georgas, J., & Berry, J. W. (1995). An ecocultural taxonomy for cross-cultural psychology. *Cross-Cultural Research, 29,* 121–157. doi:10.1177/106939719502900202

George, S., & Sreedhar, K. P. (2006). Globalisation and the prevalence of superstitious beliefs. *Journal of the Indian Academy of Applied Psychology, 32*(3), 337–343.

Gershman, N. H. (2008). *Besa: Muslims who saved Jews in World War II.* Syracuse, NY: Syracuse University Press.

Gerstein, L. H., Heppner, P. P., Ægisdóttir, A., Seung-Ming, A. L., & Norsworthy, K. L. (Eds.). (2009a). Cross-cultural counseling: History, challenges, and rationale (Ch. 1). In L. H. Gerstein, P. P. Heppner, S. Ægisdóttir, A. L. Seung-Ming, & K. L. Norsworthy (Eds.), *International handbook of cross-cultural counseling: Cultural assumptions and practices worldwide* (pp. 3–8). Los Angeles, Sage.

Gerstein, L. H., Heppner, P. P., Ægisdóttir, A., Seung-Ming, A. L., & Norsworthy, K. L. (Eds.). (2009b). A global vision for the future of cross-cultural counseling: Theory, collaboration, research, and training (Ch. 38). In L. H. Gerstein, P. P. Heppner, S. Ægisdóttir, A. L. Seung-Ming, & K. L. Norsworthy (Eds.), I*nternational handbook of cross-cultural counseling: Cultural assumptions and practices worldwide* (pp. 503–522). Los Angeles, Sage.

Gerstein, L. H., Heppner, P. P., Ægisdóttir, A., Seung-Ming, A. L., & Norsworthy, K. L. (Eds.). (2009c). *International handbook of cross-cultural counseling: Cultural assumptions and practices worldwide* (pp. 503–522). Los Angeles, Sage.

Gessmann, H-W. (Ed.). (1987). *Humanistisches psychodrama, Vol. 1-4.* Duisburg, Germany: Institute of Psychotherapeutishen Bergerhausen.

Getz, F. (1998). *Medicine in the English middle ages.* Princeton, NJ: Princeton University Press.

Gibson, E. J., & Pick, A. D. (2003). *An ecological approach to perceptual learning and development.* New York: Oxford University Press.

Gielen, U. P., Fish, J. M., & Draguns, J. G. (Eds.). (2004). *Handbook of culture, therapy, and healing.* Mahwah, NJ: Lawrence Erlbaum Associates.

Gil, M. (1976). The Radhanite merchants and the land of Radhan. *Journal of the Economic and Social History of the Orient, 17*(3), 299–328.

Gilman, S. L., King, H., Porter, R., Rousseau, G., & Showalter, E. (1993). *Hysteria beyond Freud.* Berkeley, CA: University of California.

Gilovich, T. (1993). *How we know what isn't so: The fallibility of human reason in everyday life.* New York: The Free Press.

Gilovich, T., Griffin, D., & Kahneman, D. (Eds.). (2002). *Heuristics and biases: The psychology of intuitive judgment.* Cambridge, UK: Cambridge University Press.

Gladstein, G. A. (1987). Counselor empathy and client outcome. In G. A. Gladstein & associates (Eds.), *Empathy and counseling: Explorations in theory and research.* New York: Springer-Verlag.

Goddard, C. (2002). The search for the shared semantic core of all languages. In C. Goddard & A. Wierzbicka (Eds.), *Meaning and universal grammar: Theory and empirical findings, 1* (pp. 5–40). Amsterdam/Philadelphia: John Benjamins.

Goddard, C., & Wierzbicka, A. (Eds.). (1994). *Semantic and lexical universals: Theory and empirical findings.* Amsterdam/Philadelphia: John Benjamins.

Goddard, C., & Wierzbicka, A. (Eds.). (2002). *Meaning and universal grammar: Theory and empirical findings.* Amsterdam/Philadelphia: John Benjamins.

Godlas, A. (n.d.). *Women in Islam: Muslim women.* Islam and Islamic Studies Resources (Department of Religion at the University of Georgia Web site). Retrieved from http://www.uga.edu/islam/Islamwomen.html.

Goldberg, L. R. (1992). The development of markers for the Big-Five factor structure. *Psychological Assessment, 4,* 26–42. doi:10.1037/1040-3590.4.1.26

Goldberg, L. R. (1993). The structure of phenotypic personality traits. *American Psychologist, 48,* 26–34. doi:10.1037/0003-066X.48.1.26

Goldberg, S. (2003). *Fads and fallacies in the social sciences.* Amherst, NY: Humanity Books.

Goldman, A. (2006). *Simulating minds: The philosophy, psychology, and neuroscience of mindreading.* Oxford: Oxford University Press.

Goldstein, G. A., & Michaels, G. Y. (1985). *Empathy: Development training, and consequences.* Hillsdale, NJ: Erlbaum.

Goldstone, R. L. (1994). Influences of categorization on perceptual discrimination. *Journal of Experimental Psychology* [General], *123*(2), 178–200.

Goodall, J. (1986). *The chimpanzees of Gombe: Patterns of behavior.* Cambridge, MA: Harvard University Press, Belknap Press.

Goodheart, A. (1994). *Laughter therapy: How to laugh about everything in your life that isn't really funny.* Santa Barbara, CA: Less Stress Press.

Goodyear, R. K., & Parish, T. S. (1978). Perceived attributes of the terms client, patient, and typical person. *Journal of Counseling Psychology, 25,* 356–358. doi:10.1037/0022-0167.25.4.356

Gould, S. J. (1981). *The mismeasurement of man.* New York: Norton & Company.

Gould, S. J., & Vrba, E. S. (1982). Exaptation: A missing term in the science of form. *Paleobiology, 8*(1), 4–15.

Gove, W. R. (1982). The current status of the labeling theory of mental illness. In W. R. Gove (Ed.), *Deviance and mental illness* (pp. 273–300). Beverly Hills, CA: Sage.

Gracia, A., Arsuaga, J. L., Martínez, I., Lorenzo, C., Carretero, J. M., Bermúdez de Castro, J. M., & Carbonell, E. (2009). Craniosynostosis in the Middle Pleistocene human Cranium 14 from the Sima de los Huesos, Atapuerca, Spain. *Proceedings of the National Academy of Sciences [PNAS], 106,* 6573–6578. Retrieved from http://www.pnas.org/content/106/16/6573.full?sid=c45a9c64-65fb-4474-9e3d-77aea3d67528. doi:10.1073/pnas.0900965106

Graeber, D. (2001). *Toward an anthropological theory of value: The false coin of our dreams.* New York: Palgrave. doi:10.1057/9780312299064

Graff, H., Kenig, L., & Radoff, G. (1971). Prejudice of upper class therapists against lower class patients. *Psychiatric Quarterly, 45,* 475–489. doi:10.1007/BF01563209

Graham, H. (1986). *The human face of psychology: Humanistic psychology in its historical, social, and cultural contexts.* Milton Keynes, UK; Philadelphia: Open University Press.

Grawe, K. (2007). *Neuropsychotherapy: How the neurosciences inform effective psychotherapy.* Mahwah, NJ: Erlbaum.

Gray, J. (1992). *Men are from Mars, women are from Venus: A practical guide for improving communication and getting what you want in your relationships.* New York: Harper-Collins.

Graziano, A. M., & Fink, R. S. (1973, June). Second-order effects in mental health. *Journal of Consulting and Clinical Psychology, 40*(3), 356–364. doi:10.1037/h0034549

Green. T. (2009). *Inquisition: The reign of fear.* New York: Thomas Dunne Books.

Greenberg, J. H., Ferguson, C. A., & Moravcsik, E. A. (Eds.). (1978a). *Universals of human language (Vol. 1: Method and theory).* Stanford, CA: Stanford University Press.

Greenberg, J. H., Ferguson, C. A., & Moravcsik, E. A. (Eds.). (1978b). *Universals of human language (Vol. 2: Phonology).* Stanford, CA: Stanford University Press.

Greenberg, J. H., Ferguson, C. A., & Moravcsik, E. A. (Eds.). (1978c). *Universals of human language (Vol. 3: Word structure).* Stanford, CA: Stanford University Press.

Greenberg, J. H., Ferguson, C. A., & Moravcsik, E. A. (Eds.). (1978d). *Universals of human language (Vol. 4: Syntax).* Stanford, CA: Stanford University Press.

Greenberg, N., Iversen, A., Hull, L., Bland, D., & Wessely, S. (2008). Getting a peace of the action: Measures of post traumatic stress in UK military peacekeepers. *Journal of the Royal Society of Medicine, 101*(2), 78–84. doi:10.1258/jrsm.2007.070024

Greening, T. C. (Ed.). (1971). *Existential humanistic psychology.* Belmont, CA: Brooks/Cole Pub. Co.

Greenwald, A. (1980). The totalitarian ego: Fabrication and revision of personal history. *American Psychologist, 35*(7), 603–618. doi:10.1037/0003-066X.35.7.603

Grencavage L. M., & Norcross J. C. (1990). Where are the commonalities among the therapeutic common factors? *Professional Psychology: Research and Practice, 21*(5), 372–378. doi:10.1037/0735-7028.21.5.372

Grills, C. (2004). African psychology. In R. Jones (Ed.), *African psychology.* Hampton, VA: Cobb and Henry.

Groark, K. P. (2008). Social opacity and the dynamics of empathic in-sight among the Tzotzil Maya of Chiapas, Mexico. *Ethos, 36*(4), 427–448. doi:10.1111/j.1548-1352. 2008.00025.x

Grohol, J. M. (2009). 15 common cognitive distortions. *PsychCentral.* Retrieved from http://psychcentral.com/lib/2009/15-common-cognitive-distortions/.

Groth-Marnat, G. (2009). *Handbook of psychological assessment.* Hoboken, NJ: John Wiley & Sons.

Guang, P. (n.d.). *Jews in China: Legends, history and new perspectives.* Yale Initiative for the Interdisciplinary Study of Antisemitism (YIISA). New Haven, CT. http://www.yale.edu/yiisa/georgepanpaper103009.pdf.

Guilford, J. B. (1980). Cognitive styles: What are they? *Educational and Psychological Measurement, 40,* 715–35. doi:10.1177/001316448004000315

Gullotta, T. P., & Bloom, M. (Eds.). (2003). *Encyclopedia of primary prevention and health promotion.* New York: Kluwer Academic/Plenum Publishers.

Gumucio-Dragon, A., & Tufte, T. (Eds.). (2006). *Communication for social change anthology: Historical and contemporary readings.* South Orange, NY: Communication for Social Change Consortuim.

Gummere, R. M., Jr. (1988). The counselor as prophet: Frank Parsons, 1854–1908. *Journal of Counseling and Development, 66*(9), 402–05.

Gurven, M., Zanolini, A., & Schniter, E. (2008). Culture sometimes matters: Intra-cultural variation in pro-social behavior among Tsimane Amerindians. *Journal of Economic Behavior and Organization, 67*(3-4), 587–607. doi:10.1016/j.jebo.2007.09.005

Gutfield, A. (2002). *American exceptionalism: The effects of plenty on the American experience.* Brighton and Portland: Sussex Academic Press.

Guzman, G. G. (1996). European clerical envoys to the Mongols: Reports of Western merchants in Eastern Europe and Central Asia, 1231–1255. *Journal of Medieval History, 22*(1), 53–67. doi:10.1016/0304 1181(96)00008 5

Hackney, H. (1978). The evolution of empathy. *Personnel & Guidance Journal, 57*(1), 35–39.

Hackney, H. (2008). *The professional counselor: A process guide to helping.* Englewood Cliffs, NJ: Prentice-Hall.

Haeffel, G. J., Thiessen, E. D., Campbell, M. W., Kaschak, M. P., & McNeil, N. M. (2009). Theory, not cultural context, will advance American psychology. *American Psychologist, 64*(6), 570–571. doi:10.1037/a0016191

Hakluyt Society. (1990). *The mission of Friar William of Rubruck: His journey to the court of the great khan mongke, 1253–1255* (P. Jackson, & D. Morgan, Trans.). London: Author.

Hall, C. S., & Nordby, V. J. (1973). *A primer of Jungian psychology.* New York: Taplinger Pub. Co.

Hall, E. T. (1989). *Beyond culture.* New York: Anchor Books Editions.

Hall, E. T., & Hall, R. M. (1987). *Hidden differences – Doing business with the Japanese.* New York: Anchor Press Doubleday.

Hall, R. E. (2006). White women as postmodern vehicle of Black oppression: The pedagogy of discrimination in Western academe. *Journal of Black Studies, 37*(1), 69–82. doi:10.1177/0021934705277286

Hallam, E. (1989). *Chronicles of the crusades: Eye-witness accounts of the wars between Christianity and Islam.* London: Weidenfeld and Nicolson.

Hambleton, R. K., Merenda, P. F., & Spielberger, C. D. (Eds.). (2005). *Adapting educational and psychological tests for cross-cultural assessment.* Mahwah, NJ: L. Erlbaum Associates.

Hamill, J. F. (1979). Syllogistic reasoning and taxonomic semantics. *Journal of Anthropological Research, 35,* 481–494.

Hamill, J. F. (1990). *Ethno-Logic: The anthropology of human reasoning.* Urbana, IL: University of Illinois.

Hamilton, W. D. (1964). The genetical evolution of social behavior. I and II. *Journal of Theoretical Biology, 7,* 1–52. doi:10.1016/0022-5193(64)90038-4

Hamilton, W. D. (1972). Altruism and related phenomena, mainly in the social insects. *Annual Review of Ecology and Systematics, 3,* 193–232. doi:10.1146/annurev.es.03.110172.001205

Hamilton, W. D. (1975). Innate social aptitudes in man: An approach from evolutionary genetics. In R. Fox (Ed.), *Biosocial anthropology.* New York: Wiley.

Hamilton, W. D. (1996). *Narrow roads of gene land (Vol. 1): Evolution of social behavior.* Oxford: Oxford University Press.

Hammad, A., Kysia, R., Rabah, R., Hassoun, R., & Connelly, M. (1999). *Guide to Arab culture: Health care delivery to the Arab American community.* Arab Community Center for Economic and Social Services [ACCESS]. Dearborn, MI. Retrieved from http://www.accesscommunity.org/site/DocServer/health_and_research_cente_21.pdf?docID=381.

Han, Y-S. (1946). The Chinese civil service: Yesterday and today. *The Pacific Historical Review, 15*(2), 158–170. Retrieved from http://www.jstor.org/stable/3634926?seq=1.

Handler, M. W., & DuPaul, G. J. (2005). Assessment of ADHD: Differences across psychology specialty areas. *Journal of Attention Disorders, 9*(2), 402–12. doi.10.1177/1087054705278762

Haney, H., & Leibsohn, J. (1999). *Basic counseling responses: A multimedia learning system for the helping professions.* Belmont, CA: Wadsworth.

Hansen, J. T. (2007, Fall). Counseling without truth: Toward a neopragmatic foundation for counseling practice. *Journal of Counseling and Development, 85,* 423–430.

Harding, R. M., & Sokal, R. R. (1988). Classification of the European language families by genetic distance (human variation/gene frequencies). *Population Biology, 85,* 9370–9372.

Harlow, H. E., Harlow, M. K., & Meyer, D. R. (1950). Learning motivated by a manipulation drive. *Journal of Experimental Psychology, 40,* 228–234. doi:10.1037/h0056906

Harnad, S. (2005). To cognize is to categorize: Cognition is categorization. In C. Lefebvre & H. Cohen (Eds.), *Handbook of categorization in cognitive science.* New York: Elsevier Press.

Harrington, A. (Ed.). (1997). *The placebo effect: An interdisciplinary exploration.* Cambridge, MA: Harvard University Press.

Harris, A. H. S., Reeder, R., & Hyu, J. K. (2009). Common statistical and research design problems in manuscripts submitted to high-impact psychiatry journals: What editors and reviewers want authors to know. *Journal of Psychiatric Research, 43*(15), 1231–1234. doi:10.1016/j.jpsychires.2009.04.007

Harris Interactive. (2007). Large numbers of people are not very confident in their own knowledge and the safety of prescription medications and this often leads to non-adherence. *Healthcare News, 7*(5). Retrieved from http://www.harris interac tivecom/news/newsletters/healthnews/HI_HealthCareNews2007Vol7_Iss05.pdf.

Hartmann, T. (1997). *Attention deficit disorder: A different perception (A hunter in a farmer's world).* Nevada City, CA: Underwood Books.

Haserot, F. S. (1950). Spinoza and the status of universals. *The Philosophical Review, 59*(4), 469–492. doi:10.2307/2181621

Hastorf, A., & Cantril, H. (1954). They saw a game: A case study. *Journal of Abnormal and Social Psychology, 49,* 129–134. doi:10.1037/h0057880

Haviland, W. A., Prins, H. E. L., Walrath, D., & McBride, B. (2008). *Cultural anthropology: The human challenge* (12th ed.). Belmont, CA: Thomson Higher Education.

Hayes, N. (1994). *Principles of comparative psychology.* Hove, UK: L. Erlbaum.

Hays, D. G., McLeod, A. L., & Prosek, E. (2009). Diagnostic variance among counselors and counselor trainees. *Measurement and Evaluation in Counseling and Development, 42*(1), 3–14. doi:10.1177/0748175609333559

Hays, D., & Chang, C. (2003). White privilege, oppression, and racial identity development: Implications for supervision. *Counselor Education & Supervision, 43,* 134–145.

Hays, J. (2008). Chinese exploration and Zheng He. *Facts and details* (Web site). Retrieved from http://factsanddetails.com/china.php?itemid=45&catid=2.

Hays, P. A. (2008). *Addressing cultural complexities in practice: Assessment, diagnosis, and therapy* (2nd ed.) Washington, DC: American Psychological Association. doi: 10.1037/11650-000

Hearnshaw, L. S. (1989). *The shaping of modern psychology.* Great Britain: Routledge.

Hedden, T., Ketay, S., Aron, A., Markus, H., & Gabrieli, J. D. E. (2008). Cultural influences on neural substrates of attentional control. *Psychological Science, 19*(1), 12–17. doi:10.1111/j.1467-9280.2008.02038.x

Heft, H. (2001). *Ecological psychology in context: James Gibson, Roger Barker, and the legacy of William James's radical empiricism.* Hillsdale, NJ: Erlbaum.

Heine, B. (1997). *Cognitive foundations of grammar.* New York/Oxford: Oxford University Press.

Heider, F. (1958). *The psychology of interpersonal relations.* New York: Wiley. doi:10.1037/10628-000

Heil, J. (Ed.). (2003). *Philosophy of mind: A guide and anthology.* Oxford/NY: Oxford University Press.

Helfrich, H. (1999). Beyond the dilemma of cross-cultural psychology: Resolving the tension between Etic and Emic approaches. *Culture and Psychology, 5*(2), 131–153. doi:10.1177/1354067X9952002

Helm, B. (2009). Love. *Stanford encyclopedia of philosophy.* Retrieved from http://plato.stanford.edu/entries/love/.

Helms, J. E. (1982). *A practitioners guide to the Edwards Personal Preference Schedule.* Springfield, IL: Charles C Thomas.

Helman, C. G. (1994). *Culture, health, and illness: An introduction for health professionals* (3rd ed.). Oxford, England: Butterworth-Heinemann.

Help. (2011). In *Merriam-Webster's online dictionary.* Retrieved from http://www.merriam-webster.com/dictionary/test.

Helwig, D. (2001). Traditional African medicine. *Encyclopedia of Alternative Medicine.* Retrieved from http://findarticles.com/p/articles/mi_g2603/is_0007/ai_2603000708/.

Henderson, G., & Spigner-Littles, D. (1996). *A practitioner's guide to understanding indigenous and foreign cultures.* Springfield, IL: Charles C Thomas.

Hendrick, C. (2005). Evolution as a foundation for psychological theories. In S. Strack (Ed.), *Handbook of personology and psychopathology* (pp. 3–23). Hoboken, NJ: J. Wiley.

Hendricks, A. A. J., Perugini, M., Angleitner, A., Ostendorf, F., Johnson, J. A., De Fruyt, F., Hřebíčková, M., Kreitler, S., Murakami, T., Bratko, D., Conner, M., Nagy, J., Rodríguez-Fornells, A., & Ruisel, I. (2003). The five-factor personality inventory: Cross-cultural generalizability across 13 countries. *European Journal of Personality, 17*(5), 347–373.

Hergenhahn, B. R. (2009). *An introduction to the history of psychology.* Independence, KY: Cengage Learning.

Herodotus. (1998). *The histories* (R. Waterfield, & C. Dewald, Trans.). Oxford, New York: Oxford University Press.

Hersen, M., & Sledge, W. (Eds.). (2002). *Encyclopedia of psychotherapy.* Amsterdam; Boston: Academic Press.

Hervé Kuendig, H., Plant, M. A., Plant, M. L., Miller, P., Kuntsche, S., & Gmel, G. (2008). Alcohol-related adverse consequences: Cross-cultural variations in attribution process among young adults. *The European Journal of Public Health, 18*(4), 386–391. doi:10.1093/eurpub/ckn007

Herzfeld, M. (2001). *Anthropology: Theoretical practice in culture and society.* Malden, MA: Blackwell Publishers.

Hey, J. (2005). On the number of New World founders: A population genetic portrait of the peopling of the Americas. *PLoS Biol, 3*(6), e193.

Hiebert, B. (1984). Counselor effectiveness: An instructional approach. *Personnel and Guidance Journal, 62*(10), 597–601.

Hilgevoord, J. (2006). The uncertainty principle. In E. N. Zalta (Ed.), *Stanford encyclopedia of philiosophy.* Retrieved from http://plato.stanford.edu/entries/qt-uncertainty/.

Hill, H., & Jones, J. E., Jr. (Eds.). (1992). *Race in America: The struggle for equality.* Madison, WI: University of Wisconsin Press.

Hill, M. (2004). *Diary of a country counselor.* Binghamton, NY: Haworth.

Hintzman, D. L. (2011). Research strategy in the study of memory: Fads, fallacies, and the search for the "coordinates of truth." *Perspectives on Psychological Science, 6*(3), 253–271. doi:10.1177/1745691611406924

Hodge, D. R. (2002). Working with Muslim youths: Understanding the values and beliefs of Islamic discourse. *Children and Schools, 24*(1), 6–20.

Hodge, D. R. (2005). Social work and the House of Islam: Orienting practitioners to the beliefs and values of Muslims in the United States. *Social Work, 50*(2), 162–173.

Hoffman, E., McCabe, K. A., & Smith, V. L. (1998). Behavioral foundations of reciprocity: Experimental economics and evolutionary psychology. *Economic Inquiry, 36,* 335–352.

Hoffman, G. A., Harrington, A., & Fields, H. L. (2005). Pain and the placebo: What we have learned. *Perspectives in Biology and Medicine, 48*(2), 248–65. doi:10.1353/pbm.2005. 0054

Hoffman, L. (2004–2009). *Common misperceptions of existential therapy.* Retrieved from http://www.existential-therapy.com/misconceptions.htm.

Hoffman, M. L. (1981). Is altruism part of human nature? *Journal of Personality and Social Psychology, 40,* 121–137. doi:10.1037/0022-3514.40.1.121

Hoffmann, F. W., & Bailey, W. G. (1992). *Mind & society fads.* Binghamton, NY: Haworth.

Hofstede, G. (1997). *Cultures and organizations: Software of the mind.* London: McGraw-Hill.

Hofstede, G. (2001). *Culture's consequences: Comparing values, behaviors, institutions, and organizations across nations* (2nd ed.). Thousand Oaks, CA: Sage.

Hofstede, G., & Hofstede, G. J. (2005). *Cultures and organizations: Software of the mind.* New York: McGraw-Hill.

Hogan, D. B. (1980, September). *Defining what a competent psychotherapist does: Problems and prospects.* Paper presented at the Annual Convention of the American Psychological Association, Montreal, Quebec, Canada. (ED 201 929).

Hogan, R., & Blake, R. (1999). John Holland's vocational typology and personality theory. *Journal of Vocational Behavior, 55*(1), 41–56. doi:10.1006/jvbe.1999.1696

Holahan, C. J., & Moos, R. H. (1987). Personal and contextual determinants of coping strategies. *Journal of Personality and Social Psychology, 52*(5), 946–955. doi:10.1037/0022-3514.52.5.946

Hollan, D. (2008). Being there: On the imaginative aspects of understanding others and being understood. *Ethos, 36*(4), 475–489. doi:10.1111/j.1548-1352.2008.00028.x

Hollan, D. W., & Throop, J. (2008). Whatever happened to empathy?: Introduction. *Ethos, 36*(4), 385–401. doi:10.1111/j.1548-1352.2008.00023.x

Holland, J. L. (1973). *Making vocational choices: A theory of careers.* Upper Saddle, NJ: Prentice-Hall.

Holland, J. L. (1997). *Making vocational choices: A theory of vocational personalities and work environments.* Odessa, FL: Psychological Assessment Resources.

Holton, G., & Brush, S. G. (1985). *Physics, the human adventure: From Copernicus to Einstein and beyond.* Princeton, NJ: Princeton University Press.

Homans, P. (1979). *Jung in context: Modernity and the making of a psychology.* Chicago: University of Chicago Press.

Hongkai, S. (Ed.). (2008). *China's languages.* Beijing, China: Chinese Academy of Social Sciences [CASS].

Hornberger, J. C., Gibson, C. D., Wood, W., Dequeldre, C., Corso, I., Palla, B., & Bloch, D. A. (1996). Eliminating language barriers for non-English-speaking patients. *Medical Care, 34*(8), 845–856. doi:10.1097/00005650-199608000-00011

Horton, A. M., Jr., & Wedding, D. (Eds.). (2008). *The neuropsychology handbook* (3rd ed.). New York: Springer Pub.

Horwitz, A. (2002). *Creating mental illness.* Chicago: University of Chicago Press.

Hou, Z-J., & Zhang, N. (2007). Counseling psychology in China. *Applied Psychology: An International Review, 56*(1), 33–50.

Hrobjartsson, A., & Gotzsche, P. C. (2001). Is the placebo powerless? An analysis of clinical trials comparing placebo with no treatment. *New England Journal of Medicine, 344*(21), 1594–1602. doi:10.1056/NEJM200105243442106

Hsiao, F. H., Klimidis, S., Minas, H., & Tan, E. S. (2006). Cultural attribution of mental health suffering in Chinese societies: The views of Chinese patients with mental illness and their caregivers. *Journal Clinical Nursing, 15*(8), 998–1006.

Hsu, C-J.(2006). Development of an indigenous Chinese personality inventory based on the principle of Yin-Yang and the Five Elements and on the ancient Chinese text *Jen Wu Chih*. [Digital dissertation]. Retrieved from http://sunzi1.lib.hku.hk/ER/detail/hkul/3846915.

Hubble, M., Duncan, B. L., & Miller, S. D. (Eds.). (1999). *The heart and soul of change: What works in therapy.* Washington DC: American Psychological Association. doi: 10.1037/11132-000

Huda, Q-U. (2006). *The diversity of Muslims in the United States* (No. Special Report 159). Washington, DC: United States Institute of Peace.

Huffman, S. (n.d.). *Mapping the genetic relationships of the world's languages.* Retrieved from http://www.gmi.org/wlms/users/huffman/Mapping_Genetic_Relationships_World_ Languages.pdf.

Hui, H., Ng, E. C. W., & Tai, M. H. (2010). Chinese religions. In D. A. Leeming, K. Madden, &. S. Marlan (Eds.), *Encyclopedia of psychology and religion* (pp. 143–146). New York: Springer.

Hulshof, H. J., Novati, A., Sgoifo, A., Luiten, P. G. M., den Boer, J. A., & Meerlo, P. (2011). Maternal separation decreases adult hippocampal cell proliferation and impairs cognitive performance but has little effect on stress sensitivity and anxiety in adult Wistar rats. *Behavioural Brain Research, 216*(2), 552–560. doi:10.1016/j.bbr.2010.08.038

Humanistic Psychology. (n.d.). *The mission of division 32.* Humanistic Psychology [division of American Psychological Association]. Retrieved from http://www.apa.org/divisions/div32/history.html.

Hunsley, J., & Westmacott, R. (2007). Interpreting the magnitude of the placebo effect: Mountain or molehill? *Journal of Clinical Psychology, 63*(4), 391–399.

Hutchins, E. (1980). *Culture and inference: A Trobrian case study.* Cambridge, MA: Harvard University Press.

Iacoboni, M., Molnar-Szakacs, I., Gallese, V., Buccino, G., Mazziotta, J. C., & Rizzolatti, G. (2005). Grasping the intentions of others with one's own mirror neuron system. *PLoS Biology, 3*(3), 529–535. doi:10.1371/journal.pbio.0030079

Iacoboni, M., Woods, R. P., Brass M., Bekkering, H., Mazziotta, J. C., & Rizzolatti, G. (1999). Cortical mechanisms of human imitation. *Science, 286,* 2526–8. doi:10.1126/science.286.5449.2526

Iglehart, J. K. (Ed.). (2005). Putting evidence into practice. *Health Affairs, 24*(1).

Illovsky, M. E. (1994). Counseling, artificial intelligence, and expert systems. *Simulation & Gaming, 25*(1), 88–98. doi:10.1177/1046878194251009

Illovsky, M. E. (2003). *Mental health professionals, minorities, and the poor.* New York: Brunner-Routledge.

Illovsky, M. E., Gintiliene, G., Bulotaite, L., Rickman, J., Belekiene, M., & Janowitz, K. (2008). PRF cross-cultural psychological study of Lithuanian students, teachers, and special education teachers. *International Journal of Special Education, 23*(1), 93–99.

Inglehart, R. (1997). *Modernization and postmodernization: Cultural, economic, and political change in 43 societies.* Princeton, NJ : Princeton University Press.

Inglehart, R., & Baker, W. E. (2001). Modernization's challenge to traditional values: Who's afraid of Ronald McDonald? *The Futurist, March-April,* 16–21.

Inglehart, R., & Welzel, C. (2005). *Modernization, culture change and democracy: The human development sequence.* New York: Cambridge University Press.

Inglehart, R., Welzel, C., & Foa, R. (2006). Happiness trends in 24 countries, 1946–2006. *World Values Survey.* Retrieved from World Values Survey Web site: http://www.worldvaluessurvey.org/happinesstrends/.

Ingstad, H. (1969). *Westward to Vinland.* New York: St. Martins.

Institute for Family-Centered Care. (2010). *Involving patients and families in evaluation and research bibliography.* Retrieved from http://www.pfcc.org/advance/BI_Involving_pf_research_032010.pdf.

Institute of Medicine. (2011). *Clinical practice guidelines we can trust.* Retrieved from http://www.iom.edu/~/media/Files/Report%20Files/2011/Clinical-Practice-Guidelines-We-Can-Trust/Clinical%20Practice%20Guidelines%202011%20Insert.pdf.

International Society for Applied Ethology. (2010). *Ethical treatment of animals in applied animal behavior research.* Retrieved from http://www.applied-ethology.org/ethical guidelines.htm.

Intons-Peterson, M. J. (1983). Imagery paradigms: How vulnerable are they to experimenters' expectations? *Journal of Experimental Psychology: Human Perception and Performance, 9,* 394–412.

Irvine, S. H., & Berry, J. W. (Eds.). (1988). *Human abilities in cultural context.* New York: Cambridge University Press.

Irwin, H. J. (1992). Origins and functions of paranormal belief: The role of childhood trauma and interpersonal control. *Journal of the American Society for Psychical Research, 86*(3), 199–208.

Irwin, H. J. (2009). *The psychology of paranormal belief: A researcher's handbook.* Hertfordshire, Great Britain: University of Hertfordshire.

Israeli, R. (2000). Medieval Muslim travelers to China. *Journal of Muslim Minority Affairs, 20*(2), 313–321.

Ivey, A. E., & Ivey, M. B. (2007). *Intentional interviewing and counseling: Facilitating client development in a multicultural society* (6th ed.). Belmont, CA: Thomson-Brooks/Cole.

Iwai, H., & Reynolds, D. K. (1970). Morita psychotherapy: The views from the west. *American Journal of Psychiatry, 126,* 1031–1036. doi:10.1176/appi.ajp.126.7.1031

Jackson, D. N. (1997). *Personality research form.* Port Huron, MI: Sigma Assessment Systems.

Jackson, S. W. (1999). *Care of the psyche: A history of psychological healing.* New Haven, CT: Yale University Press.

Jackson, Y. (Ed.). (2006). *Encyclopedia of multicultural psychology.* Thousand Oaks, CA: Sage.

Jacobi, J. (1973). *The psychology of C. G. Jung: An introduction with illustrations* (K. W. Bash, Trans.). New Haven, CT: Yale University Press. (First published in 1942)

Jacobs, S-E., Thomas, W., & Lang, S. (Eds.). (1997). *Two-spirit people: Native American gender identity, sexuality, and spirituality.* Urbana: University of Illinois Press.

Jacobson, J. W., Foxx, R. M., & Mulick, J. A. (Eds.). (2005). *Controversial therapies for developmental disabilities: Fad, fashion, and science in professional practice.* Mahwah, NJ: Lawrence Erlbaum Associates.

Jacobson, K. (2009). Considering interactions between genes, environments, biology, and social context. *Psychological Science Agenda. American Psychological Association, 23*(4).

Jackson, P. L., Brunet, E., Meltzoff, A. N., & Decety, J. (2006). Empathy examined through the neural mechanisms involved in imagining how I feel versus how you feel pain: An event-related fMRI study. *Neuropsychologia, 44,* 752–761. doi:10.1016/j.neuropsychologia.2005.07.015

Jaeggi, A. V., Burkart, J. M., & Van Schaik, C. P. (2010). On the psychology of cooperation in humans and other primates: Combining the natural history and experimental evidence of prosociality. *Philosophical Transactions of the Royal Society B: Biological Sciences, 365,* 2723–2735. doi:10.1098/rstb.2010.0118

Jaffe, E. (2010, July/August). Is clinical psychology broken? *Observer, 23*(6).

Jahoda, G. (1969). *The psychology of superstition.* Harmondsworth, England: Penguin.

Jahoda, G. (1993). *Crossroads between culture and mind.* Cambridge, MA: Harvard University Press.

Jahoda, G. (2007). Superstition and belief. *The Psychologist, 20*(10), 594–595.

Jairazbhoy, R. A. (1974). *Ancient Egyptians and Chinese in America.* Totowa: Rowman and Littlefield.

Jamieson, I. G. (1989). Behavioral heterochrony and the evolutions of birds helping at nest: An unselected consequence of communal breeding. *American Naturalist, 133,* 394–406. doi:10.1086/284925

James, S. A. (1994). John Henryism and the health of African Americans. *Culture, Medicine, and Psychiatry, 18,* 163–182. doi:10.1007/BF01379448

James, W. (1907). *Pragmatism, A new name for some old ways of thinking: Popular lectures on philosophy by William James.* New York, London, Bombay, Calcutta: Longmans, Green, and Co.

James, W. (1918). *The principles of psychology.* New York: H. Holt & Co.

Jandt, F. E. (Ed.). (2009). *An introduction to intercultural communication: Identities in a global community.* Thousand Oaks, CA: Sage Publ.

Jannsen, S., Liu, M. L., & Badgett, N. (Eds.). (2012). *World almanac and book of facts 2012* [International statistics – Area and population of the world by continent/region, p. 731]. New York: Infobase Learning.

Jastrow, J. (1900). *Fact and fable in psychology.* Boston: Houghton Mifflin. doi:10.1037/10919-000

Jaynes, G. (2009, October 16). Famine confronts 150 million in Africa. *New York Times.* Retrieved from http://www.nytimes.com/1981/03/26/world/famine-confronts-150-million-in-africa.html).

Jilek, W. G. (2001, July). *Cultural factors in psychiatric disorders.* Paper presented at the 26th Congress of the World Federation for Mental Health, Vancouver, Canada. Retrieved from http://www.mentalhealth.com/mag1/wolfgang.html.

Jin, J., Sklar, G. E., Oh, V. M. S., & Li, S. C. (2008). Factors affecting therapeutic compliance: A review from the patient's perspective. *Doverpress, 4*(1), 269–286.

Jo, J. K. (2005). Traditional and cultural healing among the Chinese. In R. Moodley, & W. West (Eds.), *Integrating traditional healing practices into counseling and psychotherapy.* Thousand Oaks, CA: Sage Publications.

John, O. P. (1989). Towards a taxonomy of personality descriptors. In D. M. Buss & N. Cantor (Eds.), *Personality psychology: Recent trends and emerging directions* (pp. 261–271). New York: Springer-Verlag.

John, O. P. (1990). The "Big Five" factor taxonomy: Dimensions of personality in the natural languages and in questionnaires. In L. Pervin (Ed.), *Handbook of personality theory and research* (pp. 66–100). New York: Guilford.

John, O. P., Angleitner, A., & Ostendorf, F. (1988). The lexical approach to personality: A historical review of trait taxonomic research. *European Journal of Personality, 2,* 171–203. doi:10.1002/per.2410020302

Johnson, A. (1991). Regional comparative field research. *Behavior Science Research, 25*(1-4), 3–22.

Johnson, B. (2008). Just what lies "beyond the pleasure principle?" *Neuro-Psychoanalysis, 10*(2), 201–212.

Johnson, L. (n.d.). *Native-American medicine.* Retrieved from http://www. healingther apies.info/Native-American%20Medicine.htm.

Johnson, S. B. (2012, July/August). In support of APA's treatment guidelines efforts. *Monitor on Psychology, 43*(7), 5.

Johnstone, T., van Reekum, C. M., Urry, H. L., Kalin, N. H., & Davidson R. J. (2007). Failure to regulate: Counter-productive recruitment of top-down prefrontal-subcortical circuitry in major depression. *Journal of Neuroscience, 27,* 8877–8884. doi: 10.1523/JNEUROSCI.2063-07.2007

Jones, C. R., Campbell, S. S., Zone, S. E., Cooper, F., DeSano, A., Murphy, P. J., Jones, B., Czajkowski, L., & Ptácek, L. J. (1999). Familial advanced sleep-phase syndrome: A short-period circadian rhythm variant in humans. *Nature Medicine, 9,* 1062–1065.

Jones, E. E., & Nisbett, R. E. (1972). The actor and the observer: Divergent perceptions of the causes of behavior. In E. E. Jones et al. (Eds.), *Attribution: Perceiving the causes of behavior* (pp. 79–84). Morristown, NJ: General Learning Press.

Jones, E. E., & McGillis, D. (1976). Correspondent inferences and the attribution cube: A comparative reappraisal. In J. Harvey, W. Ickes, & R. Kidd (Eds.), *New directions in attribution research* (Vol. 1, pp. 389–420). Hillsdale, NJ: Lawrence Erlbaum.

Jopling, D. (2008). *Talking cures and placebo effects.* Oxford University Press.

Jordan, E. G., & Mogil, J. S. (2006, October). Mice, pain, and empathy. *Science, 13*(314), 253.

Jung, C. G. (1968). *The archetypes and the collective unconscious.* London: Routledge & Kegan Paul.

Jung, C. G. (1990). *The archetypes of the collective unconscious.* Princeton, NJ: Princeton University Press. (First published in 1959)

Jung, C., Nam, S., Kam, S., Yeh, M., & Park, J. (2003). Therapeutic compliance and its related factors in lung cancer patients. *Lung Cancer, 41*(Issue null), S185–S185.

Kaasinen, V., Aalto, S., Någren, K., & Rinne, J. O. (2004). Expectation of caffeine induces dopaminergic responses in humans. *European Journal of Neuroscience, 19*(8), 2352–6. doi:10.1111/j.1460-9568.2004.03310.x

Kagan, J., & Kogan, N. (1970). Individual variation in cognitive processes. In P. H. Mussen (Ed.), *Carmichael's manual of child psychology* (Vol. 1, 3rd ed.). New York: Wiley.

Kahane, H., & Cavender, N. M. (2006). *Logic and contemporary rhetoric: The use of reason in everyday life.* Australia; Belmont, CA: Thomson/Wadsworth.

Kahn, P., & Cleaves, F. W. (1998). *The secret history of the Mongols.* Boston: Cheng & Tsui Company.

Kahneman, D., Slovic, P., & Tversky, A. (Eds.). (1982). *Judgment under uncertainty: Heuristics and biases.* Cambridge, UK: Cambridge University Press.

Kahneman, D., Knetsch, J. L., & Thaler, R. H. (1991). Anomalies: The endowment effect, loss aversion, and status quo bias. *The Journal of Economic Perspectives, 5*(1), 193–206.

Kale, R. (1995). Traditional healers in South Africa: A parallel health care system. *British Medical Journal, 310*(6988), 1182–5.

Kalipeni, E. (1979). Traditional African healing of mental illness as compared with western psychiatry (clinical psychology). *Dansk Psykolog Nyt (Danish Journal of Psychology), 14 & 15,* 377–381 & 402–409.

Kalisch, R., Wiech, K., Critchley, H. D., Seymour, B., O'Doherty, J. P., Oakley, D. A., Allen, P., & Dolan, R. J. (2005). Anxiety reduction through detachment: Subjective, physiological, and neural effects. *Journal of Cognitive Neuroscience, 17,* 874–883. doi:10.1162/0898929054021184

Kapferer, J-N. (1990). *Rumors: Uses, interpretations, and images* (B. Fink, Trans.). New Brunswick, NJ: Transaction Publishers.

Kaplan, B. H. (1971). *Psychiatric disorder and the urban environment: Report of the Cornell Science Center.* New York: Behavioral Publications.

Kaplan, H. I., & Sadock, B. J. (2003). *Synopsis of psychiatry: Behavioral sciences/clinical psychiatry* (9th ed.). Philadelphia, PA: Lippincott Williams & Wilkins.

Kaplan, R. M., & Saccuzzo, D. P. (2009). *Psychological testing: Principles, applications, and issues.* Belmont, CA: Wadsworth.

Kappeler, P. M., & van Schaik, C. P. (Eds.). (2006). *Cooperation in primates and humans: Mechanisms and evolution.* New York: Springer.

Karch, S. B. (1997). *A brief history of cocaine.* New York: CRC Press.

Karsh, E. (2006). *Islamic imperialism: A history.* New Haven, CT: Yale University Press.

Kaslow, F. W. (Ed.). (2002). *Comprehensive handbook of psychotherapy* (Vol. 3: Interpersonal/humanistic/existential). Chichester, NY: John Wiley & Sons.

Kaslow, F. W., Massey, R. F., & Massey, S. D. (Eds.). (2002). *Comprehensive handbook of psychotherapy* (Vol. 3: Interpersonal/humanistic/existential). Chichester, NY: John Wiley & Sons.

Kasser, T. (2002). *The high price of materialism.* Cambridge, MA: MIT Press.

Kasser, T., & Kanner, A. D. (Eds.). (2004). *Psychology and consumer culture: The struggle for a good life in a materialistic world.* Washington, DC: American Psychological Association.

Kast, V. (1992). *The dynamics of symbols: Fundamentals of Jungian psychotherapy* (S. A. Schwarz, Trans.). New York: Fromm International.

Kazdin, A. E. (Ed.). (2000). *Encyclopedia of psychology.* Washington, D.C.: American Psychological Association; Oxford [Oxfordshire]; New York: Oxford University Press.

Keats, D. M. (1985). Strategies in formal operational thinking: Malaysia and Australia. In I. Reyers Lagunes & Y. H. Poortinga (Eds.), *From a different perspective: Studies in behavior across cultures* (pp. 306–318). Lisse, Nederland: Swets & Zeitlinger.

Kehoe, A. B. (2000). *Shamans and religion: An anthropological exploration in critical thinking.* Long Grove, IL: Waveland Press.

Keirsey, D. K. (1998). *Please understand me II: Temperament, character, intelligence.* Del Mar, CA: Prometheus Nemesis Book Company.

Keirsey, D., & Bates, M. (1984). *Please understand me: Character and temperament types.* Del Mar, CA: Gnosology Books, Prometheus Nemesis.

Kelly, G. A. (1955). *The psychology of personal constructs* (Vols. 1 & 2). New York: Norton.

Kelly, G. A. (1970). A brief introduction to personal construct theory. In D. Bannister (Ed.), *Perspectives in personal construct theory.* London: Academic Press.

Kelley, H. H. (1972a). Attribution in social interaction, In E. E. Jones, D. E. Kanouse, H. H. Kelley, R. E. Nisbett, S. Valins, & B. Weiner (Eds.), *Attribution: Perceiving the causes of behavior* (pp. 1–26), Morristown, NJ: General Learning Press.

Kelley, H. H. (1972b). Causal schemata and the attribution process. In E. E. Jones et al. (Eds.), *Attribution: Perceiving the causes of behavior* (pp. 151–174). Morristown, NJ: General Learning Press.

Keltner, D. (2009). *Born to be good: The science of a meaningful life.* New York: W. W. Norton & Co.

Kendell, R. E. (1975). *The role of diagnosis in psychiatry.* Oxford, England: Blackwell Scientific.

Kennair, L. E. O. (2002). Evolutionary psychology: An emerging integrative perspective within the science and practice of psychology. *The Human Nature Review, 2,* 17–61.

Kenneally, C. (2007). *The first word: The search for the origins of language.* New York: Penquin Group.

Kennedy, W. P. (1961). The Nocebo reaction. *Medical World, 95,* 203–205.

Kerr, B., Feldman, M. W., & Godfrey-Smith, P. (2004). What is altruism? *Trends in ecology and evolution, 19,* 135–140. doi:10.1016/j.tree.2003.10.004

Kessler, R. C., & Ustun, T. B. (Eds.). (2008). *The WHO world mental health surveys: Global perspectives on the epidemiology of mental disorders.* Geneva: World Health Organization/Cambridge University Press.

Keysers, C., Wicker, B., Gazzola, V., Anton, J., Fogassi, L., & Gallese, V. (2004). A touching sightSII/PV activation during the observation and experience of touch. *Neuron, 42*(2), 335–346. doi:10.1016/S0896-6273(04)00156-4

Khan, H. K. (2005). Arab-Islamic constructive discipline practices: To eliminate corporal punishments. *International Society for Prevention of Child Abuse and Neglect (ISPCAN).* Retrieved from http://www.ispcan.org/documents/VID/Constructive_Discipline_Practices.pdf.

Khoapa, B. A. (1980). *The African personality.* Tokyo, Japan: United Nations University.

Kim, B. S. K., Liang, C. T. H., & Li, L. C. (2003). Counselor ethnicity, counselor non-verbal behavior, and session outcome with Asian American clients: Initial findings. *Journal of Counseling and Development, 81*(2), 202–207. doi:10.1002/j.1556-6678.2003.tb00243.x

Kim, H. S., Sherman, D. K., & Taylor, S. E. (2009). The irony of cultural psychology research. *American Psychologist, 64*(6), 564–565. doi:10.1037/a0016680

Kim, N., & Ahn, W. (2002). Clinical psychologists' theory-based representations of mental disorders predict their diagnostic reasoning and memory. *Journal of Experimental Psychology: General, 131*(4), 451–476. doi:10.1037/0096-3445.131.4.451

Kim, U., Triandis, H. C., Kağitçibaşi, Ç., Choi, S-C., & Yoon, G. (Eds.). (1994). *Individualism and collectivism: Theory, method, and applications (cross cultural research and methodology)*. Thousand Oaks, CA: Sage Publications.

Kim, U., Yang, K. S., & Hwang, K. K. (Eds.). (2006). *Indigenous and cultural psychology: Understanding people in context*. New York: Springer.

Kimmel, A. J. (2004). *Rumors and rumor control: A manager's guide to understanding and combatting rumors*. Mahwah, NJ: Lawrence Erlbaum.

Kindlon, D., & Thompson, M. (2000). *Raising Cain: Protecting the emotional life of boys*. New York: Random House.

King, A. Y. C., & Bond, M. H. (1985). The Confucian paradigm of man: A sociological view. In W. S. Tseng & D. Y. H. Wu (Eds.), *Chinese culture and mental health*. New York: Academic Press.

Kirk, S. A., & Kutchins, H. (1992). *The selling of DSM: The rhetoric of science in psychiatry*. New York: Aldine De Gruyter.

Kirk, S. A., & Kutchins, H. (1994). The myth of the reliability of DSM. *Journal of Mind and Behavior, 15*(1&2), 71–86.

Kirmayer, L. J. (2008). Empathy and alterity in cultural psychiatry. *Ethos, 36*(4), 457–474.

Kirmayer, L. J., & Young, A. (1998). Culture and somatization: Clinical, epidemiological, and ethnographic perspectives. *Psychosomatic Medicine, 60,* 420–430.

Kirsch, I., Deacon, B. J., Huedo-Medina, T. B., Scoboria, A., Moore, T. J., & Johnson, B. T. (2008). Initial severity and antidepressant benefits: A meta-analysis of data submitted to the food and drug administration. *Public Library of Science (PLoS – Medicine.* Retrieved from http://www.plosmedicine.org/article/info. doi:10.1371/journal.pmed.0050045

Kitayama, S., & Cohen, D. (Eds.). (2007). *Handbook of cultural psychology*. New York: Guilford Press.

Kitayama, S., Duffy, S., Kawamura, T., & Larsen, J. T. (2003). Perceiving an object and its context in different cultures: A cultural look at New Look. *Psychological Science, 14,* 201. doi:10.1111/1467-9280.02432.

Kite, M. E., & Deaux, K. (1987). Gender belief systems: homosexuality and the implicit inversion theory. *Psychology of Women Quarterly, 11,* 83–96. doi:10.1111/j.1471-6402.1987.tb00776.x

Klein, D. F. (1996). Preventing hung juries about therapy studies. *Journal of Consulting and Clinical Psychology, 64*(1), 81–87. doi:10.1037/0022-006X.64.1.81

Kleinman, A., & Lin, T-Y. (Eds.). (1981). *Normal and abnormal behavior in Chinese culture*. Dordrecht, Holland: D. Reidel Publishing.

Klima, G. (2008). The medieval problem of universals. In E. N. Zalta (Ed.), *Stanford encyclopedia of philosophy*. Retrieved from http://plato.stanford.edu/archives/win2008/entries/universals-medieval.

Kluckhohn, F., & Strodtbeck, F. (1961). *Variations in value orientations*. Evanston: Row, Peterson.

Koller, J. M. (July 2000). Syadvada as the epistemological key to the Jaina middle way metaphysics of Anekántavāda. *Philosophy East and West* (Honululu), *50*(3), 400–407. doi:10.1353/pew.2000.0009

Koenig, H. (1999). *The healing power of faith*. New York: Simon & Schuster.

Konigsberg, R. D. (2011, January). Good news about grief. *Time, 177*(3), 42–46.

Kopelman, R. E., & Rovenpor, J. L. (2006). Allport-Vernon-Lindzey Study of Values. In J. Greenhaus & G. Callanan (Eds.), *Encyclopedia of career development* (pp. 15–18). Thousand Oaks, CA: Sage.

Kopelman, R. E., Rovenporb, J. L., & Guanc, M. (2003). The study of values: Construction of the fourth edition. *Journal of Vocational Behavior, 62*(2), 203–220. doi:10.1016/S0001-8791(02)00047-7

Koss, M., Tromp, S., & Tharan, M. (1995). Traumatic memories: Empirical foundations, forensic and clinical implications. *Clinical Psychology: Science and Practice, 2*(2), 111–132. doi.org/10.1111/j.1468-2850.1995.tb00034.x

Krämer, G., Matringe, D., Nawas, J., & Rowson, E. (Eds.). (2007). *Encyclopaedia of Islam*. Leiden, the Netherlands: E. J. Brill.

Krasner, L., & Ullman, L. P. (Eds.). (1965). *Research in behavior modification: New developments and implications*. New York: Holt, Rinehart and Winston.

Kraus, R., Zack, J. S., & Stricker, G. (2004). *Online counseling: A handbook for mental health professionals*. London, UK: Elsevier Academic Press.

Kring, A. M., Davison, G. C., Neale, J. M., & Johnson, S. (2007). *Abnormal psychology*. Chichester, UK: Wiley.

Kripke, S. (1982). *Wittgenstein on rules and private language: An elementary exposition*. Cambridge, MA: Harvard University Press.

Krippner, R. (2002). Conflicting perspectives on shaman and shamanism: Points and counterpoints. *American Psychologist, 57,* 962–978. doi:10.1037/0003-066X.57.11.962

Kroeber, A. L., & Kluckhohn, C. (1952). *Culture: A critical review of concepts and definitions*. New York: Vintage.

Kroll, J., & Bachrach, B. (1984). Sin and mental illness in the Middle Ages. *Psychological Medicine, 14*(3), 507–514. doi:10.1017/S0033291700015105

Kuhn, T. S. (1962). *The structure of scientific revolutions*. Chicago: University of Chicago Press.

Kumari, V. (2006). Do psychotherapies produce neurobiological effects? *Acta Neuropsychiatrica, 18,* 61–70. doi:10.1111/j.1601-5215.2006.00127.x

Kundtz, D. (2004). *Managing feelings: An owner's manual for men*. Boston, MA: Conari Press.

Kuo, C-L., & Kavanagh, K. H. (1994). Chinese perspectives on culture and mental health. *Issues in Mental Health Nursing, 15*(6), 551–567. doi:10.3109/01612849409040533

Kutchins, H., & Kirk, S. A. (1997). *Making us crazy. DSM: The psychiatric bible and the creation of mental disorders*. New York: The Free Press.

LaFollette, H. (2002). *Ethics in practice: An anthology* (2nd ed.). Malden, MA: Blackwell.

Lai, E. Y. P. (Ed.). (2003). *The new face of Asian Pacific America: Numbers, diversity & change in the 21st century*. San Francisco, CA : San Francisco: AsianWeek, with UCLA's Asian American Studies Center Press, in cooperation with the Organization of Chinese Americans and the National Coalition for Asian Pacific American Community Development.

Laing, R. D. (1986). *Wisdom, madness and folly: The making of a psychiatrist*. New York: McGraw-Hill Book Co.

Lam, C. S., Tsang, H. W. H., Corrigan, P. W., Lee, Y-T., Angell, B., Shi, K., & Larson, J. E. (2010). Chinese lay theory and mental illness stigma: Implications for research and practices. *Journal of Rehabilitation*. Retrieved from http://findarticles.com/p/articles/mi_m0825/is_1_76/ai_n50152439/.

Lambert, M. J. (1992a). Implications of outcome research for psychotherapy integration. In J. C. Norcross & M. R. Goldstein (Eds.), *Handbook of psychotherapy integration* (pp. 94–129). New York: Basic Books.

Lambert, M. J. (1992b). Psychotherapy outcome research: Implications for integrative and eclectic counselors. In J. C. Norcross & M. R. Goldfried (Eds.), *Handbook of psychotherapy integration*. New York: Basic.

Lambert, M. J. (2004). *Bergin and Garfield's handbook of psychotherapy and behavior change* (5th ed.). New York: John Wiley & Sons.

Lambert, M. J., & Barley, D. E. (2001). Research summary on the therapeutic relationship and psychotherapy outcome. *Psychotherapy, 38*(4), 357–361. doi:10.1037/0033-3204.38.4.357

Lambert, M. J., & Bergin, A. E. (1992). Achievements and limitations of psychotherapy research. In D. K. Freedheim (Ed.), *History of psychotherapy: A recent change* (pp. 360–390). Washington, DC: American Psychological Association. doi:10.1037/10110-010

Lambert, M. J., & Bergin, A. E. (1994). The effectiveness of psychotherapy. In A. E. Bergin & S. L. Garfield (Eds.), *Handbook of psychotherapy and behavior change* (4th ed., pp. 143–89). New York: Wiley.

Lambert, M. J., Garfield, S. L., & Bergin, A. E. (2004). Overview, trends, and future issues. In A. E. Bergin & S. L. Garfield (Eds.), *Handbook of psychotherapy and behavior change* (5th ed., pp. 805–821). New York: Wiley.

Landheer, B. (1973). European integration and national decentralization. In *European Yearbook 1971* (Vol. XIX, pp. 81–94). Council of Europe/Conseil de L'Europe. The Hague, Netherlands: Martinus Nijhoff.

Lane, C. (2007). *Shyness: How normal behavior became a sickness*. Yale University Press.

Langer, E. J., & Abelson, R. P. (1974). A patient by any other name: Clinician group difference in labeling bias. *Journal of Consulting and Clinical Psychology, 42,* 4–9. doi: 10.1037/h0036054

Lankford, R. D. (2006). *Is American society too materialistic?* San Diego CA: Greenhaven Press.

Lasker, R. D., & Weiss, E. S. (2003). Broadening participation in community problem solving: A multidisciplinary model to support collaborative practice and research. *Journal of Urban Health, 80*(1), 48–60. doi:10.1093/jurban/jtg014

Lassiter, J. E. (1999). African culture and personality: Bad social science, effective social activism, or a call to reinvent ethnology? *African Studies Quarterly, 3*(2), 1. [Online]. Retrieved from http://www.africa.ufl.edu/asq/v3/v3i3a1.htm.

Lattal, K. E., & Chase, P. N. (Eds.). (2003). *Behavior theory and philosophy.* New York: Kluwer Academic/Plenum.

Laughlin, C. D., & d'Aquili, E. G. (1974). *Biogenetic structuralism.* New York: Columbia University Press.

Laungani, P. (2007). *Understanding cross-cultural psychology: Eastern and Western perspectives.* London: Sage.

Lawrence, V., Murray, J., Banerjee, S., Turner, S., Sangha, K., Byng, R., Bhugra, D., Huxley, P., Tylee, A., & Macdonald, A. (2006). Concepts and causation of depression: A cross-cultural study of the beliefs of older adults. *The Gerontologist, 46,* 23–33.

Lawson, W., Hepler, N., Holladay, J., & Cuffel, B. (1994). Race as a factor in inpatient and outpatient admissions and diagnosis. *Hospital and Community Psychiatry, 45,* 72–74.

Leaman, O. (1998). *Averroes and his philosophy* (Rev. ed.). Richmond, UK: Curzon Press.

Learning Disabilities Association of America. (2011). Retrieved from http://www.ldanatl.org/.

Lebel, S., Trinkaus, E., Faure, M., Fernandez, P., Guérin, C., Richter, D., Mercier, N., Valladas, H., & Wagner, G. A. (2001). Comparative morphology and paleobiology of Middle Pleistocene human remains from the Bau de l'Aubesier, Vaucluse, France. *Proceedings of the National Academy of Sciences, 98,* 11097-11102. doi:10.1073/pnas.181353998

Lebow, J. (2002). Integrative and eclectic therapies at the beginning of the twenty-first century. In F. W. Kaslow (Ed.), *Comprehensive handbook of psychotherapy: Integrative/eclectic* (Vol. 4, pp. 1–10). Hoboken, NJ: John Wiley & Sons.

Lee, C. C., & Armstrong, K. L. (1995). Indigenous models of mental health interventions. In J. C. Ponterroto, J. M. Casas, L. A. Suzuki, & C. M. Alexander (Eds.), *Handbook of multicultural counseling* (pp. 441–456). Thousand Oaks, CA: Sage.

Lee, E. (1997). Cross-cultural communication: Therapeutic use of interpreters. In E. Lee (Ed.), *Working with Asian Americans: A guide for clinicians* (pp. 477–489). New York: Guilford Press.

Lee, S. (2002). Socio-cultural and global health perspectives for the development of future psychiatric diagnostic systems. *Psychopathology, 35*(2-3), 152–7. doi:10.1159/000065136

Lee, W. M. L., Blando, J. A., Mizelle, N., & Orozco, G. L. (2007). *Introduction to multicultural counseling for helping professionals* (2nd ed.). New York: Routledge.

Lee, Y. K., & Son, B. K. (1998). The relationship between therapeutic compliance and emotional variables in the patients on maintenance hemodialysis. *Journal of Korean Neuropsychiatric Association, 37*(5), 869–877.

Lehmann, L., & Keller, L. (2006). The evolution of cooperation and altruism: A general framework and classification of models. *Journal of Evolutionary Biology, 19,* 1365–1725. doi:10.1111/j.1420-9101.2006.01119.x

Lehmann, S., Joy, V., Kreisman, D., & Simmens, S. (1976). Responses to viewing symptomatic behaviors and labeling of prior mental illness. *Journal of Community Psychology, 4,* 327–334. doi:10.1002/1520-6629(197610)4:4<327::AID-JCOP2290 040403>3.0.CO;2-M

Leong, F. T. L. (Ed.). (2008). *Encyclopedia of counseling* (Vol. 2). Thousand Oaks, CA: Sage.

Leu, J., Wang, J., & Koo, K. (2011, August). Are positive emotions just as "positive" across cultures? *Emotion, 11*(4), 994–999. doi:10.1037/a0021332

Leuchter, A. F., Cook, I. A., Witte, E. A., Morgan, M., & Abrams, M. (2002). Changes in brain function of depressed subjects during treatment with placebo. *American Journal of Psychiatry, 159*(1), 122–9. doi:10.1176/appi.ajp.159.1.122

Leung, S. A. (2003). A journey worth traveling: Globalization of counseling psychology. *Counseling Psychologist, 31*(4), 412–419. doi:10.1177/0011000003031004004

Levant, R. F., & Kopecky, G. (1995). *Masculinity reconstructed: Changing the rules of manhood – At work, in relationships, and in family life.* New York: Dutton.

Levathes, L. (1997). *When China ruled the seas: The treasure fleet of the dragon throne, 1405–1433.* Oxford University Press.

Levenson, R. W. (2009). Psychological clinical science and accreditation: The good, the bad, and the ugly. *Observer, 22*(3).

Levenson, R. W., & Ruef, A. M. (1992). Empathy: A physiological substrate. *Journal of Personality and Social Psychology, 63,* 234–246. doi:10.1037/0022-3514.63.2.234

Leventhal, A. L., & Martell, C. R. (2006). *The myth of depression as disease: Limitations and alternatives to drug treatment.* Westport, CT: Praeger Publishers/Greenwood Publishing Group.

Levine, R. V., Norenzayan, A., & Philbrick, K. (2001). Cross-cultural differences in helping strangers. *Journal of Cross-Cultural Psychology, 32*(5), 543–560. doi:10.1177/0022022101032005002

Levinson, D., & Ember, M. (Eds.). (1997). *American immigrant cultures: Builders of a nation.* New York: Macmillan.

Levinson, D., & Ember, M. (Eds.). (2009). *Encyclopedia of cultural anthropology.* New York: Henry Holt and Company.

Lévi-Strauss, C. (1966). *The savage mind.* Chicago: University of Chicago Press. (First published in French in 1962)

Levy, N. (2004). Evolutionary psychology, human universals, and the Standard Social Science Model. *Biology and Philosophy, 19*(3), 459–472. doi:10.1023/B:BIPH.0000 036111.64561.63

Liamputtong, P. (Ed.). (2008). *Doing cross-cultural research: Ethical and methodological perspectives.* New York: Springer.

Lilienfeld, S. O. (2002). Scientific review of mental health practice: Our raison d'etre. *Scientific Review of Mental Health Practice, 1*(1), 5–10.

Lillard, A. S. (1997). Other folks' theories of mind and behavior. *Psychological Science, 8*(4), 268–274.

Lim, R. F. (Ed.). (2006). *Clinical manual of cultural psychiatry.* Washington, DC: American Psychiatric Pub.

Lin, Y-N. (1994). Conceptualizing common factors in counseling. *Journal of Guidance and Counseling (China), 27*(1), 1–21. Retrieved from http://agc.ncue.edu.tw/text 27.1-1.pdf.

Lin, K-M. (2010). Cultural and ethnic issues in psychopharmacology – Addressing both instrumental and symbolic effects of treatment. *Psychiatric Times, 27*(1). Retrieved from http://www.consultantlive.com/diabetes/content/article/10168/150 5053.

Lin, T-Y. (1983). Psychiatry and Chinese culture. *Western Journal of Medicine, 139*(6), 862–867.

Lindzey, G. (Ed.). (1954). *Handbook of social psychology.* Cambridge, MA: Addison-Wesley.

Lindzey, G. (Ed.). (1958). *Assessment of human motives.* New York: Rinehart and Company.

Link, B. G., & Cullen, F. T. (1990). The labeling theory of mental disorder: A review of the evidence. *Research in Community and Mental Health, 6,* 75–105.

Link, B. G., Cullen, F. T., Struening, E., Shrout, P. E., & Dohrenwend, B. P. (1989). A modified labeling theory approach to mental disorders: An empirical assessment. *American Sociological Review, 54,* 400–423. doi:10.2307/2095613

Lipsitz, G. (1995). The possessive investment in whiteness: Racialized social democracy and the "White" problem in American studies. *American Quarterly, 47*(3), 369–87. doi:10.2307/2713291

Li-Repac, D. (1980). Cultural influences on clinical perception: A comparison between caucasian and Chinese-American therapists. *Journal of Cross-Cultural Psychology, 11*(3), 327–342. doi:10.1177/0022022180113006

List of cognitive biases. (2010). *StateMaster.com.* Retrieved from http://www.statemas ter.com/encyclopedia/List-of-cognitive-biases.

Litz, B. T., Orsillo, S. M., Friedman, M., Ehlich, P., & Batres, A. (1997). Posttraumatic stress disorder associated with peacekeeping duty in Somalia for U.S. military personnel. *American Journal of Psychiatry, 154,* 178–84.

Liu, W. M., Soleck, G., Hopps, J., Dunston, K., & Pickett, T. (2004). A new framework to understand social class in counseling: The social class worldview and modern classism theory. *Journal of Multicultural Counseling and Development, 32,* 95–122.

Livesley, W. J. (2001). A framework for an integrated approach to treatment. In W. J. Livesley (Ed.), *Handbook of personality disorders: Theory, research, and treatment* (pp. 570–600). New York: Guilford Press.

Livesley, W. J. (Ed.). (2001). *Handbook of personality disorders: Theory, research, and treatment.* New York: Guilford Press.

Livesley, W. J. (2010). Confusion and incoherence in the classification of personality disorder: Commentary on the preliminary proposals for DSM-5. *Psychological Injury and Law, 3,* 304–313. Retrieved from http://dx.doi.org/10.1007/s12207-010-9094-8.

Loeb, K. L., Wilson, G. T., Labouvie, E., Pratt, E. M., Hayaki, J., Walsh, G. T., Agras, W. S., & Fairburn, C. G. (2005). Therapeutic alliance and treatment adherence in two interventions for bulimia nervosa: A study of process and outcome. *Journal of Consulting and Clinical Psychology, 73*(6), 1097–1107. doi:10.1037/0022-006X.73. 6.1097

Loewenstein, G. (2008). *Exotic preferences: Behavioral economics and human motivation.* New York: Oxford University Press.

Loewenstein, G., & Lerner, J. S. (2003). The role of affect in decision making. In R. Davidson, K. Scherer, & H. Goldsmith (Eds.), *Handbook of affective science* (pp. 619–642). New York: Oxford University Press.

Loewenstein, G., & Thaler, R. H. (1989). Anomalies: Intertemporal choice. *The Journal of Economic Perspectives, 3*(4), 181–193.

Loftus, E., & Ketcham, K. (1994). *The myth of repressed memory: False memories and allegations of sexual abuse.* New York: St. Martin's Press.

Loftus E., & Pickrell, J. (1995). The formation of false memories. *Psychiatric Annals, 25,* 720–725.

Logic. (2010). In *Merriam-Webster's online dictionary.* Retrieved from http://www.merri am-webster.com/dictionary/logic.

Lonner, W. J. (1980). The search for psychological universals. In H. C. Triandis & W. W. Lambert (Eds.), *Handbook of cross-cultural psychology* (Vol. 1, pp. 143–204). Boston: Allyn and Bacon.

Lonner, W. J. (2000). Revisiting the search for psychological universals. *Cross-Cultural Psychology Bulletin, 34*(1-2), 34–37.

Lopez, S. R. (1989). Patient variable biases in clinical judgment: Conceptual overview and methodological considerations. *Psychological Bulletin, 106,* 184–203. doi:10. 1037/0033-2909.106.2.184

LoSchiavo, F. M., & Shatz, M. A. (2009). Reaching the neglected 95%. *American Psychologist, 64*(6), 565–566. doi:10.1037/a0016192

Lott, B. (2002). Cognitive and behavioral distancing from the poor. *American Psychologist, 57*(2), 100–110. doi:10.1037/0003-066X.57.2.100

Löttker, P., Huck, M., Zinner, D. P., & Heymann, E. W. (2007). Grooming relationships between breeding females and adult group members in cooperatively breeding moustached tamarins (Saguinus mystax). *American Journal of Primatology, 69*(10), 1159–72. doi:10.1002/ajp.20411

Loue, S., & Sajatovic, M. (Eds.). (2008). *Diversity issues in the diagnosis, treatment, and research of mood disorders.* Oxford; New York: Oxford University Press.

Loux, M. J. (2001). The problem of universals. In M. J. Loux (Ed.), *Metaphysics: Contemporary readings* (pp. 3–13). New York: Routledge.

Lowrie, R. H. (1917). Edward B. Tylor. *American Anthropologist* [New Series], *19*(2), 262–268.

Lowry, J. L., & Ross, M. J. (1997). Expectations of psychotherapy duration: How long should psychotherapy last? *Psychotherapy, 34,* 272–277. doi:10.1037/h0087657

Luborsky, L., Rosenthal, R., Diguer, L., Andrusyna, T. P., Berman, J. S., Levitt, J. T., Seligman, D. A., & Krause, E. D. (2002). The Dodo bird verdict is alive and well – mostly. *Clinical Psychology: Science and Practice, 9,* 2–12. doi:10.1093/clipsy/9.1.2

Luborsky, L., Singer, B., & Luborsky, L. (1975). Comparative studies of psychotherapies: Is it true that "everyone has won and all must have prizes"? *Archives of General Psychiatry, 32,* 995–1008.

Lucal, B. (1996). Oppression and privilege: Toward a relational conceptualization of race. *Teaching Sociology, 24*(3), 245–55. doi:10.2307/1318739

Lucki, I. (1998). The spectrum of behavior influenced by serotonin. *Biological Psychiatry, 44,* 151–162. doi:10.1016/S0006-3223(98)00139-5

Lumsden, C. J., & Wilson, E. O. (1981). *Genes, mind and culture: The coevolutionary process.* Cambridge, MA: Harvard University Press.

Lyddon, W. J. (1990). First- and second-order change: Implications for rationalist and constructivist cognitive therapies. *Journal of Counseling & Development, 69,* 122–127.

MacFarlane, A. (2004). To contrast and compare. In V. K. Srivastava, *Methodology and fieldwork* (pp. 91 111). Delhi: Oxford University Press.

MacLean, P. D. (1990). *The triune brain in evolution: Role in paleocerebral functions.* New York: Plenum Press.

MacLeod, M., & Rubenstein, E. (2006). Universals. In J. Fieser & B. Dowden (Eds.), *Internet encyclopedia of philosophy.* Retrieved http://www.iep.utm.edu/universa/.

MacNutt, F. (2001). *The power to heal.* Notre Dame, IN: Ave Maria Press.

Macrae, C. N., & Bodenhausen, G. V. (2000). Social cognition: Thinking categorically about others. *Annual Review of Psychology, 51,* 93–120. doi:10.1146/annurev.psych.51.1.93

Macron, M. H. (1979). *Arab-Americans and their communities of Cleveland.* Retrieved from http://www.clevelandmemory.org/ebooks/arabs/tableoc.html.

Madden, J. (Ed.). (1991). *Neurobiology of learning, emotion and affect.* New York: Raven Press.

Maddux, W. W., & Yuki, M. (2006). The "ripple effect": Cultural differences in perceptions of the consequences of events. *Personality & Social Psychology Bulletin, 32,* 669–684. doi:10.1177/0146167205283840

Madelung, W., & Daftary, F. (Eds.). (2008–2010). *Encyclopaedia Islamica.* Leiden, the Netherlands: E. J. Brill.

Maimonides, M. (1904). *The guide for the perplexed* (M. Friedländer, Trans.). London: Routledge & Kegan Paul.

Manderscheid, R. W., & Berry, J. T. (Eds.). (2006). *Mental health, United States, 2004.* Rockville, MD: U.S. Department of Health and Human Services – Substance Abuse and Mental Health Services Administration – Center for Mental Health Services. DHHS Publication no. (SMA)-06-4195.

Manglitz, E (2003). Challenging white privilege in adult education: A critical review of the literature. *Adult Education Quarterly, 53*(2), 119–134. doi:10.1177/0741713602238907

Mairal, R., & Gil, J. (Eds.). (2006). *Linguistic universals.* Cambridge: Cambridge University Press.

Majid, A., Enfield, N. J., & Van Staden, M. (Eds.). (2006). Parts of the body: Cross-linguistic categorisation [Special Issue]. *Language Sciences, 28*(2-3).

Malinowski, B. (1927). *Sex and repression in savage society.* London; New York: Routledge.

Malloy, P., Noel, N., Longabaugh, R., & Beattie, M. (1990). Determinants of neuropsychological impairment in antisocial substance abusers. *Addictive Behaviors, 15*(5), 431–8. doi:10.1016/0306-4603(90)90029-W

Manusov, V., & Spitzberg, B. H. (2008). Attribution theory. In L. A. Baxter & D. O. Braithwaite (Eds.), *Engaging theories in interpersonal communication: Multiple perspectives.* Thousand Oaks, CA: Sage.

Marangoni, C., Garcia, S., Ickes, W., & Teng, G. (1995). Empathic accuracy in a clinically relevant setting. *Journal of Personality and Social Psychology, 68*(5), 854–869. doi:10.1037/0022-3514.68.5.854

Marenbon, J. (1997). *The philosophy of Peter Abelard.* Cambridge: Cambridge University Press. doi:10.1017/CBO9780511582714

Margolis, J. (1982). Berkeley and others on the problem of universals (Ch. 14). In C. Turbayne (Ed.), *Berkeley: Critical and interpretive essays.* Minneapolis, MN, University of Minnesota Press.

Marias, J. (1967). *History of philosophy* (S. Applebaum, & C. C. Strowbridge, Trans.). Mineola, NY: Dove Publications.

Markus, H. (1977). Self-schemata and processing information about the self. *Journal of Personality and Social Psychology, 35,* 63–78. doi:10.1037/0022-3514.35.2.63

Markus, H. R., & Kitayama, S. (1991). Culture and the self: Implications for cognition, emotion, and motivation. *Psychological Review, 98,* 224–253. doi:10.1037/0033-295X.98.2.224

Marshall, A., & Batten, S. (2003). Ethical issues in cross-cultural research. *Connections, 3,* 139–151. Retrieved from http://www.educ.uvic.ca/Research/conferences/connections 2003/10 Marshall105.pdf.

Marshall, A., & Batten, S. (2004). Researching across cultures: Issues of ethics and power. *Forum Qualitative Sozialforschung / Forum: Qualitative Social Research Home, 5*(3). Retrieved from http://www.qualitative-research.net/index.php/fqs/article/view Article/572/1241.

Marston, W. M. (1979). *Emotions of normal people.* Minneapolis: Persona Press.

Martin, J. B. (2002). The integration of neurology, psychiatry, and neuroscience in the 21st century. *American Journal of Psychiatry, 159,* 695–704. doi:10.1176/appi.ajp.159.5.695

Marx, K. (1959). *Economic and philosophic manuscripts of 1844* (M. Mulligan, Trans.). Moscow: Progress Publishers, Moscow. (Original work published in 1932) Retrieved from http://www.marxists.org/archive/marx/works/1844/manuscripts/preface.htm.

Maslow, A. (1954). *Motivation and personality.* New York: Harper.

Maslow, A. (1968). *Toward a psychology of being* (2nd ed.). New York: D. Van Nostrand Co.

Maslow, A. (1971). *The farther reaches of human nature.* New York: The Viking Press.

Massey, D., & Denton, N. (1993). *American apartheid: Segregation and the making of the underclass.* Cambridge, MA: Harvard University Press.

Masson, J. M. (1988). *Against therapy: Emotional tyranny and the myth of psychological healing.* New York: Atheneum.

Masson, J. M., & McCarthy, S. (1995). *When elephants weep: The emotional lives of animals.* New York: Delacorte Press.

Matsumoto, D., Hirayama, S., & LeRoux, J. A. (2006). Psychological skills related to intercultural adjustment. In P. T. P. Wong & L. C. J. Wong (Eds.), *Handbook of multicultural perspectives on stress and coping* (pp. 387–405). Dallas, TX: Spring Publications.

Matsumoto, D., Yoo, S. H., & LeRoux, J. A. (2010). Emotion and intercultural adjustment. In D. Matsumoto (Ed.), *APA handbook of intercultural communication* (pp. 41–57). Washington, DC: American Psychological Association.

Maximino, C., de Brito, T. M., da Silva Batista, A. W., Herculano, A. M., Morato, S. & Gouveia, A., Jr. (2010). Measuring anxiety in zebrafish: A critical review. *Behavioural Brain Research, 214*(2), 157–171. doi:10.1016/j.bbr.2010.05.031

Mayberg, H. S., Silva, J. A., Brannan, S. K., Tekell, J. L., Mahurin, R. K., McGinnis, S., & Jerabek, P. A. (2002). The functional neuroanatomy of the placebo effect. *American Journal of Psychiatry, 159*(5), 728 37. doi:10.1176/appi.ajp.159.5.728

Maynard Smith, J. (1998). The origin of altruism. *Nature, 393,* 639–640. doi:10.1038/31383

Mayo, E. (1949). *Hawthorne and the Western Electric Company: The social problems of an industrial civilisation.* New York: Routledge.

Mayo, E. (1933). *The human problems of an industrial civilization.* [Ch.3.]. New York: MacMillan.

Mazrui, A. A., & Mazrui, A. M. (1995). *Swahili state and society: The political economy of an African language.* Nairobi: East African Educational Publishers.

Mbiti, J. S. (1969). *African religions and philosophy.* New York: Praeger Publishers.

McBurney, D. H., & White, T. L. (2009). *Research methods* (8th ed.). Florence, KY: Wadsworth.

McCarthy, J. (2005). Individualism and collectivism: What do they have to do with counseling? *Journal of Multicultural Counseling and Development, 33*(2), 108–117.

McClain, P. D. (Ed.). (1993). *Minority group influence: Agenda setting, formulation, and public policy [Contributions in political science, No. 333].* Westport, CT: Greenwood Press.

McCrae, R. R. (2002). NEO-PI-R data from 36 cultures: Further intercultural comparisons. In R. R. McCrae & J. Allik (Eds.), *The five-factor model across cultures* (pp. 105–126). New York: Kluwer Academic/Plenum Publishers.

McCrae, R. R., & Allik, J. (Eds.). (2002). *The five-factor model of personality across cultures.* New York: Kluwer Academic/Plenum Publisher.

McCrae, R. R., & Costa, P. T., Jr. (1990). *Personality in adulthood.* New York: Guilford.

McDermott, J. J. (Ed.). (1981). *The philosophy of John Dewey.* Chicago: University of Chicago Press.

McDevitt, T. M., & Ormrod, J. E. (2007). *Child development and education* (3rd ed.). Upper Saddle River, NJ: Carlisle.

McDonogh, G. W., Gregg, R., & Wong, C. H. (Eds.). (2002). *Encyclopedia of contemporary American culture.* New York: Taylor & Francis.

McFall, R. M. (2006). Doctoral training in clinical psychology. *Annual Review of Clinical Psychology, 2,* 21–49. doi:10.1146/annurev.clinpsy.2.022305.095245

McFall, R. M. (Ed.). (2010). *Relevant publications and links* [effectiveness of psychological treatment]. [Psychological Clinical Science Accreditation System]. Retrieved from http://www.pcsas.org/links.html.

McGruder, J. H. (1999). Madness in Zanzibar: 'Schizophrenia' in three families in the 'developing' world. (Tanzania, Third world). *Dissertation Abstracts International Section A: Humanities and Social Sciences, 60*(4-A), 1208.

McGruder, J. H. (2010). The shifting mask of schizophrenia in Zanzibar. In E. Watters, *Crazy like us: The globalization of the American psyche* (pp. 127–187). New York: Free Press.

McGuigan, F. J. (1993). *Biological psychology: A cybernetic science.* Englewood Cliffs, NJ: Prentice-Hall.

McHenry, W. (2006). *What therapists say and why they say it: Effective therapeutic responses and techniques.* Englewood Cliffs, NJ: Prentice-Hall.

McIntire, S. A., & Miller, L. A. (2007). *Foundations of psychological testing: A practical approach.* Thousand Oaks, CA: Sage Publications.

McKay, M., Wood, J. C., & Brantley, J. (2007). *Dialectical behavior therapy skills workbook: Practical DBT exercises for learning mindfulness, interpersonal effectiveness, emotion regulation, & distress tolerance.* Oakland, CA: New Harbinger Publication.

McLaren, N. (2009). *Humanizing psychiatry: The biocognitive mode.* Ann Arbor, MI: Future Psychiatry Press.

McNeilly, C. L., & Howard, K. I. (1991). The effects of psychotherapy: A reevaluation based on dosage. *Journal Psychotherapy Research, 1*(1), 74–78. doi:10.1080/10503309112331334081

MD Anonymous. (2006). *Unprotected: A campus psychiatrist reveals how political correctness in her profession endangers every student.* New York: Penguin.

Meade, C. D., Menard, J., Martinez, D., & Calvo, A. (2007). Impacting health disparities through community outreach: Utilizing the CLEAN look (culture, literacy, education, assessment, and networking). *Cancer Control, 14*(1), 70–74.

Meier, S., & Davis, S. R. (2004). *The elements of counseling* (5th ed.). Florence, KY: Cengage Learning.

Meltzoff, A. N., & Prinz, W. (2002). *The imitative mind: Development, evolution, and brain bases.* Cambridge, England: Cambridge University Press.

Mendelowitz, E., & Schneider, K. (2008). Existential psychotherapy. In R. Corsini & D. Wedding (Eds.) *Current psychotherapies* (8th ed., pp. 295–326). Belmont, CA: Thomson-Brooks/Cole.

Mental Health America. (2011). *We are mental health America!* Retrieved from http://www.mentalhealthamerica.net/go/mission-vision.

Meri, J. W., & Bacharach, J. (Eds.). (2005). *Medieval Islamic civilization: An encyclopedia* (pp. 359–60). New York: Routledge.

Mertens, D. M. (2005). *Research and evaluation in education and psychology: Integrating diversity with quantitative, qualitative, and mixed methods.* Thousand Oaks, CA: Sage.

Mesquita, B., & Frijda, N. H. (1992) Cultural variations in emotions: A review. *Psychological Bulletin, 112,* 179–204. doi:10.1037/0033-2909.112.2.179

Messer, S. B. (1992). A critical examination of belief structures in interpretive and eclectic psychotherapy. In J. C. Norcross & M. R. Goldfried (Eds.), *Handbook of psychotherapy integration* (pp. 130–165). New York: Basic Books.

Meuret, A. E., Rosenfield, D., Seidel, A., Bhaskara, L., & Hofmann, S. G. (2010). Respiratory and cognitive mediators of treatment change in panic disorder: Evidence for intervention specificity. *Journal of Consulting and Clinical Psychology, 78*(5), 691–704. doi:10.1037/a0019552

Mezzich, J. E., Honda, Y., & Kastrup, M. (Eds.). (1994). *Psychiatric diagnosis: A world perspective.* [World Psychiatric Association]. New York: Springer-Verlag.

Michalko, M. (2012, June 15). Political correctness run amok. *[Psychology Today]*. Retrieved from http://www.psychologytoday.com/blog/creative-thinkering/2012 06/political-correctness-run-amok.

Migden, D. R., & Braen, G. R. (1998). The Jehovah's Witness blood refusal card: Ethical and medicolegal considerations for emergency physicians. *Academic Emergency Medicine, 5*(8), 815–24. doi:10.1111/j.1553-2712.1998.tb02510.x

Miller, I. (1990). Neuropsychodynamics of alcoholism and addiction: personality, psychopathology, and cognitive style. *Journal of Substance Abuse Treatment, 7*(1), 31–49. doi:10.1016/0740-5472(90)90034-N

Miller, N. E., & Dollard, J. (1941). *Social learning and imitation.* New Haven: Yale University Press.

Miller, S. D., Duncan, B. L., & Hubble, M. A. (1997). *Escape firm Babel: Toward a unifying language for psychotherapy practice.* New York: Norton.

Millon, T. (1991). Classification in psychopathology: Rationale, alternatives, standards. *Journal of Abnormal Psychology, 100,* 245–261. doi:10.1037/0021-843X. 100.3.245

Millon, T. (2004). *Masters of the mind: Exploring the story of mental illness from ancient times to the new millennium.* Hoboken, NJ: John Wiley & Sons.

Millon, T., Millon, C., & Grossman, S. (2006). *MCMI-III manual* (3rd ed.). Minneapolis, MN: Pearson.

Mills, J. A. (2000). *Control: A history of behavioral psychology.* New York: New York University Press.

MindFreedom International. (2008). *World Health Organization study comparing mental health recovery in developed & developing nations.* Retrieved from http://www.mind freedom.org/kb/mental-health-global/sartorius-on-who.

Minogue, M., & Molloy, J. (1974). *African aims & attitudes: Selected documents.* London; New York: Cambridge University Press.

Minturn, L. (1965). A cross-cultural linguistic analysis of Freudian symbols. *Ethnology, 4*(3), 336–342. doi:10.2307/3772992

Minzenberga, M. J., Fan, J., New, A. S., Tang, C. Y., & Sievera, L. J. (2008). Frontolimbic structural changes in borderline personality disorder. *Journal of Psychiatric Research, 42*(9), 727–733. doi:10.1016/j.jpsychires.2007.07.015

Mischel, W. (1968). *Personality and assessment.* New York: Wiley.

Mischel, W. (1973). Toward a cognitive social learning reconceptualization of personality. *Psychological Review, 80,* 252–283. doi:10.1037/h0035002

Mischel, W. (2008). Connecting clinical practice to scientific progress [Editorial]. *Psychological Science in the Public Interest, 9*(2), i–ii.

Mischel, W., & Shoda, Y. (1995). A cognitive-affective system theory of personality: Reconceptualizing situations, dispositions, dynamics, and invariance in personality structure. *Psychological Review, 102,* 246–268. doi:10.1037/0033-295X.102.2.246

Mischel, W., Shoda, Y., & Ayduk, O. (2008). *Introduction to personality: toward an integrative science of the person* (8th ed.). Hoboken, NJ: John Wiley & Sons.

Mishra, R. C. (1980). Cognition and cognitive development. In J. W. Berry, P. R. Dasen, & T. S. Saraswath (Eds.), *Handbook of cross-cultural psychology* (pp. 143–176). Boston: Allyn & Bacon.

Mitchell, K. M., Bozarth, J. D., & Krauft, C. C. (1977). A reappraisal of the therapeutic effectiveness of accurate empathy, nonpossessive warmth, and genuineness. In A. S. Gurman & A. M. Razin (Eds.), *Effective psychotherapy: A handbook of research* (pp. 482–502). New York: Pergamon.

Mitchell, S. A., & Black, M. J. (1995). *Freud and beyond: A history of modern psychoanalytic thought.* New York: Basic Books.

Moerman, D. E. (2000). Cultural variations in the placebo effect: Ulcers, anxiety, and blood pressure. *Medical Anthropology Quarterly [New Series], 14*(1), 51–72.

Moerman, D. E., & Jonas, W. B. (2002). Deconstructing the placebo effect and finding the meaning response. *Annals of Internal Medicine, 136*(6), 471–476.

Mogahed, D. (2010). Perspectives of women in the Muslim world. *Gallup Center for Muslim Studies.* Retrieved from http://www.muslimwestfacts.com/mwf/105673/Perspectives-Women-Muslim-World.aspx.

Mohan, J. (Ed.). (2000). *Personality across cultures: Recent developments and debates.* New Delhi; New York: Oxford University Press.

Mombour, W., Spitzner, S., Reger, K. H., von Cranach, M., Dilling, H., & Helmchen, H. (1990). Summary of the qualitative criticisms made during the ICD-10 field trial and remarks on the German translation of ICD-10. *Pharmacopsychiatry, 4,* 197–201. doi:10.1055/s-2007-1014565

Montgomery, C. (2002). Role of dynamic group therapy in psychiatry. *Advances in Psychiatric Treatment, 8,* 34–41.

Montgomery, K. C. (1954). The role of the exploratory drive in learning. *Journal of Comparative & Physiological Psychology, 47,* 60–64. doi:10.1037/h0054833

Moodley, R., & West, W. (Eds.). (2005). *Integrating traditional healing practices into counseling and psychotherapy.* Thousand Oaks, CA: Sage Publications.

Moore, D. (2005). *Three in four Americans believe in paranormal.* [Gallup poll]. Retrieved from http://www.gallup.com/poll/16915/three-four-americans-believe-paranormal.aspx.

Moore, M. E., Stunkard, A., & Srole, L. (1962). Obesity, social class, and mental illness. *Journal of the American Medical Association, 181*(11), 962–966. doi:10.1001/jama.1962.030503700

Moreland, J. P. (2001). *Universals.* Montreal: McGill-Queens University Press.

Morey, L. C. (1991a). *Personality assessment inventory.* Lutz, FL: Psychological Assessment Resources.

Morey, L. C. (1991b). Classification of mental disorder as a collection of hypothetical constructs. *Journal of Abnormal Psychology, 100,* 289–293. doi:10.1037/0021-843X.100.3.289

Morita, M., & LeVine, P. (Eds.). (1998). *Morita therapy and the true nature of anxiety-based disorders (Shinkeishitsu)* (A. Kondo, Trans.). Albany, NY: State University of New York Press.

Morrison, A. R., Evans, H. L., Ator, N. A., & Nakamura, R. K. (Eds). (2002). *Methods and welfare considerations in behavioral research with animals: Report of a national institutes of health workshop.* National Institute of Mental Health (NIH Publication No. 02-5083). Washington, DC: U.S. Government Printing Office.

Moseley, A. (2010). Philosophy of love. *Internet Encyclopedia of Philosophy.* Retrieved November 20, 2010, from http://www.iep.utm.edu/love/.

Moses, D. N. (2009). *The promise of progress: The life and work of Lewis Henry Morgan.* Columbia, Missouri, & London: University of Missouri Press.

Moskowitz, M. (1996). The social conscience of psychoanalysis. In R. M. Perez-Foster, M. Moskowitz, & R. A. Javier (Eds.), *Reaching across boundaries of culture and class* (pp. 21–46). Northvale, NJ: Aronson.

Moskowitz, J. H., & Stephens, M. (Eds.). (2004). *Comparing learning outcomes: International assessment and education policy.* London; New York: Routledge Falmer.

Moss, S., & Francis, R. (2007). *The science of management: Fighting fads and fallacies with evidence-based practice.* Bowen Hills, Qld.: Australian Academic Press.

Moughrabi, F. M. (1978). The Arab basic personality: A critical survey of the literature. *International Journal of Middle East Studies, 9*(1), 99–112. doi:10.1017/S002074 3800051722

Moyo, D. (2000). *Dead aid: Why aid is not working and how there is a better way for Africa.* New York: Farrar, Straus and Giroux.

Mozelle, J., & Thompson, C. L. (1971). Counselor: Characteristics and attitudes. *Journal of Counseling Psychology, 18*(3), 249–254.

Mueller, M., & Pekarik, G. (2000). Treatment duration prediction: Client accuracy and its relationship to dropout, outcome, and satisfaction. *Psychotherapy, 37,* 117–123. doi:10.1037/h0087701

Muller-Oerlinghausen, B (1982). Psychological effects, compliance, and response to long-term lithium. *The British Journal of Psychiatry, 141,* 411–419. doi:10.1192/bjp. 141.4.411

Muntaner, C., Borrell, C., & Chung, H. (2007). Class relations, economic inequality and mental health: Why social class matters to the sociology of mental health. In W. R. Avison, J. D. McLeod, & B. A. Pescosolido (Eds.), *Mental health, social mirror.* New York: Springer.

Murchison, C. A. (Ed.). (1935). *A handbook of social psychology.* Worcester, MA: Clark University Press.

Murdock, G. P. (1949). *Social structure.* New York: Macmillan.

Murdock, G. P. (1967). *Ethnographic atlas: A summary.* Pittsburgh: The University of Pittsburgh Press.

Murdock, G. P. et al. (Ed.). (2004). Outline of cultural materials (5th ed.). *Human Relations Area Files* [Web site]. Retrieved from http://www.yale.edu/hraf/outline. htm.

Murdock, G. P., & White, D. R. (1969). Standard cross–cultural sample. *Ethnology, 8,* 329–369.

Murphy, J. (1976). Psychiatric labeling in cross-cultural perspective. *Science, 191,* 1019–1028. doi:10.1126/science.1251213

Murphy, K. R. (Ed.). (2006). *A critique of emotional intelligence: What are the problems and how can they be fixed?* Mahwah, N.J.: Lawrence Erlbaum Associates.

Murray, R. (2002). The phenomenon of psychotherapeutic change: Second-order change in one's experience of self. *Journal of Contemporary Psychotherapy* [On-line], *32*(2-3), 167–177. doi:10.1023/A:1020592926010

Murray, H. (2008). *Explorations in personality.* Oxford; New York: Oxford University Press.

Musch, J., & Ehrenberg, K. (2002). Probability misjudgment, cognitive ability, and belief in the paranormal. *British Journal of Psychology, 93,* 169–177. doi:10.1348/000712602162517

Myers, I. B., & McCaulley, M. H. (1985). *Manual: A guide to the development and use of the Myers-Briggs type indicator.* Palo Alto, CA: Consulting Psychologists Press.

Nardi, D. (2011). *Neuroscience of personality: Brain savvy insights for all types of people.* Los Angeles, CA: Radiance House.

Nanda, S., & Warms, R. L. (2009). *Culture counts: A concise introduction to cultural anthropology.* Belmont, CA: Wadsworth.

Naroll, R. (1983). *The moral order.* Beverly Hills, CA: Sage.

National Trust. (2010). *Volunteers for archaeology.* Retrieved from http://www.national-trust.org.uk/main/w-chl/w-countryside_environment/w-archaeology/w-archaeol ogy-historic_environment/w-archaeology-volunteers.htm.

National Working Group on Evidence-Based Health Care. (August, 2008). *The role of the patient/consumer in establishing a dynamic clinical research continuum: Models of patient/consumer inclusion.* Available from http://www.evidencebasedhealthcare.org/.

Ndetei, D. M. (1988). Psychiatric phenomenology across countries: Convolutional, cultural, or environmental? *Acta Psychiatrica Scandinavica Supplemenfum, 344,* 33–44. doi:10.1111/j.1600-0447.1988.tb09000.x

Nedelcu, A. M., & Michod, R. E. (2006). The evolutionary origin of an altruistic gene. *Molecular Biology and Evolution, 23*(8), 1460–1464. doi:10.1093/molbev/msl016

Nehamas, A. (1975). Confusing universals and particulars in Plato's early dialogues. *The Review of Metaphysics, 29*(2), 287–306.

Neill, J. (2005). Key players in the history & development of intelligence & testing. Wilderdom. Retrieved from http://wilderdom.com/personality/L1-5KeyPlayers.html.

Neimeyer, R. A., & Neimeyer, G. J. (Eds.). (2002). *Advances in personal construct psychology.* New York: Praeger.

Neimeyer, R. A., & Raskin, J. (Eds.). (2001). *Constructions of disorder: Meaning making frameworks in psychotherapy.* Washington, DC: American Psychological Association.

Nelson, D. W., & Baumgarte, R. (2004). Cross-cultural misunderstandings reduce empathic responding. *Journal of Applied Social Psychology, 34,* 391–401. doi:10.1111/j.1559-1816.2004.tb02553.x

Nelson, E. E., & Winslow, J. T. (2009). Non-human primates: Model animals for developmental psychopathology. *Neuropsychopharmacology, 34,* 90–105. doi:10.1038/npp.2008.150

Nelson, M. L., Englar-Carlson, M., Tierney, S. C., & Hau, J. M. (2006). Class jumping into academia: Multiple identities for counseling academics. *Journal of Counseling Psychology, 53*(1), 1–14. doi:10.1037/0022-0167.53.1.1

Nesse, R. M. (1990). Evolutionary explanations of emotions. *Human Nature, 1,* 261–89. doi:10.1007/BF02733986

Nesse, R. M. (1999). On Darwinian medicine. *Life Science Research (China), 3*(1), 1–17, & 79–91.

Nesse, R. M. (2005). Twelve crucial points about emotions, evolution and mental disorders. *Psychology Review, 11*(4), 12–14.

Nesse, R. M., & Williams, G. C. (1995). *Evolution and healing: The new science of Darwinian medicine.* London: Weidenfeld and Nicolson.

Neumann, M., Bensing, J., Mercer, S., Ernstmann, N., Ommen, O., & Pfaff, H. (2009). Analyzing the "nature" and "specific effectiveness" of clinical empathy: A theoretical overview and contribution towards a theory-based research agenda. *Patient Education and Counseling, 74*(3), 339–46. doi:10.1016/j.pec.2008.11.013

Nevill, D. D. (Ed.). (1977). *Humanistic psychology: New frontiers.* New York: Gardner Press.

Newman, W. R., & Grafton, A. (Eds.). (2001). *Secrets of nature: Astrology and alchemy in early modern Europe.* Cambridge, MA: MIT Press.

Newton, K. (2010). A two-fold unveiling: Unmasking classism in group work. *Journal for Specialists in Group Work, 35*(3), 212–219. doi:10.1080/01933922.2010.492906

Neyland, R. S. (1992). The seagoing vessels on Dilmun seals. In D. H. Keith & T. L. Carrell (Eds.), *Underwater archaeology proceedings of the Society for Historical Archaeology Conference at Kingston, Jamaica 1992* (pp. 68–74). Tucson, AZ: Society for Historical Archaeology.

Nicholson, I. A. M. (2003). *Inventing personality: Gordon Allport and the science of selfhood.* Washington, DC: American Psychological Association.

Nicolle, D. (2009). *The great Islamic conquests, AD 632–750.* Westminster, MD: Osprey Publishing.

Nicotera, A. M., Clinkscales, M. J., & Walker, F. R. (208). *Understanding organizations through culture and structure: Relational and other lessons from the African American organization.* Mahwah, NJ: Lawrence Erlbaum.

Nisbett, R. E. (2003). *The geography of thought.* New York: Free Press.

Nisbett, R. E., Borgida, E., Crandall, R., & Reed, H. (1976). Popular induction: Information is not necessarily informative. In J. S. Carroll & J. W. Payne (Eds.), *Cognition and social behavior.* Hillsdale, NJ: Lawrence Erlbaum Associates.

Nisbett, R. E., & Cohen, D. (1996). *Culture of honor: The psychology of violence in the south.* Denver, CO: Westview Press.

Nisbett, R. E., Peng, K., Choi, I., & Norenzayan, A. (2001). Culture and systems of thought: Holistic versus analytic cognition. *Psychological Review, 108,* 291–310. doi:10.1037/0033-295X.108.2.291

Nisbett, R. E., & Ross, L. (1980). *Human inference: Strategies and shortcomings of social judgment.* Englewood Cliffs, NJ: Prentice-Hall.

Nisbett, R. E., & Wilson, T. D. (1977). The halo effect: Evidence for unconscious alteration of judgments. *Journal of Personality and Social Psychology, 35*(4), 250–256. doi:10.1037/0022-3514.35.4.250

Nordal, K. C. (2012, July/August). Overcoming the barriers to serving Medicaid patients. *Monitor on Psychology, 43*(7), 59.

Norenzayan, A., & Heine, S. J. (2005). Psychological universals: What are they and how can we know? *Psychological Bulletin, 131*(5), 763–784. doi:10.1037/0033-2909.131.5.763

Norman, W. T. (1963). Toward an adequate taxonomy of personality attributes: Replicated factor structure in peer nomination personality ratings. *Journal of Abnormal and Personality Psychology, 66,* 574–583. doi:10.1037/h0040291

Norsworthy, K. L., Heppner, P. P., Ægisdóttir, A., Gerstein, L. H., & Pedersen, P. B. (2009). Exportation of U.S.-based models of counseling and counseling psychology: A critical analysis. (Ch. 4). In L. H. Gerstein, P. P. Heppner, S. Aegisdottir, A. L. Seung-Ming, & K. L. Norsworthy (Eds.), *International handbook of cross-cultural counseling: Cultural assumptions and practices worldwide* (pp. 69–88). Los Angeles, Sage.

Novotney, A. (2012, July/August). Money can't buy happiness. *Monitor on Psychology, 43*(7), 24–27.

Nuckolls, C. W. (1998). *Culture: A problem that cannot be solved.* Madison: University of Wisconsin Press; London: Eurospan.

Nudler, O. (1975). Behavior therapy. Bases and criticism. *Acta Psiquiatrica y Psicologica de America Latina [Acta Psiquiatr Psicol Am Lat], 21*(1), 35–40.

Nyasani, J. M. (1997). *The African psyche.* Nairobi: University of Nairobi and Theological Printing Press Ltd.

Oboler, S., & González, D. J. (Eds.). (2005). *The Oxford encyclopedia of Latinos and Latinas in the United States.* New York: Oxford University Press.

O'Connell, S. (1983). The placebo effect and psychotherapy. *Psychotherapy: Theory, research and practice, 20*(3), 337–345.

O'Connor, D. (1982). *The metaphysics of G. E. Moore.* Dordrecht, Holland: D. Reidel Publishing. doi:10.1007/978-94-009-7749-5

O'Donnell, M. (1911). Demonical possession. In *The Catholic encyclopedia.* New York: Robert Appleton Company. Retrieved from http://www.newadvent.org/cathen/12315a.htm.

Okasha, A. (2000). The impact of Arab culture on psychiatric ethics. In A Okasha, J. Arboldeda-Florez, & A. Sartorius (Eds.), *Ethics, culture, and psychiatry* (pp. 15–28). Washington, DC: American Psychiatric Press.

Okasha, A. (2002). Mental health in Africa: The role of the WPA. *World Psychiatry, 1*(1), 32–35.

Okasha, S. (2008). Biological altruism. In E. N. Zalta (Ed.), *The Stanford Encyclopedia of Philosophy.* Retrieved from http://plato.stanford.edu/entries/altruism-biological/.

Oken, B. S. (2008). Placebo effects: Clinical aspects and neurobiology. *Brain, 131*(11), 2812–2823. doi:10.1093/brain/awn116

Oliver, G. J. (1993). *Real men have feelings too.* Chicago: Moody Press.

Olorundare, S. (1998). Superstitious beliefs as constraints in the learning of science. *The Nigerian Journal of Guidance & Counselling, 6*(1-2), 133–149.

O*NET (n.d.). *Counselors.* U.S. Department of Labor/Employment and Training Administration. Retrieved from http://online.onetcenter.org/find/quick?s=coun selors.

Ornithological Societies of North America. (2010). *Ornithological jobs.* Retrieved from http://www.osnabirds.org/on/ornjobs.htm.

Orr, R. D., Marshall, P. A., & Osborn, J. (1995). Cross-cultural considerations in clinical ethics consultations. *Archives of Family Medicine, 4,* 159–164. doi:10.1001/archfami.4.2.15

Osei, G. K. (1971). *The African philosophy of life.* London: The African Publication Society.

Osherson, S. (1986). *Finding our fathers: How a man's life is shaped by his relationship with his father.* Chicago, IL: McGraw-Hill Companies.

Ostergren, R. C., & Rice, J. G. (2004). *The Europeans: A geography of people, culture, and environment.* New York: Guilford Press.

O'Tuathaigh, C. M. P., & Waddington, J. L. (2010). Mutant mouse models: Phenotypic relationships to domains of psychopathology and pathobiology in schizophrenia. *Schizophrenia Bulletin, 36*(2), 243–245. doi:10.1093/schbul/sbq004

Overmier, J. B., & Murison, R. (2002). Animal models. In W. E. Craighead & C. B. Nemeroff (Eds.), *The Corsini encyclopedia of psychology and behavioral science* (3rd ed., Vol. 1, pp. 105–108). New York: Wiley.

Owen, J., Smith, A., & Rodolfa, E. (2009). Clients' expected number of counseling sessions, treatment effectiveness, and termination status: Using empirical evidence to inform session limit policies. *Journal of College Student Psychotherapy, 23*(2), 118–134. doi:10.1080/87568220902743660

Oyserman, D., Uskula, A. K., Yodera, N., Nesse, R. M., & Williams, D. R. (2007). Unfair treatment and self-regulatory focus. *Journal of Experimental Social Psychology, 43*(3), 505–512. doi:10.1016/j.jesp.2006.05.014

Ozawa-de Silva, C. (2006). *Psychotherapy and religion in Japan: The Japanese introspection practice of Naikan.* New York: Routledge.

Ozkan, E. D. (2004). The relationship between paranormal beliefs and the personality trait Openness to Experience: A comparison of psychology majors with students in other disciplines. *Dissertation Abstracts International: Section B: The Sciences and Engineering, 64*(11-B): 5830.

Palmer, C. A. (Ed.). (2006). *Encyclopedia of African-American culture and history: The Black experience in the Americas* (2nd ed.). Detroit: Macmillan.

Palmer, J. A., & Palmer, L. K. (2002). *Evolutionary psychology: The ultimate origins of human behavior.* Boston: Allyn and Bacon.

Pan, C., Pfeil, B. S., & Geistlinger, M. (2004). *National minorities in Europe.* West Lafayette, IN: Purdue University Press.

Paniagua, F. A. (2005). *Assessing and treating culturally diverse clients: A practical guide* (3rd ed.). Thousand Oaks, CA: Sage Publications.

Paper, J. D. (2007). *Native north American religious traditions: Dancing for life.* Westport, CT: Greenwood Publ.

Paranormal. (2012). In *Merriam-Webster's online dictionary.* Retrieved from http://www.merriam-webster.com/medical/paranormal.

Paredes, D. M., Choi, K. M., Dipal, M., Edwards-Joseph, A. R. A. C., Ermakov, N., Gouveia, A. T., Jain, S., Koyama, C., Hinckle, J. S., & Benshoff, J. M. (2008). Globalization: A brief primer for counselors. *International Journal for the Advancement of Counselling, 30*(3), 155–166. doi:10.1007/s10447-008-9053-1

Paris, J. (2012). *The bipolar spectrum: Diagnosis or fad?* New York: Routledge.

Parloff, M., Waskow, I., & Wolfe, B. (1978). Research on therapist variables in relation to process and outcome. In S. L. Garfield & A. E. Bergin (Eds.), *Handbook of psychotherapy and behavior change: An empirical analysis* (2nd ed., pp. 233–282). New York: Wiley.

Parpola, A. (2005). Study of the Indus script. International Conference of Eastern Studies [Tokyo]. Retrieved from http://www.harappa.com/script/indusscript.pdf.

Parsons, O. A., Butters, N., & Nathan, P. E. (Eds.). (1987). *Neuropsychology of alcoholism: Implications for diagnosis and treatment.* New York: Guilford Press.

Pasick, R. (1992). *Awakening from the deep sleep: A powerful guide for courageous men.* New York: Harper Collins.

Patel, V. (1995). Explanatory models of mental illness in sub-Saharan Africa. *Social Science & Medicine, 40*(9), 1291–1298. doi:10.1016/0277-9536(94)00231-H

Patel, V., & Stein, G. (2007). Cultural and international psychiatry. In G. Stein & G. Wilkinson (Eds.), *Seminars in general adult psychiatry* (pp. 782–810). [Royal College of Psychiatrists]. London: RCPsych Publications.

Patka, F. (1964). *Value and existence: Studies in philosophic anthropology.* New York: Philosophical Library. doi:10.1017/S0012217300036106

Patterson, C. H. (1985). What is the placebo in psychotherapy? *Psychotherapy: Theory, research, practice, training, 22*(2), 183–169. doi:1037/h0085489

Patton, P. (2008). One world, many minds: Intelligence in the animal kingdom. *Scientific American Mind, 19*(6), 72–79.

Paul, A. M. (2004). *The cult of personality: How personality tests are leading us to miseducate our children, mismanage our companies, and misunderstand ourselves.* New York: Free Press/Simon & Schuster.

Pavlov, I. P. (1927/1960). *Conditional reflexes.* New York: Dover Publications.

Pavlov, I. P. (1957). *Experimental psychology, and other essays.* New York: Philosophical Library.

Pavlov, I. P. (1994). *Psychopathology and psychiatry.* New Brunswick, NJ: Transaction Publishers.

Pawlak, C. R., Ho, Y-J., & Rainer K. W., & Schwarting, R. K. W. (2008). Animal models of human psychopathology based on individual differences in novelty-seeking and anxiety. *Neuroscience and Biobehavioral Reviews, 32,* 1544–1568. doi:10.1016/j.neubiorev.2008.06.007

Peacocke, C. (1992). *A study of concepts (representation and mind).* Cambridge, MA: MIT Press.

Pearn, J. (2000). Traumatic stress disorders: A classification with implications for prevention and management. *Military Medicine, 165,* 434–40.

Pederson, P. (1995). *The five stages of culture shock: Critical incidents around the world.* Westport, CT: Greenwood Press.

Pedersen, P., Draguns, J. G., Lonner, W., & Trimble, J. (1996). (Eds.). *Counseling across cultures* (4th ed.). Newbury Park, CA: SAGE.

Pedersen, P., Draguns, J. G., Lonner, W. J., & Trimble, J. E. (Eds.). (2002). *Counseling across cultures* (5th ed.). Thousand Oaks, CA: Sage.

Peirce, C. S. (1958). *Collected papers of Charles Sanders Peirce.* Cambridge, MA: Harvard University Press.

Peltzer, K. (2003). Magical thinking and paranormal beliefs among secondary and university students in South Africa. *Personality and Individual Differences, 35*(6), 1419–1426. doi:10.1016/S0191-8869(02)00359-8

Pembrey, M. E., Bygren, L. O., Kaati, G., Edvinsson, S., Northstone, K., Sjöström, M., Golding, J., & ALSPAC Study Team. (2006). Sex-specific, male-line transgenerational responses in humans. *European Journal of Human Genetics, 14,* 159–66. doi:10.1038/sj.ejhg.5201538

Pence, D. J., & Fields, J. A. (1999). Teaching about race and ethnicity: Trying to uncover white privilege for a white audience. *Teaching Sociology, 27*(2): 150–8. doi:10.2307/1318701

Pentony, P. (1981). *Models of influence in psychotherapy.* New York: Free Press.

Perez-Teran Mayorga, R. M. (2007). *From realism to 'realicism': The metaphysics of Charles Sanders Peirce.* Lanham, MD: Lexington Books.

Perin, C. (2007). Substantial universals in Aristotle's categories. *Oxford Studies in Ancient Philosophy, 33,* 125–143.

Perkins, D. N., & Salomon, G. (1987). Tranfer and teaching thinking. In Perkins, D. N., Lochhead, J., & Bishop, J. C. (Eds.), *Thinking: The second international conference* (pp. 285–304). Hillsdale, NJ: Lawrence Erlbaum Associates.

Perls, F., Hefferline, R., & Goodman, P. (1951). *Gestalt therapy: Excitement and growth in the human personality.* New York: Julian.

Peters, W. (1987). *A class divided: Then and now.* New Haven, CT: Yale University Press.

Pew Forum on Religion & Public Life. (2010). *U.S. religious landscape survey. Report 1: Religious affiliation.* Washington, DC: Author. Retrieved from http://religions.pewforum.org/reports.

Pew Global Attitudes Project. (2002, December 19). *Among wealthy nations: U.S. stands alone in its embrace of religion.* Retrieved from http://pewglobal.org/2002/12/19/among-wealthy-nations/.

Pew Global Attitudes Project. (2004, January 14). *Canadians, Americans happiest.* Retrieved from http://pewglobal.org/2004/01/14/americans-and-canadians/.

Pezdek, K., Finger, K., & Hodge, D. (1997). Planting false childhood memories: The role of event plausibility. *Psychological Science, 8*(6), 437–441. http://dx.doi.org/10.1111/j.1467-9280.1997.tb00457.x

Pfeiffer, C. C. (1988). *Nutrition and mental illness: An orthomolecular approach to balancing body chemistry.* Rochester, VT: Healing Arts Press.

Phillipsen, E. (2004). Reflection of feelings: An essential counseling skill; Skill can be particularly difficult for recovering counselors. *Addiction Professional, 2*(4). Retrieved from http://findarticles.com/p/articles/mi_m0QTQ/is_4_2/ai_n25102192/.

Pina-Lopez, J. A., & Sanchez-Sosa, J. J. (2007). Psychological model for investigation of therapeutic compliance behaviors in people with HIV. *Universitas Psychologica* [On-line], *6*(2), 399–407.

Pinel, J. P. J. (2007). *Biopsychology* (6th ed.). Boston: Pearson Allyn and Bacon.

Pinker, S. (1994). *The language instinct: How the mind creates languages.* New York: Penguin Press.

Pinker, S. (2002), *The blank slate: The modern denial of human nature.* New York: Penguin Putnam.

Pinxten, R. (1976). Epistemic universals: A contribution to cognitive anthropology. In R. Pinxten (Ed.), *Universalism versus relativism in language and thought.* The Hague: Mouton.

Pirie, M. (1985). *The book of the fallacy: A training manual for intellectual subversives.* London: Routledge & Kegan Paul.

Pittenger, D. J. (2005). Cautionary comments regarding the Myers-Briggs Type Indicator. *Consulting Psychology Journal: Practice and Research, 57*(3), 210–221. doi:10.1037/1065-9293.57.3.210

Pittman, F. (1993). *Man enough: Fathers, sons, and the search for masculinity.* New York: Penguin.

Piya, A. (2007). *Non-verbal communication* [Spiny Blabber]. Retrieved from http://spinybabbler.org/programs/education_focus/articles/non-verbal_communication.php.

Pizzari, T., & Foster, K. R. (2008). Sperm sociality: Cooperation, altruism, and spite. *Public Library of Science* [PLoS Biol.], *6*(5), e130. doi:10.1371/journal.pbio.0060130

Plomin, R., DeFries, J. C., & McClellearn, G. E. (1990). *Behavioral genetics: A primer* (2nd ed.). New York: Freeman.

Plous, S. (1993). *The psychology of judgment and decision making.* New York: McGraw-Hill.

Poland, J., Von Eckardt, B., & Spaulding, W. (1994). Problems with the DSM approach to classification of psychopathology. In G. Graham & L. Stephens (Eds.), *Philosophical psychopathology* (pp. 235–60). Cambridge, MA: MIT Press.

Polasky, R. (2002). *Archaeological volunteer opportunities.* Retrieved from http://www.archaeolink.com/archaeology_volunteer_opportunit.htm.

Political advocacy groups in the United States. (2010). In *Wikipedia.* Retrieved July 14, 2010, from http://en.wikipedia.org/wiki/Category:Political_advocacy_groups_in_the_United_States.

Pollack, W. (1998). *Real boys: Rescuing our sons from the myths of boyhood.* New York: Henry Holt & Co.

Pollitt, K. (2009, June 24). Muslim women's rights. *The Nation.* Retrieved from http://www.the nation.com/doc/20090713/pollitt.

Polski, M. (2008). *Wired for survival: The rational (and irrational) choices we make, from the gas pump to terrorism.* Upper Saddle River, NJ: FT Press.

Ponterotto, J. G., Suzuki, L. A., Casas, J. M., & Alexander, C. M. (2010). *Handbook of multicultural counseling.* Thousand Oaks, CA: Sage.

Pope, P. E. (1997). *The many landfalls of John Cabot.* Toronto, Buffalo, & London: University of Toronto Press.

Pope-Davis, D. B., Coleman, H. L. K., Liu, W. M., & Toporek, R. L. (Eds.). (2003). *Handbook of multicultural competencies in counseling and psychology.* Thousand Oaks, CA: Sage.

Population Reference Bureau. (2009). *The 2010 census questionnaire: Seven questions for everyone*. Washington, D.C.: Author. Retrieved from http://www.prb.org/Articles/2009/questionnaire.aspx.

Porges, S. W. (2003). The polyvagal theory: Phylogenetic contributions to social behavior. *Physiology & Behavior, 79,* 503–513. doi:10.1016/S0031-9384(03)00156-2

Porges, S. W. (2005). The vagus: A mediator of behavioral and physiologic features associated with autism. In M. L. Bauman & T. L. Kemper (Eds.), *The neurobiology of autism* (pp. 65–78). Baltimore: Johns Hopkins University Press.

Porter, R. (1997). *The greatest benefit to mankind: A medical history of humanity from antiquity to the present*. New York: HarperCollins.

Possehl, G. L. (Ed.). (1982). *Harappan civilization: A contemporary perspective*. New Delhi: Oxford and IBH Publishing.

Powell, A. A., Branscombe, N. R., & Schmitt, M. T. (2005). Inequality as ingroup privilege or outgroup disadvantage: The impact of group focus on collective guilt and interracial attitudes. *Personality and Social Psychology Bulletin, 31*(4), 508–21. doi:10.1177/014 6167204271713

Prilleltensky, I. (1992). Humanistic psychology, human welfare and the social order. *The Journal of Mind and Behaviour, 13*(4), 315–327.

Prince, R. H. (1980). Variations in psychotherapeutic procedures. In H. C. Triandis & J. G. Draguns (Eds.), *Handbook of cross-cultural psychology* (Vol. 6: Psychopathology, pp. 291–350). Boston: Allyn & Bacon.

Prince, R. (2004). Western psychotherapy and the Yoruba: Problems of insight and non directive techniques. In U. P. Gielen, J. Fish, & J. G. Draguns (Eds.), *Handbook of culture, therapy, and healing*. Mahwah, NJ: Erlbaum.

Prochaska, J. O., & DiClemente, C. C. (2005). The transtheoretical approach. In J. C. Norcross & M. R. Goldfried (Eds.), *Handbook of psychotherapy integration* (2nd ed). New York: Oxford University Press.

Prochaska, J. O., Norcross, J. C., & DiClemente, C. C. (1994). *Changing for good: The revolutionary program that explains the six stages of change and teaches you how to free yourself from bad habits*. New York: W. Morrow.

Prochaska, J. O., Redding, C. A., & Evers, K. E. (2008). The transtheoretical model and stages of change. In K. Glanz, B. K. Rimer, & K. Viswanath (Eds.), *Health behavior and health education* (4th ed., p. 105). San Francisco: Jossey-Bass.

Prout, H. T., Chard, K. M., Nowak-Drabik, K. M., & Johnson, D. M. (2000). Determining the effectiveness of psychotherapy with persons with mental retardation: The need to move toward empirically based treatment. *NADD Bulletin, 3,* 83–86.

Psychology: A reality check [Editorial]. (2009, Oct. 15). *Nature, 461,* 847. doi:10.1038/461847a

Puryear Keita, G. (2012, July/August). How psychologists are helping to reduce health disparities. *Monitor on Psychology, 43*(7), 42.

Rabin, M. (1993). Incorporating fairness into game theory. *American Economic Review, 83,* 1281–1302.

Racca, A., Amadei, E., Ligout, S., Guo, K., Meints, K., & Mills, D. (2010). Discrimination of human and dog faces and inversion responses in domestic dogs (Canis familiaris). *Animal Cognition, 13*(3), 525–533. http://dx.doi.org/10.1007/s10071-009-0303-3

Rachlin, H. (1991). *Introduction to modern behaviorism* (3rd ed.). New York: Freeman.

Rahula, W. P. (1978). *What the Buddha taught.* London: Gordon Fraser.

Ralston, D. A., & Pearson, A. (2010). The cross-cultural evolution of the subordinate influence ethics measure. *Journal of Business Ethics, 96,* 149–168. doi:10.1007/s10551-010-0457-6

Rambo, L. (1995). *Understanding religious conversion.* New Haven, CT: Yale University Press.

Randy, K. (1987). Facilitating second-order change in the counseling encounter. *Journal of Humanistic Education and Development, 25*(4), 150–54.

Rashidi, A., & Rajaram, S. S. (2001). Culture care conflicts among Asian-Islamic immigrant women in U.S. hospitals. *Holistic Nursing Practice, 16*(1), 55–64.

Raskin, J. D., & Bridges, S. K. (Eds.). (2002). *Studies in meaning: Exploring constructivist psychology.* New York: Pace University Press.

Rassool, G. H. (2000). The crescent and Islam: Healing, nursing and the spiritual dimension. Some considerations towards an understanding of the Islamic perspectives on caring. *Journal of Advanced Nursing, 32*(6), 1476–1484.

Ratchnevsky, P. (1991). *Genghis Khan: His life and legacy* (T. Haining, Trans.). Oxford: Blackwell.

Rate it all. (2008). Discriminated groups of people (Rated by most concerning). Retrieved from http://www.rateitall.com/t-3466-discriminated-groups-of-people-rated-by-most-concerning.aspx.

Ratnagar, S. (2006). *Trading encounters: From the Euphrates to the Indus in the bronze age.* India: Oxford University Press.

Razali, M. S., & Yahya, H. (1995). Compliance with treatment in schizophrenia: A drug intervention program in a developing country. *Acta Psychiatrica Scandinavica, 91*(5), 331–335. doi:10.1111/j.1600-0447.1995.tb09790.x

Real, T. (1997). *I don't want to talk about it: Overcoming the secret legacy of male depression.* New York: Schribner.

Reiter, M. D. (2007). *Therapeutic interviewing: Essential skills and contexts of counseling.* Englewood Cliffs, NJ: Prentice-Hall.

Rice, E. (1990). *Captain sir Richard Francis Burton.* New York: Charles Schribner's Sons.

Richardson, L. K., Frueh, B. C., & Acierno, R. (2010). Prevalence estimates of combat-related PTSD: A critical review. *Australian and New Zealand Journal of Psychiatry, 44*(1), 4–19. doi:10.3109/00048670903393597

Rickman, R. (2012, Mar/ Apr). *Is psychology a science?* [Philosophy Now]. Retrieved from http://www.philosophynow.org/issues/74/Is_Psychology_Science.

Rienits, R., & Rienits, T. (1968). *The voyages of Captain Cook.* London; New York: Hamlyn.

Riley, C. L., Kelly, J. C., Pennington, C. W., & Rands, R. L. (Eds.). (1971). *Man across the sea: Problems of Pre-Columbian contacts.* Austin & London: University of Texas Press.

Riley-Smith, J. (1999). *The Oxford history of the crusades.* New York: Oxford University Press.

Ritterband, L. M., Andersson, G., Christensen, H. M., Carlbring, P., & Cuijpers, P. (2006). Directions for the international society for research on internet interventions. *Journal of Medical Internet Research, 8*(3), e23. doi:10.2196/jmir.8.3.e23

Rivalan, M., Grégoire, S., & Dellu-Hagedorn, F. (2007). Reduction of impulsivity with amphetamine in an appetitive fixed consecutive number schedule with cue for optimal performance in rats. *Psychopharmacology, 192*(2), 171–182. doi:10.1007/s00213-007-0702-6

Rizzolatti, G. (1995). Motor facilitation during action observation: A magnetic stimulation study. *Journal of Neurophysiology, 73*(6), 2608–2611.

Rizzolatti, G., & Craighero, L. (2004). The mirror-neuron system. *Annual Review of Neuroscience, 27,* 169–192. doi:10.1146/annurev.neuro.27.070203.144230

Rizzolatti, G., Craighero, L., & Fadiga, L. (2002). The mirror system in humans. In A. Stamenov & V. Gallese (Eds.), *Mirror neurons and the evolution of brain and language* (pp. 37–59). Amsterdam/Philadelphia: John Benjamins Publishing Company.

Rochberg, F. (2010). *In the path of the moon: Babylonian celestial divination and its legacy.* Leiden; Boston: Brill.

Roethlisberger, F. J., & Dickson, W. J. (1939) *Management and the worker.* Cambridge, MA: Harvard University Press.

Roger, A., Powell, R. A., & Fried, J. J. (1992). Helping by juvenile pine voles (Microtus pinetorum), growth and survival of younger siblings, and the evolution of pine vole sociality. *International Society for Behavioral Ecology, 3*(4), 325–333. doi:10.1093/beheco/3.4.325

Rogers, C. R. (1951). *Client-centered counselling.* Boston: Houghton-Mifflin.

Rogers, C. R. (1957). The necessary and sufficient conditions for therapeutic personality change. *Journal of Consulting Psychology, 21,* 95–103. doi:10.1037/h0045357

Rogers, P., Qualter, P., Phelps, G., & Gardner, K. (2006). Belief in the paranormal, coping and emotional intelligence. *Personality and Individual Differences, 41,* 1089–1105. Retrieved from http://mysteriousuniverse.org/uploads/2007/03/paranormal_coping.pdf. doi:10.1016/j.paid.2006.04.014

Roig, M., Bridges, K. R., Renner, C. H., & Jackson, C. R. (1997). Belief in the paranormal and its association with irrational thinking controlled for context effects. *Personality and Individual Differences, 24*(2), 229–236. doi:10.1016/S0191-8869(97)00162-1

Rokhin, L., Pavlov, I., & Popov, Y. (1963). *Psychopathology and psychiatry.* Moscow: Foreign Languages Publication House.

Rolland, J-P. (2002). The cross-cultural generalizability of the five-factor model of personality. In R. R. McCrae & J. Allik (Eds.), *The five-factor model of personality across cultures.* New York: Kluwer Academic/Plenum Publishers.

Rollins, J. (Ed.). (2011a). Technology's role in counseling [Part 1]. *Counseling Today, 54*(4).

Rollins, J. (Ed.). (2011b). Technology's role in counseling [Part 2]. *Counseling Today, 54*(5).

Rorty, R. (1999). *Philosophy and social hope.* New York: Penguin Books.

Rosch, E., Mervis, C. B., Gray, W. D., Johnson, D. M., & Boyes-Braem, P. (1976). Basic objects in natural categories. *Cognitive Psychology, 8*(3), 382–439. doi:10.1016/0010-0285(76)90013-X

Rosenberg, A. (1992). Altruism: Theoretical contexts. In E. F. Keller and E. A. Lloyd (Eds.), *Keywords in evolutionary biology.* Cambridge MA: Harvard University Press.

Rosenhan, D. L. (1973). On being sane in insane places. *Science, 179,* 250–258. doi: 10.1126/science.179.4070.250

Rosenhan, D. L. (1975). The contextual nature of psychodiagnosis. *Journal of Abnormal Psychology, 84,* 462–474.

Rosenthal, D. M. (Ed.). (1991). *The nature of mind.* Oxford/New York: Oxford University Press.

Rosenzweig, S. (1936). Some implicit common factors in diverse methods of psychotherapy. *American Journal of Orthopsychiatry, 6,* 412–415.

Rosenthal, D., & Frank, J. D. (1956). Psychotherapy and the placebo effect. *Psychological Bulletin, 53,* 294–302. doi:10.1037/h0044068

Rosenthal, R. (1966). *Experimenter effects in behavioral research.* New York: Appleton.

Rosenthal, R., & Jacobson, L. (1968, 1992). *Pygmalion in the classroom: Teacher expectation and pupils' intellectual development.* New York: Irvington Publishers.

Rosenthal, R., & Rosnow, R. L. (2009). *Artifacts in behavioral research: Robert Rosenthal and Ralph Rosnow's classic books.* Oxford; New York: Oxford University Press.

Rosenzweig, S. (1936). Some implicit common factors in diverse methods of psychotherapy. *American Journal of Orthopsychiatry, 6,* 412–415.

Rosnow, R. L. (1988). Rumor as communication: A contextualist approach. *Journal of Communication, 38,* 12–28.

Rosnow, R. L. (2001). Rumor and gossip in interpersonal interaction and beyond: A social exchange perspective. In R. M. Kowalski (Ed.), *Behaving badly: Aversive behaviors in interpersonal relationships* (pp. 203–232). Washington, DC: American Psychological Association.

Rosnow, R. L., Yost, J. H., & Esposito, J. L. (1986). Belief in rumor and likelihood of rumor transmission. *Language and Communication, 6,* 189–194.

Ross, A. C. (2002). *David Livingstone: Mission and empire.* London: Hambledon.

Ross, L. (1977). The intuitive psychologist and his shortcomings: Distortions in the attribution process. In L. Berkowitz (Ed.), *Advances in experimental social psychology* (Vol. 10). New York: Academic Press.

Ross, P. E. (1992). New whoof in whorf: An old language theory regains its authority. *Scientific American, 266*(2), 24–26.

Rossier, J. (2005). A review of the cross-cultural equivalence of frequently used personality inventories. *Journal International Journal for Educational and Vocational Guidance, 5*(2), 175–188. doi:10.1007/s10775-005-8798-x

Rothblum, E. D., Solomon, J. L., & Albee, G. W. (1994). A sociopolitical perspective of the DSM-III. In T. Millon & G. L. Klerman (Eds.), *Contemporary directions in psychopathology: Towards the DSM-IV* (pp. 167–189). New York: Guilford.

Rothenberg, P. S. (2005). *White privilege.* New York: Worth Publishers.

Rotter, J. B. (1966). Generalized expectancies for internal versus external control of reinforcement. *Psychological Monographs, 80,* [whole issue].

Rowan, J. (1998). *The reality game: A guide to humanistic counselling and psychotherapy.* New York: Routledge.

Rowe, W., Murphy, H. B., & De Csipkes, R. A. (1975). The relationship of counselor characteristics and counseling effectiveness. *Review of Educational Research, 45*(2), 231–246. doi:10.3102/00346543045002231

Rubinstein, G. (1995). The decision to remove homosexuality from the DSM: Twenty years later. *American Journal of Psychotherapy, 49,* 416–427.

Rudnick, H. (2002). *The links between western psychotherapy and traditional healing.* Unpublished doctoral thesis. Johannesburg: University of Johannesburg – Rand Afrikaans University. Retrieved from http://hdl.handle.net/10210/1641.

Ruitenbeek, H. M. (Ed.). (1964). *Varieties of personality theory.* New York: Dutton.

Ruscio, J. (2004). Diagnoses and the behaviors they denote: A critical evaluation of the labeling theory of mental illness. *Scientific Review of Mental Health Practice, 3*(1), 5–22.

Rushton, J. P. (1991). Is altruism innate? *Psychological Inquiry, 2*(2), 141–143. doi:10.1207/s15327965pli0202_11

Russell, A. F., & Lummaa, V. (2009). Maternal effects in cooperative breeders: From hymenopterans to humans. *Philosophical Transactions of the Royal Society B (biological sciences), 364*(1520), 1143–1167. doi:10.1098/rstb.2008.0298

Russell, B. (1997). *The problems of philosophy.* New York: Oxford University Press.

Russell, D. (1986). Psychiatric diagnosis and the oppression of women. *Women and Therapy, 5,* 83–89. doi:10.1300/J015V05N04_09

Russell, D., & Jones, W. H. (1980). When superstition fails: Reactions to disconfirmation of paranormal beliefs. *Personality and Social Psychology Bulletin, 6*(1), 83–88. doi:10.1177/014616728061012

Russell, M. T., & Karol, D. (2002). *16PF fifth edition administrator's manual.* Champaign, IL: Institute for Personality and Ability.

Russo, T. (2005). Cognitive counseling for health care compliance. *Journal of Rational-Emotive & Cognitive-Behavior Therapy, 5*(2), 125–134. doi:10.1007/BF01074382

Ryuzo, N. (2002). Naikan therapy: Principle and practice. *Japanese Journal of Psychosomatic Medicine, 42*(6), 355–362.

Sachs, J. (2004). Superstition and self-efficacy in Chinese postgraduate students. *Psychological Reports, 95*(2), 485–486. doi:10.2466/pr0.95.2.485-486

Sachs, J. L. (2004). The evolution of cooperation. *The Quarterly Review of Biology, 79,* 135–160. doi:10.1086/383541

Sadler-Smith, E. (2011). The intuitive style: Relationships with local/global and verbal/visual styles, gender, and superstitious reasoning. *Learning and Individual Differences, 21*(3), 263–270. doi:10.1016/j.lindif.2010.11.013

Salmon, D. P., & Butters, N. (1995). Neurobiology of skill and habit learning. *Current Opinion in Neurobiology, 5*(2), 184–90. doi:10.1016/0959-4388(95)80025-5

Sam, D. L., & Moreira, V. (2002). The mutual embeddedness of culture and mental illness. In W. J. Lonner, D. L. Dinnel, S. A. Hayes, & D. N. Sattler (Eds.), *Online readings in psychology and culture.* Western Washington University, Department of Psychology, Center for Cross-Cultural Research. Retrieved from http://www.ac.wwu.edu/~culture/Sam_Moreira.htm.

Samuels, A. (1985). *Jung and the post-Jungians.* London; Boston: Routledge & K. Paul.

Sandweiss, D. A., Slymen, D. J., Leardmann, C. A., Smith, B., Boyko, E. J., Hooper, T. I., Gackstetter, G. D., Amoroso, P. J., & Smith, T. C. (2011). Preinjury psychiatric status, injury severity, and postdeployment posttraumatic stress disorder. *Archives of General Psychiatry, 68*(5), 496–504. doi:10.1001/archgenpsychiatry. 2011.44

Santa Barbara County Board of Education. (1972). *The emerging minorities in America: A resource guide for teachers. Contributions of significance which members of minority groups have made to the historical and cultural development of the United States of America.* Santa Barbara, CA: Author.

Sapir, E. (1929). The status of linguistics as a science. *Language, 5*(4), 207–214. doi:10. 2307/409588

Sarason, I. G., & Sarason, B. R. (1980). The historical background of modern abnormal psychology. In M. Harrison (Ed.), *Abnormal psychology* (3rd ed., pp. 21–40). Englewood Cliffs, NJ: Prentice-Hall.

Sarbin, T. R., & Mancuso, J. C. (1980). *Schizophrenia: Medical diagnosis or moral verdict?* Elmsford, NY: Pergamon Press.

Saretsky, G. (1975, March-April). *The John Henry effect: Potential confounder of experimental vs. control group approaches to the evaluation of educational innovations.* Paper presented at the annual meeting of the American Educational Research Association, Washington, DC.

Sarner, H. (1972). *Rescue in Albania: One hundred percent of Jews in Albania rescued from holocaust.* Cathedral City, CA: Brunswick Press; co-published by the Boston, MA: Frosina Foundation (name has been changed to Frosina Information Network).

Sartorius, N. (2008). *Brief description of World Health Organization studies comparing mental health recovery in developed and developing nations.* Retrieved from http://www. mindfreedom.org/kb/mental-health-global/sartorius-on-who.

Sartorius, N., & Ustun, T. B. (Eds.). (1995). *Mental illness in general health care: An international study.* Chichester, NY: J. Wiley & Sons.

Sawyer, G. J., Deak, V., Sarmiento, E., Milner, R., Tatters, I., Leakey, M., & Johanson, D. C. (2007). *The last human: A guide to twenty-two species of extinct humans.* New Haven, CT: Yale University Press.

Sayed, M. A. (2003). Conceptualization of mental illness within Arab cultures: Meeting challenges in cross-cultural settings. *Social Behavior and Personality, 31*(4), 333–342. doi:10.2224/sbp.2003.31.4.333

Scaife, M., & Bruner, J. (1975). The capacity for joint visual attention in the infant. *Nature, 253,* 265–266. doi:10.1038/253265a0

Schacter, D. L. (1999). The seven sins of memory: Insights from psychology and cognitive neuroscience. *American Psychologist, 54*(3), 182–203. doi:10.1037/0003-066X.54.3.182

Scheff, T. J. (1974). The labeling theory of mental illness. *American Sociological Review, 39,* 444–452. doi:10.2307/2094300

Scheppler, B. (2006). *Al-Biruni: Master astronomer and Muslim scholar of the eleventh century.* New York: The Rosen Publishing Group.

Scherer, S. (2012). *Bias in psychology: Bring in all significant results.* JEPS Bulletin. Retrieved from http://jeps.efpsa.org/blog/2012/06/01/falsification-of-previous-results/.

Schneider, B., Carnoy, M., Kilpatrick, J., Schmidt, W. H., & Shavelson, R. J. (2007). *Estimating causal effects using experimental and observational designs: A think tank white paper.* Washington, DC: American Educational Research Association.

Schneider, K. J. (Ed.). (2008). *Existential-integrative psychotherapy: Guideposts to the core of practice.* New York: Routledge.

Schneider, K. J., Bugental, J. F. T., & Pierson, J. F. (Eds.). (2001). *The handbook of humanistic psychology: Leading edges in theory, research, and practice.* Thousand Oaks, CA: Sage Publications.

Schneider, K. J., & Krug, O. T. (2010). *Existential-humanistic therapy* [Theories of Psychotherapy Series]. Washington, DC: American Psychological Association.

Schofield, W. (1988). *Pragmatics of psychotherapy: A survey of theories and practices.* New Brunswick: Transaction Publishers.

Schorr, A. (1985). Behaviorism, ethics and the utopian society. In S. Bem, H. Rappard, & W. van Hoorn (Eds.), *Studies in the history of psychology and the social sciences, 3,* 212–228.

Schorr, A. (1987) . Behavior modification: Operant conditioning and reinforcement technology. In H. J. Eysenck & I. Martin (Eds.), *Theoretical foundations of behavior therapy* (pp. 37–54). New York: Plenum Press.

Schreck, J. H. (2008). *A patient's guide to Chinese medicine: Dr. Shen's handbook of herbs and acupuncture.* Point Richmond, CA: Bay Tree Publishing.

Schreck, K. A., & Miller, V. A. (2010). How to behave ethically in a world of fads. *Behavioral Interventions, 25,* 307–324. doi:10.1002/bin.305

Schultz, W. (2006). Behavioral theories and the neurophysiology of reward. *Annual Review of Psychology, 57,* 87–115. doi:10.1146/annurev.psych.56.091103.070229

Schwartz, A. H., Perlman, B., Paris, M., Schmidt, K., & Thornton, J. C. (1980). Psychiatric diagnosis as reported to Medicaid and as recorded in patient charts. *American Journal of Public Health, 7,* 406–408. doi:10.2105/AJPH.70.4.406

Schwartz, J. H. (1993). *What the bones tell us.* New York: Henry Holt.

Schwartz, S. H. (1994a). Are there universal aspects in the content and structure of values? *Journal of Social Issues, 50,* 19–45. doi:10.1111/j.1540-4560.1994.tb01196.x

Schwartz, S. H. (1994b). Beyond Individualism/Collectivism: New cultural dimensions of values. In U. Kim, H. C. Triandis, Ç. Kağitçibaşi, S-C. Choi, & G. Yoon (Eds.), *Individualism and collectivism: Theory, method and applications* (pp. 85–119). Newbury Park, CA: Sage.

Schwartz, S. H. (2004). Mapping and interpreting cultural differences around the world. In H. Vinken, J. Soeters, & P. Ester (Eds.), *Comparing cultures: Dimensions of culture in a comparative perspective* (pp. 43–73). Leiden, The Netherlands: Brill.

Schwartz, S. H., & Bardi, A. (2001). Value hierarchies across cultures: Taking a similarities perspective. *Journal of Cross-Cultural Psychology, 32*(3), 268–290. doi:10.1177/00220 22101032003002

Scofield, B., & Orr, B. C. (2007). *How to practice Mayan astrology: The Tzolkin calendar and your life path.* Rochester, VT: Bear & Co.

Scott, O., Lilienfeld, S. O., Lynn, S. J., & Lohr, J. M. (Eds.). (2003). *Science and pseudoscience in clinical psychology.* New York: Guilford Publications.

Scott, W. T. (1967). *Erwin Schrodinger: An introduction to his writings.* Amherst, MA: University of Massachusetts Press.

Sears, D. O., Huddy, L., & Jervis, R. (Eds.). (2003). *Oxford handbook of political psychology*. New York: Oxford University Press.

Segal, R. A. (Ed.). (1998). *Jung on mythology*. Princeton, NJ: Princeton University Press.

Segall, M. H., Dasen, P. R., Berry, J. W., & Poortinga, Y. H. (1999). *Human behavior in global perspective: An introduction to cross-cultural psychology* (2nd ed.). Boston: Allyn and Bacon.

Segall, M. H., Lonner, W. J., & Berry, J. W. (1998). Cross-cultural psychology as a scholarly discipline: On the flowering of culture in behavioral research. *American Psychologist, 53,* 1101–1110. doi:10.1037/0003-066X.53.10.1101

Seligman, L. (2008). *Fundamental skills for mental health professionals*. Englewood Cliffs, NJ: Prentice-Hall.

Seligman, M. E., & Beagley, G. (1975). Learned helplessness in the rat. *Journal of Comparative and Physiological Psychology, 88*(2), 534–541. doi:10.1037/h0076430

Semiotics. (2009). In *Merriam-Webster Online Dictionary*. Retrieved from http://www.merriam-webster.com/dictionary/semiotic.

Sen, T. (2006). The travel records of Chinese pilgrims Faxian, Xuanzang, and Yijing: Source of cross-cultural encounters between ancient China and ancient India. *Education about Asia, 11*(3), 24–33. Retrieved http://afe.easia.columbia.edu/special/travel_records.pdf.

Senerdem, E. D. (July 2010, July 28). Volunteer meteorologists assist Turkey's state weather service. *Daily News and Economic Review* [Turkey's English Daily]. Retrieved from http://www.hurriyetdailynews.com/n.php?n=voluntary-meteorologists-assist-the-dmi-2010-07-28.

Seung-Ming, A. L., Clawson, T., Norsworthy, K. L., Tena, A., Szilagyi, A., & Rogers, J. (2009). Internationalization of the counseling profession: An indigenous perspective. In L. H. Gerstein, P. P. Heppner, S. Aegisdottir, A. L. Seung-Ming, & K. L. Norsworthy (Eds.), *International handbook of cross-cultural counseling: Cultural assumptions and practices worldwide* (pp. 111–123). Los Angeles, Sage.

Sexton, T. L., Whiston, S. C., Bleuer, J. C., & Walz, G. R. (1997). *Integrating outcome research into counseling practice and training*. Alexandria, VA: American Counseling Association.

Shaffer, J. B. P. (1978). *Humanistic psychology*. Englewood Cliffs, NJ: Prentice-Hall.

Shapiro, A. K. (1971). Placebo effects in medicine, psychotherapy, and psychoanalysis. In A. E. Bergin & S. L. Garfield (Eds.), *Handbook of psychotherapy and behavior change: An empirical analysis*. New York: Wiley.

Shapiro, A. K., & Morris, L. A. (1978). The placebo effect in medical and psychological therapies. Placebo effects in medicine, psychotherapy, and psychoanalysis. In A. E. Bergin & S. L. Garfield (Eds.), *Handbook of psychotherapy and behavior change: An empirical analysis* (2nd ed.). New York: Wiley.

Shapiro, A. K., & Shapiro, E. (1997). *The powerful placebo: From ancient priest to modern physician*. Baltimore, MD: Johns Hopkins University Press.

Shapiro, S. (2007). *Jews in old China: Studies by Chinese scholars*. Beijing, China: Foreign Languages Press.

Shea, J. D. (1985). Studies in cognitive development in Papua New Guinea. *International Journal of Psychology, 20,* 33–61.

Sheldon, W. H. (1940). *The varieties of human physique: An introduction to constitutional psychology*. New York: Harper & Brothers.

Sheldon, W. H. (1954). *Atlas of men*. New York: Harper and Brothers.

Sherman, P. W. (1988). The levels of analysis. *Animal Behavior, 36,* 616–619. doi:10.1016/S0003-3472(88)80039-3

Sherif, M. (1936). *The psychology of social norms*. New York: Harper Collins.

Shields, S. A. (2002). *Speaking from the heart: Gender and the social meaning of emotion.* Cambridge, UK: Cambridge University Press.

Shigemura, J., & Nomura, S. (2002). Mental health issues of peacekeeping workers. *Psychiatry and Clinical Neurosciences, 56*(5), 483–491. doi:10.1046/j.1440-1819.2002.01043.x

Shkolyar, S. (2009). People's astronomy. *Engineering and Technology magazine, 12*. Retrieved from http://kn.thcict.org/magazine/issues/0912/peoples-astronomy-0912.cfm.

Shore, B. (1996). *Culture in mind: Cognition, culture and the problem of meaning.* New York: Oxford University Press.

Shorter, E. (1997). *A history of psychiatry: From the era of the asylum to the age of Prozac.* New York: John Wiley & Sons.

Shweder, R. (1991). *Thinking through cultures*. Cambridge, MA: Harvard University Press.

Shweder, R. A., & Levine, R. A. (Eds.). (1984). *Culture theory: Essays on mind, self, and emotion*. New York: Cambridge University Press.

Siegel, D. J. (1999). *The developing mind: Toward a neurobiology of interpersonal experience.* New York: Guilford Press.

Sieverding, M. (2009). 'Be cool!': Emotional costs of hiding feelings in a job interview. *International Journal of Selection and Assessment, 17*(4), 391–401. doi:10.1111/j.1468-2389.2009.00481.x

Silk, J. B. (2007). The adaptive value of sociality in mammalian groups. *Philosophical Transactions of the Royal Society B (biological sciences), 362*(1480), 539–559. doi:10.1098/rstb.2006.1994

Silk road. (2009). In *Encyclopædia Britannica*. Retrieved from Encyclopædia Britannica Online: http://www.britannica.com/EBchecked/topic/544491/Silk-Road.

Simmons, J. P., Nelson, L. D., & Simonsohn, U. (2011). False-positive psychology: Undisclosed flexibility in data collection and analysis allows presenting anything as significant. *Psychological Science, XX*(X), 1–8. doi:10.1177/0956797611417632

Simon, H. A. (1993). Decision making: Rational, nonrational, and irrational. *Educational Administration Quarterly, 29*(3), 392–411. doi:10.1177/0013161X93029003009

Simpson, E. L., & House, A. O. (2003). User and carer involvement in mental health services: From rhetoric to science. *The British Journal of Psychiatry, 183,* 89–91. doi:10.1192/bjp.183.2.89

Singaravelu, H. D., & Pope, M. (Eds.). (2007). *Handbook for counseling international students in the United States*. Alexandria, VA: American Counseling Association.

Singer, B., & Benassi, V. A. (1981). Occult beliefs. *American Scientist, 69*(1), 49–55.

Skinner, B. F. (1938). *The behavior of organisms*. New York: Appleton-Century-Crofts.

Skinner, B. F. (1945). The operational analysis of psychological terms. *Psychological Review, 52,* 270–277, 290–294. doi:10.1037/h0062535

Skinner, B. F. (1969). *Contingencies of reinforcement: A theoretical analysis.* New York: Appleton-Century-Crofts.

Skinner, B. F. (1991). *Behavior of organisms.* Acton, MA: Copley Pub Group.

Skinner, L. J., Berry, K. K., Griffith, S. E., & Byers, B. (1995). Generalizability and specificity associated with the mental illness label: A reconsideration twenty-five years later. *Journal of Community Psychology, 23,* 3–17. doi:10.1002/1520-6629(199501)23:1<3::AID-JCOP2290230102>3.0.CO;2-W

Skyrms, B. (1996). *Evolution of the social contract.* Cambridge: Cambridge University Press.

Sloan, J. M., & Ballen, K. (2008). SCT in Jehovah's Witnesses: The bloodless transplant. *Bone Marrow Transplant. 41*(10), 837–44. doi:10.1038/bmt.2008.5

Smith, H. (1958). *The religions of man.* New York: Harper.

Smith, K. U., & Smith, M. F. (1966). *Cybernetic principles of learning and educational design.* New York: Holt, Rinehart, and Winston.

Smith, L. (2010). *Psychology, poverty, and the end of social exclusion: Putting our practice to work.* New York: Teachers College Press.

Smith, P. B., Bond, M. H., & Kağitçibaşi, Ç. (2006). *Understanding social psychology across cultures: Living and working in a changing world* (3rd rev. ed.). London, UK: Sage.

Smithsonian Institution National Museum of Natural History. (2009). *Cro-Magnon 1.* Retrieved from http://anthropology.si.edu/humanorigins/ha/cromagnon.html.

Smits, J. A., & Otto, M. W. (2009). *Exercise for mood and anxiety disorders.* New York: Oxford University Press.

Snyder, C., Scott, T., & Cheavens, J. (1999). Hope as a psychotherapeutic foundation of common factors, placebos, and expectancies. In M. Hubble, B. L. Duncan, & S. Miller (Eds.), *The heart and soul of change: What works in therapy* (pp. 179–200). Washington DC: American Psychological Association. doi:10.1037/11132-005

Sober, E. (1984). *The nature of selection: Evolutionary theory in philosophical focus.* Cambridge, MA: MIT Press.

Society for Humanistic Psychology. (2012). *About us.* Retrieved from http://www.apadivisions.org/division-32/about/index.aspx.

Sober, E., & Wilson, D. S. (1998). *Unto others: The evolution and psychology of unselfish behavior.* Cambridge, MA: Harvard University Press.

Solecki, R. S. (1972). *Shanidar: The humanity of Neanderthal man.* London: Allen Lane.

Solis, M. (2012, May). Personality traits correlate with brain activity. *Scientific American MIND.* Retrieved from http://www.scientificamerican.com/article.cfm?id=personality-circuits.

Sommers, C. H., & Satel, S. (2005). *One nation under therapy: How the helping culture is eroding self-reliance.* New York: St. Martin's Press.

Sommers-Flanagan, J., & Sommers-Flanagan, R. (2004). *Counseling and psychotherapy theories in context and practice: Skills, strategies, and techniques.* Hoboken, NY: John Wiley and Sons.

Song, Y., Skinner, J., Bynum, J., Sutherland, J., Wennberg, J. E., & Fisher, E. S. (2010). Regional variations in diagnostic practices. *New England Journal of Medicine, 363,* 45–53. doi.10.1056/NEJMsa0910881

Sonnard, S. R. (2000). Self-fulfilling prophecy. In W. E. Craighead & C. B. Nemeroff (Eds.), *Corsini encyclopedia of psychology and behavioral science, 4,* (3rd ed., pp. 1476–1479). New York: Wiley.

Sorensen, R. (2004). *A brief history of the paradox: Philosophy and the labyrinths of the mind.* Oxford/New York: Oxford University Press.

Sorenson, J. L., & Raish, M. H. (1996). *Pre-Columbian contact with the Americas across the oceans: An annotated bibliography.* (2v. 2d ed., rev.). Provo, Utah: Research Press.

Specter, M. (2009, October 12). *The fear factor.* The New Yorker.

Spence, K. W. (1956). *Behavior theory and conditioning.* New Haven, CT: Yale University Press. doi:10.1037/10029-000

Spering, M. (2001). *Current issues in cross-cultural psychology: Research topics, applications, and perspectives.* Institute of Psychology, University of Heidelberg, Germany. Retrieved from http://www.psychologie.uni-heidelberg.de/ae/allg/mitarb/ms/cross-cultural%20psy.pdf.

Sperry, L. (2006). Family-oriented compliance counseling: A therapeutic strategy for enhancing health status and lifestyle change. *The Family Journal, 14*(4), 412–416. doi:10.1177/1066 480706290972

Spikins, P. A., Rutherford, H. E., & Needham, A. P. (2010). From Homininity to humanity: Compassion from the earliest Archaics to modern humans. *Time and Mind, 3*(3), 303–325. doi:10.2752/175169610X12754030955977

Spindler, G. D., & Spindler, L. (1983). Anthropologists view American culture. Annual *Review of Anthropology, 12,* 49–78. doi:10.1146/annurev.an.12.100183.000405

Spitzer, R. L. (1975). On pseudoscience in science, logic in remission, and psychiatric diagnosis: A critique of Rosenhan's "On being sane in insane places." *Journal of Abnormal Psychology, 84,* 442–452. doi:10.1037/h0077124

Spitzer, R. L. (1976). More on pseudoscience in science and the case for psychiatric diagnosis. *Archives of General Psychology, 33,* 459–470.

Sprenkle, D. H., & Blow, A. J. (2004, April). Common factors and our sacred models. *Journal of Marital & Family Therapy, 30*(2), 113–129. doi:10.1111/j.1752-0606.2004.tb01228.x

Staddon, J. (2001). *The new behaviorism: Mind, mechanism and society.* Philadelphia, PA: Psychology Press.

Shadish, W. R., Cook, T. D., & Campbell, D. T. (2002). *Experimental and quasi-experimental designs for generalized causal inference.* Boston, MA: Houghton Mifflin.

Stanford, M. S. (2007). Demon or disorder: A survey of attitudes toward mental illness in the Christian church. *Mental Health, Religion & Culture, 10*(5), 445–449. doi:10.1080/13674670600903049

Stanford, M. S. (2008). *Grace for the afflicted: A clinical and biblical perspective on mental illness.* Colorado Springs, CO: Paternoster.

Stark, M. (1999). *Modes of therapeutic action: Enhancement of knowledge, provision of experience, and engagement in relationship.* Northvale, NJ: Aronson.

Steele, C. M. (1997). A threat in the air: How stereotypes shape the intellectual identities and performance of women and African Americans. *American Psychologist, 52,* 613–629. doi:10.1037/0003-066X.52.6.613

Stefferud, B., & Bolton, B. (1981). Nonverbal counseling behavior and therapists' stated value orientations. *Counseling and Values, 26*(1), 19–25. doi:10.1002/j.2161-007X.1981.tb01093.x

Steinhorn, L., & Diggs-Brown, B. (1999). *By the color of our skin: The illusion of integration and the reality of race.* New York: Dutton.

Stelmack, R. M. (Ed.). (2004). *On the psychobiology of personality: Essays in honor of Marvin Zuckerman.* New York: Elsevier Ltd.

Sternberg, R. J., & Lubart, T. I. (1995). *Defying the crowd: Cultivating creativity in a culture of conformity.* New York: Free Press.

Stevens, M. J., & Uwe, P. G. (Eds.). (2007). *Toward a global psychology: Theory, research, intervention, and pedagogy* (Global and cross-cultural psychology series). Mahwah, NJ: Lawrence Erlbaum Associates.

Stevenson, L. (Ed.) (2000). *The study of human nature: A reader.* New York: Oxford University Press.

Stewart, T. L., LaDuke, J. R., Bracht, C., Sweet, B. A. M., & Gamarel, K. E. (2003). Do the 'eyes' have it? A program evaluation of Jane Elliott's 'blue-eyes/brown-eyes' diversity training exercise. *Journal of Applied Social Psychology, 33*(9), 1898–1921. doi:10.1111/ j.1559-1816.2003.tb02086.x

Stewart-Williams, S., & Podd, J. (2004). The placebo effect: Dissolving the expectancy versus conditioning debate. *Psychological Bulletin, 130*(2), 324–340. doi:10.1037/0033-2909.130.2.324

Stirling, J. D., & Hellewell, J. S. E. (1999). *Psychopathology.* London: Routledge.

Stolz, S. B. (1978). Ethics of social and educational interventions: Historical contexts and a behavioral analysis. In A. C. Catania & T. S. Brigham (Eds.), *Handbook of behavior analysis: Social and instructional processes.* New York: Irvington.

Stone, F. E., & Ward, C. (1990). Loneliness and psychological adjustment of sojourners: New perspectives on culture shock. In D. Keats, D. Munro, & L. Mann (Eds.), *Heterogeneity in cross-cultural psychology* (pp. 537–547). Lisse, Netherlands: Swets and Zeitlinger.

Straub, R. O. (2006). *Health psychology: A biopsychosocial approach.* New York: Worth Publishers.

Straus, M. B. (1999). *No-talk therapy for children and adolescents.* New York/London: W. W. Norton.

Stricker, G. (2012). Psychotherapy integration. In *Encyclopedia of mental health.* Retrieved from http://www.minddisorders.com/Ob-Ps/Psychotherapy-integration.html.

Stricker, G., & Gold, J. (Eds.). (1993). *Comprehensive handbook of psychotherapy integration.* New York: Plenum.

Strickland, B. R. (Ed.). (2001). *The Gale encyclopedia of psychology* (2nd ed.). Detroit, MI: Gale Group.

Strickland, T. L., Jenkins, J. O., Myers, H. F., & Adams, H. E. (1988). Diagnostic judgments as a function of client and therapist race. *Journal of Psychopathology and Behavioral Assessment, 10*(2), 141–151. doi:10.1007/BF00962639

Striker, G. (2009). *Aristotle's prior analytics book* (I. G. Striker, Trans.). New York: Oxford University Press.

Stroebe, W., & Nijstad, B. (2009). Do our psychological laws apply only to Americans? *American Psychologist, 64*(6), 569. doi:10.1037/a0016090

Strong, E. K., Jr., Donnay, D. A. C., Morris, M. L., Schaubhut, N. A., & Thompson, R. C. (2004). *Strong interest inventory* (Rev. ed.). Mountain View, CA: Consulting Psychologists Press.

Strupp, H. H., & Bloxom, A. L. (1973). Preparing lower-class patients for group psychotherapy. *Journal of Consulting and Clinical Psychology, 41,* 373–384. doi:10.1037/h0035380

Sturtevant, W. C. (Ed.). (1978–2004). *Handbook of North American Indians.* Washington, DC: Smithsonian Institution.

Sudhoff, K. (1926). *Essays in the history of medicine.* New York: Medical Life Press.

Superstition. (2012). In *Merriam-Webster's online dictionary.* Retrieved from http://www.merriam-webster.com/dictionary/superstition.

Stueber, K. (2006). *Rediscovering empathy: Agency, folk psychology, and the human sciences.* Cambridge, MA: MIT Press.

Sue, D. W. (2001). Multidimensional facets of cultural competence [Abstract]. *The Counseling Psychologist, 29*(6), 790–821. doi:10.1177/0011000001296002

Sue, D. W. (2004). Whiteness and ethnocentric monoculturalism: Making the "invisible" visible. *American Psychologist, 59,* 761–769. doi:10.1037/0003-066X.59.8.761

Sue, D. W., & Sue, D. (1977). Barriers to effective cross-cultural counseling. *Journal of Counseling Psychology, 24*(5), 420–429. doi:10.1037/0022-0167.24.5.420

Sue, S. (1999). Science, ethnicity, and bias: Where have we gone wrong? *American Psychologist, 54*(12), 1070–7. doi:10.1037/0003-066X.54.12.1070

Sugiyama, L. S., Tooby, J., & Cosmides, L . (2002). Cross-cultural evidence of cognitive adaptations for social exchange among the Shiwiar of Ecuadorian Amazonia. *Proceedings of the National Academy of Sciences, 99*(17), 11537–11542. doi:10.1073/pnas.122352999

Suh, E., Diener, E., Oishi, S., & Triandis, H. C. (1998) The shifting basis of life satisfaction judgments across cultures: Emotions versus norms. *Journal of Personality and Social Psychology, 74*(2), 482–493. doi:10.1037/0022-3514.74.2.482

Suomi, S. J. (2000). A biobehavioral perspective on developmental psychopathology: Excessive aggression and serotonergic dysfunction in monkeys. In A. J. Sameroff, M. Lewis, & S. M. Miller (Eds.), *Handbook of developmental psychopathology* (2nd ed., pp. 237–256).

Sushinsky, L. W., & Wener, R. (1975). Distorting judgments of mental health: Generality of the labeling bias effect. *Journal of Nervous and Mental Health, 161,* 82–89. doi:10.1097/00005053-197508000-00002

Sussman, L. K. (2004). The role of culture in definitions, interpretations, and management of illness. In U. P. Gielen, J. M. Fish, & J. G. Draguns (Eds.), *Handbook of culture, therapy, and healing* (pp. 37–66). Mahwah, NJ: Lawrence Erlbaum Associates.

Suthahar, J., & Elliott, M. (2004). *Asian-Indian women's views on mental health and illness.* Paper presented at the annual meeting of the American Sociological Association, Hilton San Francisco & Renaissance Parc 55 Hotel, San Francisco, CA. Retrieved from http://www.allacademic.com/meta/p110072_index.html.

Swets, J. A., Dawes, R. M., & Monahan, J. (2000). Psychological science can improve diagnostic decisions. *Psychological Science in the Public Interest, 1,* 1–26. doi:10.1111/1529-1006.001

Swoyer, C. (2003). The linguistic relativity hypothesis. *Stanford Encyclopedia of Philosophy* [Web site]. Retrieved from: http://plato.stanford.edu/entries/relativism/supplement2.html.

Sylvers, P., Lilienfeld, S. O., & LaPrairie, J. L. (2011). Differences between trait fear and trait anxiety: Implications for psychopathology. *Clinical Psychology Review, 31*(1), 122–137. doi:10.1016/j.cpr.2010.08.004

Symons, D. (1992). On the use and misuse of Darwinism in the study of human behavior. In J. Barkow, L. Cosmides, & J. Tooby (Eds.), *The adapted mind: Evolutionary psychology and the generation of culture* (pp. 137–159). New York: Oxford University Press.

Szasz, T. (1961). *The myth of mental illness: Foundations of a theory of personal conduct.* New York: Hoeber-Harper.

Szasz, T. (1970). *The manufacture of madness: A comparative study of the inquisition and the mental health movement.* Syracuse, NY: Syracuse University Press.

Szasz, T. (1978, 1988). *The myth of psychotherapy: Mental healing as religion, rhetoric, and repression.* Syracuse, NY: Syracuse University Press.

Szasz, T. (2001). *Pharmacracy medicine and politics in America.* Westport, CT: Thomas Praeger Trade.

Szimhart, J. P. (2008). [Review of the book *Shamans and religion: An anthropological exploration in critical thinking,* by A. B. Kehoe]. *Cultic Studies Review, 7*(2), 182–187. Retrieved from http://www.icsahome.com/infoserv_bookreviews/bkrev_shamans_dreamcatchers.asp.

Tagg, J. (1996). *Cognitive distortions* [Web site]. Anker Publishing [now Jossey Bass]. Retrieved from http://daphne.palomar.edu/jtagg/cds.htm.

Tallman, K., & Bohart, A. C. (2004). The client as a common factor: Clients as self-healers. In M. Hubble, B. L. Duncan, & S. Miller (Eds.), *The heart and soul of change: What works in therapy* (pp. 91–132). Washington, DC: American Psychological Association.

Tankersley, D., Stowe, C. J., & Huettel, S. A. (2007). Altruism is associated with an increased neural response to the perception of agency. *Nature Neuroscience, 10,* 150–151. doi:10.1038/nn1833

Tata, S. P., & Leong, F. T. L. (1994). Individualism-collectivism, social-network orientation, and acculturation as predictors of attitudes toward seeking professional psychological help among Chinese-Americans. *Journal of Counseling Psychology, 41,* 280–287. doi:10.1037/0022-0167.41.3.280

Tattersall, I. (2007). How did modern human cognition evolve? In H. Cohen & B. Stemmer (Eds.), *Consciousness and cognition: Fragments of mind and brain.* London: Academic Press. doi:10.1016/B978-012373734-2/50002-9

Temerlin, M. K. (1968). Suggestion effects in psychiatric diagnosis. *Journal of Nervous and Mental Disease, 147,* 349–353. doi:10.1097/00005053-196810000-00003

Temkin, O. (1994). *The falling sickness: A history of epilepsy from the Greeks to the beginnings of modern neurology.* Baltimore, MD: Johns Hopkins University Press.

Teo, T. (2005). *The critique of psychology: From Kant to postcolonial theory.* New York: Springer.

Test. (2010). In *Merriam-Webster's online dictionary.* Retrieved from http://www.merriam webster.com/dictionary/test.

Tetlock, P. E. (2005). *Expert political judgment: How good is it? How can we know?* Princeton: Princeton University Press.

Therapy. (2011). In *Merriam-Webster's online dictionary.* [Medical]. Retrieved from http://www.merriam-webster.com/dictionary/therapy.

Thernstrom, S. (Ed.). (1980). *Harvard encyclopedia of American ethnic groups.* Cambridge, MA: Belknap Press of Harvard University.

Thompson, C. M. (1950). *Psychoanalysis: Evolution and development.* New York: Thomas Nelson & Sons.

Thompson, W., & Hickey, J. (2005). *Society in focus.* Boston: Pearson.

Thorndike, E. L. (1920). A constant error on psychological rating. *Journal of Applied Psychology, IV,* 25–29. doi:10.1037/h0071663

Throop, C. J., & Hollan, D. W. (Eds.). (2008). Whatever happened to empathy? *Special issue of Ethos, 36*(4), 385–401.

Tierney, J. (2008, February 23). The hazards of politically research. *The New York Times.* Retrieved from http://tierneylab.blogs.nytimes.com/2008/02/23/the-hazards-of-politically-correct-research/.

Tishkoff, S. A., Reed, F. A., Friedlaender, F. R., Ehret, C., Ranciaro, A., Froment, A., Hirbo, J. B., Awomoyi, A. A., Bodo, J-M., Doumbo, O., Ibrahim, M., Juma, A. T., Kotze, M. J., Lema, G., Moore, J. H., Mortensen, H., Nyambo, T. B., Omar, S. A., Powell, K., Pretorius, G. S., Smith, M. W., Thera, M. A., Wambebe, C., Weber, J. L., & Williams, S. M. (2009). The genetic structure and history of Africans and African Americans. *Science Express, 324*(5930), 1035–1044. doi:10.1126/science. 1172257

Tobacyk, J., & Milford, G. (1983). Belief in paranormal phenomena: Assessment instrument development and implications for personality functioning. *Journal of Personality and Social Psychology, 44*(5), 1029–1037. doi:10.1037/0022-3514.44.5.1029

Todes, D. (2000). *Ivan Pavlov: Exploring the animal machine.* New York: Oxford University Press.

Tolle, E. (2004). *The power of now: A guide to spiritual enlightenment.* Vancouver: Namaste Publishing.

Toth, A. L., Varala, K., Newman, T. C., Miguez, F. E., Hutchison, S. K., Willoughby, D. A., Simons, J. F., Egholm, M., Hunt, J. H., Hudson, M. E., & Robinson, G. E. (2007). Wasp gene expression supports an evolutionary link between maternal behavior and eusociality. *Express Science* [On-line], *318,* 441–444. doi:10.1126/science.1146647

Tracy, A. B., & Shephard, C. (1994). *Prozac: Panacea or Pandora? The rest of the story on the new class of SSRI antidepressants (Prozac, Zoloft, Paxil, Lovan, Luvox & more).* Salt Lake City, Utah: Cassia Publ.

Travis, J. (1999). Animal genes illuminate human sleep. *Science News, 156,* 100. doi:10. 2307/4011715

Trevifio, J. G. (1996). Worldview and change in cross-cultural counseling. *Counseling Psychologist, 24*(2), 198–215. doi:10.1177/0011000096242002

Triandis, H. C. (1989). The self and social behavior in differing cultural contexts. *Psychological Review, 96,* 506–520. doi:10.1037/0033-295X.96.3.506

Triandis, H. C. (1995). *Individualism and collectivism.* Boulder, CO: Westview Press.

Triandis, H. C., Brislin, R. W., & Hui, C. (1991). Cross-cultural training across the individualism-collectivism divide. In L. Samovar & R. Porter (Eds.), *Intercultural communication: A reader* (pp. 370–382). Belmont, CA: Wadsworth.

Trivers, R. L. (1971). The evolution of reciprocal altruism. *Quarterly Review of Biology, 46,* 35–57. doi:10.1086/406755

Trivers, R. L. (1985). *Social evolution.* Menlo Park, CA: Benjamin/Cummings.

Trompenaars, F., & Hampden-Turner, C. (1998). *Riding the waves of culture.* New York: McGraw-Hill.

Thompson, C. L. (1989). Psychoanalytic psychotherapy with inner city patients. *Journal of Contemporary Psychotherapy, 19,* 137–148. doi:10.1007/BF00946067

Trevithick, P. (1998). Psychotherapy and working-class women. In I. B. Seu & M. C. Heenan (Eds.), *Feminism and psychotherapy* (pp. 115–134). Thousand Oaks, CA: Sage.

Trierweiler, S. J., Muroff, J. R., Jackson, J. S., Neighbors, H. W., & Munday, C. (2005). Clinician race, situational attributions, and diagnoses of mood versus schizophrenia disorders. *Cultural and Ethnic Minority Psychology, 11*(4), 351–364. doi:10.1037/1099-9809.11.4.351

Trochim, W. (1986). *Advances in quasi-experimental design and analysis.* San Francisco: Jossey-Bass.

Trochim, W., & Land, D. (1982). Designing designs for research. *The Researcher, 1*(1), 1–6.

Truax, C. B., & Carkhuff, R. R. (1967). *Toward effective counseling and psychotherapy.* Chicago, IL: Aldine.

Truax, C. B., & Carkhuff, R. R. (2008). *Toward effective counseling and psychotherapy: Training and practice.* Piscataway, NJ: Transaction Publishers.

Trull, T. J., & Geary, D. C. (1997). Comparison of the big-five factor structure across samples of Chinese and American adults. *Journal of Personality Assessment, 69*(2), 324–341.

Trusty, J., & Sandhu, D. S. (2002). *Multicultural counseling: Context, theory and practice, and competence.* Huntington, NY: Nova Science.

Tseng, W. S. (1999). Culture and psychotherapy: Review and practical guidelines. *Transcultural Psychiatry, 36*(2), 131–179. doi:10.1177/136346159903600201

Tseng, W. S. (2003). *Clinician's guide to cultural psychiatry.* London, UK: Academic Press.

Tsoi, W. F. (1985). Mental health in Singapore and its relation to Chinese culture. In W. S. Tseng & D. Y. H. Wu (Eds.), *Chinese culture and mental health* (pp. 229–250). Orlando: Academic Press.

Turnbull, S. (1980). *The Mongols.* Oxford: Osprey Publishing.

Turnbull, S. (1985). *The book of the medieval knight.* London: Arms and Armour Press.

Turnbull, S. (2003). *Genghis Khan & the Mongol conquests 1190–1400.* Oxford: Osprey Publishing.

Twitchell, J. B. (1999). *Lead us into temptation: The triumph of American materialism.* New York: Columbia University Press.

Tyerman, C. (2006). *God's war: A new history of the crusades*. London: Allen Lane.

Union of International Associations. (2009a). *Encyclopedia of world problems and human potential*. Retrieved from http://www.uia.be/.

Union of International Associations. (2009b, November, 21). Human values project – commentaries: 2.1 Defining values: Value confusion. In Union of International Associations, *The Encyclopedia of world problems and human potential*. Retrieved from http://www.uia.be/node/152?kap=4.

Union of International Associations. (2009c, November 21). Volume 2: Human potential: Transformation and values. In *The Encyclopedia of world problems and human potential* (Vol. 2). Retrieved from http://www.uia.be/node/318529.

United Nations, Department of Economic and Social Affairs, Population Division. (2011). *World population prospects, the 2010 revision*. Retrieved from http://esa.un.org/unpd/wpp/index.htm.

United Nations Population Division. (2010). *The world at six billion*. [Department of Economic and Social Affairs] Geneva: United Nations. Retrieved from http://www.un.org/esa/population/publications/sixbillion/sixbilpart1.pdf.

United Nations Volunteers. (n.d.). *Online volunteers*. [United Nations Development Programme]. Retrieved from http://www.unv.org/how-to-volunteer/online-volunteers.html.

United States Census. (2000). *Profile of General Demographic Characteristics: 2000 [Table DP-1] CenStats Databases*. Retrieved from http://censtats.census.gov/data/US/01000.pdf.

United States Census Bureau. (2008). *Race data: Racial and ethnic classifications used in census 2000 and beyond*. Retrieved from http://www.census.gov/population/www/socdemo/race/race factcb.html.

United States Census Bureau. (2009). *2010 census materials*. Retrieved from http://2010.census.gov/2010census/promotional_materials/009579.html.

United States Congress Senate Committee on Small Business. (1982). *Minority business and its contributions to the U.S. economy: Hearing before the committee on small business, United States senate, ninety-seventh congress, second session, on minority business and its contributions to the U.S. economy*. Washington: U.S.G.P.O.

United States Department of Justice. (1997). *The CIA-Contra-crack cocaine controversy: A review of the justice department's investigations and prosecutions*. Retrieved from http://www.usdoj.gov/oig/special/9712/ch01p1.htm.

United States National Library of Medicine. (2010). *NLM databases & electronic resources*. Bethesda, MD: Retrieved from http://www.nlm.nih.gov/databases/.

United States Public Health Service. (1999a). Overview of cultural diversity and mental health services. In *Mental Health: A report of the surgeon general*. Retrieved from http://www.surgeongeneral.gov/library/mentalhealth/chapter2/sec8.html.

University of Dayton School of Law. (2001). *Oppressed groups*. Retrieved from http://academic.udayton.edu/race/06hrights/OppressedGroups/index.htm.

Ussher, J. M. (2010). Gender differences in self-silencing and psychological distress in informal cancer carers. *Psychology of Women Quarterly, 34*(2), 228–242. doi:10.1111/j.1471-6402.2010.01564.x

Utay, J., & Miller, M. (2006). Guided imagery as an effective therapeutic technique: A brief review of its history and efficacy research. *Journal of Instructional Psychology, 33*(1), 40–43.

Uzoka, A. F. (1983). Active versus passive counselor role in didactic psychotherapy with Nigerian clients. *Social Psychiatry, 18,* 1–6. doi:10.1007/BF00583381.

Vacc, N. A., & Loesch, L. C. (2000). *Professional orientation to counseling* (3rd. ed.). Philadelphia, PA: Brunner-Routledge.

van Deurzen, E. (2002). *Existential counselling and psychotherapy in practice* (2nd ed.). London: Sage.

van Eenwyk, J. R. (1997). *Archetypes & strange attractors: The chaotic world of symbols.* Toronto, CAN: Inner City.

Van Maanen, J. (1996). Ethnography. In A. Kuper & J. Kuper (Eds.), *The social science encyclopedia* (2nd ed., pp. 263–265). London: Routledge.

Vanman, E. J., Paul, B. Y., Ito, T. A., & Miller, N. (1997). The modern face of prejudice and structural features that moderate the effect of cooperation on affect. *Journal of Personality and Social Psychology, 73,* 941–959. doi:10.1037/0022-3514.73.5.941

van Sertima, I. (Ed.). (1992). *The golden age of the Moor.* New Brunswick: Transaction Publishers.

Vasquez, Melba J. T. (2007). Cultural difference and the therapeutic alliance: An evidence-based analysis. *American Psychologist, 62*(8), 878–885. doi:10.1037/0003-066X.62.8.878

Vassaf, G. Y. H. (1982). Mental massacre: The use of psychological tests in the third world. *School Psychology International, 3*(1), 43–47. doi:10.1177/0143034382031007

Vendramini, D. (2009). *Them and us: How Neanderthal predation created modern humans.* Armidale, N.S.W.: Kardoorair Press.

Vezina, P. (2007). Sensitization, drug addiction and psychopathology in animals and humans. *Progress in Neuro-Psychopharmacology & Biological Psychiatry, 31*(8), 1553–1555. doi:10.1016/j.pnpbp.2007.08.030

Viamontes, G. I., & Beitman, B. D. (2009). Brain processes informing psychotherapy. In G. Gabbard (Ed.), *Textbook of psychotherapeutic treatments* (pp. 781–808). Arlington, VA: American Psychiatric Pub.

Virginia State Police. (2009). *Volunteers: A valuable asset.* Retrieved from http://www.vsp.state.va.us/Employment_Volunteers.shtm.

Virine, L., & Trumper, M. (2007). *Project decisions: The art and science.* Vienna, VA: Management Concepts.

Vogt, E. Z., & Albert, E. M. (1966). *People of Rimrock: A study of values in five cultures.* Cambridge, MA: Harvard University Press.

Vohs, K. D., Baumeister, R. F., & Loewenstein, G. (Eds.). (2007). *Do emotions help or hurt decisionmaking? A Hedgefoxian perspective.* New York: Russell Sage Foundation.

Volunteers in Police Service. (n.d.). *About VIPS.* Retrieved from http://www.policevolunteers.org/about/.

Volkow, N. D., Wang, G. J., Ma, Y., Fowler, J. S., Wong, C., Jayne, M., Telang, F., & Swanson, J. M. (2006). Effects of expectation on the brain metabolic responses to methylphenidate and to its placebo in non-drug abusing subjects. *Neuroimage, 32*(4), 1782–92. doi:10.1016/j.neuroimage.2006.04.192

von Schenck, U., Bender-Götze, C., & Koletzko, B. (1997). Persistence of neurological damage induced by dietary vitamin B-12 deficiency in infancy. *Archives of disease in childhood, 77,* 137–139. doi:10.1136/adc.77.2.137

Vontress, C. E. (1979). Cross-cultural counseling: An existential approach. *Personnel and Guidance Journal, 58*(2), 117–122.

Vontress, C. E. (1988). An existential approach to cross-cultural counseling. *Journal of Multicultural Counseling and Development, 16*(2), 73–83.

Vroom, V. H. (1964). *Work and motivation.* New York: John Wiley.

Vyse, S. A. (2000). *Believing in magic: The psychology of superstition.* New York: Oxford University Press.

Wachtel, P. L., & Messer, S. B. (Eds.). (1998). *Theories of psychotherapy: Origins and evolution.* Washington, DC: American Psychological Association.

Wahl, O. F. (1999). Mental health consumers' experience of stigma. *Schizophrenia Bulletin, 25,* 467–478.

Wakefield, J. C. (1992). The concept of mental disorder: On the boundary between biological facts and social values. *American Psychologist, 47,* 73–388. doi:10.1037/0003-066X.47.3.373

Wakefield, J. C. (1997). Normal inability versus pathological disability: Why Ossorio's definition of mental disorder is not sufficient. *Journal of Abnormal Psychology, 108,* 374–399. doi:10.1037/0021-843X.108.3.374

Wakefield, J. C. (1999), Evolutionary versus prototype analysis of the concept of disorder. *Journal of Abnormal Psychology, 108,* 374–399. doi:10.1037/0021-843X.108.3.374

Waldemar, K. (Ed.). (2006). Part xiii – Outstanding human factors and ergonomics professionals – K. U. Smith. In K. Waldemar, *International encyclopedia of ergonomics and human factors* (Vol. 3, pp. 3481–3483). Boca Raton, FL: CRC Press/Taylor & Francis.

Walker, A., & Shipman, P. (1996). *The wisdom of the bones.* New York: Alfred Knopf.

Walker, P. M., Silvert, L., Hewstone, M., & Nobre, A. C. (2008). Social contact and other-race face processing in the human brain. *Social Cognitive and Affective Neuroscience, 3*(1), 16–25. doi:10.1093/scan/nsm035

Wall, P. D. (1999). The placebo and the placebo response. In P. D. Wall & R. Melzack (Eds.), *Textbook of pain* (4th ed., pp. 1–12). Edinburgh: Churchill Livingstone.

Wallingford, E. I., & Prout, H. T. (2000) The relationship of season of birth and special education referral. *Psychology in the Schools, 37,* 379–387.

Wampold, B. E. (2000). Outcomes of individual counseling and psychotherapy: Empirical evidence addressing two fundamental questions. In S. D. Brown & R. W. Lent (Eds.), *Handbook of counseling psychology* (3rd ed., pp. 711–739). New York: Wiley.

Wampold, B. E. (2001). *The great psychotherapy debate: Models, methods, and findings.* Mahwah, NJ: Erlbaum.

Wampold, B. E., & Imel, Z. E. (2007). The placebo effect: "Relatively large" and "robust" enough to survive another assault. *Journal of Clinical Psychology, 63*(4), 401–403. doi:10.1002/jclp.20350

Wampold, B. E., Mondin, G. W., Moody, M., Stich, F., Benson, K., & Ahn, H. (1997). A meta-analysis of outcome studies comparing bona fide psychotherapies: Empirically, "all must have prizes." *Psychological Bulletin, 122,* 203–215. doi:10.1037/0033-2909.122.3.203

Ward, C. (2001). The A, B, Cs of acculturation. In D. Matsumoto (Ed.), *Handbook of culture and psychology* (pp. 411–446). New York: Oxford University Press.

Warneken, F., Hare, B., Melis, A. P., Hanus, D., & Tomasello, M. (2007) Spontaneous altruism by chimpanzees and young children.[Public Library of Science – Biology]. *PLoS Biol, 5*(7), e184. doi:10.1371/journal.pbio.0050184

Warneken, F., & Tomasello, M. (2006). Altruistic helping in human infants and young chimpanzees. *Science, 311*(5765), 1301–1303. doi:10.1126/science.1121448

Watkins, C. E., & Campbell, V. L. (2000). *Testing and assessment in counseling practice.* Mahwah, NJ: Lawrence Erlbaum Associates.

Watson, J. B. (1913). Psychology as the behaviorist views it. *Psychological Review, 20,* 158–177. doi:10.1037/h0074428

Watters, E. (2010). *Crazy like us: The globalization of the American psyche.* New York: Free Press.

Watzlawick, P., Weakland, J. H., & Fisch, R. (1974). *Change: Principles of problem formation and problem resolution.* New York: Norton.

Webster, G. D., Nichols, A. L., & Schember, T. O. (2009). American psychology is becoming more international. *American Psychologist, 64*(6), 566–569. doi:10.1037/a0016193

Wechsler, D. (2003). *Wechsler intelligence scale for children.* San Antonio, TX: Pearson.

Weinberger, J. (1995). Common factors aren't so common: The common factors dilemma. *Clinical Psychology: Science and Practice, 2,* 45–69.

Weiner, B. (1979). A theory of motivation for some classroom experiences. *Journal of Educational Psychology, 71,* 3–25. doi:10.1037/0022-0663.71.1.3

Weiner, B. (1986). *An attributional theory of emotion and motivation.* New York: Springer-Verlag.

Weiss, A. P. (1925). Linguistics and psychology. *Language, 1*(2), 52–57.

Werbach, M. R. (1999). *Nutritional influences on mental illness.* Tarzana, CA: Third Line Press.

Westermeyer, J. (1987). Clinical considerations in cross-cultural diagnosis. *Hospital and Community Psychiatry, 38,* 160–165.

Whiston, S. C., Tai, W. L., Rahardja, D., & Eder, K. (2011). School counseling outcome: A meta-analytic examination of interventions. *Journal of Counseling & Development, 89*(1), 37–55.

White, C. S., Lambert, D. M., Millar, C. D., & Stevens, P. M. (1991, July). Is helping behavior a consequence of natural selection? *The American Naturalist, 138*(1), 246–253. doi:10.1086/285214

Whitfield, S. (1999). *Life along the silk road.* Berkeley/Los Angeles/London: University of California Press.

Whiting, J. W. (1974). A model for psychocultural research. In *American Anthropological Association, Annual Report.* Washington, DC.

Whitman, D. B. (2000). *Genetically modified foods: Harmful or helpful?* [ProQuest]. Retrieved from http://www.csa.com/discoveryguides/gmfood/overview.php.

Whitaker, R. (2002). *Mad in America: Bad science, bad medicine, and the enduring mistreatment of the mentally ill.* Cambridge, MA: Perseus Books.

WHO World Mental Health Survey Consortium. (2004). Prevalence, severity, and unmet need for treatment of mental disorders in the world health organization. *JAMA, 291*(21), 2581–2590. doi:10.1001/jama.291.21.2581

Whorf, B. (1956). *Language, thought and reality.* Cambridge, MA: MIT Press.

Whyte, J. (2004). *Crimes against logic: Exposing the bogus arguments of politicians, priests, journalists, and other serial offenders.* New York: McGraw-Hill.

Wickens, J. R., Horvitz, J. C., Costa, R, M., & Killcross, S. (2007). Dopaminergic mechanisms in actions and habits. *Journal of Neuroscience, 27*(31), 8181–8183. doi: 10.1523/JNEUROSCI.1671-07.2007

Wicker, B., Keysers, C., Plailly, J., Royet, J. P., Gallese, V., & Rizzolatti, G. (2003). Both of us disgusted in my insula: The common neural basis of seeing and feeling disgust. *Neuron, 40*(3), 655–664. doi:10.1016/S0896-6273(03)00679-2

Wier, K. (2012, July/August). Smog in our brains. *Monitor on Psychology, 43*(7), 32–37.

Wiggins, J. D., & Weslander, D. L. (1979). Personality characteristics of counselors rated as effective or ineffective. *Journal of Vocational Behavior, 15*(2), 175–185. doi: 10.1016/0001-8791(79)90036-8

Wiggins, J. S., & Trapnell, P. D. (1997). Personality structure: The return of the Big Five. In R. Hogan, J. A. Johnson, & S. R. Briggs (Eds.), *Handbook of personality psychology.* San Diego: Academic Press. 737–764. doi:10.1016/B978-012134645-4/50029-9

Wilcken, U., & Borza, E. N. (1967). *Alexander the great.* New York: W. W. Norton & Company.

Wildman, S. M., Armstong, M., Davis, A. D., & Grillo, T. (1996). *Privilege revealed: How invisible preference undermines America.* New York: NYU Press.

Wilkins, D. P. (1993). *From part to person: Natural tendencies of semantic change and the search for cognates (Working paper No. 23).* Cognitive Anthropology Research Group at the Max Planck Institute for Psycholinguistics.

Willi, J. (1999). *Ecological psychotherapy.* Seattle, WA: Hogrefe & Huber.

Winerman, L. (2012, July/August). Psychology's 'ideas worth spreading.' *Monitor on Psychology, 43*(7), 28–30.

Witkin, H. A., Moore, C. A., Goodenough, D. R., & Cox, P. W. (1977).Field dependent and field independent cognitive styles and their educational implications. *Review of Educational Research, 47,* 1–64.

Williams, E., Francis, L., & Lewis, C. A. (2009). Introducing the modified paranormal belief scale: Distinguishing between classic paranormal beliefs, religious paranormal beliefs and conventional religiosity among undergraduates in Northern Ireland and Wales. *Archiv für Religionspsychologie/Archive for the Psychology of Religions, 31*(3), 345–356.

Williams, G. C. (1966). *Adaptation and natural selection.* Princeton, NJ: Princeton University Press.

Williams, J. E., & Best, D. L. (1990). *Sex and psyche: Gender and self viewed cross-culturally.* Newbury Park, CA: Sage.

Williams, L. F. (2003). *Constraint of race: Legacies of white skin privilege in America.* University Park, PA: Pennsylvania State University Press.

Williamson, L. (1998). Eating disorders and the cultural forces behind the drive for thinness: Are African American women really protected? *Social Work in Health Care, 28*(1), 61–73. doi:10.1300/J010v28n01_04

Willyard, C. (2012, July/August). Psychology's peace builders. *Monitor on Psychology, 43*(7), 45–52.

Wilson, E. O. (1975). *Sociobiology: The new synthesis.* Cambridge, MA: Harvard University Press.

Wilson, E. O. (1979). *On human nature.* Cambridge, MA: Harvard University Press.

Wilson, G. T., & Abrams, D. (1977). Effects of alcohol on social anxiety and physiological arousal: Cognitive versus pharmacological processes. *Cognitive Research and Therapy, 1,* 195–210. doi:10.1007/BF01186793

Winkelman, M. (2000). *Shamanism: The neural ecology of consciousness and healing.* Westport, CT: Bergin & Garvey.

Winkelman, M. (2009). *Culture and health: Applying medical anthropology.* San Francisco, CA: Jossey-Bass.

Wiredu, K., Karp, I., & Bird, C. S. (Eds.). (1996). *Cultural universals and particulars.* Bloomington, IN: Indiana University Press.

Wiseman, N. (2002). Traditional Chinese medicine: A brief outline. *Journal of Chemical Information and Computer Sciences, 42*(3), 445–455. doi:10.1021/ci0101071

Wittgenstein, L. (1967). *Philosophical investigations* (G. E. M. Anscombe, Trans.). Oxford: Blackwell.

Wittgenstein, L. (1994). *Tractatus logico-philosophicus* (D. F. Pears & B. F. McGuinness, Trans.). London; New York: Routledge.

Wittkower, E. D., & Warms, H. (1974). Cultural aspects of psychotherapy. *Psychotherapy and Psychosomatics, 24*(4-6), 303–310. doi:10.1159/000286749)

Wolman, B. B. (Ed.). (1996). *The encyclopedia of psychiatry, psychology, and psychoanalysis.* New York: Henry Holt.

Wolpe, J. (1976). Behavior therapy and its malcontents – II. Multimodal eclecticism, cognitive exclusivism and "exposure" empiricism. *Journal of Behavior Therapy and Experimental Psychiatry, 7*(2), 109–116. doi:10.1016/0005-7916(76)90066-5

Wood, F. (2004). *The silk road: Two thousand years in the heart of asia.* Berkeley/Los Angeles/London: University of California Press.

Wood, W., & Neal, D. T. (2007). A new look at habits and the habit-goal interface. *Psychological Review, 114*(4), 843–863. doi:10.1037/0033-295X.114.4.843

Woodside, M., & McClam, T. (2009). *An introduction to human services* (6th ed.). Belmont, CA: Thomson-Brooks/Cole.

Workman, L., & Reader, W. (2008). *Evolutionary psychology: An introduction* (2nd ed.). New York: Cambridge University Press.

WorldAtlas. (2010). *Countries listed by continent.* Retrieved from at http://www.worldatlas.com/cntycont.htm.

World Factbook. (2009). *United States.* Washington, DC: Central Intelligence Agency. Retrieved from https://www.cia.gov/library/publications/the-world-factbook/index.html.

World Health Organization. (1997). *Lexicon of cross-cultural terms in mental health.* Geneva: Author.

World Health Organization. (2008). *International statistical classification of diseases and related health problems, 10 Revision, Vols. 1-3.* Geneva: Author.

World Health Organization – Mental Health Evidence and Research Team. (2005). *Mental health atlas.* Geneva: Author.

World Health Organization. (2010a). *International classification of diseases (ICD).* Retrieved from http://www.who.int/classifications/icd/en/.

World Health Organization. (2010b). *History of ICD.* Retrieved from http://www.who.int/classifications/icd/en/HistoryOfICD.pdf.

World Health Organization. (2010c). *Production of ICD-11: The overall revision process.* Retrieved from http://www.who.int/classifications/icd/ICDRevision.pdf.

World Values Survey. (2009a). *Introduction to the world values survey* [Web site]. Retrieved from http://margaux.grandvinum.se/SebTest/wvs/articles/folder_published/article_base_16.

World Values Survey. (2009b). *The Inglehart values map.* Retrieved from http://www.worldvaluessurvey.org/statistics/some_findings.html.

Worthman, C. M., & Melby, M. K. (2002). Toward a comparative developmental ecology of human sleep. In M. A. Carskadon (Ed.), *Adolescent sleep patterns: Biological, social, and psychological influences.* Cambridge, UK: Cambridge University Press. doi:10.1017/CBO 9780511499999.009

Wriggins, S. H. (2004). *The silk road journey with Xuanzang.* Cumnor Hill, Oxford: Westview Press.

Wu, S. (2005). *Chinese astrology: Exploring the eastern zodiac.* Franklin Lakes, NJ: Career Press.

Wyatt, G. (Ed.). (2001). *Rogers' therapeutic conditions: Evolution, theory and practice.* Glasgow, UK: Bell & Bain.

Wylie, M. S. (1995). The power of DSM-IV: Diagnosing for dollars. *Family Therapy Networker, 19*(3), 22–26.

Xu, X. (2003). *The Jews of Kaifeng, China: History, culture, and religion.* Jersey City, NJ: KTAV Publishing House.

Yang, K. S. (1986). Chinese personality and its change. In M. H. Bond (Ed.), *The psychology of the Chinese people* (pp. 106–170). Hong Kong: Oxford University Press.

Yang, K. S. (2006). Indigenous personality research: The Chinese case [Ch. 13]. In U. Kim, K. S.Yang, & K. K. Hwang (Eds.), *Indigenous and cultural psychology: Understanding people in context* (pp. 285–314). New York: Springer.

Yalom, I. D. (1970). *The theory and practice of group psychotherapy.* New York: Basic Books.

Yalom, I. D. (1980). *Existential psychotherapy.* New York: Basic Books.

Yeh, C. J., Hunter, C. D., Madan-Bahel, A., Chiang, L., & Arora A. K. (2004). Indigenous and interdependent perspectives of healing: Implications for counseling and research. *Journal of Counseling & Development, 82*(4), 410–419.

Yep, R. (2010). *Year-in-review 2009.* American Counseling Association. Retrieved from http://www.counseling.org/Sub/BlastEmails/YIR_2009.pdf.

Yeung, W. H., & Lee, E. (1997). Chinese buddhism: Its implications for counseling. In E. Lee (Ed.), *Working with Asian Americans: A guide for clinicians* (pp. 452–463). New York: Guilford Press.

Yin, H. H., & Knowlton, B. J. (2006). The role of the basal ganglia in habit formation. *Nature Reviews Neuroscience, 7*(6), 464–476. doi:10.1038/nrn1919

Yip, K-S. (2004). Taoism and its impact on mental health of the Chinese communities. *International Journal of Social Psychiatry, 50*(1), 25–42. doi:10.1177/0020764004 038758

Yip, K-S. (2005). Family caregiving of clients with mental illness in the People's Republic of China (Part 2: Current Situation). *International Journal of Psychosocial Rehabilitation, 10*(1), 35–42.

Yong, E. (2012, May). Replication studies: Bad copy. *Nature, 485,* 298–300. doi:10.1038/485298a

Young, G. (2010). The dsm-5 draft: Critique and recommendations. *Psychological Injury and Law, 3*(4), 320–322. doi:10.1007/s12207-010-9091-y. Retrieved from http://www.psychologytoday.com/files/attachments/52877/dsm-critique-article-2010.pdf.

Yoo, S. H., Matsumoto, D., & LeRoux, J. A. (2006). Emotion regulation, emotion recognition, and intercultural adjustment. *International Journal of Intercultural Relations, 30*(3), 345–363. doi:10.1016/j.ijintrel.2005.08.006

Yrizarry, N., Matsumoto, D., Imai, C., Kooken, K., & Takeuchi, S. (2001). Culture and emotion. In L. L. Adler & U. P. Gielen (Eds.), *Cross-cultural topics in psychology* (2nd ed.). Westport, CT: Praeger.

Yule, H., & Cordier, H. (1923). *The travels of Marco Polo.* Mineola, NY: Dover Publications.

Zafirovski, M. (2003). Human rational behavior and economic rationality. *Electronic Journal of Sociology, 7*(2). Retrieved from http://www.sociology.org/content/vol 7.2/02_zafirovski.html.

Zaimeche, S. (2004). *Aspects of the Islamic influence on science and learning in the Christian west* [Foundation for Science Technology and Civilisation]. Retrieved from http://www.muslimheritage.com/uploads/Main%20-%20Aspects%20of%20the %20Islamic%20Influence1.pdf.

Zakour, A. B. (2004). Cultural differences and information technology acceptance. *Proceedings of the 7th Annual Conference of the Southern Association of Information Systems* (SAIS), Savannah, GA., pp. 156–161. Retrieved from http://sais.aisnet.org/sais2004/Zakour.pdf.

Zane, N., Nagayama Hall, G. C., Sue, S., Young, K., & Nunez, J. (2004). Research on psychotherapy with culturally diverse populations. In H. D. Singaravelu & M. Pope (Eds.), *Handbook for counseling international students in the United States* (pp. 767–804). Alexandria, VA: American Counseling Association.

Zdep, S. M., & Irvine, S. H. (1970). A reverse Hawthorne effect in educational evaluation. *Journal of School Psychology, 8,* 89–95. doi:10.1016/0022-4405(70)90025-7

Zebrowitz, L. A., Montepare, J. M., & Lee, H. K. (1993). They don't all look alike: Individual impressions of other racial groups. *Journal of Personality and Social Psychology, 65*(1), 85–101. doi:10.1037/0022-3514.65.1.85

Zeeberg, A. (2012, 07/08). Hidden truths of health [Special issue]. *Discover,* 63.

Zeidner, M., & Beit-Hallahmi, B. (1998). Sex, ethnic, and social class differences in parareligious beliefs among Israeli adolescents. *The Journal of Social Psychology, 128*(3), 333–343. doi:10.1080/00224545.1988.9713750

Zeki, S. (1993). *A vision of the brain.* Oxford: Blackwell Scientific Publications.

Zheng He. (2010). *New world encyclopedia.* Retrieved from http://www.newworldency clopedia.org/entry/Zheng_He?oldid=751187.

Zhou, X., Saucier, G., Gao, D., & Liu, J. (2009). Factor structure of Chinese personality descriptors. *Journal of Personality, 77,* 363–400. http://dx.doi.org/10.1111/j. 1467-6494.2008.00551.x

Ziliak, S. T., & McCloskey, D. N. (2008). *The cult of statistical significance: How the standard error costs us jobs.* Ann Arbor, MI: University of Michigan Press.

Znoj, H. J., & Grawe, K. (2000). The control of unwanted states and psychological health: Consistency safeguards. In W. J. Perrig, A. Grob, & A. Flammer (Eds.), *Control of human behavior, mental processes, and consciousness. Essays in honor of the 60th birthday of August Flammer* (pp. 242–258). Mahwah, NJ, & London: Erlbaum.

Zollikofer, C. P. E., Ponce de León, M. S., Vandermeersch, B., & Lévêque, F. (2002). Evidence for interpersonal violence in the St. Césaire Neanderthal. *Proceedings of the National Academy of Sciences, 99,* 6444–6448. doi:10.1073/pnas.082111899

Zubieta, J-K., Bueller, J. A., Jackson, L. R., Scott, D. J., Xu, Y., Koeppe, R. A., Nichols, T. E., & Stohler, C. S. (2005). Placebo effects mediated by endogenous opioid activity on μ-opioid receptors. *The Journal of Neuroscience, 25*(34), 7754–7762. doi:10.1523/JNEUROSCI.0439-05.2005

Zur, O., & Nordmarken, N. (2010). *DSM: Diagnosing for money and power – Summary of the critique of the DSM.* Retrieved from http://www.zurinstitute.com/dsmcri tique.html.

Zuriff, G. E. (1985). *Behaviorism: A conceptual reconstruction.* New York: Columbia University Press.

NAME INDEX

SUBJECT INDEX

- Boone, Beverly—**BASIC TRAINING FOR RESIDENTIAL CHILDCARE WORKERS: A Practical Guide for Improving Service to Children.** '12, 224 pp. (7 x 10), $36.95, paper.

- Bowker, Art—**THE CYBERCRIME HANDBOOK FOR COMMUNITY CORRECTIONS: Managing Offender Risk in the 21st Century.** '12, 276 pp. (7 x 10), 29 il., 8 tables, $54.95, hard.

- Geldard, Kathryn & David Geldard—**PERSONAL COUNSELING SKILLS: An Integrative Approach. (Rev. 1st Ed.)** '12, 340 pp. (7 x 10), 20 il, 3 tables, $45.95, paper.

- Gottlieb, Linda J.—**THE PARENTAL ALIENATION SYNDROME: A Family Therapy and Collaborative Systems Approach to Amelioration.** '12, 302 pp. (7 x 10), $64.95, hard, $44.95, paper.

- Lester, David and James R. Rogers—**CRISIS INTERVENTION AND COUNSELING BY TELEPHONE AND THE INTERNET. (3rd Ed.)** '12, 398 pp. (7 x 10), 12 tables.

- Noltemeyer, Amity Lynn & Caven S. Mcloughlin—**DISPROPORTIONALITY IN EDUCATION AND SPECIAL EDUCATION: A Guide to Creating More Equitable Learning Environments.** '12, 288 pp. (7 x 10), 1 il., 5 tables, $61.95, hard, $41.95, paper.

- Payne, Brian K.—**CRIME AND ELDER ABUSE: An Integrated Perspective. (3rd Ed.)** '11, 374 pp. (7 x 10), 7 il., 18 tables, $68.95, hard, $48.95, paper.

- Marvasti, Jamshid A.—**WAR TRAUMA IN VETERANS AND THEIR FAMILIES: Diagnosis and Management of PTSD, TBI and Comorbidities of Combat Trauma - From Pharmacotherapy to a 12-Step Self-Help Program for Combat Veterans.** '12 356 pp. (7 x 10), $69.95, hard.

- Miller, Susan B.—**WHEN PARENTS HAVE PROBLEMS: A Book for Teens and Older Children Who Have a Disturbed or Difficult Parent. (2nd Ed.)** '12, 120 pp. (7 x 10), $19.95, paper.

- Cipani, Ennio—**DECODING CHALLENGING CLASSROOM BEHAVIORS: What Every Teacher and Paraeducator Should Know!** '11, 240 pp. (7 x 10), 9 il., 72 tables, (and a CD-ROM containing answers to fill-in-the-blank and true/false test items), $34.95, paper.

- Freeman, Edith M.—**NARRATIVE APPROACHES IN SOCIAL WORK PRACTICE: A Life Span, Culturally Centered, Strengths Perspective.** '11, 260 pp. (7 x 10), 7 il., 19 tables, $54.95, hard, $34.95, paper.

- Ensminger, John J.—**SERVICE AND THERAPY DOGS IN AMERICAN SOCIETY: Science, Law and the Evolution of Canine Caregivers.** '10, 340 pp. (7 x 10), 25 il., 1 table, $71.95, hard, $49.95, paper.

- Thyer, Bruce A., John S. Wodarski, Laura L. Myers, & Dianne F. Harrison—**CULTURAL DIVERSITY AND SOCIAL WORK PRACTICE. (3rd Ed.)** '10, 370 pp. (7 x 10), 14 tables, $79.95, hard, $59.95, paper.

- Brock, Michael G. and Samuel Saks—**CONTEMPORARY ISSUES IN FAMILY LAW AND MENTAL HEALTH.** '08, 158 pp. (7 x 10), $36.95, paper.

- Plach, Tom—**INVESTIGATING ALLEGATIONS OF CHILD AND ADOLESCENT SEXUAL ABUSE: An Overview for Professionals.** '08, 192 pp. (7 x 10), $52.95, hard, $32.95, paper.

Due Date

Date Re...